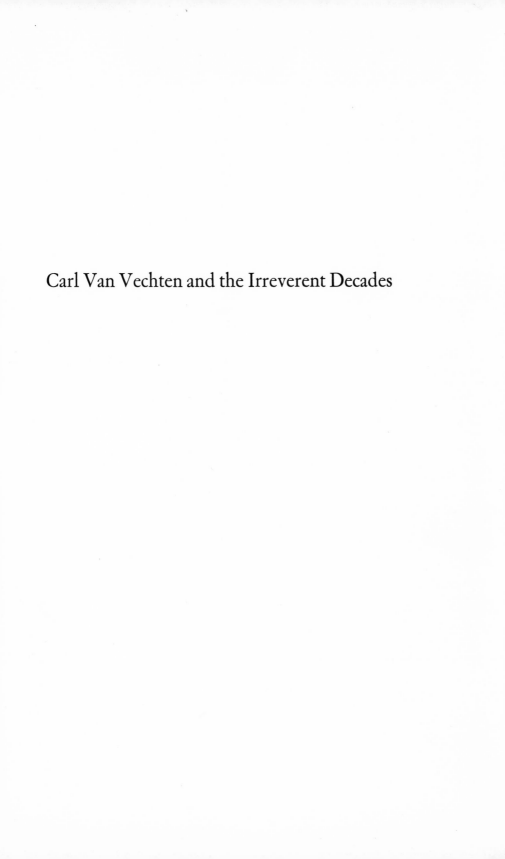

Carl Van Vechten and the Irreverent Decades

CARL VAN VECHTEN
and the
IRREVERENT
DECADES

By Bruce Kellner

UNIVERSITY OF OKLAHOMA PRESS
NORMAN

The paper on which this book is printed bears the watermark of the University of Oklahoma Press and has an effective life of at least three hundred years.

Library of Congress Catalog Card Number: 68–15683

Copyright 1968 by the University of Oklahoma Press, Publishing Division of the University. Composed and printed at Norman, Oklahoma, U.S.A., by the University of Oklahoma Press. First edition.

For Arden

A Prefatory Memoir

FOR MORE THAN HALF A CENTURY Carl Van Vechten's persuasive interests in the arts continued to enlighten the present by challenging the past.

He began dancing to the scores of Richard Strauss while everybody else still waltzed to the tunes of Johann; he championed Stravinsky long before *The Firebird* had flown across to our shores; he encouraged jazz and ragtime from the dance hall to the concert stage.

He found reasonable explanations for several literary curiosities in an alien library: Gertrude Stein and Ronald Firbank and Arthur Machen, when they were unknown and unread; Herman Melville, at a time when first editions of *Moby Dick* sold for fifty cents or so in New York secondhand bookstalls; and Langston Hughes and James Purdy—all before they had been officially discovered.

He became America's first ballet critic in the days when most theatergoers settled for the Floradora Girls.

Almost singlehandedly, he was responsible for the popular recognition of the Negro as a creative artist during the Harlem renaissance.

In addition to these various occupations, he turned out nine volumes of musical and literary criticism, two books about cats, a quasi-autobiography, dozens of prefaces and introductions to the works of others, and more than two hundred magazine articles and book reviews.

He wrote seven novels.

Carl Van Vechten

He established at least half a dozen important library collections, one of them among the most significant in America.

Finally, at an age when most men begin to think about retirement, he became a gifted photographer.

Carl Van Vechten's life was busy enough, his ear and eye felicitous enough, and his pens and lens distinctive enough to warrant a reckoning. True, while most of his fellow artists and writers seem to have gone fishing in search of mermaids, he was content with the pearls he found; but this effort will, I hope, renew their luster.

I FIRST MET CARL VAN VECHTEN on a rainy late afternoon in May, 1953, having flown into New York for a week's leave from the navy to meet a certainly curious correspondent. During World War II, Carl had written to dozens of servicemen around the globe; in the summer of 1951, he had been moved to begin again because of a book order of mine. At sea we were paid in stacks of military scrip that looked like Monopoly money, and, on the U.S.S. *Harry E. Hubbard* with nothing else on which to squander it, ten dollars did not seem very much to invest in Gertrude Stein, whose work I had started collecting in college.

The book order went off by helicopter, the weekly transportation for mail while we were at sea. A month later we returned to port, where the book—sent airmail—was waiting for me, along with an unfamiliar envelope and letter, both of elegantly heavy pale aquamarine paper, engraved in emerald green, untidily typed:

> *Dear Mr Kellner*, . . . the . . . Banyan Press has handed me your letter as I am the literary executor of Miss Stein. . . . Much of her past work is out of print, but if you will tell me what you have I may be able to supply some of your lacks. Miss Stein would be happy to hear this voice out of Korea, but she would not be surprised as the army and navy and most young people have been for her for a long time.
>
> sincerely,
CARL VAN VECHTEN

I got off an answer in the evening mail, and then waited for three

A Prefatory Memoir

weeks until another letter came. The Fleet Post Office in those days was not very prompt. This time there were dozens of questions: How old was I? Had I read any of his books? Would I like some photographs? And in conclusion, "Who the hell is Harry E. Hubbard?"

Who the hell was Carl Van Vechten? The naval base library at Yokosuka did not help: there was no *Who's Who*, and the card catalogue skipped from Anthony Trollope to Thomas Wolfe. When the librarian asked me, witheringly, if I didn't mean Carl Van Doren, I gave up. But I did answer the letter, and from then on, with faithful regularity, there were books and magazines, clippings and programs, phonograph records, an occasional package of exotic foods from Bloomingdale's and an astonishing number of letters and post cards to pass an otherwise stultifying enlistment. (Admittedly, it was disconcerting to my innocent eyes to get photographic post cards of ballet dancers and naked Florentine fountains and Anna May Wong through the mail.)

He could be contrarily instructive:

I can't answer your questions about literature. . . . LIKE what you LIKE and pay no attention to the academies. You seem to be getting on pretty well.

He could be informative:

It is curious, but while singers and actors have deteriorated, violinists, pianists, and ballerinas have improved in every department. Indeed, the whole technique of the ballet has changed to a terrific extent.

Excited and enthusiastic, when he requested (and got) a brief glossary of navy slang:

Shitkickers is now my very favorite word. I never heard it before and I know lots of sailors. I shall use it to advantage, but NOT about western movies.

Or, when I returned to the West Coast, he could wax nostalgic:

I have . . . only spent part of a day in San Diego . . . circa 1930. . . .

ix

Carl Van Vechten

Everybody was drunk; prostitutes were legion and one place advertised the longest bar in the world, of which you could scarcely see
the end. I went into the john and discovered the pissoir was like a
trough. In this was lying, extended at full length . . . a Harvard or
Yale type . . . very well dressed, as soused as they make 'em. However he managed to look at me and to say very disconnectedly, "Just
pee . . . . on me. I'm all wet anyway."

For the first four months I wrote to "Dear Mr. Van Vechten"; he
was, after all, seventy-one years old, and I had been reared to respect my elders. Then: "Dear Bruce, Why don't you address me
as Carlo; everybody else in the world does. . . ." He had been signing himself that way all along, and I had assumed it was just bad
penmanship.

Two years of steady correspondence with anybody else might
have put me at my ease; two years of it with Carl only worked to
unnerve me a little more when, finally, I was able to arrange a holiday in New York. During the interim I had boned up on the Van
Vechten canon, which came to me slowly, book by book, as gifts
or by way of battered copies in California libraries (where *The
Tattooed Countess* had not been checked out since 1936) and
secondhand shops (where half a dozen copies of *Spider Boy* had
gathered dust, side by side, at fifty cents apiece) and rare book
rooms (where a snazzy limited edition of *The Blind Bow-Boy*
carried a $12.50 price tag). Also, I had managed to piece together
enough of Carl's background and tastes, through prefaces and
essays, references and allusions, to expect a randy old dilettante.

"You are very late," he said in a dead voice when I telephoned
from La Guardia, six hours behind schedule because of inclement
weather. "I shall wait for you in the lobby of your hotel. Now,
how will I know you?" We wore neither uniform nor carnation,
but I recognized him. He stood at the registration desk, swaying
slightly, with an orange and red and black flowered tie and a
striped shirt of brown and green and black and white, and there
was a very dirty raincoat over his arm. He was not so tall as I had
expected, older because his letters had never reminded me of the

x

fifty-year difference in our ages, younger because his complexion was as fresh and unlined as a schoolboy's. His snowy hair fell forward over his forehead: he had recently seen Brandon de Wilde in *Shane*. (Brandon de Wilde has since abandoned his bangs; Carl never did.) I had a momentary start when we shook hands, for there were three rings and two beautiful bracelets. He stared a very long time, a disconcerting, petrified stare. Then he smiled, I got my first look at his incredible front teeth, and any trepidation I may have felt immediately vanished. He looked like a genial walrus.

A COUPLE OF YEARS LATER, out of the navy and back in college, I began spending my summers in New York between semesters. At some time in that period, I asked Carl to let me browse around in the enormous collection of the manuscripts, letters, scrapbooks, and periodicals he had begun giving to the New York Public Library in 1940 and, during the ensuing years, to Yale. (Much of the material remains sealed, of course, some of it until 1980, the hundredth anniversary of his birth, and some until twenty-five years after his death.) My peremptory trips, born largely of curiosity, prompted a long series of fascinating visits and led, finally, to this book.

When we first talked about it, Carl said: "I approve personally, but impersonally I am not so enthusiastic. Probably you'd be better off working on Jean Genet or Mickey Spillane." Not without reason: Carl Van Vechten's life was, at best, a success story, unfraught with personal or literary trauma, relatively calm. And some time later, when I had hit some snag or other:

> But you must remember that my life doesn't include as many scandalous, ex-curricular adventures as the biographies of Sinclair Lewis, Eugene O'Neill or Scott Fitzgerald. However times may change: a window painter strolling through the apartment addressed me as "Pop." I had no revolver, butcher knife, or ax handy, or that bold innovator would have died in his tracks. . . . Weaponless, I managed a sickly smile. Pop indeed!

Acknowledgments

M<small>Y</small> <small>PRINCIPAL SOURCE</small> for this book is, of course, Carl Van Vechten: his creative works, our personal friendship, a series of happy encounters and lively interviews, and the extensive correspondence of more than a dozen years; but I am particularly indebted, too, to Fania Marinoff, without whose conversation and advice and patience, my work would be less complete and less accurate, and to Donald Gallup, Carl Van Vechten's literary trustee, who gave me his attention and co-operation at all times. Their permission to quote from Carl Van Vechten's published and unpublished writings and correspondence is gratefully acknowledged.

Additionally, I wish to thank those whose personal reminiscence, oral and written, answered questions and questioned answers: Donald Angus, Tallulah Bankhead, Richard Banks, Bennett Cerf, Nora Holt, Edward Howell, the late Langston Hughes, the late Fannie Hurst, Grace Nail Johnson, Armina Marshall, Mark Lutz, Saul Mauriber, Dorothy Peterson, Helen Channing-Pollock, Aileen Pringle, Francis Robinson, Joseph Solomon, the late Clara Deacon Taylor, Ethel Todd, and the late Alice B. Toklas.

Edward Lueders and the late Peter David Marchant lent more assistance than they realized, because of their admirable studies of Carl Van Vechten's literary achievements; so did Donald Gallup, Robert Lescher, and Richard Rutledge, because they read the manuscript in an earlier version and offered valuable suggestions; so did my wife, Margaret Wilcox Kellner, because she proofread these pages with an eye on my syntax.

Carl Van Vechten

Grateful acknowledgment is made to the following publishers for permission to reprint excerpts from their copyrighted works: to Alfred A. Knopf, Inc., for all of Carl Van Vechten's books and various essays of his, for *The Big Sea* by Langston Hughes, for *Innocence Abroad* by Emily Clarke, for *The Flowers of Friendship: Letters written to Gertrude Stein* edited by Donald Gallup, for *The Borzoi 1920*; to Harcourt, Brace & World, Inc., for *Movers and Shakers* by Mabel Dodge Luhan; to G. P. Putnam's Sons for *Joy Ride* by Dwight Taylor; to Random House, Inc., for *Selected Writings of Gertrude Stein* edited with an introduction by Carl Van Vechten, and for Carl Van Vechten's introduction to *Four Saints in Three Acts* by Gertrude Stein; to Yale University Press for Carl Van Vechten's introduction to *A Novel of Thank You* by Gertrude Stein; to the Yale University Library for *Fragments from an unwritten autobiography*, and for articles and essays in the *Yale University Library Gazette* by Donald Gallup, Fannie Hurst, Alfred Knopf, and Carl Van Vechten; to the University of Pennsylvania Press for *Letters of Theodore Dreiser: A Selection* (in three volumes) edited with preface and notes by Robert H. Elias; to Condé Nast, Publications, Inc., for articles by Carl Van Vechten that originally appeared in *Vanity Fair*.

I am especially indebted to the Oral History Office of Columbia University for allowing me to quote from the Memoirs of Carl Van Vechten in the Oral History Collection (or from, as Carl Van Vechten preferred to call it, his "rudimentary narration").

The original letters to Carl Van Vechten in this book are permanently housed in the Yale University Library Collection of American Literature; in the Carl Van Vechten Collection in the manuscript division, and in the Henry A. and Albert W. Berg Collection of the New York Public Library (Astor, Lenox and Tilden Foundations). Letters from Carl Van Vechten to members of his family are in his collection at the New York Public Library; other letters from him, to acquaintances and business associates, are at Yale. For permission to print these letters or selections from them, I make grateful acknowledgment to the libraries as owners

Acknowledgments

of the property rights, and to the individuals, representatives, and firms listed below as owners of the publication rights.

Margaret Freeman Cabell, for James Branch Cabell; the Philadelphia Fidelity Bank and the University of Virginia, for Emily Clarke Balch; John Evans, for Mabel Dodge Luhan; Gladys Ficke, for Arthur Davison Ficke; A. P. Watt & Son, representing Colonel Thomas Firbank, for Ronald Firbank and, as literary executor, for W. Somerset Maugham; Dorothy Hergesheimer, for Joseph Hergesheimer; Nora Holt; the University of Michigan's Avery Hopwood Memorial Center, for Avery Hopwood; Grace Nail Johnson, for James Weldon Johnson; Harold Ober Associates, Inc., for Langston Hughes; Alfred A. Knopf; Ernst, Cane, Berner, & Gitlin, for Sinclair Lewis; the Baltimore Mercantile Safe Deposit & Trust Company, for H. L. Mencken; Aileen Pringle; Donald Gallup, for Gertrude Stein and for Alice B. Toklas; Joseph Solomon, for Florine, Ettie, and Carrie Stettheimer; Van Vechten Shaffer, for the Van Vechten family letters; Sir Rupert Hart-Davis, for Hugh Walpole; Poppy Cannon White, for Walter White. I also wish to express my gratitude to all other correspondents whom I endeavored unsuccessfully to reach before this book went to press.

In all matters relating to the preparation of this biography, I am beholden to Robert W. Hill and his friendly staff in the manuscript division of the New York Public Library, and to Donald Gallup, curator of the American Literature Collection of the Yale University Library. For additional research, I wish to thank John D. Gordan, curator of the Berg Collection in the New York Public Library, the Cedar Rapids Free Public Library and the Masonic Library in Cedar Rapids, Iowa, and the Hartwick College Library in Oneonta, New York.

For photographs and other illustrations, I am particularly grateful to Saul Mauriber, Carl Van Vechten's photographic executor, and to the following individuals, firms, and collections: Charles Fatone, Al Hirschfeld, Alfred A. Knopf, Inc., Mark Lutz, the New York Public Library (the Carl Van Vechten Collection, manuscript division), James Ringo, Fania Marinoff Van Vechten, United Air Lines, and Hope White, the White Studios. All photographs and illustrations, unless otherwise identified, are in my possession as gifts from Carl Van Vechten. The selection of photographs by Carl Van Vechten is largely his own, drawn from a list of which he approved to accompany this book, shortly before his death in December, 1964.

Finally, the scope and variety of illustrations was made possible through a grant-in-loan from Hartwick College. The faithful reproduction of Carl Van Vechten's photographs is the result of the care and patience of Donald W. Zuercher of the Viking Studio in Oneonta, New York.

The chapter perorations, from unpublished sources, are taken from Carl Van Vechten's letters to me (I, II, IV, V) and to Anna Marble Pollock (VIII, IX, X); those from published sources are taken from *Peter Whiffle* (III), from *Fragments from an unwritten autobiography*, volume I (VI), from *Excavations* (VII), and from the Memoirs of Carl Van Vechten in the Oral History Collection of Columbia University (XI). The unpublished verse by Witter Bynner, dedicated to Carl Van Vechten, is used as an epigraph with Mr. Bynner's permission through the kindness of Dorothy Chauvenet.

Quotations not otherwise identified are drawn from my conversations with Carl Van Vechten, and from his more than seven hundred letters and post cards to me, all of which will be deposited in the American Literature Collection of the Yale University Library.

BRUCE KELLNER

Oneonta, New York
March 20, 1968

Contents

Illustrations

xix

Carl Van Vechten

Dust-jacket for *The Tattooed Countess*
Dust-jacket for *Spider Boy*
Alfred A. Knopf, Carl Van Vechten, and Texas Guinan
Four Saints in Three Acts
Carl Van Vechten, Gertrude Stein, and Alice B. Toklas
Caricature by Miguel Covarrubias
Carl Van Vechten about 1936
Carl Van Vechten, about 1940
The Stage Door Canteen
Alice B. Toklas and Carl Van Vechten
Carl Van Vechten in 1952
Carl Van Vechten at the Thalia Theatre
Detail of a drawing by Al Hirschfeld
Dr. Carl Van Vechten and Dr. Charles Johnson
Fania Marinoff and Carl Van Vechten, 1959
Carl Van Vechten, 1961

Portrait Photographs by Carl Van Vechten

xxi

Carl Van Vechten

William Warfield
Alvin Ailey
Zero Mostel
Kim Stanley
Edward Albee
Martha Graham and Bertram Ross
Lotte Lenya
Mahalia Jackson

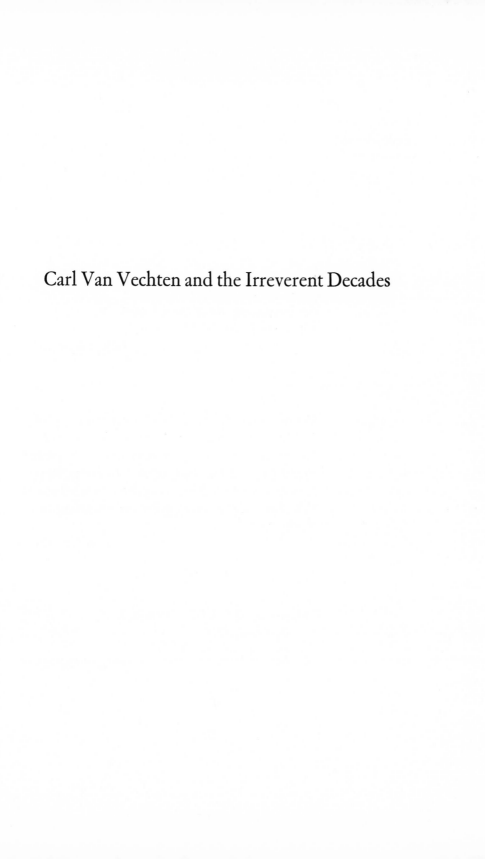

Carl Van Vechten and the Irreverent Decades

Or are you boy or are you man?
You have the eyes of Peter Pan.
Or are you barren as the whores?
Salome had a mouth like yours.
                              —*Witter Bynner*

What mattered it to her just then that the rushes
had begun to fade, and to lose all their scent and
beauty, from the very first moment that she picked
them? Even real scented rushes, you know, last
only a very little while . . . but Alice hardly noticed
this, there were so many other curious things to
think about.
                              —*Lewis Carroll*

"Have you nothing, young man, to declare?"
". . . Butterflies!"
"Exempt of duty. Pass."
                              —*Ronald Firbank*

I

The Maple Valley Years

*There was no one quite like me in
Cedar Rapids.... I couldn't wait to
get out.*

Aʟᴛʜᴏᴜɢʜ ᴡᴇ ʟɪᴋᴇᴅ ᴛᴏ ʙᴇʟɪᴇᴠᴇ ʜɪᴍ an ill-begotten son of that
period he called the "splendid drunken twenties," Carl Van
Vechten was born in Iowa in 1880. Dates and geography are matters of public record, however, gathering dust in the scrapbooks
and periodicals and newspapers of the past. Their print whispers
across the columns. Like sentimental verses on faded valentines,
records only vaguely remind us of other eras, for nothing decorates
them. So to embroider the public record:

Curiously, the time and place were much more propitious than
Carl Van Vechten ever allowed himself to admit. Born in 1880, he
was ripe just in time for the harvest of invention and experiment in
most of the arts at the turn of the century; and growing up in
Cedar Rapids, Iowa, he germinated under fortunate conditions.
Some of this, to be sure, must be credited to Carl Van Vechten
himself: the time was coincidental, and the town only peripherally
involved; but each supplied its own several fields in which any
vigorous talent could find nourishment and any inventive imagination could thrive.

He called it Maple Valley in one of his novels, and chastised its
provincialism with the good-natured malice usually reserved for
the nostalgic longings of a native son. But Carl Van Vechten did
not stay long enough really to qualify as a native son and, once he
escaped, he never longed to rejoin the alien race from which he fled
in 1899. Cedar Rapids was like one of its customary midday meals:
wholesome and plentiful, unimaginatively but well cooked, on

3

which one might grow. To stick around for second helpings, however, could only induce indigestion: the corn belt had a way of stealthily tightening around the belly.

So he was born in Iowa, and he got out just as soon as possible.

Cedar Rapids was at least geographically unique, though the manner in which it differed from its Midwestern sisters would not impress a boy whose horizons stopped at the city limits. It was a town on the make, preoccupied almost from the beginning with its industries and financial resources. Perhaps this is only pragmatic in the corn and trotter territory, where, scarcely a generation before Carl Van Vechten's own, wolves had howled across the green and gold rolling landscape. Cedar Rapids had been settled quickly after the Civil War, growing from a small village of log cabins built by Czechoslovakian emigrants.

By 1878, when Carl's parents moved there from Michigan, some of the buds of the city's fertile beginnings had blossomed. The surrounding hills had given way to at least a minor metropolis. During the years that followed, small farms circled the city at its rapidly expanding outskirts; within their circumference, the two railroad tracks doubled; and freight cars and factories lay just beyond gingerbread mansions, brick and stucco palaces, and wooden cupolaed castles, all of which Carl in his vintage liked to call "that horrible condition without character, the Style McKinley."

All this lay on one side of the Cedar River, which flowed into the Mississippi, less than a hundred miles away. On the opposite bank lay the less imposing structures of the city's Bohemy Town. Like Paris, Cedar Rapids seated its government offices on an island in the center of the dividing tributary. Unlike Paris, however, where the bohemian atmosphere—in its romantic sense—vied with the Right Bank in popularity, the Bohemian atmosphere in Cedar Rapids— nationalistic, to be sure—was conscientiously ignored. In Carl Van Vechten's home town, right and left meant right and wrong.

THE VAN VECHTEN NAME was not new to Cedar Rapids when Carl was born there in 1880. Indeed, it was not new to America:

its bearers served as latter-day pioneers in Iowa, having been, themselves, among the country's earliest pioneers 150 years before.

Carl Van Vechten once declared that ancestor worship had never been one of his fetishes, but it might easily have been, for the family clans are worth consideration. Teunis Dircksen, the first to emigrate from Holland, settled near Albany, New York, in 1638. Successively, his descendants, having come from (*van*) the fields (*Vechten*), made their livings as farmers, merchants, and landowners; one unfortunate ancestor (Carl's great-grandfather) was scalped by Indians while carrying out his duties as a government inspector. His son Gilbert fathered two children: Giles Fonda (named for Jellis, the hairless) and Charles Duane.

Gilbert ran a lumber mill in Kalamazoo, Michigan, the Van Vechtens having spread that far west gradually, over the two-hundred-year period following their arrival in America. During their youth, Giles and Charles worked for their father; but, when he died and the business dissolved, Giles followed the movement toward the west. With his half of the proceeds from the lumber inheritance, he opened a money-lending house in Minneapolis, Minnesota, the nearest approximation to a bank in the Midwest before the Civil War. There, at the age of thirty, having just eloped with the thirteen-year-old daughter of his current mistress, he embarked on a spectacularly successful career. Whether these two events are contingent has not been ascertained. The Minnesota lending house became a bank in Cedar Rapids, and within a few years he had established a second one.

Charles, more conservative, stayed in Michigan to marry Ada Amanda Fitch, the daughter of a pioneer who had hacked his home from the wilderness in the earlier days of the century and the descendant of another Fitch who had invented a primitive steamboat while Robert Fulton was still a very young man. Ada, romantically named by her father after Byron's daughter, had met Charles Van Vechten while still in her teens. The romance developed during his days at Columbia Law School and hers at Kalamazoo College, culminating in 1860 when they were married on the Fitch farm. Charles ran a store on the property for a time, during which two children were born: Ralph in 1862, and Emma in 1864. Then, fourteen years later, when fire devastated everything they owned, Charles was prompted to accept his brother Giles's persistent invitation to come west. A deep-seated conservatism—never to abandon him—had precluded an earlier move; now there was nothing else to do. Charles moved his family to Cedar Rapids in 1878.

They lived first in a small, unpretentious white house. There, on June 17, 1880, Carl Van Vechten was born, a late child to be sure; Emma was sixteen years older, Ralph eighteen.

Forty years later, Carl Van Vechten, in *The Borzoi 1920*, a volume of papers by and about writers on Alfred A. Knopf's payroll during his first five years as a publisher, wrote of the advantages of being born on the "one day in . . . the year which is in every way worthy of being a birthday": It is the day of the birth of Igor Stravinsky and of the death of Joseph Addison, of the Battle of Bunker Hill and of the celebrated ball preceding the Battle of Waterloo; it is the day on which Abraham Lincoln was first nominated. Roses bloom and strawberry shortcake is in season on June 17, and, as the date is six months removed in either direction from Christmas, one might expect a plentitude of presents; the saints of the day bear fascinating if unfamiliar names; and the stars are friendly. "It is," he concluded, "a day on which charming people are born. . . . Nothing can be expected of . . . them . . . and everything!"[1]

For various reasons, the birth was not reported in the newspaper. First of all, the family was of no importance at the time—at best they were poor relations in a singularly class-conscious society. Second, the newspaper was busy with other matters.

The front page of the *Cedar Rapids Evening Gazette* was almost entirely given over to a full account of a railroad show. A few years later, Carl Van Vechten would visit these traveling spectaculars. Concurrently, the Emma Abbott English Grand Opera Company (best remembered for having introduced a trapeze act

[1] "On the Advantages of Being Born on the Seventeenth of June," pp. 49–51.

into *Romeo and Juliet* and *Nearer, My God, to Thee* into the last act of *Faust*) had promised Cedar Rapids three operas in repertory, and seemed to be having trouble getting more than one together. Garfield and Arthur took up considerable space in the paper with their Republican admonitions; what room remained, not given over to advertisements, was occupied by dismal discussions of the local social life, including notice of the Cedar Rapids Cooking Club meeting that same June 17, which Emma Van Vechten attended. Her brother Ralph, then a "thin serious-looking boy in his youth who passed his spare time practising the violin and in printing"[2] his own magazine, *The Rounce*, was working for his Uncle Giles in one of the two banks, probably with his father.

At eleven o'clock that morning, Ada Amanda Fitch Van Vechten, at the age of forty-six, bore her third and last child. "Late children," Carl Van Vechten later observed, "are popularly supposed to be the best; they seem to resist more."[3]

His own resistance is certainly accountable. Growing up alone, without the immediate companionship of children (Ralph married when Carl was seven; Emma followed very soon thereafter), he naturally discovered at an early age the tastes and talents he would always retain. At least one of them began to develop almost immediately:

> I think of all the things he has ever played with or seen nothing pleases him so well as a cat [his mother wrote when Carl was fifteen months old]. Grandma has an old tortoise-shell and she seems to be willing to have baby fondle her as much as he likes even if he does rub her fur the wrong way sometimes.[4]

Carl was scarcely walking when two important changes took place in the Van Vechten family: first, Giles built and deeded his brother an enormous house, a three-story Victorian edifice, bay-windowed and gingerbreaded; second, at the age of forty-eight,

[2] *Sacred and Profane Memories*, p. 6.
[3] Memoirs of Carl Van Vechten, the Oral History Collection of Columbia University (hereafter cited as Van Vechten, Oral History)
[4] *Sacred and Profane Memories*, p. 191.

7

Charles went broke and subsequently entered the insurance business, a vocation in which he achieved considerable success, being publicly cited as one of Iowa's leading businessmen in 1902.

Into the new house, with the Van Vechten menagerie, came Grandmother Fitch. She had abandoned Michigan after the death of her husband, whom Carl remembered only because of his morphine tablets: an inquisitive four-year-old swallowed a whole fistful; the bitter taste brought them right back up again, of course, but at least—during the twenties when opium smoking and cocaine sniffing became an occasional pastime—Carl knew what he was missing. He remembered his Grandmother Fitch better. She smoked a pipe and prophesied that her youngest grandchild would die on the gallows. Also, to Carl's father's intense displeasure, she insisted on spreading her voluminous skirts to urinate on the front lawn: Charles feared for the grass; Ada feared for the neighbors; Carl was enchanted, watching the great bell skirts billow out as she sank into position.

He equally well recalled Grandmother Van Vechten, who lived the last of her nearly one hundred years with Giles and his child bride, and died, Carl later reflected, only because she wanted to, neither ill nor in poor health. He read to her during those final years, not from his earliest favorite J. T. Trowbridge, but from the travel books of Bayard Taylor, dull but suitable, he thought, for the old lady, who did not really listen anyway. One day while Mary, Giles's adopted daughter, was playing the piano, Grandmother Van Vechten leaned over the staircase railing to say, "Play funeral dirges, Mary." Then she went back to her room and died.

It is understandable that Carl's first memories dealt with the adults around him, since there were no other children. His brother and sister were married by the time he could remember them clearly; Cousin Mary was several years his senior; the children of his parents' friends were all much older; and his parents themselves, nearing fifty as Carl emerged from babyhood to boyhood, had reached an age when indulgence was easier than discipline. Even his introduction to the minor vices came by way of adults, if inadvertently: his first bouts with smoking occurred when he stole a couple of cubebs from his sister, who used them to relieve her asthma; and, although no intoxicating drink graced his father's table, Carl first sampled beer at the age of seven at his brother's bachelor dinner. The following morning—a Sunday—early church-goers discovered him parading around the front yard, his bare arms and legs covered with paper bands from cigars and beer bottles. He was off to a good start or perhaps a bad one: if the neighbors thought him a thoroughly nasty little boy, given to temper tantrums and show-off tactics, he must have seemed, in the years that followed, more and more a hybrid ear in the fields of conventional corn.

Dear Leah [Carl wrote to Ralph's wife's younger sister in 1889], how are you getting along I hope very well. We have found the kittens, I found them, my very own self, there are five of them, and all of them are maltee. I found them up in the hay. I saw two beautiful doves this afternoon, I mean pigeons they were black and white. We write in our copy-books at school now with ink and its fun. Teacher is reading us little lord Fauntleroy. . . . St. Nicholas, I will name some funny and pretty story books. Delightful Story book; Brownies; Edith as burglar; Fools Paradise; Picture Gallery; Our littles and the nursely; Youth's Companion. There are others but this is all I am going to write. . . . Your loving husband, Carl Van Vechten[5]

This earliest letter points up three interests that stayed with Carl throughout his life: a love for animals, an "obstinate penchant" for cataloguing, and a passion for reading. He began by adoring Trowbridge and Horatio Alger; but he was exposed also to *Harper's Weekly* and the *Atlantic Monthly*, bound files of which reposed behind glass doors in one of the Van Vechten bookcases. When he was about six, contemplating a copy of the latter, he burst into tears; his explanation, between sobs: "Someday I'll grow up and begin to like magazines without pictures."[6]

[5] Carl Van Vechten Collection, Manuscript Division, New York Public Library (hereafter cited as CVV, NYPL).
[6] *Sacred and Profane Memories*, p. 10n.

Then too, the *Woman's Journal* always lay on a table in the sitting room. Carl's mother, a college friend of Lucy Stone, endorsed the cause of women's suffrage at a time when the movement was hardly a popular one, and, in her own quiet way, proved the ability of her sex to function beyond the confines of the family: Ada Van Vechten successfully legislated in the state senate to appropriate funds for the construction of the Cedar Rapids Free Public Library. It was from there that Carl read the early Henry James, Daudet's *Sapho*, and, some time later, two volumes that left "an indelible impression": Bernard Shaw's *Plays Pleasant and Unpleasant* and George Moore's *Confessions of a Young Man*.

Somewhere between, he sandwiched *The Swiss Family Robinson* and an abridged *Arabian Nights*, and most of Ingersoll Lockwood and Frank Stockton. (At the age of eighty-four, he could still write, probably without much exaggeration, "After Sartre and Genet, Frank Stockton is my favorite writer and I am having an orgy.") Then, after a momentary acquaintance with the popular dime novels involving Nick Carter or Deadwood Dick or Nugget Nell the Waif of the Range or Double Dan the Dastard, he passed on to more fruitful orchards: Dickens in quantity, and Mark Twain and Richard Harding Davis; Chicago's bohemian *Chap-Book*, where French decadence and Brander Matthews ran in adjoining columns. He read some Shakespeare too, though admittedly without much enthusiasm except for the plays he had seen: Ellen Terry in *The Merchant of Venice*, when he visited his sister in Cincinnati in 1896; and, at the age of twelve, Otis Skinner and his wife Maud Durbin in *Romeo and Juliet* in Cedar Rapids.

Paradoxically, Carl's home town, halfway between Chicago and Omaha, was an extremely propitious place for him to have been raised; nearly every traveling theatrical company stopped there to play at least a one-night stand in Greene's Opera House. If Carl in later years could disparage the drought in Maple Valley's culture and if, alas, Greene's Opera House is now a parking garage, what better training ground could have possibly existed for a music and drama critic? At Greene's, an eight-year-old Carl saw Richard

Mansfield in *Beau Brummel* and *A Parisian Romance*. But his happiest memories in the beginning were of the entertainments: the Hanlon Brothers or Eddie Foy in their musical extravaganzas, for example, or Gilbert and Sullivan light opera.

On many of these excursions to Greene's he was accompanied by Edward Howell, a neighbor boy whom Carl remembered best because of a stuffed bird of paradise that sat in the front bow window of the Howell house. Edward remembered Carl best because of the plays that he watched, a solo audience for a solo performer, in the Van Vechten front parlor. Carl frequently presented shows there, dressing a miniature stage with scraps from his mother's ample sewing basket, and acting all the roles himself with the aid of a number of Godey's ladies cut from an 1868 volume of the fashion magazine in which they originally appeared. The shows went on for hours, improvised as they progressed, and lasting as long as Edward's attention or Carl's invention allowed them to. Neither gave out easily.

There were other productions as well. In the barn behind the Van Vechten house there was ample space to reflect and embroider upon the spectacular performances given at Greene's Opera House. Posters adorned the rough walls, pasted there by Carl's brother some years earlier: James O'Neill (the father of Eugene, later a friend of Carl's) declared that the world was his in *The Count of Monte Cristo*, and kept company with the Hanlon Brothers embarked on their *Voyage en Suisse* or tumbling in *Fantasma* or *Superba*; there were posters of by-gone circuses and portraits of race horses; Frank Mayo as Davy Crockett and Emma Abbott as Yum Yum in *The Mikado* posed along the walls; and John L. Sullivan stood in boxing stance.

Wild West shows and circuses were the mainstay, sometimes as neighborhood productions, more often as one-man shows. Later, when the barn burned to the ground in 1892, Carl turned its stone base into an elaborate garden, complete with fountains and rock designs. The loss of the barn did not, however, deter the amateur theatricals. At Crystal Lake, Michigan, where the family frequently went for summer vacations, Carl wrote plays and skits and acted in them as well. The place abounded with young people and, though nobody had any particular talent, everybody performed. Still later, in his junior year in high school, Carl and two of his classmates wrote a dramatic version of *The Prisoner of Zenda*. Carl had a rousing success as Rupert of Hentzau, the villain of the piece, by combing his hair over his forehead and pouting mysteriously.

Along with his preoccupation with the theater, other interests were developing, most often through collections: postage stamps, cigarette pictures of popular actresses, tobacco tags; but the amassing of birds' eggs seems to have been the greatest passion of those early years. His mother, picturing the despair of the mother birds, begged him to leave a single egg in each nest he chose to despoil, and for a time he agreed. Then he met his cousin Roy Fitch on a summer holiday with his father in Michigan, a cold-blooded twelve-year-old professional. After that, Carl followed Roy's experienced example and filched the whole clutch whenever he happened upon one.

Deprived of ordinary domestic pets, he cultivated, at various times: a baby alligator, chameleons, mice, a snapping turtle housed in a swill barrel, and, during a visit to Michigan in 1892, a sudden desire for pigeons:

> *Dear Mamma:*—we arrived here safely and I at least am having a nice time. Papa is too. I guess but I can't tell the feelings of others. On the train from St. Joe. Papa met a man and began talking with him. After a while the man said he was a Baptist minister. I thought that would end their conversation but it didn't. . . . Tony the dog knows me now and will come when I call him. A pair of Roy's pigeons hatched last night I think. Your son CARL

Four days later, he wrote again,

> If you can and I wish you would please send one dollar, as Uncle Charlie has money only for my clothes, and I have not money enough with me. I want to get a pair of pigeons with it.

Apparently, the dollar had not arrived at the end of the week:

Please send me eleven dollars for I've got to have it. For 12 dollars I can get 10 pair of the best pigeons Grand Rapids ever set eyes on. With the eleven dollars and the other one you are going to send it will make 12 dollars. I know you will think it is foolish but it isn't a bit, if you could see the birds once you would not think so. Please send it to me and I will not ask you for any more money to spend for pigeons. Roy advises me to get them.

Then he had a new idea, and requested that his mother go out to the barn behind the house in Cedar Rapids, close all the windows, and build a hinged screen door in the floor of the hayloft above:

Then nail up 12 peach baskets about 7 feet from the ground with about one inch of straw in the bottom with the handles broken off, for nests and I will send home the birds just as fast as I get them.

Cedar Rapids apparently remained silent; another letter followed immediately, marked "private":

Dear Mamma . . . Please tell me when you have the pigeon coop fixed so that I will know when to send on the pigeons.

And a few days later:

Please send me the money as the pigeons are a bargain. One pair alone the boy paid 12 dollars for. Please send it right away because I am afraid some one else will buy them.

Presumably the wisdom of age and an expert knowledge of her son's enthusiasms deterred Carl's mother from complying with these not altogether simple requests. In the face of silence he wrote, toward the middle of August,

I have thought the matter over and I have decided not to get any pigeons here as I have a catalogue and when I get home I can send for some if I want them.[7]

It was a dignified withdrawal for a twelve-year-old; the pigeon phase passed, and Carl moved in other directions.

Beyond the points of the compass, there were, however, few

[7] CVV, NYPL.

13

Carl Van Vechten

directions for an imaginative boy at the close of the nineteenth century. The nineties have been variously characterized: Stuart Pratt Sherman called them "yellow," echoing a familiar tag given the period because of the popularity of yellow-jacketed French novels; H. L. Mencken called them "electric," because of their revolt against the authority of their century; Richard Le Gallienne called them "romantic," because from his point of view they were; and W. L. Whittlesey called them "moulting." More often they seem to be stuck with "gay," though "innocent" seems, perhaps, more appropriate, at least in Cedar Rapids. There, movies were only a vaguely blurred image, and the horseless carriage was still called a devil wagon; doctors had never heard of insulin, farmers had never heard of tractors, bankers had never heard of the Federal Reserve; there were no chain stores, no self-service, no permanent waves, no cafeterias, no automats, no crossword puzzles; and no one had ever heard of cubism or Rotary Clubs.

Entertainment during the nineties was homegrown. Certainly, the Van Vechtens were not unique at the time in being a musical family: the phonograph was in its infancy, and "radio" was an unknown word. Carl's mother's rosewood square grand piano was an important fixture in the house, and his own lessons at its keyboard began early. By the time he was twelve he was sampling the masters on his own, since nobody else seemed to know them. Tosti's *Goodbye*, parlor pieces—like *The Butterfly*, *The Dying Poet* or *The Last Hope*, *The Rosebud Polka*—and the *King Cotton March* of John Philip Sousa were more likely to hold the attention of Cedar Rapids musicians. Nor were the audiences possessed of discriminating ears, judging from a Cedar Rapids newspaper of the period:

> Each piece whether from the piano or voice was heard with a gladsome frame of mind and a disposition to comprehend the eloquence of the player and the emotionality of the singer. So rare for the audience.[8]

The foregoing account is of a joint recital, the eloquent player

[8] *Cedar Rapids Gazette*, June 17, 1897.

14

The Maple Valley Years

Thuel Burnham; but Carl remembered only that Burnham approached the distinction only by way of his temperament, which frequently ended in his not appearing at all. Such entertainments took place irregularly in the basement of the Universalist Church, where the Van Vechten family attended services. And, if the pianist did not show up, then Carl was able to watch Herbie Newell sing "She Was a Daisy" and perform the skirt dance in an amateur production of *1492* at the Grace Episcopal Church. Beyond this, there was little regular amusement. Cedar Rapids had no symphony orchestra, no opera company, no resident company at Greene's. But Carl was able to compensate by playing Schubert and Beethoven and Bizet and Gounod and others on his mother's Gilbert grand long before their compositions were heard professionally in the town.

When Carl was seventeen, an aspiring opera singer—a connection or relative of some Cedar Rapids matron—bobbed up. He went to her with the score of *Carmen* under his arm and demanded that she sing it for him. She could not, of course; the opera was too new. Her inability was typical of the general apathy toward contemporary music at the time, a sad fact Carl was soon to discover and, later, to fight during all the years of his critical writing. By the time he got to Chicago two years later, *Carmen* and a number of other scores were familiar to him, but no one in Cedar Rapids could be held responsible for having introduced him to them.

For entertainment beyond the piano and the offerings at Greene's Opera House, Carl usually parked himself on the doorstep of Mahala Dutton Benedict Douglas, an extraordinary woman whose family lived in Cedar Rapids. Because the town considered the lady too emancipated, Carl was warned by his family to avoid her. He promptly interpreted this as an order to see her more, and did so whenever the opportunity arose.

As Mrs. Walter Douglas, she later inherited the Quaker Oats industry in Cedar Rapids. After her husband went down on the *Titanic* and she and her maid were rescued, she moved away from Iowa. But, during the years she lived there, her influence on Carl

15

was considerable. Mahala Douglas is often cited as the counterpart of Carl Van Vechten's fictional tattooed countess, the Iowa girl who married well and returned to her home town to shock the natives. Beyond the obvious parallel, there was no connection: whereas the countess carried the youthful hero off to European capitals when he was seventeen, Mrs. Douglas first encountered Carl when he was eight years old; and her reactions to him, when he reached the age of being carried off, differed slightly. "I'm so damn bored with this town," Carl exploded one evening, "I'd like to put on a bath towel and run through the streets naked." Mrs. Douglas said nothing, but she went into the house and returned a moment later with the towel. "Go ahead, Carl," she said.

Carl had a few other isolated acquaintances in those earliest years, but, on the whole, those years were singularly empty. In any society —Midwestern or not—at the close of the nineteenth century, the same difficulty beset anyone who veered from the recognizable pattern. Edward Howell, Carl's childhood friend, recalled him during the early nineties: "Carl wasn't any good at ball—he wasn't any good at the things the rest of us did—but he did almost everything we couldn't do." Howell remembered a game of some kind, perhaps a contest of physical prowess, carried on in the back yard of one of the boys, to illustrate what he meant. During the handstands, the Indian wrestling, the various feats of strength, Carl sat on the sidelines, pretending singular interest in the bark of a tree. Then the boys got around to the broad jump. Carl ambled over, with the angular undulation of a young giraffe, and put them all in their places with one gigantic stride of his yard-long eleven-year-old legs. Then he stumbled back to his tree. Such disdainful, show-off performances neither inspired friendship with, nor endeared him to, the neighborhood hearties.

The years of adolescence that followed must have been worse. At thirteen, Carl was six feet tall, his body awkward and uncoordinated in its early height, and his features actually unnerving. A latter-day description of him as looking like a domesticated werewolf would have never been inappropriate: he had the blank stare of an animal, as steady as a cat's, as cold as a snake's; and the outwardly sullen expression was disfigured by two very big and very ugly protruding front teeth, like squares of broken crockery. For nearly a dozen years during his youth, he endured the pain of trying to have them straightened, wearing elaborate primitive braces, fighting off well-meaning dentists' plans for extraction. He was a strange-looking boy, and he behaved appropriately; that, coupled with his conscious cultivation of the eccentric, raised the local eyebrows. "We thought him very odd, queer almost," a schoolmate hesitatingly admitted, remembering a couple of her dates with Carl—once to a picnic, once to a dance—when he seemed determined to attract attention. He grew one long, talon-like nail on the little finger of his right hand. He rode about town on one of the modern, low bicycles, first a Sterling ("built like a watch," the advertisements claimed) and then a Baines ("like a trusty steed"). He dressed in the fashion of the big city, which was decidedly not the fashion of Cedar Rapids. Charles Dana Gibson's creation of the ideal American girl in 1895 had its counterpart in the ideal American boy, square-shouldered and firm-jawed, his sleek hair parted mathematically in the middle. Mustaches were out, and shoulder pads were in, though nobody in Cedar Rapids knew it as soon as Carl did. He sported a derby and pointed, patent-leather boots; he affected Ascots; and he had the highest collars and the tightest trousers in town. He was, in the parlance of the period, a dude as far as Cedar Rapids was concerned, *sui generis* and *fin de siècle*, whatever those then popular but doubtless subversive expressions may have implied to Iowa during the 1890's.

THE PAIN OF ADOLESCENCE, however, was tempered slightly by what little social life existed for the young people in Cedar Rapids. But, once past puberty, Carl easily adjusted to the contemporary climate, though his interests carried him in the direction of feminine pursuits. There were lap suppers and kettle drums, the forerunners of buffet dinner parties; there were pack-wax gatherings, where concoctions of snow and maple sirup were devoured; there were picnic afternoons and front-porch evenings and boat rides on the Cedar River.

When a golf course opened in Cedar Rapids—one of the first in the country—the town's young people flocked to it. Carl frequently played the new game with Anna Elizabeth Snyder, his most constant companion through his teens. It seemed to their friends a curious relationship, for Ann was a handsome girl, nearly six feet tall, awkward in the kitchen, uncomfortable with the other girls whose domestic proclivities bored her, ill at ease with the yellow elegance of the nineties. Ann was almost remote; and, possessed of a maddening serenity, an indifference that masked her own attitude toward the town, she was a strange companion for Carl. Their families were friendly, and the courtship long; marriage, though never encouraged, was more or less expected. Ann and Carl "always went about together," Clara Deacon, a classmate, recalled. "They were not engaged or spoken; and Carl even took me out to a dance—and got his ears frostbitten on the way home—but Ann was his real pal." She thought them a peculiar couple, but no one in Cedar Rapids registered any particular surprise when they married in 1907.

Ten years earlier, however, Ann and Carl were most often in the company of others their own age, attending "evenings." Carl's sister Emma was responsible for a typical one in 1897, a supper party followed by palm reading in honor of Carl's seventeenth birthday. A partial guest list gives some indication of the social cross-section: a local dairyman's son escorting the daughter of the opera house impresario, the various teenage offspring of the Episcopal rector, a criminal lawyer, some merchants, even farmers; but, though a single high school served the city, nobody from the Czech "Bohemy Town" appeared. According to the local newspaper, which never failed to report on table decorations, menus, and entertainment for every gathering in town, "the youthful spirits triumphed over all discomforts of the temperature." (It was 107).

The same remark might stand for Carl himself, for his own predilections did much to overcome the stifling intellectual climate in Cedar Rapids. Like its temperatures, exceedingly hot and exceedingly cold, there were absolutely no half-measures in the mores and conventions of the town. Not surprisingly, Carl's eccentricities did not bother his contemporaries: an oddball, popular enough, one of them recalled. The complacency of small-town middle age is, however, not so amenable, and in a world that precluded interest in almost everything except a bumper corn crop, he must have seemed an enigma.

But Carl Van Vechten knew from the beginning where he was going and, like the youth in his Iowa novel *The Tattooed Countess*, he must have often cried to himself:

> I want to know everything, *everything* . . . and . . . I'm going to. . . . I want to get away from this town. . . . I want to visit the theatre and the opera and the art galleries. I want to meet people. I want to learn. Somewhere there must be more people like me. . . .[9]

If he was ready to leave Iowa in 1896, when at sixteen he "couldn't wait to get out," by 1899 he was on the verge of claustrophobia. The atmosphere his parents had provided carried just enough exposure to the arts to make him want more; what he knew of the theater, of music, of literature, only frustrated him because of what he did not know. Actually, Cedar Rapids had been a rather fertile garden that he had sown successfully, though at the age of nineteen Carl must have found its cuttings pale and withered and totally lacking in fragrance.

The University of Chicago may not have been the most fruitful kingdom for an early exile, but it was a step in the right direction because it was a step away from the myopic world of Maple Valley.

[9] Pp. 77–81.

II

Chicago

*Chicago actually is not much better,
but I didn't know that yet.*

The 7th Sassy Snell Soiree was held Monday, and polite society was there with the goods. Snell is the favorite haunt of the smart set, because it has a dance hall in the cellar. The dancing space runs from the potato bin to the cheese box, and dancing has all the delights and excitement of a swell fireman's ball, and then some. When the freckled Freshman essays the Hyde Park Chicken Two Step down the length of the pillared promenade he is in danger. . . . Rumor has it that a near-sighted medic lost his girl in the crush, grasped one of the pillars by mistake and waltzed wildly around it for 5 minutes by the clock trying to get it in reverse. The dust from the coalbin often makes the promenade more like a cinder track than a dance hall, but the joys of Snell Hall receptions are still multitudinous.[1]

But the dust upon this repartee, culled from the pages of *The University of Chicago Weekly*, would not yet have settled when Carl Van Vechten first invaded Chicago to begin college at midterm in 1899. He had fooled around sufficiently during his senior year in high school to flunk mathematics. Indeed, he spent most of his schooling somewhat laconically: he studied French and German, and learned neither; he prescribed his own reading; he practiced his piano lessons instead of doing homework; his indulgent parents even let him drop out for a semester to spend the winter season in Cincinnati with his sister Emma and her family. Anna Snyder graduated and went to Wellesley; other friends took local jobs or got married; Carl enrolled in Cedar Rapids's Coe College to make

[1] January 9, 1902, p. 330.

up his lost credits in mathematics, not as an entering freshman but as a probationary transient. In January, he fled toward the east.

Carl had not chosen the University of Chicago for any academic reason; it is unlikely that he really burned to go to college at all. But at least Chicago was two hundred miles away from Cedar Rapids, and Denis Campau, a summer friend from the Michigan holidays, had written enthusiastically about both the school and the town that toddled toward revolution. Just a few years later, Chicago would become an active verb in the sentence passed on nineteenth-century traditions in literature.

As early as the mid-nineties, the rumblings had sounded when several groups of artists and writers joined forces as if in defiance of the city's gentility. Chicago's peerage blamed such bohemian in-filtrations on the World's Fair, convinced that the local gypsies were simply the refuse of the 1893 exposition. Eugene Field fell into that category, even though his wildest days had already spent them-selves before he reached Chicago; Isadora Duncan came east from San Francisco to perform her religious dances; the Cypher Club and the Bohemian Club festered on Chicago's healthy brow. The city's worthies may not have approved, but they could not ignore the popularity of the *Chap-Book*, first issued in 1894, which intro-duced Paul Verlaine and Stéphane Mallarmé to America; nor could they overlook the disclosures of Henry Blake Fuller, their own resident novelist, who wrote about the Midwestern Left Bank in *Under the Skylights*.

Chicago's growth on the eve of the new century was not of course limited to literary upheavals. The City of Big Shoulders was already on its way to becoming the "Hog Butcher for the World," as Carl Sandburg called it, the "Tool Maker, Stacker of Wheat,/ Player with Railroads and the/Nation's Freight Handler." Its academic growth ran parallel: the university was already develop-ing what the Federal Writers called "the most auspicious program in university history," engineered by William Rainey Harper, whose revolutionary ideas created an amazing curriculum and an inspired faculty. Musically, Chicago generated equal excitement at the time because of Theodore Thomas. Since 1891, the Chicago Symphony Orchestra under his direction had played the compositions of César Franck, Tchaikovsky, Richard Strauss, Debussy, Ravel, Gustave Charpentier, and Edward MacDowell—many of them before they were given hearings in New York. When Carl Van Vechten arrived in Chicago, the city was seething with possibilities.

His first two years at college were sufficiently diverting. He had arrived—for all his Cedar Rapids sophistication—a pretty innocent boy, an obvious off-horse, and a technical virgin. Denis Campau talked his fraternity into pledging Carl, though the harangue that ensued delayed membership until his sophomore year. Once given the grip, however, both boys seem to have neglected the organization as often as possible. They drank too much and studied too little; but simultaneously Carl discovered that there were in the world other people who shared his interests. He heard professional musicians. He visited the art galleries. He attended the opera. He saw, for the first time, authentic ragtime in action in performances by Bert Williams and Cissie Loftus and George Walker and Aida Overton. If popular music did not pass any of its time in Chicago concert halls—as it would do one day—Carl at least could syncopate it with the serious musical endeavors of the city. Additionally, through the university and a gifted teacher named Myra Reynolds, he discovered Restoration comedy and eighteenth-century satire and read almost nothing else during his college career. Concurrently, he suffered a happy exposure to three men whose teaching had an early effect on his own work: Robert Herrick, the now neglected but then popular novelist whose books Carl worshiped, more for their author than for their content; William Vaughn Moody, the poet and dramatist then in residence at the university; and Robert Morss Lovett, who encouraged Carl to write.

The creative urge, nourished at the university, had been an early one, dating back to the days of the Crystal Lake skits and the diaries he began to keep with some regularity about 1896; but it was not until Carl's last two years in college that writing became an

22

obsession, an excuse to escape an environment with which he had grown, frankly, bored. He wrote dozens of stories and plays—one of the latter based on Robert Hichens's *The Londoners*—and attempted some verse. When Carl was a sophomore, he began contributing "really vile sketches," as he later called them, to the *University of Chicago Weekly*. They show no profoundly latent talent, and seem instead to have been inspired by Horatio Alger, the university, Nick Carter, and the sophisticated patina of youth—all at once. "The Change in Harlowe" concerned a serious fellow disinterested in the ribaldry in Snell Hall, where "songs were interspersed with stories of doubtful propriety." Harlowe, incensed, engages one of the "Old Snellers" in fisticuffs:

> A blow from Harlowe's fist effectually quenched all further desire of repartee. . . . The other fellows crowded up to seize the new man who was proving himself more of a hero than they imagined him. He hit one after another with surprising coolness and parried their blows with great success.

Suddenly he stops:

> "I can't do it, fellows; I see it all now. What an ass I've been and how I have misunderstood you. Not that there is any harm in men's fighting. But not to feel each other in the fight, not to sympathize with each other's thoughts. I imagined you a hard lot. I never thought of college as a moral training ground."

The boys are overcome and,

> already delighted with his brawn, found his changed manners irresistible. They placed him on their shoulders and gave many "rahs" for Harlowe. And the next afternoon Harlowe was on hand for football practice.[2]

In spite of the cynicism, is there not more wishful thinking than accuracy in the situation? The social columns of the *University of Chicago Weekly* are singularly devoid of Carl's name, and his only real friend in college seems to have been Denis Campau; nor did he pay court to the local Gibson girls.

[2] *Ibid.*, p. 333.

The stories in the campus paper are, however, generally objective and interesting because they contain a few Van Vechten penchants: the inclusion of actual personalities and the carrying over of characters from one tale to another. In the final story to appear in the *Weekly*, "A Relief," printed in July, 1902, Carl did apparently write directly about himself. Over a period of a year and a half under Lovett's tutelage, the actual practice of composition had wrought a number of significant changes in his work:

> Marston had stayed for the summer quarter to see *Florodora* again, as he flippantly expressed it, and, to say truth, that was as much his reason as any. His leanings toward the academic were not pronounced: Of course, there was no society in the summer: the amusements that remained were a few of his fraternity brothers, the summer gardens and the theatre. It was either summer work for him or a vacation in Mudville. . . . The first day he loafed, chatted under the trees with some of the other stayovers, and made uncomplimentary remarks about the summer students. The second day he was bored and did not go to college at all. He stayed at the house and read: "*Confessions of a Young Man*" and "*A Pair of Blue Eyes*"—at night *Florodora*.[3]

During the summer before his senior year, Carl did stay in Chicago, if not to see *Florodora*—its local appearance echoing a record-breaking run in New York—then to escape the prospect of three months in Cedar Rapids. Earlier summers had found him checking bicycles at the ball park or working in Uncle Giles's bank, the latter job a singularly stultifying chore. Early in the mornings, before the Iowa sun began to bake its citizens, Carl opened envelopes and sorted out the bills for collection; then, in the furnace heat of noon, he went round on his bicycle to make the collections. In the afternoons, he moved on to the adding machine and, in the evenings, sealed up new envelopes in order to begin all over again the following day. His salary was nine dollars a week.

Anna Snyder was in Cedar Rapids during those hot summer months, home on vacation from Wellesley, and so there was some

3 July 31, 1902, pp. 942–943.

respite. She had been to New York, where Sarah Bernhardt was playing, where opera singers from Europe made their American debuts. Moreover, Carl's affection for Ann and hers for him had continued beyond their high-school courtship. If they were not exactly in love with each other, there was at least a communion of spirit in their joint rebellion against Cedar Rapids's limited concern with the arts. And so the warm summer holidays passed not unpleasantly until the time came to return to school for the fall term.

Peter Whiffle, the hero of Carl Van Vechten's first novel, confesses that his last two years of college were "an awful strain," but that he managed to endure them because he could not think of anything else he wanted to do. Carl was doubtless talking about himself, but he later appended Peter's remarks: "I was scared to death whenever I thought of leaving college and so, although I was bored to extinction my last year at Chicago, I stuck it out, rather than plunge into a strange world." And again: "When I got out of college I had no idea I could make a living and was perfectly certain I would become a . . . public charge."

Two old interests, however, kept Carl occupied during his academic *Götterdämmerung*: theater and music; the first superficially, the second seriously. During his senior year at the University of Chicago he had undergone a period of intense creativity, resulting in a number of musical compositions, six of which were privately printed in 1904, at a cost of thirty dollars to the composer. Limited to one hundred copies, the large sheets were enclosed in maroon covers, stamped in gold: *Five Old English Ditties*, "With music by Carl Van Vechten." These songs—settings for lyrics by Congreve, Lyly, and Carl's friend Denis Campau—indicate little musical merit. The accompaniments are clumsy, and the melodies not notably tuneful, though Campau's song begins with a brief waltz of considerable charm. More interesting is the manner in which the singer is directed to perform: "ingenuously," "quizically," "hypocritically"—depending on the song.

The collection, originally entitled *The Love Songs of a Philanderer*, was dedicated in manuscript (but not in the printed version) to AES, Anna Snyder. The romance, apparently, continued to develop:

> *Dear, were you in a garden old*
> *Loved of brave troubadors,*
> *Who praised your hair bewildering gold*
> *That glimmers and adores:*
> *The greatest wondering on your face*
> *Between the ilex trees*
> *Might take his lute and thrill the place*
> *With sweeter songs than these.*[4]

The other music composed in this period was never published in any form, but among the compositions were such songs as *Absinthe* and *Chloe*, several studies for violin and piano, a number of waltzes and serenades. If the published songs are any indication of the content of the others, it becomes clear that the influences stemmed from the current ballads of the period rather than from the music Carl had studied during his youth.

Theodore Thomas, nevertheless, kept him constantly aware of serious music by way of the Chicago Symphony Orchestra. Thomas was not an inspired conductor, but—from Carl's point of view—he was an inspired arranger of programs, never afraid to give contemporary composers frequent performances. There were other felicitous discoveries. Chicago had more than a cursory opera season. The Metropolitan played four weeks every year with its greatest casts; and the New Orleans Opera Company appeared regularly in works, like *Sigurd* and *Salammbô*, that no one hears anywhere today. In the city's ancient auditorium, Carl heard Puccini's *Tosca*, shortly after its first American performance in New York, with Milka Ternina, who had introduced the role. Her Tosca was "pure gold," he later reflected of a singer who "molded her own figure" in a part she had never heard. Fritzi Scheff (before her *Kiss Me Again* days) stopped the show so completely as Papagena in *The Magic Flute* that Sembrich's Queen of the Night aria began unheard because of the storm of applause. Nellie Melba and Emma

[4] CVV, NYPL.

26

Chicago

Eames and Ernestine Schumann-Heink appeared annually during Carl's years in Chicago. But opera was expensive, and he often joined the casts on stage and "suped"; that is, he donned a robe or carried a spear, depending on the evening's offering, as a member of the nonsinging chorus that supplemented the skeleton casts of the touring companies.

For seven years, indeed, he attended nearly all the recitals and concerts available, the musical entertainments of Cissie Loftus at the roof theater of the Masonic Temple, and Fritzi Scheff in *Mlle Modiste* and other operettas of the period. Also, in Chicago, he continued to play the piano, performing violin and piano sonatas by Grieg and Franck and Richard Strauss in public with Evelyn Cooper, and, semipublicly, when he occasionally replaced a professor in a Chicago brothel on Custom House Place, playing current popular tunes for the clients and *Hearts and Flowers* and Massenet's *Elégie* for the girls. It was, altogether, a varied musical education, gradually preparing him to assume the responsibilities of assistant music critic on the *New York Times* a few years later.

Carl's interest in the theater, during his college years at least, was less profound. Having appeared in his junior year as a silent trumpeter in a production of Ben Jonson's *The Case Is Altered*, he got a chance to do considerably more when he was a senior. A musical extravaganza about Madame Du Barry, playing in Chicago at the time, inspired a "Dew Berry" show. With the assistance of a few of his fraternity brothers, Carl erected, between two large doorways in the Psi Upsilon house, a stage that consisted of nothing more than one gigantic bed, on which all the action—most of it salacious—took place. Carl played the title role, the rest of the cast was in blackface, and together they shocked their classmates. But at that point propriety had become pointless, and, ready for another of Mahala Douglas's bath towels, Carl could not wait to get free of his academic shackles.

The opportunity came later in his senior year when Sam Paquin, a former fraternity brother, employed Carl in some minor office work for the United Press. By the time he had graduated with a bachelor of philosophy degree in the spring of 1903, he had severed all his relations with the university. Newspaper life amused him more and more, and he was ready, after his brief experience as an errand boy, to embark on a career in journalism.

WITH LITTLE DIFFICULTY, Carl was hired almost immediately for the staff of William Randolph Hearst's *Chicago American*. For anyone of reasonable intelligence and a clever pen, it was easy to get a job on a newspaper staff or in an advertising office at the time, for Chicago was bursting its seams in almost every direction. In less than seventy years since its incorporation in 1833, it had grown from a village of a handful of inhabitants to a metropolis of nearly 1,700,000.

In 1904, when Carl Van Vechten left college and went to work, Chicago was a curious blend of good and bad, of astonishing progress and ruthless exploitation. At the same time that herds of ignorant immigrants invaded the stockyards at slave-labor wages, there were several bright young men from various parts of the Midwest, attracted by Chicago's glamour, who came to discover twentieth-century American literature and stayed to produce some of it themselves. Floyd Dell, Arthur Davison Ficke, Witter Bynner, Thorstein Veblen, Edgar Lee Masters, Sherwood Anderson, Ben Hecht, Vachel Lindsay, Maxwell Bodenheim, Theodore Dreiser, and Carl Sandburg, among many others, spent time in Chicago during the years that followed; but the city's great age—which included the rediscovery of free verse in America, Harriet Monroe's *Poetry* and Margaret Anderson's *Little Review*, and the Bodenheim-Hecht bohemian scandals—came several years after Carl Van Vechten had left Chicago.

The *Chicago American* at that time was housed on the second floor of a broken-down building, but its staff was excellent in spite of the office facilities: Hugh Fullerton and Charles Finnegan; Ben Hecht—so Carl claimed; and Charles Fitzmorris, who, as a school-boy, had been sent around the world by another Chicago newspaper and had returned in 60 days, 13 hours, 29 minutes, and

42 ⅘ seconds, to break Nellie Bly's 1889 record. As reporters they were so sufficiently gifted that the newest member of the organization had little opportunity to write much in the beginning.

Carl's first assignment, on the early shift at four in the morning, was to clip the rival newspapers and prepare composite articles for the editor, who arrived three hours later. To fortify himself for this chore, Carl hied himself to one of the few restaurants open in the Loop at that hour, for two pieces of heavy apple pie submerged in Welsh rarebit and "a great cup of worse coffee than any I have ever sampled before or since."[5]

Eventually, he telephoned in stories for rewrite, one of which at least gave him material for an alumni letter to the *Pulse*, his high-school newspaper in Cedar Rapids. Assigned to the Harrison Street police station on Thanksgiving ("I worked quite as usual today. The great American Daily seemed intent upon its editions, at any cost . . ."), he found ample material for a brief article: singing missionaries bringing food to the prisoners, a lost dog, a delirium-tremens patient, police matrons, and, afterward, "a chop sooey" dinner in the neighborhood; "and yet," he concluded, "not a bad Thanksgiving."[6]

Frequently, the *American* called upon him to collect photographs for the paper; it was, indeed, Carl's primary duty for a time. But on at least two occasions he was involved in important news events: the Parker-Roosevelt presidential election, which he covered in sensible, workmanlike fashion through a night-long hotel watch; and, later, the disastrous Iroquois Theatre fire.

Eddie Foy, an old Van Vechten favorite from the days of Greene's Opera House, was appearing at the Iroquois in a musical extravaganza called *Mr. Bluebeard*. A defective connection in the wiring backstage caused a fire that tore through the theater. More than a thousand persons escaped, but when the fire chief finally hacked his way through an exit door to call, "Is anybody alive here?" nobody answered. Nearly six hundred burned to death or

[5] *Sacred and Profane Memories*, p. 214.
[6] January, 1904, p. 88.

smothered, and the bodies were jammed against the doors seven feet deep. The *American* sent Carl down to cover the tragedy: he arrived to find the corpses being piled up like cordwood on the sidewalk outside the Iroquois. His particular job that night was terrifying: "I still remember it with a great deal of horror. . . . I had to go around to the different morgues and find out from searchers whether they'd found their people and why, and how some . . . got there by sitting in seats . . . someone had given them. . . ."[7]

Carl Van Vechten's actual writing for the newspaper was in many fields: births and deaths; a society belle spurning wealth to marry a miner; bogus sun worshipers; women bankers. Intermittently he wrote some articles under the general heading of "The Whirl of Society" for the *Chicago Inter-Ocean*, a paper on which a friend of his, Jessie Call, was society editor. These latter assignments led indirectly to one on the *Chicago American*: as the "Chaperone," Carl reported—in a tea-party prose all his own—the current society events around the city, in a regular column called "Gossip of the Chicago Smart Set." He may have been growing farther and farther away from Cedar Rapids, but his prose was not keeping up with his geography.

He wrote of Jessie Bulsey, who "became the wife of a Chicago millionaire, a pet of Chicago society . . . and who has recently become the favorite of the Mayfair district in London, with an introduction to the King of England as the next step." He wrote of Mrs. Potter Palmer, the acknowledged social ruler of the city, who "continues to be feted . . . in cold weather and in warm weather, in Summer, Winter, Autumn, and Spring; in Paris, Berlin, St. Petersburg, London, or Chicago. She is always being feted. It is her fate."[8] Occasionally he managed a theatrical note; once, after following Sarah Bernhardt from Pullman car to hotel room, he wrote that the actress breakfasted on two poached eggs, a porterhouse steak, fried potatoes, and a bottle of Budweiser. But most of the time his reporting was limited to groups of sedately upholstered local matrons

[7] Van Vechten, Oral History.
[8] CVV, NYPL, circa 1905.

"in very exclusive circles . . . partaking of punches and frappes and mousses and sherbets betimes and keeping up with what was going on. . . ." But, even at the age of twenty-four, Carl had, as Dorothy Parker supposedly said of him years later, his tongue in somebody else's cheek:

> The three acknowledged rivals to social queendom were being discussed with great fervor. "Mrs. Palmer has manner, she has blood and she has precedent; she has always held the reins and she won't drop them easily. But think of the women she has snubbed. Won't they be glad to join a new regime?"
>
> "You seem to forget . . . that she has taken care to snub only the right persons. She has never snubbed anyone whom the others would or could make an ally of. She has been so careful always to do her big things in the name of charity . . . isn't it ridiculous? . . . Why must we have . . . social leaders at all?"
>
> "Because," answered the hostess authoritatively, "because Barnum was right when he said that the American public likes to be humbugged."[9]

Accounts of this sort brought Carl a fashionable notoriety in the small and ephemeral world in which he moved for the nine-dollar weekly salary that the *Chicago American* paid him. His parents, supplementing with some additional cash by mail from time to time, were suitably impressed. In August, 1905, Carl's father could write: "She already thinks you a wonder and will never be satisfied until the literary or newspaper world discovers it. She didn't say so—but my she is proud of Carl—& so is his dad—even if Carl never gets but $15 a week. Money is a *mighty* small thing."[10]

Carl's own world at the time was, however, far removed from the damask and crystal splendor of Mrs. Potter Palmer's. Once out of college, his circle of friends expanded to include other fledgling writers and artists: the Call sisters, who produced the *Inter-Ocean*, and Edna Kenton, who chronicled the news in an extraordinary fashion in its pages; Charles Fitzmorris, Carl's reporter friend, who

[9] CVV, NYPL, circa 1904.
[10] CVV, NYPL.

later became Chicago's chief of police; Channing Pollock, then a young novelist and playwright but slightly known; Thorstein Veblen, who had come west to investigate the educational experiments at the University of Chicago; and Martha Baker, a young painter for whom Carl sat twice during his "Chaperone" days.

Martha Baker's "peculiar form of genius lay in the facility with which she caught her sitter's weaknesses. . . . Her sitters were exposed, so to speak; petty vices shone forth; Martha almost idealized the faults of her subjects. . . . She tore away men's masks and, with a kind of mystic understanding, painted their insides."[11] Her portraits of Carl are sufficiently telling to reinforce his comments. Painted when he was twenty-six years old, the less successful but better known of the two shows him sitting, his legs crossed, a book in his hands, an absolutely blank stare on his ageless face. The other portrait is more revealing: in a dressing gown, dark-eyed, his full lips drawn together petulantly to hide the great tusks that marred his handsome features, lank-haired, he sits with clasped hands, a Charles Dana Gibson hero bedeviled by Aubrey Beardsley. Mabel Dodge later titled it, during the days that it hung in her 23 Fifth Avenue salon in New York, *The Conscious Despair of Irrevocable Decadence*. "Martha should have painted our senators, our majors, our scientists, our authors, our college presidents, and our critics," Carl later wrote. "But most of her sitters were silly Chicago ladies, not particularly weak because they were not particularly strong."[12]

They constituted, of course, the club membership of which he gossiped when he masqueraded as "The Chaperone" for the *American* or wrote "The Whirl of Society" for the *Inter-Ocean*. In the fall of 1905, he covered the annual horse show for both, writing, however, of the clothes horses rather than the horses. The local matrons might justifiably have taken issue with his malicious jibes and those of the "Angel Child" too, a chichi companion Carl had capriciously invented to accompany him:

11 *Peter Whiffle: His Life and Works* (hereafter cited as *Peter Whiffle*), pp. 26–27.
12 *Ibid.*, p. 27.

Chicago

Go to the horse show and get the nightmare; that is, if you're sensitive to colors. With my natural artistic temperament, the week's scheme has given me a serious attack of the nerves. I dream of colors, of textiles, of floating fabrics—glimpses of Paris, shades of the Roman empire, fancies of the decadent poets. . . . Why did you do it? Why startle a mere man out of a week of sleep after wakeful evenings at the horse show with a display of your kaleidoscopic wardrobe? Why did you do it? I ask it of you? I loved the brown and I adored the rose, but why the dark blue with the cerise hat and the olive green with the lavender Gainsborough? The Angel Child went to the horse show with me this week. I told him my theory that every woman should study herself and select her color with care. "She has studied herself," answered the Child. "She has studied herself and decided that she can wear all colors at once."[13]

In light of this, it seems astonishing that Carl was ever engaged by either paper in the first place; but bad writing was not so sinful as bad manners.

The wife of the business manager of the *American* had attended, sitting in a box for the first time in her life. The boxes, presumably, got the worst notices, for she swooped into the newspaper office the following morning to demand Carl's removal. The managing editor dashed off a note, shocked that Hearst's "pleasant newspaper" had been used to "pander to 'nasty' tastes." He thought it was dirty. He thought it was vicious. He thought it was mean. And he proposed taking "The Chaperone" off the society page immediately.[14]

The man was sufficiently upset to backdate his letter an entire year to 1904, but Carl later insisted that it was this 1905 communication that moved him to begin to empty his desk. At least one of his favorite stories—about having been advised that he had "lowered the tone of the Hearst newspapers"—was apocryphal, though it received some happy mileage in the years that followed. Later in the day, the editor apologized when he discovered that Carl had considered himself fired. Fortunately, it was too late.

[13] *Inter-Ocean*, November, 1905.
[14] American Literature Collection, Yale University Library (hereafter cited as Yale).

Carl Van Vechten

There was little to hold him in the Midwest. Cedar Rapids was
certainly behind him forever: Anna Snyder was off touring Europe;
his sister and brother, though nearby—Emma back in Cedar Rapids,
and Ralph in Chicago, where he had become second vice-president
of the Commercial National Bank—were both too much older for
close companionship; following Carl's mother's death earlier that
year, his father had married Addie Lawton, an old friend of the
family; and his home town itself no longer held even the charm of
nostalgia. Nor did Chicago, though his seven years there had not
harmed him.

Had Carl Van Vechten stayed in Chicago, he would doubtless
have found himself involved in the brilliant group of writers that
would emerge a few years later, though one scarcely imagines his
being very congenial with Upton Sinclair or Maxwell Bodenheim.
"My sense of propaganda," he once wrote as an inscription, probably with more truth than he intended, "always concerned art and
never politics!"

He traveled east with his father in the early spring of 1906. He
had no job or any prospect of one, though he did have a letter
of introduction from his brother. But, for a young man of nearly
twenty-six years, Carl Van Vechten's background was enviable in
many ways, in spite of his increasing dissatisfaction with it. If he
was convinced that his success would blossom in the future, the
roots of that success were assuredly planted in the past.

III

La Belle Epoque

*It was all gay, irresponsible and
meaningless, perhaps, but gay.*

CARL VAN VECHTEN's first digs in New York City were on West
Thirty-ninth Street, a large, and largely colorless, single chamber
just down the hall from another one occupied by Sinclair Lewis.
They used to nod in passing: Lewis deferential and Van Vechten
patronizing, though each denied this to the other in later years when
their acquaintance passed on to a kind of remote friendship.

Already heavily in debt to his father, Carl had borrowed money
for the journey eastward, convinced that the town was ready for
his invasion, not an unlikely idea: on Broadway, Ruth St. Denis
had recently introduced interpretative dancing, and Fritzi Scheff
was scheduled to appear in *Mlle Modiste*; Nazimova's performance
in *Hedda Gabler* would revive memories of *Ghosts* and inspire a
new pun, "Ibscene"; Yvette Guilbert had just presented a series of
recitals, and Fay Templeton still strutted nightly in George M.
Cohan's *Forty-five Minutes from Broadway*; Geraldine Farrar
would make her American debut at the Metropolitan Opera House
in November, and Oscar Hammerstein would open his rival Manhattan Opera House a month later. In an age bereft of movie queens
and television personalities, actors and opera singers were the
celebrities of the day: certainly Carl could see vaguely where he
wanted to go, if pretty severely blinded by the stardust on the way.

He may have lived on West Thirty-ninth Street, but he spent
most of his time at the opera houses, often "suping" again when his
funds dwindled. Carl's fascination did not stop at idle adulation,
however: he sold a lengthy article on Richard Strauss's *Salome* al-

most as soon as he arrived in New York. The time was propitious, for the Metropolitan Opera had announced the American premiere for January, 1907.

Through Algernon St. John Brennon, a young newspaper reporter, Carl had heard that *Broadway Magazine* wanted to publish a piece on the then notorious music drama; and, fired by Anna Snyder's reports of the first performance in Dresden, he decided to propose himself for the chore. Carl arrived to discover a "walrus jawed" Theodore Dreiser behind the editor's desk.

The principal memory he retained of that encounter with the author of the then still-suppressed *Sister Carrie* was Dreiser's habit of "folding and refolding his handkerchief until it was a nest of tiny squares."[1] This object completed, he would unfold it and begin all over again. Somewhere in the middle of this process, he agreed to commission Carl to write an article about *Salome*.

The article, "Salome: The Most Sensational Opera of an Age," appeared, profusely illustrated, in the January, 1907, issue of Dreiser's periodical. Some of it might have been written by "The Chaperone":

> New York positively howls for novelty, and the newest sensation to be successful must eclipse the one which came before. "Salome" . . . is the latest bid for public favor and the prediction has been made that it will eclipse all previous sensations of any sort which have held the metropolitan mouth agape.[2]

Although the body of the article dealt with a detailed plot summary, incorporating suitable quotations from Oscar Wilde's text and bad puns ("Wilde at his wildest"), there were some interesting passages of the kind of minutiae that in later years lent such charm to Carl Van Vechten's criticism. When he came to the celebrated dance, for example, he recalled both Loie Fuller and Little Egypt, whose "*Danse du ventre*, a species of contortion first made popular in America through the Midway at the Chicago World's Fair . . .

[1] *Fragments from an unwritten autobiography*, Volume II (hereafter cited as *Fragments I* or *Fragments II*), p. 4.
[2] *Broadway Magazine*, p. 381.

[was] since tolerated only in the less discreet theatres." In the projected Metropolitan production, Olive Fremstad, he wrote brashly with the authority of experience he did not have, would not perform the Dance of the Seven Veils, since "no singer could possibly dance it and have any breath left for the very trying music at the close." Of the projected "double" at the Metropolitan, he concluded dogmatically that this was done "in all European productions." At that time Carl had not even heard the score.

Dreiser commissioned a second article when he accepted "Salome." This was to be about Barnard College, but, though Carl worked "long and laboriously," he never completed it. There were more interesting avenues to explore through the *New York Times*, where he had been hanging out for weeks, waiting for occasional assignments. Then, in November, the newspaper hired him as a staff reporter.

"Doesn't it all sound too good to be true?"[3] he had written to Cedar Rapids. It sounded even better a few weeks later when the *Times* appointed him assistant to music critic Richard Aldrich.

Carl investigated everything and, in a semiregular column, catalogued the fashions and the pastimes of the opera luminaries. The "Chaperone" was still apparent, but during the craze for vocal drama the style hit a right note between news and press-agentry. What he did not actually review, he anticipated, whetting his readers' appetites with projected menus. "Nordica May Sing Here," he headed an early article, and, the following day, "We May Hear Pagliacci." A few days later, he advised his readers that Caruso had shaved off his mustache. He reported on the divorce of Emma Eames and the death of Edward MacDowell. He reviewed a revival of *The Count of Monte Cristo* and welcomed the American premiere of *Caesar and Cleopatra*. He went even further afield with a piece about firebugs. He covered a Nellie Melba performance, and in the same issue wrote of wrecked railway bridges and a spiritualist funeral. He covered Saint-Saëns's first appearance as conductor with the New York Symphony before a "small but en-

[3] CVV, NYPL.

thusiastic audience," the opening of *The Merry Widow*, and the closing of a women's hotel. He wrote, during that first year with the *Times*, of many things indeed.

Carl Van Vechten was young enough and excited enough to do what he was told but to enjoy himself in the process. Nearly all the writing in his articles for the *New York Times* is routine and, on nonmusical subjects, flabby; but the interviews with opera singers and various pieces on productions have a real and innocent enchantment. He could, however, easily lose the innocence to scoop a story. After Algernon St. John Brennon had given Carl the lead on *Salome*, the two of them agreed to share news from time to time during those first months Carl was with the *Times*, an agreement the latter neglected to remember. Brennon wrote furiously about "truth telling between man and man" and Carl's "full and characteristic use" of people to whom Brennon had introduced him.

Carl was amused but unmoved by the tirade:

> The understanding you speak of as having made with me is something I know nothing of. I remember that on various occasions you assured me that we were to share stories, but I do *not* remember agreeing to such a proposition. I am sorry you feel so bitterly about your inability to get my work into your paper.[4]

Brennon called this "the cheap repartee of amateur journalism" and blathered on about exclusive stories on George M. Cohan. Carl made no reply. In time Brennon's anger subsided, and a few years later, when Carl was temporarily incarcerated in the Ludlow Street jail for failure to pay alimony to his first wife, Brennon contributed a series of amusing articles about the confinement.

In January, 1907, when Carl's "Salome" appeared on the newsstands, he wrote at even greater length of the furor aroused by the projected production at the Metropolitan Opera House. While tickets remained on sale, there were "compromises, comments and conferences" over the advisability of allowing the music drama to be presented at all. Finally, there was a single performance before

4 CVV, Yale.

the opera was withdrawn at the nervous request of certain directors, among them J. P. Morgan, who said it was so revolting and degrading that he was willing to refund the entire cost of the production to prevent a second performance.

Carl remembered the first performance well enough to document Olive Fremstad's characterization ten years later in the *Bellman*, "a splendid leopard" whose interpretation was vivid enough to suggest "the dregs of love, the refuse of gorged passion." It is not surprising then that, in 1907, *Salome* alarmed the public sufficiently to cause its withdrawal.

Two seasons later, the less conservative Oscar Hammerstein revived the opera with Mary Garden. But, by that time, the provincial tastes that had originally canceled *Salome* had canceled some of Carl's enthusiasm for New York. It was not long after the original demise of *Salome* that he felt the urge to move on. The city's conservatism had created a burning need for him to see opera in Europe, of which Anna Snyder had written so vividly and reported to him on her return.

Carl's father, characteristically, questioned the advisability of such an endeavor: "How much money do you have on hand? What particular advantage is there in listening to the opera in European cities that you don't have in New York?" A second letter did not mention the opera at all. "Cut your garment according to the money you have and make it fit," he proposed. But the urge was strong, and Carl requested that his life insurance be borrowed upon. "You take my breath," his father wrote. "But my boy, you should earn your way to such a step." Then a firm rejoinder: "We build our credit unconsciously on our conduct." Carl wrote again, trying to detail the necessities he felt: Wagner was being staged at Bayreuth; there was the Opéra-Comique in Paris; and surely the experience could improve his position with the *Times*. The elder Van Vechten finally relented:

It takes a little time to get a thing through my head—a surprise terrifies me for the moment. I lie awake nights until I get accustomed to it. Think I shall sleep tonight. As I see the matter now you are

39

right in wanting to go to Europe & I shall rejoice in whatever of good it does for you.

Then, finally, the truth Carl had originally planned to keep secret: though he and Anna were never actually engaged, they had decided to marry—in Europe, to avoid the chore of a wedding in Cedar Rapids.

Charles Van Vechten wrote feelingly:

> *Dearest boy*, why didn't you tell me what you wanted on the very start & save me the humiliation I now feel. I should not have argued with you a moment. For havent I hoped & hoped that you would marry, & wouldn't I have done almost any unreasonable thing even to know that Anna & you were preparing for a wedding? But never mind my son, I am all right now. I do regret that you are to go away for the marriage & yet your idea is all right and has my most hearty approval (I think you call it blessing—you have it anyhow) Well, I will see that you have a little extra in the way of money sometime in June. No use to send it now even if I have it . . . which I have not. But spend very carefully remembering the necessity of the case. You are a dear boy & I love you better than ever, if that be possible. I want awfully to see you before you go, but had better save the cost of the journey for your benefit. . . . with a bunch of love for my darling Carl.[5]

The letter was dated April 14; less than a month later, Carl arranged for a leave of absence from the *New York Times* and sailed for Europe from Philadelphia, in the company of Channing Pollock and his wife, on the *Westernland*, a tublike transport, for $32.50. It was not the steadiest of conveyances. In addition to having facilities that provided almost nothing for its passengers, the *Westernland* managed to break a propeller blade at sea, stranding Carl on a becalmed ocean for ten days. He was never a good sea voyager, and that initial trip may have been responsible for his chronic *mal de mer*. The boat eventually drifted into Liverpool, which only added a dismal conclusion to the journey. He left almost immediately for London to visit the theaters. But the pull to far-

[5] CVV, NYPL.

away places was strong, and by May 10, Carl had spent his first night in Paris, a holiday fully documented in *Peter Whiffle*, his first novel:

> I was . . . in my twenties when I first went to Paris—my happiness might have been even greater had I been nineteen—and I was alone. . . .
>
> Paris in the May twilight is very soft and exquisite, the grey build-ings swathed in a bland blue light and the air redolent with a strange fragrance, the ingredients of which have never been satisfactorily identified in my nasal imagination. . . . Presently we crossed the boulevards and I saw for the first time the rows of blooming chestnut trees, the kiosques where newsdealers dispensed their wares, the brilliantly lighted theatres, the sidewalk cafés, sprinkled with human figures, typical enough, doubtless, but who all seemed as unreal to me at the time as if they had been Brobdingnags, Centaurs, Griffins, or Mermaids. . . .
>
> We drove on through the Louvre and now the Seine was under us, lying black in the twilight, reviving dark memories of crime and murder, on across the Pont du Carrousel, and up the narrow Rue de Seine. . . .
>
> Paris! I cried. Paris! Good God![6]

A month later he was back in England to meet Anna Snyder, who had taken a later ship, arriving in June with a friend from her Wellesley days.

"I can see you with pleasure, tomorrow (Thursday) at 9. If you wish, the marriage can be tomorrow (Thursday) at 11 or 11:30 or on Friday at any time between 8 and 3 or on Saturday at any time between 9 and 10:30 or from 11:30 to 3," wrote J. Glendenning Nash, who arranged the ceremony.[7] They chose Saturday for the quiet wedding, and left London almost immediately afterward for the Continent, where Carl Van Vechten had his first real taste of opera. The tour had begun with Covent Garden in London; in Paris, they heard Mary Garden in *Pelléas et Mélisande* at the Opéra-Comique, and watched Colette performing in a music hall. At the

[6] Pp. 10–12, 15.
[7] Yale.

Grand Guignol, where bloodthirsty deeds outdid those of the Jacobean theater, Carl and Ann screamed for the curtain to come down, and a few days later he mustered a similar reaction at the *Folies Bergère* by climbing onto his seat to yell at one of the entertainers, "You! Young lady! Put your skirts down!"[8] In Munich, he renewed acquaintance with Olive Fremstad in the lobby of the Prinzergarten Theatre and met a then unknown American singer named Minnie Saltzmann-Stevens. By the time the summer came to an end, Carl was much better qualified—as he certainly believed—to fulfill his duties under Richard Aldrich on the *New York Times*. Once again, as usual, without funds, Carl called upon his father to help him return to America; and Olive Fremstad, a grateful friend for his attention to her in the newspaper, directed her husband, Edson Sutphen, to cable a check from Munich. Before it arrived, however, the newlyweds lived on Edam cheese—the only thing in cheap abundance—for two days. It was not the last time they would find themselves in such straits; certainly it was not the last for Carl.

BACK IN NEW YORK, Ann went to work as secretary to the Author's League, and Carl put his operatic knowledge to immediate use in an article for the *Bookman*. He promised considerable excitement, though the big news came from the Manhattan Opera House, where Oscar Hammerstein announced the engagement of Mary Garden. It was altogether fitting, Carl noted in conclusion, that "the opera year in New York should commence with *Gioconda* and end with *Parsifal*. Catholicity of taste and New York mean the same thing."[9]

He was Buddy Van Vechten in those days, a name given him in Chicago by Channing Pollock and picked up, at least momentarily, by Channing's wife Anna. She was his first friend—and compatriot—in New York. As press agent for Oscar Hammerstein's company, she supplied not only much of the information for Carl's news articles but a piano in the basement of the Victoria Theatre for

8 Yale.
9 November, 1907, p. 65.

Charles Duane Van Vechten, about 1854.
Ada Amanda Fitch, about 1856.

The Van Vechten family, about 1884.
Left to right: Emma, Charles, Ralph, Ada, and Carl.

(left) Carl Van Vechten, about 1890.

(right) Carl Van Vechten, about 1900.

Anna Elizabeth Snyder, about 1900.

Carl Van Vechten, 1906.

Carl Van Vechten, 1906.
Entitled by Mabel Dodge, about 1913,
"The Conscious Despair of Irrevocable Decadence."

Portrait by Martha Baker

Top left: Olive Fremstad, about 1906.
Top right: Luisa Tetrazzini, about 1909.
Below, left: Mary Garden, about 1909.
Below, right: Isadora Duncan, about 1906.

Mabel Dodge, about 1912.

Photograph by Jacques-Émile Blanche

The Yellow Salon at the Villa Curonia.

Carl Van Vechten and Fania Marinoff
in Venice, summer, 1914.

(left) Fania Marinoff, 1914.

(right) Carl Van Vechten, about 1917.

Photograph by Underwood and Underwood

Photograph by Mishkin

Carl Van Vechten and Fania Marinoff, 1915.

THE TIGER IN THE HOUSE

By *Carl Van Vechten*

with 32 full page illustrations from photographs and drawings.
An Edition of 2000 numbered copies.

THE most complete book yet published relating to the domestic cat. It is not a breeder's manual or a cat fancier's guide. It is an urbane, informing, and amusing history of puss, his religion, his politics, his ethics, and his manners and habits. Incidentally the author makes no attempt to conceal his opinion that the feline race is superior to the human race. He discusses the cat's relation to folklore, law music, painting, the drama, poetry, and fiction and describes his occult powers in an informal and personal style. An elaborate, handsomely made volume, fully illustrated and includes the first bibliography yet published on the subject, carefully classified, and an index.

ALFRED A. KNOPF PUBLISHER, N. Y.

Box decoration for *The Tiger in the House*,
suppressed after objections by a Philadelphia bookseller.

Fania Marinoff as Trina in *Life's Whirlpool*, 1916.

(left) Fania Marinoff as Ariel in *The Tempest*, 1916.

(right) Fania Marinoff as Wendla
in *Spring's Awakening*, 1917.

Carl Van Vechten, 1926.

Photograph by E. O. Hoppé

him to practice on. And, if the occasion demanded, she could even be persuaded to rifle the Hammerstein closets to costume him and Avery Hopwood for fancy dress balls, to one of which Buddy went as an octopus. Eventually, however, most of his friends called him Carlo. (In the ensuing half-century, the extra vowel became almost automatic at the end of his name.)

Van Vechten became acquainted with most of the singers on the current operatic scene. He escorted Luisa Tetrazzini to the *Times* tower and then photographed her emerging prettily from its entrance; Caruso produced one of his celebrated caricatures; certainly, Carl saw a great deal of Mary Garden. But opera was more than social intercourse. He interviewed Feodor Chaliapin, for example, in the dining room of the Hotel Savoy on a rainy Sunday afternoon after the Russian basso's arrival in America. He looked, Carl remembered, like a college football player. "I spik English," were his first words. "How do you do? *et puis* goodbye, *et puis* I drrrink, you drrink, he drrrinks, *et puis* I love you!"[10] Later they met again, this time for an interview about Chaliapin's concept of his role as Mephistopheles. The chat lasted twelve hours and included a continuous meal very nearly the length of the entire interview. At one point, Chaliapin put his recording of the *Marseillaise* on the phonograph and then amused himself (and Carl) by singing in unison with it, in an attempt to drown out the mechanical sound. He succeeded.

Certainly, opera and opera singers played the largest roles in Carl's work for the *Times*, particularly through his connections with the Manhattan Opera House, ferociously and benevolently supervised by the indomitable Oscar Hammerstein. The company had just been organized when Carl first came to New York in 1906. It was in his regular round of duties that he first met the redoubtable impresario in an office in the "gilded, but shabby, dusty, and dingy, and always crowded" old Victoria Theatre, "a short stubby figure of a man with a thin greyish Mephistophelan and slightly rakish beard."[11]

[10] *Interpreters and Interpretations*, p. 98.   [11] *In the Garret*, p. 237.

Hammerstein had arrived in America some forty years earlier, a penniless German immigrant who made a quick fortune by inventing machinery that eventually revolutionized the cigar-making industry. Subsequently, he built several theaters through which "he tried persistently and courageously to make [opera] a successful and popular form of entertainment."[12] For four seasons at the Manhattan Opera House, New York audiences enjoyed performances of opera as they had "never enjoyed them before or since."

> The scenery and costumes for these operas were often cheap and tawdry, not because enough money had not been spent, but because taste in this direction was not one of the man's virtues; it was the spirit of the performances that was unforgettable.[13]

These performances had dash and élan and sparkle and vitality, Carl Van Vechten recalled a dozen years later; opera, in other words, was exciting at the Manhattan. When the novelty of *Salome* eventually wore off, Hammerstein gave New York Strauss's *Elektra*; when Mary Garden's reputation was insured, he imported Luisa Tetrazzini, then at the height of her London success; when one singer became firmly identified with a role, Hammerstein replaced him with another. The man's ability to capture public attention resulted ultimately in the Metropolitan's buying him out to kill the competition.

During the four seasons at the Manhattan, Carl was provided with plenty of information for his columns—and for some extra-curricular activity as well. "The Story of My Operatic Career" appeared in *Cosmopolitan* for June, 1908, signed by Luisa Tetrazzini but ghostwritten by Carl Van Vechten. How much of the material was Luisa's and how much was Carl's is open to conjecture. The reader was advised that Tetrazzini had taken lessons for only three months; that her voice was contralto when she was ten; that her teachers admitted defeat, saying she could learn nothing from them that she did not already know; that she had sung Inez in

---

12 *Ibid.*, p. 243.
13 *Ibid.*, p. 244.

Meyerbeer's *L'Africaine* at the age of thirteen; that doctors were convinced she was consumptive during performances of *La Traviata*; that pigeons fell at her feet in Mexico because she "sang like the birds." Carl (or Luisa) concluded merrily, "To a young girl who is contemplating a career on the operatic stage I would say, let her first be sure she has a voice."[14]

Luisa Tetrazzini was not Van Vechten's only pen name. As Walter Tempest, he wrote "The Shoes of Clyde Fitch" for *Green Book Album*. His old friend Channing Pollock arranged his assignment for the article, modestly furnished most of the material, and suggested himself as the inheritor of the dramatist's shoes. In the circumstances, the pseudonym was understandable.

During that 1907–1908 season, following their return from Europe, Carl and Ann lived at the Maison Favre on Seventh Avenue, just behind the Metropolitan Opera House, where Madame Favre presided in the evening over "a good, old-fashioned table d'hôte. Bottles of wine, furnished free with the dinner—and the dinner in those days cost seventy-five cents—stood on the tables and the conversation was coevally referred to as bohemian."[15] They lived in a large single room on the first floor, without bath or kitchen, where they regularly entertained. On necessary occasions they would bring in food from the restaurant, but, more often, they simply served grapefruit, then as exotic as pomegranates. It was the scene, a gossip columnist reported, "of many a bright little afternoon affair at which stage celebrities and literary geniuses shone." Opera singers, musicians, and newspapermen attended the Maison Favre soirees, which Carl remembered as "a very amusing, delightful life." They saw a lot of Channing Pollock and his wife, and Avery Hopwood, and of course Olive Fremstad. "It wasn't formal and it wasn't rich, but it was delightful," Carl could recall many years later. "I liked the people I worked with and I liked the people I met. Everybody liked Ann, and we had a very good time."

In 1908, New York was a quieter city and, to be sure, a smaller

---

[14] P. 51.
[15] *Sacred and Profane Memories*, p. 215.

one. Carl and Ann Van Vechten became familiar figures in literary and musical circles without much difficulty, for the circles were small enough in circumference to travel in sidewalk strolls from one to the other. Anna Marble Pollock's daughter Helen clearly remembers the couple from those early days: Ann, tall and serenely handsome and friendly; and Carl, tall and serenely handsome and fish-eye cold. "I'm always a little frightened when we meet Mr. Van Vechten," she used to confide to her mother. "Never mind," Mrs. Pollock always replied, "he's probably a little frightened of you too." And so he was: terrified of children, terrified of having children; it meant responsibility, and he wanted none. The world in which he moved involved him sufficiently for him to desire no other.

If smaller and quieter than the frenetic eras that succeeded it, Carl's world nevertheless possessed its own charm and excitement. *The Merry Widow* first came to America in 1907–1908, reprieving the waltz a little longer from the inevitable onslaught of the turkey trot, the one-step, and the bunny hug a few years later. George Bernard Shaw's *Mrs. Warren's Profession,* closed by the police in 1905, reopened and ran successfully. The *New York Herald* head-lined the news that women had been discovered smoking cigarettes on their way to the opera; the *Times* asked rhetorically, "Will the ladies rebel as the ladies of New Amsterdam did when Peter Stuyvesant ordered them to wear broad flounces?"

But the Van Vechtens' stay in New York did not last long. Late in the spring of 1908, Carr Van Anda, the managing editor of the *Times,* appointed Carl its Paris correspondent. They sailed for Europe in May.

CARL AND ANN lived on the rue Jacob that year, on fifty dollars a week and their living expenses from the newspaper. The venture was pleasant, if not a very successful one. But it did prove to Carl that he could call himself a newspaperman only in the loosest sense of the word: he wanted to write about music, and the *Times* expected him to write about everything; about opera and the theater, his reporting could delight, but about alien subjects, it could easily bore.

In October, the New York office seemed pleased: "Your work has been excellent. . . . & I congratulate you." In November, however, the forecast was already gloomy: Carl was paying too much attention to "theatricals," and the *Times* wanted "more general news if you can possibly get it."[16]

Carl tried, but the effort was halfhearted. He wrote of sports events and politics when absolutely necessary; of the adoption of life imprisonment in France; of murders and suicides; of autumn fashions and Americans in Paris. He wrote of the flavor of the city, as if he meant to take up space: "Paris insists on modernity. To be truly Parisian one must be of the minute. The Boulevardiers demand a new catch word, a new idea, every day."[17]

More often, he was interviewing Rodin, surrounded by twenty of the sculptor's works, or writing of Odette Valéry's dance recitals or Mary Garden's performances at the Opéra-Comique. The *New York Times* could have wanted a broader frontier for newsgathering.

But Carl was too involved with Olive Fremstad's *Salome*; with *Spring's Awakening* by Frank Wedekind, a production that actually utilized children to delineate its probing of adolescent sexuality; with Gluck's *Orfeo*, of which he witnessed every performance during the season. Not surprisingly, his weekly communications to New York were largely devoted to his own interests. Between these endeavors, he renewed some old acquaintances and made some new ones.

Mahala Douglas, vacationing in Paris, took Carl and Ann to dinner, at a cost of forty dollars for a single concoction—of chicken, brandy, cream, butter, truffles, and wine—that sent them to bed, ill, for three days. They emerged on the fourth to attend the *Folies Bergère*.

Carl ran into Feodor Chaliapin, just back from a South American

16 Yale.
17 CVV, NYPL, *circa* 1908.

tour, on the boulevard, and was promptly dragged off to see his zoo. Chaliapin had, indeed, transformed the bathroom in his suite at the Grand Hotel into a menagerie: there were several brightly plumed birds, a cockatoo, a couple of monkeys, and two large alligators, the latter dozing in the bathtub.

On another occasion, he went to see Elinor Glyn, then in search of a singer for a projected operatic version of her scandalous *Three Weeks*. At the Ritz, Mrs. Glyn sent word to the desk that she was lunching with the king of Greece but that she would see Carl later. He cooled his heels in the lobby until she was ready to receive him. During their talk, Carl discovered that she wanted a European for her hero. "I want no American with padded coat sleeves to play Paul," she announced. Carl crossed his arms, clutching his own fashionably enlarged protrusions, and flushed. "Oh, I didn't mean you, dear boy," she commiserated. "It isn't *your* fault that you haven't centuries of breeding behind you!"[18]

In Paris that fall, he renewed acquaintance with Mary Garden, by way of a telegram from her: "*Venez ce soir à 5½ chez Mlle. Chasles 112 Boulevard Malesherbes me voir en Salome.*"[19] The invitation was to a rehearsal—her last before those in New York preceding her initial performance in the part. She intended to break tradition and perform the dance herself as well as sing the role. To prove that it could be done, she sang the final taxing scene at the conclusion of her dance before a select audience that afternoon: the Paris Opéra manager, the choreographer, Mlle Chasles, an accompanist, a maid, a hairdresser, and Carl Van Vechten.

Although he did not see her "impetuous and highly curious interpretation" as its premiere in New York, the *Times* arranged for Carl to be on hand the following season. In April, 1909, he was relieved of his duties as correspondent, when Van Anda wrote him to return immediately. Carl was allowed a first-class passage but was advised to provide personally for Ann's return.

Although the Van Vechtens' money was not plentiful at the time, Ann had means, through her family, to return. Nevertheless,

[18] *Fragments II*, p. 53.   [19] *Interpreters and Interpretations*, p. 79.

she decided to stay in Europe temporarily, and Carl returned alone —not without some relief for both of them. The whole relationship had begun to wear a little thin. The move precipitated some mother-in-law trouble when Mrs. Snyder, fearing that the home fires would not keep burning long, cajoled Ann into a quick return, falsely cabling that Mr. Snyder, whom Ann adored, was at the point of death. The lie prolonged the marriage temporarily, but a separation was inevitable. Ann and Carl, each other's final tie with the background they had sought to escape, their attitudes vastly different, had ultimately grown apart. The return to New York only aggravated the difficulties.

The European interlude ended. Carl returned to New York without regret, to the happier prospect of resuming his duties as assistant music critic for the *Times*.

SEVERAL YEARS LATER, Carl Van Vechten observed that most music critics fall automatically into two classes: one, who tries to render his feeling by quoting poets or otherwise coupling Milton and Handel, Byron and Tchaikovsky; the other, who soberly feels it his duty to avoid all florid language in an effort to impress listeners with the "sublime seriousness of the art he is so laboriously striving to keep within academically prescribed limits."[20]

The assistant music critic for the *Times* fell into neither category. He attacked his assignments with a youthful enthusiasm that his competitors lacked or had otherwise forgotten how to utilize. It is perhaps this alone that makes his early criticism worth more than a cursory glance. Relegated to reviewing those performances that did not sufficiently interest Richard Aldrich, Carl instituted, under his own steam, a series of "Monday Interviews," as they were called in the paper. These pieces were personal in their approach and peripheral as criticism. In untutored hands, material of this kind—open wider than a soprano's high C to the dangers of high-pressure press-agentry—could have easily lapsed into fan-club coverage. Sometimes it did. The aura of glamour that automatically

20 *Ibid.*, p. 358.

49

seems to accompany people of celebrity never completely escaped Van Vechten; but that artless combination of sense and nonsense, anecdote and erudition, enthusiasm and reservation—gradually becoming his trademark—cast the weekly articles in a role both unequaled and original. Carl's "Interpreters," as they were later called in a volume of that name, chronicled an ephemeral but nevertheless exciting art: performance. No other critic ever made this particular facet of music so brilliant. Olive Fremstad, Mary Garden, Geraldine Farrar, Feodor Chaliapin, Enrico Caruso, Yvette Guilbert, Marietta Mazarin: half a century later, the revised pieces about these performers still hold their initial fascination. "No photograph can duplicate Van Vechten's *Interpreters*," Francis Robinson of the Metropolitan Opera once said in conversation. "But of course no music critic today writes like Van Vechten either. He wasn't afraid to say so when he liked something."

Because of Aldrich's apparent conservatism, Carl was able to review most of the controversial figures, like Mary Garden, and the debuts of Europeans, like Rachmaninoff. Occasionally, the *Times* sent him off to cover police parades or cobra operations at the Bronx Zoo; occasionally, he wrote minor articles for such publications as the *New Music Review*; but most of his energy went into operatic coverage for the *Times*. At the end of the season, however, the music world afforded him material he did not relish covering.

Oscar Hammerstein, whose revolutionary Manhattan Opera House had been a potent attraction in New York, was paid the sum of $1,200,000—a handsome price in 1910—to give up opera production in New York for a period of ten years. He had set such a pace for his rivals that the only alternative for the Metropolitan Opera House was to make him an attractive enough offer to insure his removal from the scene. At the time of the demise of the Manhattan Opera House, its repertoire was unexcelled. *Aïda, Thaïs, Cavalleria Rusticana, Pagliacci, Sapho, La Fille du Regiment, Le Jongleur de Notre Dame, Tannhäuser, Carmen, Mefistofele, I Puritani, Otello, Les Huguenots, L'Elisir d'Amore, Don Giovanni, La Traviata, Mignon, Il Trovatore, La Boheme, Grisélidis, Elektra,*

La Belle Epoque

Rigoletto, Louise, Salome, Pelléas et Mélisande, Lakmé, La Sonnambula, Lohengrin, and *Die Meistersinger*—all were among Hammerstein's offerings, many of them introduced to America through his auspices.

At the time of the transaction, Hammerstein held contracts with, among others, Luisa Tetrazzini, Mary Garden, and John McCormack, all of which had to be purchased by the rival house. Additionally, the rights to Strauss's *Salome* and *Elektra* and Debussy's *Pelléas et Mélisande,* another of Hammerstein's introductions to America, were disposed of by performance: five hundred dollars each for six of *Salome* a year, eight hundred dollars for six of *Elektra,* and four hundred dollars for the season for *Pelléas* plus an additional one hundred dollars for each performance. There was also an $800,000 mortgage on the opera house to be taken over.

Financially, Hammerstein had benefited enormously, though money had never concerned him very much; artistically, the agreement was his destruction, for never again did he achieve any success equaling the four seasons at the Manhattan. A gala performance was a memorable event for the audience: selections from *Contes d'Hoffmann, Hérodiade, Samson et Dalila, Romeo et Juliette* (with Charles Dalmorés and Mary Garden as the young lovers), and *Faust* comprised the program. The following evening, March 26, 1910, a complete performance of *Lucia di Lammermoor,* with Luisa Tetrazzini, brought down the final curtain at the Manhattan Opera House.

The great days of opera in New York were at an end for Carl Van Vechten. Occasionally, he wrote extended pieces—analyses of Strauss's new opera, *Der Rosenkavalier* and Wagner's *Tristan und Isolde* when they appeared at the Metropolitan Opera—for Pitts Sanborn, a music critic friend on the *Evening Globe*; or gossipy articles full of anticipation over Puccini's much heralded operatic version of David Belasco's *The Girl of the Golden West* (*La Fanciulla del West*), which opened only to prove a disappointment. But Carl Van Vechten's time was already being taken up with a new art form.

Anna Pavlova had been invited that season for a limited engagement at the Metropolitan Opera House, and Isadora Duncan made her second appearance in New York. Once again Richard Aldrich demurred, in favor of his assistant, and Carl Van Vechten was put in the fortuitous position of becoming America's first dance critic.

ISADORA DUNCAN, a San Francisco girl who had evolved a curious style of choreography, gave her second New York season in November, 1909, just after Carl had returned from Paris to resume his music duties on the *New York Times*. Until that time, dancing in America had been a secondary art form, relegated to the chorus lines of operettas and the shaggy corps at the Metropolitan Opera House. With the arrival on the scene of Miss Duncan, and Loie Fuller, Maud Allan, and Anna Pavlova a few weeks later, New York was introduced to Dancing—with a capital "D"—and, through Carl Van Vechten's enthusiastic if layman-like coverage, to its possibilities as a conceivable contender for the city's major theatrical interest. The art was new to America and, though Carl had seen a few performances in Europe during his year as Paris correspondent, new to him as well.

Miss Duncan, he told his readers, was at her best in dances "which depict life and gaiety and motion. In this she is always communicating her meaning to an audience."[21]

Of a second performance a week later, when Miss Duncan chose to dance to Beethoven's Seventh Symphony, he was less solicitous: "It is quite within the province of this recorder of musical affairs to protest against this perverted use . . . which Beethoven certainly never had in mind when he wrote it." He was moved to add, by way of compensation, that the dancer had seldom been "more poetical, more vivid in her expression of joy, more plastic in her poses, more rhythmical in her effects."[22]

A year later, she returned for a third engagement, but in the meantime Carl Van Vechten's acquaintance with the dance had

21 *New York Times*, November 10, 1909.
22 *Ibid.*, November 17, 1909.

broadened. In December, 1909, Loie Fuller danced in New York. A dozen years before, Carl had seen her perform her celebrated Skirt Dance in Cincinnati; now the passage of time had added several variations (on Isadora's themes) to the Fuller repertoire: modern dance had another exponent.

The following month, Maud Allan brought her *Salome* to the American stage. In 1907, it had caused a sensation in London, where she had continued the characterization nightly for more than a year. In New York, the performance "differed in no marked respect" from the earlier operatic version. There were, however, a few differences in the audience:

> It is true that in Paris she had caressed the severed head of John the Baptist. Yesterday the head itself was left to the imagination but none of the caressing. However, New York has seen so many dances of this sort by now that there were no exclamations of shocked surprise, no one fainted, and at the end there was no very definite applause. . . . Miss Allan yesterday executed steps and curved her body in contortions which are now conventionally supposed to suggest Salome.[23]

Latter-day dance fans may pause over Carl Van Vechten's use of phrase; "executed steps" and "curved her body" seem curiously prosaic terminology for America's avowedly first balletomane. It must be remembered that the music critic was writing in 1910 from his own vocabulary for lack of a more precise one. An argument might be made, with a preference for academic scholarship over primitive excitement, that Carl's accounts of dance recitals were purposely avoiding unfamiliar words in order to suit his reader's needs; but it is more likely to assume that these accounts were expressed in phrases simply invented for the occasion. In any event, they made up in ardor what they lacked in erudition.

In March, 1910, scarcely a month after Miss Allan's departure, Carl saw for the first time a kind of dancing that was to become of passionate interest to him, when Anna Pavlova made her American debut at the Metropolitan Opera House after a complete perform-

[23] *Ibid.*, January 30, 1910.

ance of Massenet's opera *Werther*. More than two-thirds of an already taxed audience remained in their seats when the final curtain fell on the opera. It rose again, after midnight.

Pavlova appeared on stage to a dead silence. There was no welcome for the small, porcelain-like figure, and her conventional ballet costume elicited no response. But after the first brief number, a waltz, and at every other opportunity thereafter, an unbelieving audience burst into vociferous applause.

It was well after one o'clock in the morning before the performance ended, but Pavlova had no difficulty in holding her audience. Carl Van Vechten said the following day in his column, "It is safe to say that such dancing has not been seen on the local stage during the present generation." Indeed, there was an ovation:

> And her dancing deserved it. To begin with, her technique is of a sort to dazzle the eye. The most difficult tricks of the art of the dancer she executed with supreme ease. She even went further. There were gasps of astonishment and bursts of applause after several of her remarkable feats, all of which were accomplished with the greatest ease and lightness. Grace, a certain sensuous charm, and a decided sense of humor are other qualities which she possesses. In fact, it would be difficult to conceive a dancer who so nearly realizes the ideal of this sort of dancing.[24]

The following evening, Pavlova made a second appearance. This time the house was filled to capacity, and the receipts totaled $15,000. Dancing with Mikail Mordkin, she

> twirled on her toes. With her left toe pointed out behind her, maintaining her body poised to form a straight line with it, she leapt backward step by step on her right foot. She swooped into the air like a bird and floated down. She never dropped. At times she seemed to defy the laws of gravitation. The divertissement ended with Pavlowa, supported by Mordkin, flying through the air, circling his body around and around. The curtain fell. The applause was deafening.[25]

[24] *Ibid.*, March 1, 1910.
[25] *Ibid.*, March 2, 1910.

Two weeks later, she and Mordkin appeared at The New Theatre, and Pavlova performed her first *Dying Swan* for an American audience, "an achievement of the highest order of imagination. It is the most exquisite specimen of her art which she has yet given to this public."[26]

Between dance recitals, Carl Van Vechten contributed to the *New Music Review* an essay and a column called "Facts, Rumors, and Remarks," but the latter smacked of his "Chaperone" days in Chicago and the subject matter was not much of an improvement:

> Mary Garden has broken out again. She always does, so that mere statement will cause no one to start. But she has a keen sense of variety. One time it is this and another time it is that—never is it twice the same thing. One moment she is going into a convent. Another moment she is going elsewhere. . . .[27]

In the fall of 1910, there were further performances by Pavlova and Duncan and the first American performance of Tchaikovsky's *Swan Lake* to occupy Carl's time. But he had not been idle during the summer interim. He prepared the program notes for the *Symphony Society Bulletin*, writing about composers whose works were relatively new to this country, and wrote ninety-three biographies for the *Century Cyclopedia of Names*. His salaries were small—for this latter chore he received less than fifty dollars—but he was being read and, more important, his writing was beginning to be recognized. Dance enthusiasts could look forward to his accounts of the new season's recitals.

Pavlova and Mordkin, appearing with their own company, began their second, brief New York sojourn with *Giselle*, probably the first performance of this ballet in the country since 1842. "It is impossible to describe the poetry of her dancing in the second act," Van Vechten wrote on October 16.[28]

He was less sympathetic toward Isadora Duncan the following February when she chose to dance to the *Liebestod* from Wagner's

26 *Ibid.*, March 18, 1910.
27 December, 1909, p. 26.
28 *New York Times.*

Tristan und Isolde. It was scheduled for the end of the program in order that those who did not wish to see it—so the conductor, Walter Damrosch, announced—might leave. Nobody did, but Carl Van Vechten was apparently not the only member in the audience who wondered why Miss Duncan had bothered, since her "conception of the music did not seem to suggest a pantomimic Isolde, nor was it exactly dancing. In other words, she puzzled those who knew the music drama, and did not interest those who did not."[29]

These remarks turned up a day or two later in the *New York Times.* Between the recital and their appearance, a very large party was given Miss Duncan at the Plaza Hotel to celebrate the close of her performances with the New York Symphony. The champagne flowed as freely as Miss Duncan's gown, which, at one point, she proposed to remove. "For you, Mr. Damrosch, I shall dance nude!" The conductor's wife hastily propelled him out of the room, but Isadora carried out her threat anyway. At dawn, the remaining guests, Carl included, all piled into a single taxi to see the lady off for Europe.

The dance craze continued throughout the season and into the following one. Pavlova's performances ultimately drew larger crowds at the Metropolitan than the operas did. Carl continued to chronicle the musical events of the city, by that time attending, on occasion, parts of two or three different performances, concerts, recitals, and plays in a single evening. If he had functioned as a kind of publicity hound during those early days in New York, he assuredly ended up leading something other than a dog's life by 1912. The preparatory legwork gave him an enviable access to the musical scene. The assistant music critic for the *New York Times* had turned what might have been a thankless job into an exciting one. It was a full life, but not one that allowed for a conventional marriage. Carl's chores kept him away from the apartment on Fortieth Street most of the time; his afternoons and evenings were taken up by those events he covered, and much of the remaining time was spent at the newspaper office. Very little was left for Ann.

29 *Ibid.*, February 16, 1911.

La Belle Epoque

DURING THE FIVE YEARS of their marriage, Carl and his wife had grown slowly away from each other. Nothing classifiable as violence, argument, or even serious disagreement seems to have marred the relationship; the lack of something, rather than the presence of something, estranged the always curiously matched pair. The early bond for an amicable relationship—their mutual desire to flee the stifled life in Cedar Rapids—was strained by the passage of time. Certainly, Carl had developed different tastes, moving in a world inhabited by musicians and writers and newspaper reporters; certainly Ann, the more knowledgeable of the two in the beginning, was aware of their changing roles. They shared fewer and fewer friends—Channing and Anna Marble Pollock, a photographer named Paul Thompson and his wife Daisy—but Carl's own circle grew, while Ann's did not. Assuredly, money had something to do with their eventual agreement to separate; there was never enough for anything—the bills, the food, the rent, Ann's clothes— anything. Through his job with the *Times*, Carl attended most of the musical events and many of the theatrical ones as well, all without charge. Ann shared his enthusiasms but not his invitations. Domestic activity bored her; then, too, the role of housewife in a place like New York rated second billing not only to Carl but to everyone else in the cast. She grew, indeed, to view his friends with suspicion, Pitts Sanborn and Avery Hopwood particularly. Hatred and frustration easily followed.

In the spring of 1912, the situation had grown, if not exactly frantic, certainly beyond any solution but a divorce. So Carl sauntered forth one evening, "a little terrified"—he claimed years later in recalling the incident—picked up a local *fille de joie*, and took her to a predetermined hotel room, where Paul Thompson arrived, "almost too late," in order legally to swear as a witness for Ann that he had discovered Carl *en situation*.

The court directed Carl to pay Ann twenty-five dollars a week as alimony. This they considered a formality—at least at the time. Aside from the painful fact that Carl could have scarcely afforded such an amount, the parting did not occur in anger. For a time, Ann returned to Cedar Rapids, where she taught in the high school as Ann Van Vechten—no Miss, no Mrs.

Carl saw her only twice after the divorce, and then briefly. Free at last of all ties with the past, he began to live an easier life, a freer existence. He had not resented Anna Snyder, who had helped him a great deal in growing up. "Women are always older than men," he later reflected, "although she was almost exactly my age. . . . I am sure she influenced me in many ways and was very good for my progress, or I would still be a reporter on the *Times*—maybe doing ship news. Who knows?"[30] It was, after all, Anna Snyder whose accounts of opera in Europe had first moved Carl away from New York and whose stories of music in New York had first moved him away from Chicago.

Two months after the divorce, Carl dined alone at Claridge's, a favorite restaurant of the period where singers and actors frequently gathered. There, across the room at another table, he spied Paul Thompson with a young woman, her dark hair worn low on her forehead over black and beautiful eyes. He crossed the room to ask for an introduction. Does love at first sight really exist? He always liked to think so.

"Hello, Carlo," Thompson said. "I'd like you to meet Fania Marinoff."

[30] Van Vechten, Oral History.

IV

Fania Marinoff

To me, discovery is nine-tenths of
the interest in life.

IF CARL VAN VECHTEN'S CHILDHOOD had been a reasonably happy
one, Fania Marinoff's could not have been more appallingly unhappy; if his exposure to the arts had been reasonably broad, that of
the dark-eyed Russian who was to become his second wife could
not have been more limited.

Born in Odessa, Fania Marinoff came to America in the nineties,
when she was five, the thirteenth child and seventh daughter of
aging Russian-Jewish parents. Her mother died when Fania was
still a baby. Her father remarried, and the family emigrated to
America, Fania hiding under her stepmother's voluminous skirts
most of the way, to avoid paying transportation fares.

For Mayer Marinoff, the move to the United States should have
been a propitious one, away from the conditions in Russia that
could allow one son to die of consumption in the army, away from
the medieval superstitions that surrounded Jewish culture in Europe. But, like so many emigrants of so many nationalities, both
the youngest and the oldest—Fania and her parents—were quickly
swallowed up in one of the ghettos that festered along the Eastern
Coast—for them, Boston's Salem Street. There, until his death,
Mayer Marinoff sat in the dark of a honeycomb tenement poring
over the Talmud.

While Carl Van Vechten was collecting birds' eggs a thousand
miles to the west, Fania Marinoff was running wild in the narrow
streets of Boston, like a child in one of the miserably sentimental
ballads of the period, selling matches for the few pennies they might

59

bring and returning only at night to the Salem Street flat. By the time she was six years old, Fanny—as she was called then—could cajole like a professional hawker, mimicking for attention, flashing the expressive dark eyes that were to become an asset on the stage a few years later. An innate dramatic sense followed her from the beginning, and on more than one occasion saved her from the abysmal fate of most children in similar situations. She could barely speak English when she followed the other neighborhood offspring to school. There she simply adopted the name of the boy in front of her; during her brief stay in school, she was known as Fanny Epstein. On another occasion, hiding near a lighted street lamp out of fear of the dark—Mayer infrequently interrupted his Talmud study to spin terrifying ghost stories—Fanny was befriended by the benevolent Sarah Carpenter, whose lovely house and protective wing offered a briefly happy respite from Fanny's dismal environment. The following year, when Jacob, the next in age to Fanny but several years her senior, went to Denver to join their older brother Michael, the child was taken along. Younger guardians were thought best to raise the almost wild child; certainly, a change could hardly be worse.

Denver was not, however, a noticeable improvement. Michael's wife, a waspish girl, had no children of her own, and loathed the latest addition to the household. At the age of seven, Fanny was no more than a kitchen slavey in her own home. Nor did being left alone in a darkened apartment when Michael and his wife went out for the evening strengthen the child's security. The following year, when Jacob married a would-be singer (whose fruitless voice lessons were to take most of the income from her husband's tailor trade), the situation was no better. The new member of the family had no interest in Fanny; Jacob was too involved with the then rising socialist movement to concern himself with his younger sister. Also, he was learning to write, his attempts leading eventually to his popular Yiddish newspaper *Der Grosse Kundes* (*The Big Stick*). To get Fanny out of the way, Jacob's wife sent her out to work in another household in exchange for her room and board.

Fania Marinoff

But Fanny was inventive enough to hire herself out very shortly, staying in houses where she could live as well as work, where she was allowed to attend school—though the exposure to formal education was perfunctory, haphazard, and nomadically arranged as her jobs moved her from one district to another. When she was eight or nine, she was employed as a waitress in a boarding house, where she met Margaret Fealy, who ran a dramatic arts school in Denver. Fanny begged for lessons. Her gift for mimicry and imitation, which had developed during her match-selling days in Boston and in the make-believe world she had had to invent for herself, found a natural outlet in recitation. But Mrs. Fealy charged five dollars a month, and Fanny did not have five dollars. She did study, nevertheless, at the Robert E. Bell School of Oratory, where her talent sufficiently moved the directors to offer her free lessons. Even at the age of nine, she "put herself in the part," as they told her after the tryouts. By the time she was ten, Fanny could recite extensively from *Hamlet*, and had in her repertoire a number of other readings and orations. Her first public appearances took place, however, before the elocution lessons had begun. Her brother Jacob, who had known George Bernard Shaw through the Fabian Society in London, was a rabid socialist, and Fanny was put to work reciting and singing at rallies in Denver.

Shortly thereafter she appeared on stage, at Elitch Gardens, the city's resident theater. Stage-struck before she could properly read and write, Fanny hung around the stage door until they allowed her behind the footlights. "I was always carrying somebody's train," she remembered later, but recalled that her first actual role was that of the little boy in the bakery scene from *Cyrano de Bergerac*.

By the time she was twelve, she had joined the Camilla Martinson St. George Company for a princely eight dollars a week (which she never received). The popularity of the traveling theatrical troupe was at its height, and, though the youthful Fanny Marinoff did not play Greene's Opera House in Cedar Rapids, she did journey as far as Ogalalla, Nebraska, where for three nights the company gave "excellent satisfaction" to the town. The local newspaper called her a bright little soubrette: "Fanny Marinoff is a very young miss, but possesses 'the divine spark' of real dramatic talent, and all who have seen her perform predict a great future for her."[1] But in spite of the notices, the company folded in Ogalalla, and Fanny was stranded, without money, without transportation. Traveling theater in those days was a precarious life. She wired her brothers for return fare, but there was no reply; so the bright little soubrette of Ogalalla went to work washing dishes to earn enough to get back to Denver.

The experience had done her no harm. Almost immediately she was engaged for some small roles at the Tabor Grand Opera House in Denver, and then to play with Blanche Walsh in *A Broken Heart*. The local critics suggested that her acting was of a "clever order." The regular seventeen-dollar weekly salary certainly boosted Fanny's ego as well. Later, when the star took the play to New York, friends from Fanny's Elitch Gardens days collected money to send the young actress east with the troupe.

Her first notice in New York came almost immediately when her performance in *A Japanese Nightingale* was singled out for commendation in several newspapers. The following year she began a series of regular appearances: with Cissie Loftus in *The Serio-Comic Governess*; with Mrs. Patrick Campbell in *The Sorceress*; as Dolly in Bernard Shaw's *You Never Can Tell*; and in Max Figman's 1907 *The Man on the Box*. The following season she toured the West Coast and, somewhere between Los Angeles and Seattle, changed her name to Fania.

Back in New York for the 1911–12 season, she found her career given a boost when she lost a role, an incident that may indicate her gifts as an actress. *The Rainbow* had been designed as a vehicle for Henry Miller, with a small role assigned to Fania Marinoff. "They're going to cut this part," she confided to a friend while the play was on its pre-Broadway tour. "It's too good to leave in." Her fears were realized shortly before the New York opening, though

[1] Fania Marinoff's scrapbook.

it was not the part that was cut—it was the actress. Most theatrical pages of the city's newspapers explained that she had "been too good for the role." Henry Miller, "desiring that it be known to the profession generally," explained that she "was so interesting in her brief scene and by her acting made the character so sympathetic that throughout the remainder of the play the audience was curious to see more of her. . . ."[2]

By the time she encountered Carl Van Vechten at Claridge's, Fania Marinoff's name was fairly well known in theatrical circles in New York. Several weeks later, when they met for the second time, again at Claridge's, Carl's heart was still on his sleeve. But it was firmly pinned to hers very shortly, and within the year the affair had blossomed in the gossip columns: "Clever Carl Van Vechten remains constant in his devotion to the fascinating Miss Marinoff, a darksome and delightful slip of a girl. Play-going, table d'hoting and turkey-trotting, they are quite inseparable."[3]

In February, 1913, at a dinner party, Carl Van Vechten met Mabel Dodge, a woman whose spirit had a profound influence on him, and on almost everyone else who ever met her. Carl first described her as "a new kind of woman, or else the oldest kind" and then as "a Madonna who had lived long enough to learn to listen."[4] Mrs. Dodge remembered Carl as being "funny-looking," with eyes full of good-natured malice and teeth that made him look like a wild boar. "He seemed amused at everything; there wasn't a hint of boredom in him," she later wrote in her memoirs. " 'A young soul,' I thought to myself in my superior way. . . ."[5]

It was, doubtless, that lack of boredom that first attracted Mrs. Dodge to Van Vechten, for she was in a kind of desperate need of diversion when she met him.

Mabel Evans Dodge (who turned up as Edith Dale in Van Vechten's *Peter Whiffle* several years later) had returned to New

[2] *New York Telegram, circa* October, 1911.
[3] CVV, NYPL.
[4] *Peter Whiffle*, p. 119.
[5] Mabel Dodge Luhan, *Movers and Shakers*, p. 15.

York after three years in Italy, where she had occupied her time in restoring the Villa Curonia, a palatial ghost-ridden estate near Florence. In its garden, cypresses and gardenias became settings for white peacocks and imported statues; and in its rooms, Mrs. Dodge incorporated Renaissance and Venetian furnishings into a "perfect expression of her moods." She had gone to Europe as a young widow, but arrived there engaged to marry Edwin Dodge of Boston, whom she had met on the boat going over. Ten years later, anxious to enter her son John Evans in school, she returned to America.

Carl Van Vechten and Mabel Dodge met, that first night, at Mrs. Jack Oakman's Italian town house. (Greta Oakman, whom Carl called "the heroine of a thousand adventures," had been involved years before in a *cause célèbre*: during her first marriage, to Edward Everett Hale, Jr., her face had been substituted for Lady Eden's in the celebrated case that later inspired Whistler's *The Baronet and the Butterfly*.) Mrs. Dodge had given Mr. Oakman a copy of a curious pamphlet called *Portrait of Mabel Dodge at the Villa Curonia* by someone named Gertrude Stein. It was handsomely printed and bound in Florentine wallpaper. "Why did you give that to Jack Oakman?" Carl demanded. "I'm sure you would rather have given it to me."[6] The evening did not promise to be easy. Carl was alternately put off and fascinated by Mrs. Dodge's remoteness and sphinxlike silence; she responded similarly to his flamboyance. And she was not a little alarmed by his appearance: his long body bent in two places, at waist and neck, throwing his stomach and his jaw forward; his knees wobbled; and little shrieks flew past his strange teeth when he laughed. " 'Really, those teeth,' I thought. 'They seem to have a life of their own apart from the rest of him.' "[7]

What began uncomfortably, however, ended pleasantly enough, for a kind of mutual affection developed almost immediately, or, as Mrs. Dodge put it, "a mutual stimulation with none of the usual

[6] "The Origin of the Sonnets from the Patagonian," p. 51.
[7] *Movers and Shakers*, p. 15.

elements of sex." Years later, following a minor disagreement (of which there were several, one lasting sixteen years), Carl wrote to Mabel Dodge of those early days:

> Somehow I wanted you to know, because you have played a very important part in my life making me acquainted with beauty when I didn't even know how to spell the word. More than that, indeed. . . . But you know how callow I was, and what you did. Perhaps better than I do.[8]

When the Oakmans' dinner party concluded, the Dodges dropped Carl off at the Metropolitan Opera House:

> I have to meet some fellows in the lobby in the last act and see what we're going to say about it tomorrow. . . . And if Mary fainted or anything . . . or if the Opera House caught fire, or if the President was there . . .; after all, one takes one's job seriously, I hope. . . .[9]

With Carl, Mrs. Dodge later reflected, only amusing things were really essential: "Whimsicality was the note they must sound to have significance. Life was perceived to be a fastidious circus, and strange conjunctions were more prized than in the ordinary relationships touted in eternity."[10] Her tour of his circus began almost immediately. Carl telephoned for an interview; in addition to all his fascination with Mabel Dodge, he had already foreseen the possibility of articles about Gertrude Stein.

He first arrived in the sunny parlor at 23 Fifth Avenue on a cold morning, with a terrible head cold. Then, fortified with Mrs. Dodge's whiskey and soda, he began to "animate" her "lifeless rooms," giving them "a gently vibrating awareness," as she later wrote in her memoirs. She had decorated the apartment exquisitely with French and Italian furniture against white draperies and walls and woodwork; but it was Carl whose appreciation brought "an instant response from all those inanimate things and the place became alive for us and for all others who ever afterwards entered

[8] Yale.
[9] *Movers and Shakers*, p. 15.
[10] *Ibid.*, p. 16.

there."[11] He was indeed the first of Mabel Dodge's *Movers and Shakers*.

He began telephoning her at nine o'clock every morning, addressing her as "Mike," doubtless a carry-over from Oscar Hammerstein's practice of calling those he liked—including Carl—by that name. In the weeks that followed, Carl introduced her to New York and very probably saw her as often as he saw Fania Marinoff. The relationship was understandable for both of them at that particular time; a few months later the "mutual stimulation" Mrs. Dodge spoke of had tempered, as her affair with John Reed developed and as Carl began to admit to himself that he had fallen hopelessly in love with Fania.

Mabel Dodge observed that the Van Vechten–Marinoff alliance was another of his strange conjunctions, but one firmly "rooted in eternity, odd and everlasting." Although Carl's "dead sweet affectionateness,"[12] as Mrs. Dodge termed it, was demonstrated throughout his life in warm and intimate friendships, it was Fania whom he loved. But during that winter and spring of 1913, Carl was terrified of marriage after the shambles that concluded his five years with Anna Snyder. And during that same period, Mabel Dodge was suffering from what she called a "peculiar instability," a deep depression filled with hopelessness as her marriage to Edwin Dodge began quietly to die. In her memoirs, Mabel Dodge recalled part of a conversation between her and Carl that may explain both their points of view, toward each other and individually:

> "Do you know what love is?" asked Carl of me one day, with earnest eyes, allowing a mocking smile to twist his inadequate lips sideways over his unfriendly and unaccommodating teeth. "It is to feel the way a kitten feels when a man holds it high up in the air in the palm of his hand." I didn't know whether he meant the kitten didn't know enough to be scared of falling, or whether it knew with panic the man would let it down.[13]

[11] *Ibid.*
[12] *Ibid.*, p. 45.
[13] *Ibid.*

Fania Marinoff

In February, 1913, a revolution took place in New York of the sort Carl Van Vechten delighted in. No guns were fired and no bombs exploded, but the repercussions of the Sixty-ninth Regiment Armory Show were sufficient to change forever the face of art in America. "It was the first, and possibly the last, exhibition of paintings held in New York," Carl declared, "which everybody attended."[14] He heard about it first through Mabel Dodge, who was in on the plans after she had visited Alfred Stieglitz's 291 Gallery. Actually, her support consisted primarily of lending her car and chauffeur for organizational errands. In peripheral connection with the show, already well under way, she wrote an article about Gertrude Stein for *Arts & Decoration*, copies of which were sold at the armory.

Long before this, 291 had functioned as an informal exhibition hall for the kind of work that turned up at the armory; in 1913, it functioned additionally as an underground headquarters for the revolutionists to organize their revolution. The younger American artists, especially the progressive ones, had no place to exhibit their work. No dealer's gallery was open to them.

Walt Kuhn, the executive secretary of the Armory Show as well as one of its contributors, suggested this as a primary reason for the exhibition; but he knew of other equally important ones: a desire to learn about art in Europe and to destroy the local conditions that ignored American painters and sculptors.

Initially, the exhibition had been conceived as a showcase for American art, with some European work thrown in for additional interest. After a quick trip to Germany and France and England, however, Kuhn and Arthur B. Davies, another American painter, realized the important effect the exhibition might possibly have on the United States. The government agreed to let the European paintings be imported free of duty for the show, and Kuhn and Davies prepared to improve the country's artistic vision. They adopted the Pine Tree flag of the American Revolution as their

[14] *Peter Whiffle*, p. 123.

emblem, and reproduced it on campaign buttons and posters to signify the "New Spirit."

The show opened on February 17, 1913. The critics and the public may not have liked what they saw, but neither could they ignore it. After two weeks of relatively slow attendance, the Pine Tree bombed New York with a barrage of cones: the criticism, the indignation—both artistic and moral—and the adverse publicity suddenly propelled everyone to the Sixty-ninth Regiment Armory. Newspapers cartooned and vaudeville comedians lampooned; Brancusi's sculptures were called indecent, and Marcel Duchamp's *Nude Descending a Staircase* was renamed by one critic "explosion in a shingle factory." Carl Van Vechten supplied a full account several years later in his *Peter Whiffle*:

> Everybody went and everybody talked about it. Street-car con-
> ductors asked for your opinion of the Nude Descending the Stair-
> case, as they asked you for your nickel. Elevator boys grinned about
> Matisse's Le Madras Rouge, Picabia's La Danse á la Source, and
> Brancusi's Mademoiselle Pogany, as they lifted you to the twenty-
> third floor. Ladies, you met at dinner, found Archipenko's sculpture
> very amusing, but was it art? Alfred Stieglitz, whose 291 Gallery
> had nourished similar ideas for years, spouted like a geyser for three
> weeks and then, after a proper interval, like Old Faithful, began
> again. Actresses began to prefer Odilon Redon to Raphael Kirschner,
> To sum up, the show was a bang-up whale of a success. . . .[15]

With the close of the Armory Show, Mabel Dodge found herself a minor celebrity. People began to call at 23 Fifth Avenue unexpectedly. Before the exhibit, to be sure, there had been a few callers; Hutchins Hapgood, a writer on the *Globe*, and Carl Van Vechten were regulars from the beginning, and Edwin Dodge (the shadowy husband who subsequently removed himself from Mabel's life forever) brought along Jo Davidson, the sculptor, who, in turn, introduced Lincoln Steffens. It was Steffens who solved the problem of mushrooming guests. When the practice of calling without

15 *Ibid.*

invitation threatened to get out of hand, he suggested that Mrs. Dodge have "Evenings."

"I don't mean that you should *organize* the *Evenings*," he said. "I mean, get people here at certain times and let them feel absolutely free to be themselves, and see what happens." (It was not a new idea to Mabel Dodge. Something similar had already occurred at the Villa Curonia, where Gordon Craig and Eleonora Duse and Gertrude Stein had visited.) "Let everyone come!" Steffens continued. "All these different kinds of people that you know, together here, without being managed or herded in any way! Why, something wonderful might come of it! You might even revive General Conversation!"[16]

Something wonderful did come of it. Usually on Wednesdays, but frequently on Mondays and Thursdays as well, socialists and suffragettes, artists and atheists, poets and journalists, and free thinkers and free lovers—all invaded 23 Fifth Avenue. Carl documented the phenomenon in *Peter Whiffle*:

> Well, she's a woman, but a new kind of woman, or else the oldest kind; I'm not sure which [he tells Peter, of Mabel Dodge—called Edith Dale—and her Evenings]. I'm going to take you there. Bill Haywood goes there. So does Doris Keane. Everybody goes there. Everything is all mixed up. Everybody talks his own kind of talk, and Edith, inscrutable Edith sits back and listens. . . . She spends her energy in living, in watching other people live, in watching them make their silly mistakes, in helping them make their silly mistakes. She is a dynamo. She will give you a good deal. At least these gatherings will give you a good deal.[17]

Of the Evenings themselves, the narrator of *Peter Whiffle* continues: "Arguments and discussions floated in the air, were caught and twisted and hauled and tied, until the white salon itself was no longer static. There were undercurrents of emotion and sex." There was always a simple dinner for Mrs. Dodge's guests, there was always plenty of drink, and there was certainly plenty of conversa-

[16] *Movers and Shakers*, p. 81.
[17] P. 119.

tion: "The groups separated, came together, separated, came together, separated, came together: syndicalists, capitalists, revolutionists, anarchists, artists, writers, actresses ... feminists, and malthusians were all mixed in this strange salad."[18] Max Eastman and Hutchins Hapgood rubbed shoulders with Emma Goldman; Marsden Hartley and Max Weber and Charles Demuth talked about painting with Big Bill Haywood and Walter Lippmann; and they, in turn, discussed socialism with Amy Lowell and Edwin Arlington Robinson; Neith Boyce and Fania Marinoff and Margaret Sanger and Frank Norris and Alan Seeger and Harry Kemp—all "came together, separated, came together." "Greenwich Village stands aghast at your performance," Carl wrote to Mrs. Dodge at the height of the salon's popularity. "Somebody who has really done something is too much for the villagers. . . . Admiration mixed with awe describes them."[19]

Occasionally the Evenings were organized: a Poetry Evening, a Prison Reform Evening, a Birth Control Evening. Carl was responsible for one of them—a particularly bad one—when he proposed inviting two Negro entertainers to perform. Why not, thought Mrs. Dodge. For the customary crowd in the salon, a Negro Evening should prove ethnic enough. The audience, at Carl's insistence, had been selected in advance, and the doors were closed to casual droppers-in. Following Mrs. Dodge's usual, excellent buffet, the assembled guests sat down to witness an absolute disaster: the duet began a grotesque "darky" routine, with "coon" songs and cakewalks, a gross imitation of current vaudeville entertainments. The evening broke up earlier than usual.

In the late spring, after months of what had amounted to a regular open house, Mabel Dodge began to weary of it all, partly because of the tedium of repetition, but primarily because she had fallen in love with John Reed, a young journalist and poet—the wonder boy of Greenwich Village, as Van Wyck Brooks later called him. Fresh from Harvard in 1910, Reed had published several stories and some verse; but his energies were soon directed toward the vigorous

[18] P. 145.   [19] Yale.

socialist movement. The strike of the silk workers in Paterson, New Jersey, and its appalling repercussions were a torture and preoccupation the night he met Mrs. Dodge at Bill Haywood's apartment. Catching his enthusiasm almost immediately, she suggested the possibility of staging a pageant to re-enact the Paterson strike, showing the closed mills, the gunmen, the murderer of the striker, and the funeral. The idea took hold, and the salon was soon abandoned. Having rented the deserted Madison Square Garden, she devoted all her time and interest to Reed and, ostensibly, the pageant.

To recuperate from the rigors of this endeavor—the show at Madison Square Garden had been a triumph—she suggested they go to her villa in Italy, inviting Robert Edmond Jones, the stage designer, and Carl Van Vechten to come along with her and Reed for the holiday.

Just at this time, Carl was offered a new job. The *New York Press* had been looking for a dramatic critic for some time, and they wrote to him, "If you are still in the mind to consider a change of position . . . ."[20] He accepted the challenge, resigning from the *New York Times* in May, 1913. He sailed for Europe with Pitts Sanborn, before Mrs. Dodge and her other *"jeunes gens assortis,"* as Jacques-Émile Blanche later dubbed them, agreeing to meet her in Paris and motor to Florence the following month.

Mrs. Dodge's pageants were of no particular interest to Carl Van Vechten, but the appearance of Sergei Diaghilev's ballet in Paris most emphatically was. He had missed, by a few weeks, Diaghilev's first season there, when the *Times* recalled him to America. Carl arranged to be present for the fifth one.

There was another reason for his desiring some extra time in Paris. Mabel Dodge had given him a letter of introduction to Gertrude Stein, a woman whose work he knew only slightly. Two weeks later, a lifelong friendship began.

The other day I got a note from the representative of the New York Times who lives in Paris asking for an interview. He wants me to

20 Yale.

tell him about myself. I hope I will be satisfactory. He is coming here Saturday.[21]

Mabel Dodge received the note from Gertrude Stein about the same time Carl Van Vechten received one that said: "Will you dine with us tomorrow Saturday evening at 7:30. Let me know immediately. Yrs sincerely, Gtde Stn."[22]

Her name was not unfamiliar to him. Earlier that year in New York, he had seen the pamphlet *Portrait of Mabel Dodge at the Villa Curonia*, first a copy at the Oakman party and later a whole stack of them on the foyer table at 23 Fifth Avenue. Written during the summer of 1912, the *Portrait*, as all lovers of roses and tender buttons know, begins, "The days are wonderful and the nights are wonderful and the life is pleasant." Immediately after this initial encounter, Van Vechten read Miss Stein's *Three Lives* and her word portraits of Matisse, Picasso, and Cézanne in the June, 1912 issue of *Camera Work*. By the time she received Mrs. Dodge's letter of introduction, Miss Stein already had a sympathetic and affectionate admirer. Moreover, she was familiar with Carl Van Vechten's name. Mabel Dodge had written to her three months earlier:

> You are just on the eve of *bursting*! . . . There is an article about you coming out in the N.Y. Times this Sunday & the editor sent a young man around to see me & talk about you. . . . I had met the young man . . . at dinner, & found him temperamental . . . but rather nice! . . . His name is Van Vechten.[23]

That first article on Gertrude Stein, probably the first notice of her work in America, except for a few reviews of *Three Lives*, did not appear on Sunday after all. Carl first took his essay to *Bookman*, which turned it down. Then the *New York Times Sunday Magazine* turned it down. Finally, it did appear in the *Times*—in a single edition (one of four for the day) on the Monday morning financial page. "My original article was 3 times as long and 4 times as amus-

[21] Yale.
[22] Yale.
[23] Yale; Donald Gallup, ed., *The Flowers of Friendship*, p. 74.

ing," Carl wrote to Mrs. Dodge, "but for a daily paper one must have to exclude style."[24]

Gertrude Stein had recently encountered the name. In *The Autobiography of Alice B. Toklas*, she reported that an acquaintance had brought a "depressed and unhappy" Anna Snyder Van Vechten to dinner: "Mrs. Van Vechten told the story of the tragedy of her married life but Gertrude Stein was not particularly interested."[25]

About a week later, Gertrude Stein and her companion Alice Toklas attended the second performance of Stravinsky's *Le Sacre du Printemps*. It was there that Carl first saw the magnetic woman who was to become one of his greatest friends.

He had already attended the first performance of the controversial work at the Théâtre des Champs-Élysées. From the moment the music began, with a bassoon solo in an unnaturally high register, there was such an uproar that the dancers were unable to hear the orchestra, even when it swelled to include all of its 128 instruments. Pierre Monteux tried to keep the score together; Nijinsky stood in the wings, beating out the rhythm with his feet and crying to the dancers on stage; Stravinsky clutched the choreographer's coattails to prevent him from going on stage and creating a scandal. Further to complicate the hullabaloo, composers in the audience were storming out indignantly (Saint-Saëns) or shouting blasphemously (Florent Schmitt); Diaghilev, from his box, rose to implore the audience to be silent. The lights were never lowered, and to the dancers the audience's performance must have appeared as frenetic as their own. From another box, Carl Van Vechten remembered:

> Cat-calls and hisses succeeded the playing of the first few bars, and then ensued a battery of screams, countered by a foil of applause. We warred over art (some of us thought it was and some thought it wasn't). . . . Some forty of the protestants were forced out of the theatre but that did not quell the disturbance. The lights in the

[24] Yale.
[25] *Selected Writings of Gertrude Stein*, p. 112.

73

auditorium were fully turned on but the noise continued and I remember Mlle. Piltz executing her strange dance of religious hysteria on a stage dimmed by the blazing light in the auditorium, seemingly to the accompaniment of the disjointed ravings of a mob of angry men and women.[26]

This account appeared in Carl Van Vechten's "Music and Bad Manners," an essay written in 1916. His memory was equally vivid in a paper about the composer, called "Igor Strawinsky, A New Composer":

> I was sitting in a box in which I had rented one seat. Three ladies sat in front of me and a young man occupied the place behind me. He stood up during the course of the ballet to enable himself to see more clearly. The intense excitement under which he was laboring, thanks to the potent force of the music, betrayed itself presently when he began to beat rhythmically on the top of my head with his fists. My emotion was so great that I did not feel the blows for some time. They were perfectly synchronized with the beat of the music. When I did, I turned around. His apology was sincere. We had both been carried beyond ourselves.[27]

Carl either shared a box with three other women at the second performance of *Le Sacre du Printemps*, or he confused the two evenings in his excitement; at any rate, he did not recognize Gertrude Stein until a couple of days later when he went to call. She and Miss Toklas had, however, noticed him when he entered the box, just before the performance began:

> A tall, well-built young man, he might have been a dutchman, a scandanavian or an american and he wore a soft evening shirt with the tiniest pleats all over the front of it. It was impressive, we had never even heard that they were wearing evening shirts like that. That evening when we got home Gertrude Stein did a portrait of the unknown called a Portrait of One.[28]

There was little of Stravinsky's music in Miss Stein's portrait, but

[26] *Music and Bad Manners*, p. 34.
[27] *Music after the Great War*, p. 88.
[28] *Selected Writings of Gertrude Stein*, p. 113.

a good deal about the shirt that, curiously enough, Carl had worn the first night he met Mrs. Dodge. She too had commented on the pleats, though not so vividly as Miss Stein: "touching white shining sash and a touching white green undercoat and a touching white colored orange and a touching piece of elastic,"[29] perhaps the most lucid statement in her portrait. When he called on Saturday evening, following that second performance of *Le Sacre du Printemps*, Carl was familiar with only a few of Gertrude Stein's writings, most of them hermetic; but they were new and they were exciting, and the enthusiasm he frequently felt for the pioneer and the outlaw in all the creative arts compensated for knowledge yet unlearned. He arrived promptly at 7:30 at 27 rue de Fleurus, the address so many Americans had visited before him, would visit after him, to view the paintings—the early Matisses and Picassos just then known to the outside world, the Cézannes, the work of other new artists—and to meet Gertrude Stein:

> He came and he was the young man of the soft much-pleated evening shirt and it was the same shirt. Also of course he was the hero or villain of Mrs. Van Vechten's tragic tale. . . . Gertrude Stein began to tease Carl Van Vechten by dropping a word here and there of intimate knowledge of his past life. He was naturally bewildered. It was a curious evening.[30]

The acquaintance, begun that Saturday evening in May, quickly developed into a warm friendship, and in the following month Carl and Gertrude Stein saw considerably more of each other. He saw considerably more of the Diaghilev ballets as well: Nijinsky's *Jeux*, *Les Sylphides, Carnaval, Scheherazade, The Firebird, Petrouchka, L'Après-midi d'un Faune*. By the time the company reached America a few years later, Carl was already familiar with the superb repertoire, the astonishing settings and costumes of Léon Bakst, the great dancing of Nijinsky. It was all material he later put to good use in a number of essays on the ballet.

[29] *Geography and Plays*, p. 199.
[30] *Selected Writings of Gertrude Stein*, p. 114.

In July, he motored south with Mabel Dodge to join her ménage at the Villa Curonia. In addition to John Reed—now Mrs. Dodge's lover, though the affair began to pall almost immediately—and Robert Edmond Jones, Artur Rubinstein was there, playing the piano in the great salon.

The pianist had arrived with Muriel Draper, whose Edith Grove Salon in London had been the scene of evenings attended by Henry James and Pablo Casals and others. In her entourage at the Villa Curonia she included, in addition to Rubinstein, Robin de la Condamine, an occasional actor, and Johnny McMullin, a New York publicist. The two groups were not exactly congenial, however, and actually saw little of each other. The Dodge boys held out on the loggia, while the Draper boys camped in the damasked-draped salon.

Carl had already met Mrs. Draper several weeks before in London, by way of an introductory letter from Mabel Dodge; but the beginning was bad, and the situation at the villa did not improve matters. When the assembled guests did meet, the encounter constituted more an attack than a social intercourse: the battles were verbal, the contention aesthetics, and Carl's reactions largely posturing, according to Muriel Draper's *Music at Midnight*.

The holiday at the Villa Curonia was memorable, nevertheless: Carl discovered Italy for the first time: he scaled the walls at Campo Santo to pick oranges from the heavy trees; he dined on ortolons at Arles; and he passed an afternoon, as all good tourists did, in the bar at the Hotel Spezia. The villa itself offered incredible beauty: from Mabel's blue room (under which Edwin Dodge had reposed, and to which he had approached her by means of a rope ladder) to the pepper trees and rows of cypresses. The façade of its loggia was attributed to Raphael, and its cortile designed by Brunelleschi. There Carl sat in the evening, as he wrote in *Peter Whiffle*, "under the red brocaded walls, illuminated by wax tapers set in girandoles of green and rose faience."[31] Or he strolled in the gardens where the atmosphere was tinged with green, while peasants sang in the road

[31] Pp. 168–169.

below and nightingales sang in the olive copse; he breakfasted there also while white peacocks strutted about and the bells of Florence sounded softly in the distance.

The summer came to a close, and, reluctantly, they all returned to New York: Mabel and Reed to 23 Fifth Avenue, where the Evenings began again; Carl to the *New York Press*, where he assumed his new duties.

> The new dramatic editor of the Press is not taking chances of being late with his copy [wrote one of the gossip columnists], for one of his adornments on first nights is a bracelet worn on the left wrist containing a tiny watch which is frequently consulted so that the writer can make a hasty exit from the theatre when it is time for him to be in with his editorial on the new play. This new dramatic editor is Carl Van Vechten.[32]

Carl had brought the wrist watch—apparently the first one in New York—back from Paris. It was put to excellent use during that single season he covered the theater for the *New York Press*, for between September and June he reviewed more than 130 productions: plays, musical comedies, and operettas. It was a season that included the first American performance of Bernard Shaw's *Pygmalion*, a production, curiously enough, given in German. Nothing else of extraordinary dimensions occurred, though Fania Marinoff's "grace and beautiful voice" in Percy MacKaye's *A Thousand Years Ago* were of some interest to the reviewer.

"What has become of Carl Van Vechten's wife," an unenlightened columnist wanted to know, "that the Press critic can lavish so much attention upon the little Russian actress with whom he is seen so much? . . . No one seems to recall that there was a divorce or anything of that sort. What is the solution of the mystery?"[33]

There was of course no mystery. Carl and Fania had fallen in love. "There is contentment in single blessedness," he advised an

[32] CVV, NYPL.
[33] *Ibid.*

interviewer, "but contentment is an awful bore . . . and [I] might take a dip into matrimony soon."[34] Miss Marinoff may have questioned the advisability of such a move a few weeks later:

> We had dinner at the Brevoort [Van Vechten wrote to Mabel Dodge] and I got very drunk and read . . . out loud to the assembled dining room . . . The Portrait of Mabel Dodge and Avery was drunk enough by that time to say that he understood it. I went to Evangeline in a terrible condition but it didn't do any good; it was too dull. However, during the course of the piece, Fan and I had a rotten row and she left with authority, nor did I see her again that night. . . . She adjudged my condition to be due to my having seen you and Avery—after all not far wrong. . . . Scenes from the Younger Generation were freely enacted.[35]

The inebriated Avery referred to was Avery Hopwood. A playwright best remembered for his collaboration with Mary Roberts Rinehart on *The Bat*, Hopwood was one of the most prolific and popular playwrights in America during the period when he and Carl were friends. They met shortly after Carl's arrival in New York, at a party given by two maiden ladies who lived in an apartment near Carl and Ann's digs on Fortieth Street. A warm if erratic companion, Hopwood came closest to Carl Van Vechten's Peter Whiffle, with one major distinction: Peter never managed to write anything; Avery Hopwood, though now cobwebbed with neglect, wrote continuously and with apparent ease. In the 1919–20 season, four of his plays ran simultaneously on Broadway.

In Peter Whiffle there may be more of another friend of this period, an oddball named Donald Evans who entered Carl's life at about the same time. A conventional copy reader for the *Times*, Evans was a most unconventional poet. He suggested to Carl of his latest effort, in a note written in March, 1913:

> Please show this to 100 persons today. It's the cleverest thing done since the Pyramids were built and I'm in awe of myself at having written it. Please have it published. I really can't wait for the volume

34 *Ibid.*
35 Yale.

to hold it. Make Town Topics take it. And if you're particularly nice you'll wire me Wednesday (tonight) c/o Plymouth Inn, Northampton, Mass. I want to know you like my poem.[36]

The poem, one of his "Sonnets from the Patagonian," finally got printed, but not through Carl Van Vechten's efforts. Evans founded his own publishing house, Claire-Marie, to serve the "seven hundred civilized people" in America to whom his first brochure was distributed. Most of the material was local, the work of his friends—indeed, he even announced an apocryphal Van Vechten volume entitled *Sacral Dimples*—though, primarily, he published his own verse. But he persuaded Carl to ask Gertrude Stein for a manuscript. She, in turn, submitted *Tender Buttons*, though Mabel Dodge begged her not to publish with Evans. Following the advice of Edwin Arlington Robinson, one of the regulars at 23 Fifth Avenue, Mrs. Dodge wrote, fearfully:

> Claire Marie Press which Evans runs is absolutely third rate, & in bad odor here, being called for the most part "decadent" & Broadwayish & that sort of thing. . . . I think it would be a pity to publish with him *if* it will emphasize the idea in the opinion of the public, that there is something degenerate & effete & decadent about the whole of the cubist movement which they *all* connect you with, because, hang it all, as long as they don't understand a thing they think all sorts of things. . . .[37]

Miss Stein wrote for the return of her manuscript, but it was too late. *Tender Buttons* appeared in the spring of 1914, neither degenerate nor effete nor decadent. And Evans could boast that there were no typographical errors, a considerable achievement in light of the contents, which the *Chicago Tribune* called a "nightmare journey in unknown and uncharted seas." The volume, printed in an edition of only one hundred copies, was a *succès d'estime*, and several of Miss Stein's cryptic poems were quoted widely. "Red Roses," for example, Miss Stein advised her readers, was easily ex-

[36] Yale; "The Origin of the Sonnets from the Patagonian," p. 52.
[37] Yale; Gallup, ed., *The Flowers of Friendship*, pp. 96–97.

pressed in a single line: "A cool red rose and a pink cut pink, a collapse and a sold hole, a little less hot"; and "Chicken": "Alas a dirty word, alas a dirty third alas a dirty third, alas a dirty bird."[38]

Miss Stein's new publisher could be as capricious as she. "I have found why restlessness has driven me like Orestes for years," he wrote to Carl. "I have satisfied neither of the two great hungers in my life—the love of being swathed in bedclothes and my desire for hourly baths."[39] On other occasions, the tone differed slightly. "Call me up immediately at the Yorkville Prison,"[40] he telegraphed after being thrown in jail for one of his frequent drinking bouts. The following day, he was back in the city, breakfasting on raw eggs, black coffee, and a glass of raw beef blood, his customary repast. A week later, he announced he would embrace the Episcopal ministry to combat the evangelistic derring-do of Billy Sunday. His verse did not long survive his suicide at the age of thirty-two, either as influence or as art; but, as Mabel Dodge observed in her *Movers and Shakers*, he left "a curiously strong impression upon the friends who were nearest to him . . . ."[41] The legend these friends sought to perpetuate in a memorial volume seems now as remote as Patagonia, where of course Donald Evans never ventured.

Between these "scenes from the younger generation" and his duties as drama critic for the *Press*, Carl prepared a number of articles for *Trend* magazine, run by his old friend Pitts Sanborn. These began with a general review of the season in retrospect in the April, 1914, issue, with an early consideration of animated cartoons. Having remarked that enthusiasm outweighs sophistication, Carl went on to defy "the most sophisticated Roman of us all" to witness *Gertie the Dinosaur* "without experiencing thrills of the first order . . . ."[42] Another article, the following month, reviewed an American Negro drama, *Granny Maumee*, which he called the "most important contribution which has yet been made to the

38 *Selected Writings of Gertrude Stein*, pp. 417, 436.
39 Yale; "The Origin of the Sonnets from the Patagonian," p. 51.
40 Yale; *ibid*.
41 P. 78.
42 "The Dying Audience," p. 111.

American stage."[43] With an extraordinary devotion, he spent the rest of his life trying to widen the audience for contributions of the Negro to the various fine arts; this article was his first publicly to call attention to one of them—more than fifty years ago.

Subsequent issues of *Trend* carried pieces on George Moore and George Bernard Shaw and, more important from Carl Van Vechten's point of view, Gertrude Stein, his first extensive article on the latter:

> The English language is a language of hypocrisy and evasion. How not to say a thing has been the problem of our writers from the earliest times. . . . Miss Stein . . . has really turned language into music, really made its sound more important than its sense.[44]

The last article of the series, written in the spring of 1914, was an expanded revision of an essay about stage decoration that Carl had prepared for the *New York Press*, an essay that Frank Munsey, the "eccentric owner" of the paper, had chided for its initial length. The arrangement with the *Press*, which had begun so promisingly in September, was not altogether felicitous. In January, Carl's work was accused of being too strongly press agent; in February, his diction and vocabulary came under criticism; in March, Munsey suggested that Carl review the early efforts of the movies; in April, he wanted less coverage and more news; in May, he dispensed with Carl altogether. (And, for the record, it should be added that in June he dispensed with the paper.)

Carl had two weeks' severance pay and two weeks' vacation salary, several scheduled *Trend* articles, and an invitation to join Mabel Dodge for the summer at the Villa Curonia, where she was taking a vacation from John Reed. Carl sailed on June 29, 1914, just as the rumblings of the first world war were about to sound.

BACK IN PARIS ONCE AGAIN, Carl tried to see Gertrude Stein and Alice Toklas, to deliver the latest gossip about *Tender Buttons* and

43 "A Cockney Flower Girl and Some Negroes," p. 111.
44 "How to Read Gertrude Stein," p. 553.

81

to introduce "a little Russian called Fania,"[45] who had accompanied him on the European jaunt. But Miss Stein was on her way to London to interview publishers, and missed the visitors.

Europe offered sufficient consolation. Carl and Fania were in love, and young, and without responsibility. They spent an enchanted summer, investigating first Paris and Venice and then London, leisurely passing away the warm days until Fania had to return to America around the first of August to begin rehearsals for a new play, *Consequences*, and Carl planned to meet Mabel Dodge.

The trip to London was Carl's first since his first marriage, but the prospect of introducing the town to Fania easily offset the earlier visit. They saw everything, from Windsor Castle to Billingsgate Market, where they watched Cockney fishwives chopping the heads from live eels. It was an incident Carl Van Vechten chose to document the following fall in another essay (which, incidentally, had nothing to do with eels) about George Moore:

> Won't they bite you? was Fania's query. Not if you looks out for 'em, replied the girl and she showed signs for expertness. At a brewery hard by lager beer was brewing and Fania stood treat at the tap to perhaps fifty women, many with children at breast. There were four in the beginning, but the news spread and if we had stayed a little longer all Shoreditch and Whitechapel would have arrived.[46]

At the end of the month, they returned to Paris. Mrs. Dodge telegraphed Carl to meet her in Florence; but the following day, traveling south, he realized that what he really wanted to do was to return with Fania Marinoff to New York.

He arrived at the Villa Curonia to find Mabel Dodge packing to leave for Vallombrosa, a mountain retreat; it was likely that communications would be momentarily cut with America. The next day, August 1, Germany declared war on Russia; two days later, Germany declared war on France and invaded Belgium and Luxembourg. First cabling John Reed, who was visiting his family in

---

[45] Yale; Gallup, ed., *The Flowers of Friendship*, p. 97.
[46] *Sacred and Profane Memories*, pp. 65–66.

Oregon at the time, Mrs. Dodge and her son deserted the villa in favor of the mountains, dragging Hutchins Hapgood's wife and children and Carl Van Vechten with her on the journey.

For the next few days, they led a frantic existence: money was growing tighter; rumors were that Italian ships had stopped sailing; Mabel was waiting impatiently for Reed to arrive and wanting desperately to get her son out of Europe. Americans crowded the streets of towns and villages, unable to cash checks, unable to cable for money, unable to book passage on ships that would probably never leave their Italian ports.

In a moment of frugality, Mabel Dodge quietly decided that her party would give up tobacco and liquor and servants and sit out the war in a cottage in Vallombrosa; obviously, they were not going to leave Italy. Others disagreed. Neith Boyce Hapgood, saddled with two small children and a couple of pet owls at the time, did not like the idea, and Carl did not look forward to an extended stay in Italy or anywhere else in Europe. In spite of the fact that his tickets were good only as far as the borders of the country, he continued to act as legman, making hurried trips back to the Villa Curonia and into Florence in a desperate effort to find a means of escape. "My feeling most of the time," he wrote in early August, "was one of anxiety, insecurity. I did not unpack. I did no writing. I was waiting for some catastrophe which never actually occurred."[47]

Then they learned by telephone that two Italian steamships were booked to sail from Naples in less than a week. They returned to Florence to secure visas. "Write down the name of your nearest male relative," the assistant consul suggested, "and if you are killed we shall know whom to notify."[48] There was no panic in this, Carl Van Vechten later reflected, but, instead, a listless despair. The re-establishment of communications with America offered a little hope. Among the cables to reach Mabel's entourage was one from Fania Marinoff informing Carl that she had arrived safely. Meanwhile, the consul in Florence advised them to go to Naples, in case

[47] *Ibid.*, p. 134.
[48] *Ibid.*, p. 135.

passage became available. By the time they reached that port, Italian banks were no longer recognizing drafts cabled from the United States. Eavesdropping in the hotel lobby, Carl learned that an Italian lugger (as Carl called it), the *San Guglielmo*, was sailing that night for America. Other ships, he knew, had been scheduled to sail later, but if Italy did declare war, all ships might be requisitioned for government service.

Advertisements for the *San Guglielmo*, a rusting tank that in peacetime transported emigrants from Naples to the United States, indicated that United States citizens "would be taken back to their native land at the purely nominal rates of $110 to $150 a head."[49] Carl's first trip to Europe, scarcely a decade earlier, had cost him $32.50. The owners of the *San Guglielmo* were apparently prepared to cash in on the desperate plight of the tourists and expatriates in search of escape.

Borrowing money from Mrs. Dodge, Neith Hapgood and Carl handed over the substantial sum of 2,200 lire for passage for themselves, the Hapgood children, and Mrs. Dodge's son. Mabel Dodge was determined to await the arrival of John Reed, who, authorized by the government as a war correspondent, had already sailed for Europe. For Reed, this was the beginning of the journey that would end six years later behind the walls of the Kremlin, where he died at the age of thirty-two.

At the dock where the *San Guglielmo* was tied up, the sight was lively, to be sure: men were changing lire into dollars, not infrequently doling out counterfeit American bills with the greenbacks, all the while waving them in the air and screaming frantically to advertise their activity; fruit vendors were hawking along the docks and in small boats; steamer chairs, hastily improvised from indifferent wood and castoff canvas, were going for three or four dollars apiece; merchants were peddling pots and pans and washbasins. There was, additionally, a regiment of beggars—blind, lame, deaf, armless, legless, and whole—all demanding *soldi*; and frenzied, shrieking porters were doing an equal amount of begging to be

49 *Ibid.*, p. 149.

allowed to carry baggage on board. One offered to carry Carl's trunks a distance of fifty feet for two dollars. He was not engaged.

Carl and Neith Hapgood, her children and John Evans in tow, left a bitter Mabel Dodge dockside. They could think only of returning to New York as quickly as possible; she could not understand their deserting her while she was waiting for Reed. She did not speak to Carl for several years afterward.

The party boarded the *San Guglielmo* to discover a nightmare. Carl had been advised that the ship's hasty renovations would meet the present crisis: bunk partitions, fresh paint, new bedding; indeed, their cabin—a single cabin for all five of them—had a skylight, or so they had been told. Mrs. Hapgood had wanted to check the accommodations before purchasing the tickets, but Carl had refused, convinced they would never sail if they knew in advance what faced them. He was right. Two weeks later a piece appeared in a New York newspaper, announcing that the "globe-trotting . . . Van Vechten . . . is safe again in the land of the free. He arrived yesterday from Naples on a cattle steamer . . . and although the cattle aboard were comfortably stabled, Mr. Van Vechten's cabin was the upper deck where he slept every night."

Carl's own account, printed in *Trend*, was more graphic. The promised skylight was nonexistent, and the dingy cabin itself was too small for two adults and three children. The narrow bunks were merely lead-pipe frames covered with canvas, and the freshly painted red deck was still wet. He procured steamer chairs for a dollar each, and for the entire trip slept outside on the upper deck, even after the initial good weather had passed and a nightly drizzle set in. On at least one evening, wrapped in a voluminous Italian army cape, he weathered a heavy storm rather than submit to the tortures of the transport's interior. It was sufficient to enter there for the nightmarish meals:

> The room smelled badly; the tablecloth was filthy; so were the napkins—no one got his own; there were hard biscuits and *café au lait*—on dishes that were not very clean. There was no jam, no toast, no rolls, no butter. Someone informed me that some of the stewards

had been forced to sleep on the tables. Cockroaches abounded. They ran over the walls and occasionally at mess the boys amused themselves by killing them.[50]

That was breakfast; for dinner, they served, at least for their first meal, a dubious bouillabaisse of eel and squid and baby octopus, their several tentacles still attached to their bodies. After the *San Guglielmo* passed Gibraltar the food improved slightly, but the accommodations did not, and chaos threatened. Ultimately, a committee was formed to organize the confusion. The bar was transformed daily into an altar for Mass; meal tickets were arranged and a bath schedule posted, the latter doing little good because of the limited facilities. Most of the bathing that was done took place in the corridors, where ladies and gentlemen communally, in dressing gowns or underclothes or less, performed such ablutions as were necessary. Carl did not even bother to change his clothes during the eleven-day voyage.

Fortunately, there was little sickness, after an initial *mal de mer en masse*. The crowded conditions kept most of the passengers topside, and, fortunately, the weather was good almost continuously. For diversion, someone always seemed to be entertaining with recitations or songs at the untuned piano in the salon, and there were a couple of organized dances to pass the time away. But the cigarettes were moldy, and the liquor was rotten to the taste and raw to the throat; only the mutual despair of the passengers kept morale alive.

The issue of *Trend* with Carl's article about the trip included another Van Vechten piece, "Glimpses of the European Stage." For this issue and two successive ones, he acted as editor. The magazine had been slowly dying for some time, and, at the instigation of Pitts Sanborn, then serving as its secretary-treasurer, Carl assumed the editorial responsibilities. "I came back to find the Trend moaning and lying flat on its back," he wrote to Mabel Dodge.

Sanborn was crying that he had lost the Trend, which seems to be his hold on life at present. . . . The editor was fuming; the backer

[50] "Once Upon the Lugger, San Guglielmo," p. 15.

refused to put up money. . . . In 4 hours, Mike, I got a check for $2000 out of the backer which I put in the bank in the name of the Trend, wiped Sanborn's tears away and put him on a boat, and every thing was all right again.[51]

Then he established a new policy under which the *Trend* would be determined to exclude "stupidity, banality, cant, clap-trap morality, Robert W. Chambersism, sensationalism for its own sake."[52] He signed his testament "Atlas," and in his new capacity featured the work of Edna Kenton, an old friend from Chicago, Sanborn, Allen Norton, Hutchins Hapgood, Donald Evans, and Wallace Stevens.

But the new policy of *Trend* expired almost immediately when the magazine's angel stopped paying the bills. Carl's third issue as editor was also the final issue. Walter Arensberg and Wallace Stevens helped celebrate the wake, which began at the Brevoort and ended several hours later in Arensberg's apartment. Between rounds, "Peter Quince at the Clavier" had one of his first public hearings, a happening Carl immediately committed to paper but then withheld from publication for nearly fifty years because of its unpleasant references to Mrs. Stevens.

Those final three issues of *Trend* carried of course several Van Vechten essays as well as the work of his friends. And he took time from his editorial chores almost immediately to write at least one other note: "I am enclosing my application for a marriage license, and will call for the license during the next week."[53] That was on the first day of October; two weeks later, Carl Van Vechten and Fania Marinoff were secretly married in Connecticut. A few weeks later, as an indirect result, Carl was in jail.

THE PAYMENTS Van Vechten had been directed by the court to make to his first wife had never begun. The process of separation and divorce had been neither bitter nor unpleasant; the agreement,

[51] Yale.
[52] "The Editor's Work Bench," p. 101.
[53] Yale.

a mutual one. But her former husband's remarriage had moved Anna Snyder Van Vechten to demand her back alimony. When he refused to pay—actually, he was unable to pay—she secured a legal order of commitment.

It has already been suggested that Van Vechten's meager income had been one of the motivating factors in the divorce. Consequently, it is reasonable to assume that Ann considered a second wife sufficient justification for demanding her $25 a week, which by that time would have amounted to about $750. It is equally reasonable to assume a marked degree of jealousy: the young critic had come a long way since his divorce. Certainly, Ann did not need the money; her family in Cedar Rapids had enough.

On December 6, as a result of the court order, Carl Van Vechten was hauled off to Ludlow Street jail in downtown Manhattan. Ludlow was not an unfashionable place to be imprisoned at the time, and Carl made use of the incident several years later in *The Blind Bow-Boy.*

The first newspaper coverage suggested that Carl had been carried screaming into jail. A few days later, Algernon St. John Brennon's account told a considerably different story:

Carl Van Vechten Happy in Jail
Resents the Intrusion of the Turbulent Outer World
Revels in Turgenieff
Recipient of Many Gifts
Aroused in His Epicurean Calm the Envy of Those
Who Must Toil and Spin

He was whistling that which in the coagulated phrase of the higher musical criticism would be called a simple melism in the pentatonic scale. The words ran, "So the walls do not a prison make nor iron bars a cage." The music was an excerpt from Debussy's Pelleas and Melisande.

He wore a Byronic collar, an oxblood tie and a silken shirt of many colors, and other more prosaic vestments. He was striking contrast to the wreck of nerves and liver that had come to prison.

"Oh—ah—you, of course. You are working. Journalism, always, I

88

suppose? Yes, of course," said he, undoing a package of costly hot-house fruits sent him by one of the great ladies of the theatre. "You are working. You have very little time for reading, study, original composition and so on. Uncommonly good grapes, these. And how is the food out there," he jerked a disdainful finger at the outer world. "Bad as ever?

"If Mrs. Van Vechten the First heard of it she would have me turned out into the cold, cruel world."

"And Fania Marinoff Van Vechten?" said I.

"Ah, she will be here in a few minutes with a dozen plover's eggs and some caviar from the Ural River. . . ."[54]

Certainly, the incarcerated Carl was not abandoned in jail. The cell was usually filled with flowers, sent by well-wishers, by singers from the Metropolitan and actors whose work he had praised or whose friendship he held. And of course Pitts Sanborn and Anna Marble Pollock and Donald Evans were regularly in attendance. There was even a piano in his quarters at Ludlow. Fania Marinoff was, however, in no position to purchase plover's eggs and caviar. She served double duty that season: acting with the Greenwich Village Players, and then, in a valiant effort to raise money, return-ing to motion pictures. She had made a few films a couple of years earlier.

While Fania worked, others played. Donald Evans wrote to Carl in jail:

Green moons on the soapsud staircase churned
Chinese candles within his sweetbreads burned[55]

He asked how Carlo liked *De Profundis*. From Chicago, Edna Kenton wired at length to amuse her imprisoned friend:

Hello child of the glades of Ludlow Street where the days are wonderful and the nights are wonderful and the life is pleasant out here a university professors wife holds Mary Garden to be illiterate because she did not finish sophomore year at Hyde Park High love

[54] *Morning Telegraph*, December 9(?), 1914.
[55] Yale.

to you and Fan as for Ann see Stein on chicken we have explained this telegram to the operator who sends her sympathy[56]

Later, she suggested that Claire-Marie, Evans's printing house, bring out "Letters from Ludlow," bound in prison-striped black and white boards.

Carl may not have written many letters from Ludlow, but at the same time he did not idle away his time, as Brennon's newspaper interview had suggested. In the four months of his internment, he wrote at least three interesting pieces and a number of others of less value. A few of these—some of them in French—appeared in *Rongwrong*, an odd little magazine Marcel Duchamp got out for three or four issues.

These Ludlow papers, most of which appeared in *Rogue*, were actually Carl Van Vechten's first attempts to write fiction, the first at least since his days at the University of Chicago. He had, from time to time over the years, turned his attention to playwriting, but without any success. Now, in Ludlow, a number of quasi-fictional pieces began to develop for the audacious little periodical that advertised itself as "The Cigarette of Literature" that "sells the truth and the untruth for $1 a year." "The Nightingale and the Peahen," an enchanting tale about these birds in mating season at the Villa Curonia, appeared in *Rogue* in April, 1915; a couple of others were in the May and August issues; and in October there was a trio of brief fictional sketches entitled "Three Lives." One other piece of fiction, "The Fifth Alternative," appeared in the December issue of *Snappy Stories*. But the lives were barely alive, and the alternative scarcely snappy; they were never reprinted.

If composition occupied his time in jail, it did not compensate for his loss of freedom. Carl's brother Ralph could write early in the year: "While I hope you will effect a settlement with Ann before long, I think it unwise to appear anxious in the matter. She has done her worst now and you might as well profit by it."[57] But in March, he was not so encouraging, and his patronizing attitude did not help:

[56] Yale.
[57] CVV, NYPL.

There is no use of talking about settlements now. You have nothing with which to settle and Father will not pay any amount which she will consider. It is therefore up to you to take your medicine and after she has had you in jail a few days or weeks, she will be glad to settle on any reasonable terms, but mind you after having gone through that ordeal if I were you I would not think of settling for more than $1000 or $2000. I have talked with a number of attorneys who tell me that there is nothing serious in . . . going to jail on a matter of this kind and so I am beginning to look at it entirely differently from what I did on the start. I want you to know that really my sympathies are with you and I hope you will brace up and take the matter philosophically.[58]

Carl's father suggested that Ann be offered half within ten days and the balance within thirty, a plan she refused. Indeed, she refused every offer but the awarded amount, plus the $750 in arrears. The elder Van Vechten commiserated: "Malice and selfishness are short lived in the face of patience. Courage, my boy."[59]

Finally, in early April, Carl was released. Ann had grumpily agreed to a not altogether happy settlement—a thousand dollars cash. He went into debt for one thousand dollars to meet her requirements, but as a result he was legally free forever. Ann exiled herself in Europe, where she wandered about for nearly twenty years. Then, in 1933, afflicted with a cancer from which she could not recover, she committed suicide by leaping from the third-story window of a Paris sanitorium.

THE NEWSPAPERS covered Carl's release from jail in a manner typical of the earlier accounts:

Carl Van Vechten, poet, aesthete and mystic is out of Ludlow Jail. The heavy doors opened yesterday morning and after a violent struggle in which Van Vechten resisted for some time the efforts of six turnkeys and four wardens to set him free, he was finally vanquished and stood on the corner of Ludlow and Grand Streets, a free but miserable and foreboding man.[60]

[58] CVV, NYPL.   [59] CVV, NYPL.   [60] CVV, NYPL.

Carl Van Vechten

The dark countenance (if there really was one) would have masked something considerably more serious than a prison release. Carl Van Vechten had neither the poet's temperament nor the mystic's patience; and his aestheticism was largely decorative. When he left Ludlow—forcibly evicted or not—he was nearly thirty-five years old. He was without funds. He was in debt. He had no job or any immediate hope of one. At the *New York Times*, Alexander Woollcott had recently assumed the duties of drama critic, a position Carl had applied for, only to be chided for having been "disloyal." From prison he had written to the *Evening Sun*, but the reply was not encouraging: they were going to "try out several 'youngsters.' " And the *Tribune* did not expect to make any additions "at the present time."

A few weeks later, "Town Topics" gossiped:

> It seems to have been the impression that Carl Van Vechten, erstwhile "assistant" critic on the daily newspaper, was still languishing in the city's Ludlow Street Hostelry at the instigation of his former wife. Not so. From an alimony debtor's pen to apparent affluence is but a step in the strange life of Gotham. I saw the gay and festive Carl—wrist-watch and all—emerging from a 5th Avenue banking institution on Monday, accompanied by Fania Marinoff, his current wife, and clinging affectionately to a large roll of yellow backs which he counted over and over to make sure that the paying teller had made no mistake....[61]

This was in late May. Carl still had no hope of a permanent job, but Fania Marinoff had been engaged for a revival of Shaw's *Arms and the Man*. Several years earlier, she had read for the role of Louka when the play was first presented in America, but Arnold Daly, responsible for Shaw's first productions in this country, turned her down because of her youth. This time, in 1915, when she heard about the planned revival and asked again, there was no question about the casting. As the pert Bulgarian chambermaid in Shaw's comedy, Fania Marinoff had the critic's praise in the papers and the customer's praise at the box office. When *Arms and the*

[61] CVV, NYPL.

Man closed, she was engaged to play in a film version of George Barr McCutcheon's *Nedra*. After a brief holiday in Cedar Rapids with Carl's father and stepmother, Fania and Carl sailed for the Bahamas, where the first "location" movie was made.

As early as 1914, Fania had played in the film *One of Our Girls* with Hazel Dawn. Following this, she appeared in several other motion pictures of equally little value, but one of them—*Life's Whirlpool*—is worthy of consideration. Based on Frank Norris's *MacTeague*, it marked the first serious attempt to translate the naturalistic fiction of that period into a dramatic medium. The film was not well received in 1916, when it was first released, and Erich von Stroheim's more popular version, *Greed*, in 1924, all but buried it. At the present time no known print exists; at least, none is available to the public. Even before she was engaged for *Nedra*, however, Fania Marinoff's name was already well known on the movie screen; but the film did mark one debut: Carl put in a very brief appearance as a warship captain when the director failed to engage an actor for the role. He was apparently not encouraged to pursue the vocation.

Additionally, the trip to the Bahamas supplied material for some new essays. One of them, written four years later, described the place at that time of year ("Out of season, indeed, Nassau is the most uninhabitable, unsociable town I have ever visited"[62]) but used it only as a framework for some remarks on minor writers, works of whose were often found in the deserted public libraries of such places. It was called, appropriately, "On Visiting Fashionable Places out of Season." The second essay, written while he was there but not published until 1920, was called "The Holy Jumpers." It dealt with a native evangelistic sect by that name, which was summed up by one of the waitresses in the hotel where the Van Vechtens stayed: "I'se a Baptist. I don't hold no stock in dem jumpers. De females jump an' de males jump after 'em."[63]

Three weeks later, *Nedra* completed, Carl and Fania returned to

[62] *Excavations*, p. 9.
[63] *In the Garret*, p. 145.

New York and a new apartment. When they first married, just a year before, they had maintained separate residences. "He'd come over to see me and I'd go over to see him and sometimes we visited each other for a day or so," Fania announced to a newspaper interviewer some years later.[64]

When they first met, Carl had lived over Brown's Chop House, opposite the Metropolitan Opera. Some months afterward, living at the Longacre on Forty-seventh Street, he was just down the street from Fania at the St. Margaret Hotel. Another move occurred shortly after Carl returned from Europe in the fall of 1914. John Astor had converted a theater between Forty-third and Forty-fourth streets into an apartment house for men, to which Carl moved, and Fania took a one-room flat a block or two away. After their marriage, faced with leases on the two tiny apartments, they lived in both. "The tradesmen were horrified," she confided in the newspaper interview. "As for me, I was having an affair with my husband. Living in sin, you know."[65] It was then that the first Mrs. Van Vechten made her play for back alimony. With all that behind them, Carl and Fania finally settled into married life at 151 East Nineteenth Street, on the top floor of an apartment house, where they covered the living room walls with gold-dotted Chinese red tea paper, skipping the hidden spaces behind the bookshelves and chests.

For a while longer, Fania continued to bring home the bacon, and Carl cooked it—on a two-burner stove atop the icebox in the new digs on East Nineteenth Street. He continued to write, to be sure, but he sold very little. In January, ten months earlier, *Musical Quarterly* had bought "Shall We Realize Wagner's Ideals?" for sixty-three dollars, and *Forum*, "Music after the Great War" and "Adolphe Appia and Gordon Craig." But other magazines regularly rejected his pieces. *New Republic*, for example, turned down "Music for Museums" as "not quite suited to our purposes"; and

[64] Nunnally Johnson, "The Actress-Wife and Writer-Husband Who Maintain One Home and Two Professions," *Brooklyn Eagle*, March 9, 1924.
[65] *Ibid.*

though that piece, along with a few others, was accepted by *Rogue*, *Rogue* did not pay.

Then Carl began to consider a casual suggestion made by George Moore two years earlier. "Why don't you make this the nucleus of a book of essays?" he had asked of one of their conversations recorded in a Van Vechten paper.[66] In the fall of 1915, however, Carl believed that his best writing dealt with music and the ballet. He gathered together and reworked seven essays written in the preceding three years. Then he posted a note to Rudolph Schirmer, of the Schirmer Music Company, whom Carl had known during his days as reporter for the *New York Times*: "I have gathered together enough of my essays on musical subjects to make a short volume and would like to submit it to you for publication if you would care to consider it."[67]

Schirmer agreed to look at the papers, though without much enthusiasm; but a longer-sighted staff reader suggested he take a second look. Less than two weeks later, Schirmer was writing Carl to ask about dedication pages and complimentary copies.

A new career had begun.

[66] *Sacred and Profane Memories*, p. 228.
[67] Yale.

V

From a Garret Window

First drafts are already more than half the battle.
They give me the form and most of the content.
Everything else is either additional fact or embroi-
dery. I love the embroidery.

A FEW OF THE ESSAYS in *Music after the Great War* had already
appeared in periodicals. *Rogue* and *Forum* had of course carried
several, but two had never been published: *Musical America* had
rejected one and accepted the other, only to reject it as well in the
space of three days. These discards were, however, the most significant sections of an otherwise slight book and—for the time at which
they appeared—the most extreme in their contentions: "The Secret
of the Russian Ballet," written when America was not even aware
that the Russian ballet kept secrets; and an extended article about a
Russian whose name meant little to most readers, "Igor Strawinsky:
A New Composer."

The book attracted some favorable attention, though the reviews
were few and it did not sell. The *Smart Set* liked it, even though
H. L. Mencken sneered at Stravinsky and all those other Russians
whose work he had not bothered to listen to. An extended and
thoughtful review in *Musical America* brought some publicity. It
was praised by another reviewer for its "conversational style with a
minimum of technical terms." From Carl's home town, he received
a minor accolade in the local newspaper:

> Carl Van Vechten, former Cedar Rapids resident, later of New
> York and London, where he was engaged on the staff of various
> journals, has made a noteworthy contribution to the field of art
> criticism in his recent . . . small volume which contributes seven en-

gaging essays each written with the facile touch of sympathetic com-
prehension of the work involved.[1]

The book even had two small printings. But notices do not set the
table, and the larder on East Nineteenth Street remained bare.
There was no money, and there was no food except when Carl and
Fania journeyed to the local pawnbrokers to dispose of possessions
from luckier days. During the winter of 1915–16 they subsisted almost entirely on potatoes, not exactly nourishing food for an
actress about to enter—with some trepidation—a production of *The
Tempest*.

Fania Marinoff had attended the early tryouts at her agent's suggestion, but she was not particularly enthusiastic when asked if she
could sing the several songs of Ariel. That evening, Carl asked about
the readings. "It was for Ariel in *The Tempest*," she replied offhandedly. There was scarcely time for her to say anything else.
Ariel was a role she could certainly do, Carl was convinced, if he
taught her the songs by rote. He shoved a volume of Shakespeare
into Fania's hands and sent her off to read the play. The next
morning she returned to the producer's office, to "pound on the
door to read for the part again." That particular version of *The
Tempest*, the tercentenary production of 1916, found Fania's Ariel
playing spirit slave to Louis Calvert's Prospero and Walter Hamp-
den's Caliban. The hard times were suspended, at least temporarily,
in light of Fania's four-hundred-dollar weekly salary.

She cut an exotic swath in those days, in the fashionable hobble
skirts and a necklace that moved Louis Sherwin to suggest that she
looked as if she had just rifled a pool table. Most of the time Carl
passed as Mr. Marinoff; he was much better known for his wife's
Ariel than for his own *Music after the Great War*.

The title article of the book and the following one, "Music for
Museums," characteristically pleaded for attention to contemporary music. The arguments were scarcely profound, but they did

[1] *Cedar Rapids Gazette*, December 31, 1915.

97

illustrate the mounting frustration Carl felt with the comfortable tastes of the average concertgoer. The meat of the slender book appeared in the two papers that followed, though the first of these was pretty pallid for hearty appetites. The influence of the Russian ballet on dancing as well as on painting, music, *décor*, indeed, on fashion, could not be overestimated, he contended at considerable and unnecessary length. "It takes a true keenness of wit," a reviewer declared, "to be brilliantly silly or subtly paradoxical." *Musical America* echoed the remark by calling the essay "delightfully naive and absurd," as, to a musical America almost totally ignorant of Russian ballet, it must have seemed in 1916.

The piece on Igor Stravinsky was the first to appear in America about the composer of such compositions as *Le Sacre du Printemps*, which Carl translated as "The Sacrifice to the Spring," having no official title from which to work at the time. M. D. Calvocoressi had been the first to write about Stravinsky in England, and it was from his comments that Carl drew some of his own material, though most of it was first-hand information gleaned from performances by the Diaghilev company and from actual orchestral scores. "He is, perhaps, the most vital of the modern forces in the music world," Carl Van Vechten insisted, months before Stravinsky's music was performed in America.

By comparison, the following article seemed doubly superficial. "Massenet and Women," a featherweight document of that composer's various ladies (on and off the stage) had been written in October, 1912, and published in *New Music Review* in February, 1913. It might have been better left in the pages of its periodical; certainly, it was a letdown after the Stravinsky piece. *Music after the Great War* concluded with two articles on stage decoration: the first concerned with American production, the second a brief study of Gordon Craig and Adolphe Appia.

The book appeared in December, 1915, just two months after its initial submission to Schirmer. In a modest format, it was bound in unfriendly, rather soiled-looking lavender cloth, on which a paper label printed in black announced the contents. The following month, Carl took some time off from his writing chores, long enough to welcome the dregs of the Russian ballet to New York.

Sergei Diaghilev brought the company over for a public that drank none too greedily "after a first . . . gulp, inspired by curiosity, to get a taste of his highly advertised beverage."[2] Given a two-week season at the Century Theatre with a poor repertoire and, at best, second-string dancers, audiences went on the wagon. When, following a brief tour, the company entered a four weeks' engagement at the Metropolitan Opera House, included in the regular subscription season of opera, the subscribers groaned aloud, with letters to the management and the newspapers. Then Nijinsky arrived. He had come to New York, following an incarceration in a prison camp in Austria, to prove that he had "added to the refinement and polish of his style"—so Carl later wrote. But even before the Russian dancer's arrival, a publicity campaign got under way that threatened to eclipse the earlier efforts of P. T. Barnum to advertise the voice of Jenny Lind. Not only did Nijinsky's official press representatives lay groundwork, but critics and private citizens did so as well. When he finally danced in April, the public discovered there had been no exaggeration. If Nijinsky had already surpassed his rivals in the past, now he had surpassed himself, first in *Le Spectre de la Rose* and then in Stravinsky's *Petrouchka*. But he achieved his greatest success in this country in *Scheherazade*.

The passage of time has softened the impact of this ballet, but in 1916 *Scheherazade* seemed an erotic and blasphemous skin show. There had been talk of Jim Crowing the performance in order to separate the Negro slaves from the white ones in the harem, and rumors that the local magistrates wanted to replace the "mattresses," as the divans were described in court, with rocking chairs. Whatever may have happened to these abortive efforts, Nijinsky's appearance with the company pushed them into oblivion and the company back into popularity. *Scheherazade* remained integrated and divaned.

The company returned to Europe in May, and Carl returned to

2 *Interpreters and Interpretations*, p. 149.

his garret to complete a second collection of music essays that would appear six months later. It was not, however, his second book.

FOLLOWING THE PUBLICATION of *Music after the Great War*, he put together a collection of fugitive pieces on a variety of subjects. They dealt primarily with painters and writers and musicians; there were a few sketches of a semifictional nature; a dadaist piece or two; and half a dozen pronouncements and aphorisms. None of them was very profound; most of them were worldly and sophisticated: pretty to listen to and pretty empty-headed. A thin volume, both in pages and in erudition, *Pastiches et Pistaches* was rejected by every publisher to whom Carl submitted it.

After Schirmer had turned the manuscript down, Carl shipped it to John Lane in England. But Lane replied that the book market was "unsettled," probably a polite way of saying he was not interested. A month later, the book began its rounds of American publishers. Duffield and Company said they appreciated the "literary quality" but could not publish a volume of sketches for "only a small audience." Next it went to B. W. Huebsch—just then preparing James Joyce's *A Portrait of the Artist as a Young Man* for its initial appearance—who begged off because there was "too much else." Macmillan did not want it; McBride did not want it; Doubleday did not want it. Eventually, thirteen publishers read and rejected *Pastiches et Pistaches*. Then the fourteenth—Alfred A. Knopf—received Carl's second effort in the mail. Fortunately, Knopf was young enough and adventurous enough to show some sympathetic interest beyond a simple refusal or a standard rejection slip. It is of course unlikely that he even had rejection slips at that early date; his publishing house was less than a year old, and he was only twenty-three.

Three years earlier, Alfred Knopf had held his first job, with Doubleday and Company. In 1914, having moved on to a smaller house, he met Joseph Hergesheimer; and in 1915, setting up an office of his own in the Candler Building in mid-Manhattan, he began to build a list of his own. H. L. Mencken—a friend of Knopf's

from the days of his choreboy efforts at Doubleday—and Hergesheimer were soon to become regular contributors. When Carl
Van Vechten joined them, Knopf had a literary trinity that was to
prove critically and commercially successful during the 1920's.

Knopf had read *Music after the Great War* shortly after its appearance, probably at the instigation of Mencken's highly laudatory
review of it in the *Smart Set*, which Mencken was then editing with
George Jean Nathan. Knopf wrote Carl Van Vechten and invited
him for an interview.

"He looked like a Persian Prince," Carl later recalled, "and certainly behaved like one."[3] Knopf reinforced Carl Van Vechten's
own original belief about his writing: that he knew more about
music than anything else and should stick to it. In other words,
Knopf suggested that *Pastiches et Pistaches* be put aside permanently. The new book that resulted from the conversation was
titled after one of its essays, "Music and Bad Manners." Offered first
to Schirmer, the book, like its breezy predecessor, was rejected,
since it was not up to his "usual excellent standards."[4] But Knopf
did not share Schirmer's myopia. He wrote from Boston in August,
1916: "Send up that mss and I'll give you a decision at the earliest
possible moment. I'll be back in my office in a day or two."[5] He
accepted the book immediately, even before he had finished reading all of it.

Some of the pieces had already appeared in print. "A New Prin-
ciple in Music," for example, another article about Stravinsky, had
been published in the April issue of the *Russian Review*; "Shall We
Realize Wagner's Ideals" was in the July *Musical Quarterly*, an article for which the author received sixty-three dollars. The pieces
were embroidered with anecdote and aphorism, a method rapidly
becoming a Van Vechten trademark, for which the reviewers alternately praised and roasted him: attractive lessons that amused with
gossip and ephemera and, at the same time, instructed. The formula
was simple, direct, unacademic, and highly readable.

[3] *Sacred and Profane Memories*, p. 229.
[4] Yale.   [5] CVV, NYPL.

Music and Bad Manners, his first Knopf book, appeared on November 14, 1916. Carl had submitted the manuscript toward the end of August, with his own blurb for the dust jacket advising prospective readers of a facile style, diverting lessons, and "no dull pages." The format resembled that of *Music after the Great War*, but the volume was thicker by seventy-five pages and bound in pale robin's-egg blue boards. The paper label listed the contents, which were, in part at least, prophetic: "Music for the Movies" clearly predicted film scores at a time when theaters were content with orchestras or pit pianists who played whatever occurred to them. Then, too, there was a long and thoughtful study of contemporary music, "The Bridge Burners," which considered the general apathy and critical approach of Carl's old boss on the *New York Times*.

The book was most favorably reviewed, particularly by H. L. Mencken in the *Smart Set*. His "modest hymn of praise" for the earlier *Music after the Great War* had warmed him for this second volume, "thicker, livelier, better," by a "bird of very bright plumage and, after Huneker, the best now in the tonal aviary."[6]

The comparison was appropriate. Certainly, Carl had been strongly influenced by his predecessor. The man who could indirectly call himself "a stubborn, prejudiced, well-trained musician and well-read man, one who was not devoid of irony"[7] was only a few steps behind. Clearly, he was the organizer of the parade Carl had joined. James Gibbons Huneker had been embracing iconoclastic subjects in a private love affair for twenty years; moreover, the cosmopolitan combination of personal anecdote and criticism had been his fairly exclusive property for the same length of time. Huneker's contribution to criticism is more significant than Carl's, if only because of his literary seniority, but Carl's own version of the particular genre was distinctive enough to demand comparison. H. L. Mencken was the first—but assuredly not the last—to speak of Van Vechten and Huneker simultaneously.

Before his review appeared in print, Mencken had already writ-

[6] May, 1917.
[7] James G. Huneker, *Old Fogey*, p. 9.

ten to Carl: "Your new book is just in. Excellent stuff."[8] By that time he and Mencken had firmly established the beginning of a long and fruitful friendship. How they first met, Carl was never able to recall, but they probably encountered each other in the Knopf offices. The publisher issued Van Vechten first, but he had known Mencken since 1913, when his passionate interest in Joseph Conrad found a kindred spirit in Baltimore's good-natured son. Mencken's regular trips to New York—in connection with the *Smart Set*—became friendly visits almost as regularly. He and Carl ate together in any number of German restaurants, for which Mencken had an enormous fondness, or they hied themselves to Hoboken to pay their respects to a favorite pub there, consuming an inordinate amount of good German beer. On less frequent occasions, they were house guests of Alfred Knopf and his wife Blanche in Hartsdale, sometimes in the company of Joseph Hergesheimer.

"You know so much you make me sick," Hergesheimer cheerfully complained when *Music and Bad Manners* was published. "The chapter on opera technique is so inevitable and good that it seems almost foolish to read—if you see what I mean."[9] From Paris, Gertrude Stein joined the chorus: "Thanks so much for the book, I really did enjoy it. . . . Do write and tell me about yourself. Are you going to be a soldier."[10] (At the time Gertrude Stein and Alice Toklas were busily driving about in an ambulance—converted from an ancient Ford named Auntie—for the French government.)

Other reviewers, neither acquaintances nor friends, found the book equally diverting. *Vogue* decided that Carl Van Vechten had "the good taste and good temper to write without rancour"; and *Bellman*, later to publish many of Carl's "interpreters," said that his comments "betray a rare quality of clear and independent thought . . . [and] stimulate . . . a healthy desire to climb out of deep-worn ruts."[11] The Chicago *Herald* found the book "intensely interest-

[8] Yale.
[9] CVV, NYPL.
[10] CVV, NYPL.
[11] Henry Adams Bellows, "Musical Criticism and Readable English," December 23, 1916.

ing," and the New York *Evening Sun* called the writer bold and entertaining.

Riding high on the crest of this critical wave—there was almost no adverse criticism of *Music and Bad Manners*—Carl had a busy 1917. The book's success moved *Seven Arts* to accept "Electrical Picture Concerts" for publication, though the editor objected to the "cataloguing of a thousand musical pieces." Carl was more interested in publication than in minor cuts. "It is a matter of complex indifference," he wrote to *Seven Arts*, ". . . altho I feel it is the most amusing passage in the article."[12] The editor paid him twenty dollars by way of reply, and added, "I'm not sure we won't leave in all the names."[13] The piece appeared in the May issue, Carl sharing the table of contents with Sherwood Anderson, S. N. Behrman, John Dewey, Kahlil Gibran, Marsden Hartley, Leo Stein, and Van Wyck Brooks. Minus only a brief passage, his article was concerned, once again, with new music for films, perhaps Debussy and Schoenberg or even Louis A. Hirsch and Irving Berlin to write it.

Seven Arts was not the only magazine with which Carl corresponded in 1917. Frank Crowninshield accepted a few articles for publication in *Vanity Fair*, though others did not "hit hard enough" in spite of their being "interesting and amusing." Finally, in August, Crowninshield wrote to request a list of subjects and blurbs so that he would not have to go through the "ritual of refusing something by you."[14] That same month *Vanity Fair* printed its first Van Vechten article, and in November a second appeared. Between the two, Carl's third book, *Interpreters and Interpretations*, had reached the bookshops.

TEN YEARS LATER, an older Van Vechten could reflect that musical criticism was poorly paid because it was poorly read; but in 1917, he was grateful enough to get his work into print—an understatement for the debt to Knopf's faith in Carl's writing.

[12] Yale.
[13] Yale.
[14] Yale.

The publishing agreements between the two men would doubt-less terrify the U.S. Internal Revenue Service today. They became close friends almost immediately, and, during the long years of their association, operated in a most unorthodox manner. Carl liked to boast in later years that he never received or asked for an advance against royalties for a book. Knopf echoed this as well, though in at least one reminiscence, he thought, wistfully, that Carl might have asked once for an advance of two hundred dollars. Nor were contracts necessarily issued ahead of finished books. Knopf even pointed out that they were often not even signed until the books were on sale. But the publisher's relations with his writers extended beyond the conventional limitations of friendly business. In New York or Boston or West Chester or Baltimore, a kind of camaraderie existed by frequent post and infrequent encounter. Mencken raf-fishly wrote Carl about their mutual publisher's familiar insignia on one of their books: "My lawsuit against him, for disfiguring the title-page with a portrait of a dog, will be tried next month. In this great cause I expect the support of all authors." A year or so later, Mencken decided to "form a soviet and take over Knopf's business. If you think well of it, let us approach Hergesheimer, Nathan, Delafield, Eunice Tietjens, Louis Wilkinson and Gustave Flau-bert."[15] Hergesheimer attacked Knopf's borzoi in a different direc-tion. On one of his occasional weekends with Carl at the Knopf house in Hartsdale, Hergesheimer spent a sleepless night because of the howling hounds beneath his window. At breakfast the next morning, he groggily speculated, "I'll bet Scribner hasn't any such damn dogs."[16]

The affection of Mencken and Hergesheimer and Van Vechten went considerably beyond the limitations of good-natured ribbing. Their work formed a solid cornerstone of the house of Knopf, which in its first few years of existence issued books by writers whose work has played a significant part in the development of con-temporary letters. Even a partial listing is impressive: Conrad Aiken,

[15] Yale; *Fragments I*, p. 52–53.
[16] *Fragments I*, p. 10.

Witter Bynner, Willa Cather, Max Beerbohm's *Seven Men*; the early poetry of T. S. Eliot, Kahlil Gibran, Ezra Pound, and Robert Graves; novels by E. M. Forster and Thomas Mann; the stream-of-consciousness excursions of Dorothy Richardson; and the criticism of George Jean Nathan, Wyndham Lewis, and T. S. Eliot. Carl Van Vechten was in good company, even if his books did not sell.

Interpreters and Interpretations, however, had good reviews. At least one friend had discovered part of the Van Vechten formula when Mabel Dodge wrote:

> I would claim it for my own perpetuity did I not fear it more than I desire it. For there is a terror lurking in your pages though I don't know exactly wherein it lies. Maybe your smile is full of little daggers! Anyway pinpricks. . . . It's the only George Moore spoiled child thing that clings to you—for he does it too—he *always has* to stick his tongue out at the last minute to make *some* one laugh. He'd rather make 'em laugh at him than love him.[17]

Joseph Hergesheimer reflected some of this in his decision publicly to call Carl "the most personal writer in America," even if the *New Republic* did say that the proportion between scholarship and thought was not maintained, and that in *Interpreters and Interpretations* there could have been more of the latter.

Interpreters and Interpretations was the first of Carl's books to have what amounted to a limited edition. For reasons now forgotten, Knopf had ten copies issued uncut, that is, with the folded octavo sheets unopened and with the binding about a quarter of an inch taller than that of the trade edition. There was, however, no statement in the book to indicate this fact to collectors, had Carl had any at that early date.

The "interpreters" in the book were, for the most part, gossipy essays about Olive Fremstad, Mary Garden, Yvette Guilbert, and Nijinsky—all developed from the *Times'* "Monday Interviews." The paper on Feodor Chaliapin, on the other hand, was a full-

17 CVV, NYPL.

blown portrait, based on Carl's brief acquaintance with the Russian basso. Quoting him in the essay, Carl established the Van Vechten creed in regard to the criticism of music drama and its singers:

> Criticism in New York is not profound. It is the most difficult thing in the world to be a good critical writer. I am a singer, but the critic has no right to regard me merely as a singer. He must observe my acting, my makeup, everything. And he must understand and know about these things.[18]

Chaliapin had merely distilled Carl's home brew. If James Huneker invented the recipe, the "interpreters" illustrated how delightful it tasted. From them, Carl then moved to his less conversational but equally informative "interpretations." These covered a variety of subjects: style in opera production, a discussion of Gluck's *Armide*, the *Seven Arts* article on musical movies, and a piece on Erik Satie that *Seven Arts* had turned down the preceding year. Three other pieces, concluding the collection, were of more personal reflection.

"Modern Musical Fiction," printed for the first time, was a selection of reviews of books on musical subjects: after another interminable Van Vechten catalogue, Carl commented on Robert Hichens's *The Way of Ambition*, Willa Cather's *The Song of the Lark* (based in part on Olive Fremstad's life), George Bernard Shaw's *Love among the Artists*, Henry Handel Richardson's *Maurice Guest*, and Gertrude Atherton's *The Tower of Ivory*, the latter "a flamboyant and breathless romance." It was long thereafter that Carl met Mrs. Atherton, when he was at an age "young enough (or old enough) to appreciate her wit and beauty, her gem-like hardness, and her dignified (if somewhat smug) self-esteem." Mrs. Atherton's particular aversion, Carl discovered, was to Edith Wharton, whom she considered her most formidable rival, and whose literary abilities she frequently denounced. "But what about *Ethan Frome?*" Carl once tentatively inquired. Mrs. Atherton fixed

---

[18] *Interpreters and Interpretations*, p. 100.

her beady green eyes on him, and asked, "Do you *really* believe that Mrs. Wharton wrote *Ethan Frome?*"[19] Carl's Uncle Charlie had the last word for Gertrude Atherton when, a few years later, he wrote to his nephew about her *Black Oxen,* "It is a book for flappers to laugh at, for middle aged women to weep over, and for really aged ladies to be thankful for."[20]

The two remaining pieces in *Interpreters and Interpretations,* "The Great American Composer" and "Why Music Is Unpopular," had appeared in *Vanity Fair* earlier in 1917. Both were worthy of inclusion in the book. In the first of these, Carl suggested several popular composers—among them Irving Berlin—as the true grandfathers of the great American composer, men who had "brought a new quality into music." And, he concluded breathlessly, "I am inclined to believe that . . . 'Waiting for the Robert E. Lee' . . . [is] among the first twenty-four beautiful things produced in America."[21]

In "Why Music Is Unpopular," Carl Van Vechten set up three disarmingly simple rules for critics to follow: "Have something to say and say it as well as you know how; say it with charm or say it with force but say it naturally; do not be afraid to say to-day what you may regret tomorrow. . . ."[22]

Certainly, charm and force were the two motivating traits in his own writing during the years when his annual volumes appeared with Knopf's imprint. That the charm usually outweighed the importance of the subject, and the force often spent itself on ephemeral matters, only reinforced the personal point of view in Carl Van Vechten's work that was often lacking in conventional criticism. A Philadelphia critic summed up intelligently and tellingly the value of books like *Interpreters and Interpretations:*

> There would be less profound cant and meaningless ceremony about the art of music if more musical critics wrote with the simplicity and directness of Carl Van Vechten. He says divertingly

[19] *Fragments II,* pp. 25–26.
[20] CVV, NYPL.
[21] *Interpreters and Interpretations,* p. 284.
[22] *Ibid.,* p. 362.

what he has to say; and agree with him or not, you feel the mental stimulation which only a keen, ardent intelligence can bring to a subject.

These remarks prefaced a small brochure, distributed a year or so later, that advertised all Carl Van Vechten's books to date. It also contained a portrait photograph of Carl by the popular and fashionable Mishkin. Although he was then only in his late thirties, Carl's hair had turned completely gray, an almost silver-white. Otherwise, there was little change in his appearance from the days when Martha Baker had painted his portrait in Chicago. He was heavier, the jaw less firmly modeled, but the frozen stare was still present. The photograph was taken in the fall of 1917, an exciting year in New York. It was the season that Sarah Bernhardt was "operated on at the age of seventy-three and had several kidneys removed," Carl wrote to Gertrude Stein. It was the season of the Salon des Independents, to which a toilet bowl had been submitted for exhibition and which Stieglitz had later photographed from every angle until it looked "like anything from a Madonna to a Buddha."[23]

The year 1917 also saw a single performance of Frank Wedekind's *Spring's Awakening*, with Fania Marinoff in the lead. The twenty-five-year-old play, dealing with adolescent sexual discovery, had never had an English production; it very nearly missed this one as well. Shortly before the curtain was scheduled to rise, the city commissioner of licenses arrived to prevent its doing so; but a last-minute injunction allowed the performance to go on. "With many sniggers, rollings of the eye, and gestures indicating intellectual freedom,"[24] the *New York Times* reported, the audience witnessed the solo matinee performance before the police stepped in to close the controversial curtains. Nor did a partial second performance in court persuade the judge to reopen them.

That same 1917, Isadora Duncan reappeared in New York, dancing—"draped in an American flag"—into the loyal hearts of

[23] Yale; Donald Gallup, ed., *The Flowers of Friendship*, p. 116.
[24] Quoted in Eric Bentley, *The Modern Theatre*, Volume VI, p. 286.

her native countrymen, who promptly ran out to enlist. Fania and Carl met the dancer on the street one evening. The Van Vechtens were on their way home from the Greenwich Village Theatre in the company of its owner. When they met Miss Duncan, the quartet went to the owner's nearby apartment, where Isadora proceeded to dance not only by herself but with the assembled guests, including Carl, who carried her about the room in his arms.

For some people connected with the arts in 1917, the war presumably took second place. Patriotism, in any event, was only relative for Donald Evans. He wrote to Carl from his temporary quarters in an army camp:

> I am glad I enlisted. As I take it, we are fighting not to make the world safe for democracy, but for the aristocracy of thought, to make life comfortable once more for the decadent, the iconoclyst [*sic*], the pessimist, for surely, since 1914, there has been no stage for dissolving this most needful leaven in a too healthy and normal world.[25]

The close of the year brought three further articles for the Van Vechten canon, all of which, revised or otherwise reworked, were to appear in his next Knopf volume, *The Merry-Go-Round*. For Carl, 1917 had been an encouraging year, and almost a successful one. He had seen more of his work in print than ever before, and it had received serious consideration from the critics. His pay did not, however, keep up with his promise. His writing brought no regular income, and Fania's desire to forgo the commercial theater in favor of repertory and plays like *Spring's Awakening* allowed for only an unsteady remuneration. The new year dawned bleak for both of them.

BETWEEN ESSAYS, Carl took time for an interview, printed in both the *New York Morning Telegraph* and the *Chicago Daily News Book Review*, most of which he wrote himself. "Do you like to write?" the mythological interviewer asked. "I have never yet

25 Yale; "The Origin of the Sonnets from the Patagonian," p. 56.

found an author who likes to write," Carl answered. "There are people who like to paint, really enjoy putting paint on canvas, but I have yet to find the man who likes to pen or typewrite ideas. Even dictation is odious to some people. . . ."[26]

The year threatened to pass without further publication. Then, toward the end of the summer, the first article in *The Merry-Go-Round* appeared in *Bellman*. Not a new piece, "In Defence of Bad Taste" had been written during Carl's holiday in Nassau while Fania was filming *Nedra*. At least one reviewer of *The Merry-Go-Round* wished he had left it there. Certainly, *Chronicle Magazine* had better things in mind when it editorialized: "It has been said he has too much knowledge to permit him to hold a position on any of the Metropolitan newspapers. Intrepid and experienced, Mr. Van Vechten is able to solve many of the complicated musical affairs of America. . . ."[27]

In September, another of the prancing horses from *The Merry-Go-Round* found a publisher: "Music and Cooking" turned up in *Smart Set*, for which Carl received thirty-five dollars. Mencken would have preferred a piece "on the grotesque amours of musicians and especially of singers—unprecedented polygamy, . . . marriage between eminent divas and obscure barbers, and inspired carnalities. . . ."[28] Carl Van Vechten's article was, however, the kind his regular readers might easily label as unmistakably Carl Van Vechten's own: a series of amusing incidents involving musicians and, in this instance, food and their passion for it, going on the not altogether remarkable premise that people who enjoyed good music enjoyed good food. The article also made brief mention of a restaurant, operated by Giacomo Pogliani, that played a more important role at that time than "Music and Cooking" indicated. A favorite haunt for Joseph Hergesheimer, David Belasco, and many prominent singers, the restaurant was run by a former musician who "gave up the bassoon for the fork, spoon, and saucepan."[29]

[26] "How I Do It," March 13, 1918.
[27] April, 1918, p. 15.
[28] Yale; *Fragments I*, p. 54.
[29] *The Merry-Go-Round*, p. 157.

Van Vechten and Hergesheimer usually dined there on the latter's trips to New York. For them at least, this gustatory address rivaled in popularity the Algonquin Hotel on West Forty-fourth Street, where the famous Round Table held court with nearly all the current well-known writers.

The other pieces in *The Merry-Go-Round* were equally diversified, less than half of them concerned with music. In the past three years, Carl's writing had grown steadily broader in its subject matter, more casual in its approach, more personal in its discourse. The papers were filled with his recognizable idiocyncrasies: too many catalogues, too many quotations, too many ephemeral references; but the perverse mixture of "startling candour and conscious posing," as Emily Clarke once called his concoctions, gives Carl Van Vechten's writing its singularity. There is often a well-baked cake under the frosting, and it does not always stale with the passage of time. Several of the pieces concerned the theater: "Old Days and New," a brief and sentimental memoir of entertainments in the past; one on the playwrights Philip Moeller and Avery Hopwood; and four impressions of the period: on a Spanish entertainment called *The Land of Joy*, on a 1914 production of *As You Like It*, on Mimi Aguglia, and on Isadora Duncan. Of the four, "The New Isadora" commanded the most attention, as an extension of his early reviews of her performances:

> Those who like to see pretty dancing, pretty girls, pretty things in general, will not find much pleasure in contemplating the art of Isadora. She is not pretty; her dancing is not pretty. She has been cast in nobler mould and it is her pleasure to climb higher mountains. Her gesture is titanic; her mood generally one of imperious grandeur. She has grown larger with the years—and by this I mean something more than the physical build. But this is the secret of her power and force. There is no suggestion of flabbiness about her and so she can impart to us the soul of the struggling moujik, the spirit of a nation, the figure on the prow of a Greek bark. . . . And when she interprets the Marseillaise she seems indeed to feel the mighty moment.[30]

[30] *Ibid.*, pp. 316–317.

From a Garret Window

The Merry-Go-Round (which Mencken wrote he was reviewing "with a bladder") was dedicated to Mary Garden. It appeared
the last day of September, 1918, bound in black paper-covered
boards with orange labels on the spine and front cover. Once again,
Carl Van Vechten provided his own dust jacket note: "Our author
mounts his wooden horse and dashes gaily round the circle of the
merry-go-round of the arts. This book is more intimate, lighter in
touch, more personal, than Mr. Van Vechten's earlier works. . . ."
To round out the carousel, there were four other essays, one of
them devoted to Edgar Saltus, the initial example in print of Carl's
"discovery" of a neglected writer. Two other papers—"Au Bal
Musette" and "An Interrupted Conversation"—were actually fiction, or rather essays in the guise of fiction. The first concerned a
visit to a back-street Parisian dance hall in Montmartre; the second
—ostensibly a discussion of George Moore's literary methods—was
framed in the context of a whorehouse. The final piece in *The
Merry-Go-Round* was not really an essay at all but an "Impertinent
Catalogue" of modern composers, included "more to interest my
reader than to prove anything," and included here for the same
reason:

Igor Stravinsky: Paul Revere rides in Russia.
Cyril Scott: A young man playing Debussy in a Maidenhead villa.
Balilla Pratella: Pretty noises in funny places.
Englebert Humperdinck: His master's voice.
Leo Ornstein: A small boy upsetting a pushcart.
Giacomo Puccini: Pinocchio in a passion.
Erik Satie: A mandarin with a toy pistol firing into a wedding cake.
Paul Dukas: A giant eating bonbons.
Riccardo Zandonai: Brocade dipped in garlic.
Erich Korngold: The white hope.
Arnold Schoenberg: Six times six is thirty-six—and six is ninety-two!
Maurice Ravel: Tomorrow . . . and tomorrow . . . and tomorrow . . .
Claude Debussy: Chanticleer crows *pianissimo* in whole tones.
Richard Strauss: An ostrich not hiding his head.
Sir Edward Elgar: The footman leaves his accordion in the bishop's
    carriage.

113

Italo Montemezzi: Three Kings—but no aces.
Percy Aldridge Grainger: An effete Australian chewing tobacco.[31]

The Merry-Go-Round was the first of Carl's books to have an index, one he prepared himself. *The Music of Spain*, published less than two months later, also contained an index that was even more important and extensive, since the volume was actually the first book on Spanish music to appear in the United States. It was, substantially, a volume of reprints: "Spain and Music" from *Music and Bad Manners* and "The Land of Joy" from *The Merry-Go-Round* were printed from the original plates, in spite of the statement on the dust jacket that these pieces had been completely revised. Carl did, however, append nearly fifty pages of "notes on the text," more than half the length of the original articles. To these he added a history of the development of *Carmen*, "from George Borrow to Mary Garden." The volume, bound in bright orange boards and stamped in blood red, was dedicated "pour Blanche," Alfred Knopf's wife.

Although *The Music of Spain* fared well with the critics—it was called "indispensable to libraries" and written "with a perfect knowledge of the material it handles"—*The Merry-Go-Round* was chided, by Randolph Bourne in *Dial*, but more gently than usual: "The trouble with his school, with the Menckens and the Nathans, is not that their taste is bad, but that it is all disintegrated . . . . Mr. Van Vechten, however, deserves some mitigation from these strictures . . . . What saves him in the end is the freshness and warmth of his appreciations."[32]

George Moore called the "charming volume . . . witty and far-seeing," concluding that everywhere "the intelligence of the writer sparkles." From Chicago, Fanny Butcher, an early fan, wrote that Carl had "the jauntiest pen that ever graced the ear of a literary gentleman." But for all the publicity, the books continued to interest only a few readers, and neither the meager royalties nor the

---

[31] *Ibid.*, pp. 329–330.
[32] "The Light Essay," November 16, 1918, p. 20.

small sums for periodical articles brought in enough money to support Carl and Fania.

As early as February, 1917, Ralph Van Vechten had begun sending monthly checks of twenty-five dollars to Fania, "until you and Carl get work." To a Midwestern banker steadily piling up a considerable fortune in Chicago, writing and acting apparently did not qualify as work. By the end of 1918, the situation was desperate. Fania had no engagement, and Carl's royalties were almost nonexistent. Carl wrote Ralph asking him to send whatever principal he had at his disposal. There was no alternative. Ralph replied smugly: "It would seem to me that you ought to begin to cut your garment according to your cloth. . . . You are evidently determined to get rid of what little estate you have. It seems to me that it is high time you turned right about face and began to treat your principal as sacred."[33]

But it was not advice that Carl needed. Ralph's suggestion that he and Fania cut down expenses made no sense; there were no expenses on which they could cut down. On Ralph's occasional trips to New York, he might spend as much on a single dinner as they did on all their living expenses in a fortnight. The year 1919 had begun hopelessly. The rent was unpaid, and there was no food in the apartment. Carl replied to his brother's proposals heatedly:

> The point is that I have determined to be a writer, not a journalist or a scribbler but a writer. This does not as a rule make money; it usually takes it. . . . It is one thing or the other for me, either to settle down to a career of a mediocre journalist or to strive to be something better. The first does not content me and I have decided . . . to make no compromises. . . . I may or may not spend all my principal. At present there seems to be no alternative to spending a little of it, except dropping my career . . . or borrowing more money from people who would sell their principal to lend it to me. What I am doing now undoubtedly costs more than it brings in; and it is likely to do so for some time. . . . I am perfectly capable of earning my living, indeed,

[33] CVV, NYPL.

in a dozen different ways at the present moment. But my intention and desire is for something else and until I have failed at that I wish you would not add to my list of worries.[34]

IN THE EARLY MONTHS OF 1919, Carl set to work on a subject that had interested him for a long time: cats. Since the days of Grandmother Fitch's old tortoise-shell, when Carl was two years old, he had been in love with the "fireside sphinx." In Paris, he and Anna Snyder had shared their apartment with a tail-less kitten—Carl's first since Cedar Rapids—that had followed him one day as he left the *Daily Mail* office. The cat took a dislike to an engraving of Salome that hung on the wall, leaped at it, and pulled it down daily. It was not this habit but its unwillingness to patronize the sandbox that convinced Carl and Ann to ask it to leave. In New York, on East Nineteenth Street, an "ugly, gaunt, gray tabby with a white belly," metamorphosized into a "sleek and smooth fellow through the new janitor's collar and a daily ration of liver,"[35] used to pay frequent calls on Carl and Fania on the sixth floor; and Ariel, an orange and white female, later shared their lodgings.

Working at the New York Public Library, Carl Van Vechten now began to collect material for a large book—one that would detail the history of the cat not from the point of view of anthropologist or zoölogist but from his own, as an admirer. Simultaneously, he was preparing a new series of essays for a fifth Knopf volume, *In the Garret*; but before it appeared, the remaining copies of *Music and Bad Manners* were issued in a format resembling that of *The Merry-Go-Round*. The boards were black, and the paper labels were ivory. There were no changes in the text, but the dust jacket carried quotations from various reviewers of the books that had been published in the intervening years.

In June, Carl's first preface to a book by another writer appeared. Knopf published Philip Moeller's *Sophie*. Dedicated to Emily Stevens and to Carl Van Vechten "who first gave me the key to Sophie's dressing room," the play was a failure. Carl Van Vechten's

34 CVV, NYPL.
35 *Sacred and Profane Memories*, p. 193.

"Prologue for the Reader" historically introduced the protagonist, Sophie Arnould, actress-singer-demimondaine—indeed, an "interpreter" of the eighteenth century. Earlier, Moeller had dedicated a one-act farce of unstageable proportions to Carl, who had suggested a play about American Indians. It was an idea inspired, perhaps, by Mabel Dodge's removal to New Mexico.

In the summer of 1919, the *Chicago Daily News Book Review* contracted for a series of reviews for its weekly pages. In the following months, Carl Van Vechten evaluated books by Arthur Symons, John McCormack, Edgar Saltus, Artemus Ward, and Lafcadio Hearn. A December notice of a do-it-yourself book on violins coincided with the publication of *In the Garret*, from which only four essays had already been printed in periodicals.

Bound once again in black paper boards—there was a second binding in black cloth—and with blue paper labels, the volume was dedicated to Joseph and Dorothy Hergesheimer, "with warm affection." In turn, Hergesheimer dedicated his *Linda Condon* to Carl in the same year, by which time their friendship was firmly sealed. Although they usually met in New York, Carl infrequently traveled to West Chester, Pennsylvania, to visit Hergesheimer in his own familiar surroundings. The townspeople looked on their local celebrity as a latter-day member of the landed gentry luxuriously ensconced in a kind of baronial splendor, first in a Victorian mansion complete with shell flowers under glass bells that could remind Carl of similar displays in Cedar Rapids parlors, and later in Hergesheimer's renovated Dower House, an elegant eighteenth-century re-creation of early America. Hergesheimer once wrote Carl: "I am incapable of generous enthusiasm, except in the very grand manner. I like perfect writing, superfine friends, a Ramos gin fizz; lilacs, lovely females—embrace Fania for me—some tobacco; all, you see, the very best."[36] In loudly checked tweeds and Charvet cravats, Hergesheimer worked at being a conscious artist. Carl remembered his reflecting, on more than one occasion, that "There are only a few of us left" whenever he spoke of good writing, a sub-

[36] Yale.

ject he rarely abandoned in conversation. He included Carl in the general category: *In the Garret* was "a very engaging piece of writing that promises more than the table of contents reveals."[37]

The book began with pieces on Philip Thicknesse, a neglected seventeenth-century figure; "The Folksongs of Iowa," which dealt with the great Midwest's lack of necessary response to evolving a culture of its own; and essays on Isaac Albéniz, Sir Arthur Sullivan, and the redoubtable Oscar Hammerstein. *In the Garret* concluded with four evaluations of the theater: Negro, Italian, Yiddish, and a note on Mimi Aguglia as Salome. In another paper, "La Tigresse," readers discovered a fellow named Peter Whiffle and a subtle growth in Carl Van Vechten's talents as a creative writer.

He had turned once again to the semifictional essay. "La Tigresse" tells of a visit to a New York bistro in the company of a friend, Peter Whiffle, who had already put in an off-stage appearance in "A Note on Philip Thicknesse" as one who very much wanted Carl's collection of Lafcadio Hearn. "La Tigresse" sings a hymn of praise to New York and its multicolored cityscape, and then describes a stop at a pub, where Carl and Peter hear an aging chanteuse.

La Tigresse lives upstairs and appears late in the evening to sing, unaccompanied. She is, in the Van Vechten parlance, another "interpreter":

> It was two o'clock. The crowd had thinned to two groups. The *patron* yawned behind the counter. The pianist had gone home. Suddenly *la Tigresse* arose and backing into the middle of the room, hands in the pockets of her skirt, she began to sing without accompaniment. . . . Her hips swayed, her eyes flashed fire, her voice bawled out the tones. She became, indeed, immediately a different person and I recognized the artist in her at once. What fervour! What animation! What power of characterization! What sensuous appeal! . . .
>
> "The woman is a find," I said to Peter. "She should have a great success here if we could arrange some drawing room appearances

[37] Yale.

for her." And as we talked over the possibilities, a great pity surged into my heart, a pity for her warm but unfashionable apparel, the signs of her poverty. . . .[38]

Then Carl and Peter learn that she has money, that she sings alone, her triumphs in Paris behind her, because "It is her life. It is what she is accustomed to: it is what she likes." To revert to type, to settle back in middle age to the pleasure of youth, Carl concludes, is something that comes only with time and success. But Peter says he does not want to settle back, nor does he believe that Carl wants to; too much of the future lies ahead of them.

In the Garret received generally favorable notices. *Bookman* declared that Van Vechten's "culture is Hunekeresque. His scholarship is musicianly, sometimes jazzy."[39] The *Times* (London) said that when Carl Van Vechten was viewing the American scene, the reviewer was "with him all the way." Other notices questioned his frequent brashness, his unqualified opinions, his casual pedantry. To answer all such charges, Carl once said, "If every time I expressed a personal feeling (and all my feelings are intensely personal) I followed with something like this, 'it seems to me,' or 'Mr. Thing does not agree with me,' my utterances would lose whatever force or charm they possess and they would be so clogged with extraneous qualifications that no one would read them."[40]

Friends were more perspicacious in praise of the book, among them, the Stettheimer sisters, three maiden ladies Avery Hopwood had known in Germany before the war. When Carl met them in 1916, Ettie's writings were relatively unknown, Carrie's elaborate and beautiful dollhouse was only just begun, and Florine's paintings had been seen by a very favored few. They made an exotic, if somewhat strange, trio: Ettie in red wig, brocades, and diamonds; Carrie, who dressed never in the fashions of the day but in the elegance of a past era; Florine in white satin pants. Today Ettie's *Love Days* brings handsome prices in second-hand bookstores;

[38] *In the Garrett*, pp. 276–277.
[39] April, 1920, p. 192.
[40] "How I Do It."

Carrie's dollhouse is on permanent exhibition at the Museum of the City of New York; Florine's paintings—first seen briefly in a show at the Knoedler gallery in 1916—have been given a memorial exhibition at the Museum of Modern Art. To the Stettheimer sisters, the arts were a vital issue. The salon they created did much to shape the intellectual and artistic efforts of the twenties a few years later.

During the months that followed the publication of *In the Garret*, Carl Van Vechten was thoroughly occupied with the cat book, which threatened to reach mammoth proportions. For fourteen months, he worked steadily at it, writing a final sentence to a final second draft early in March, 1920. He called it "Everybody's Tiger," and delivered it to Alfred A. Knopf, with a letter of explanation: There were six chapters epitomizing the history and character of the cat, the history "inserted subtly, like castor oil in a sweet drink." These were followed by another six dealing with the cat in relation to the arts. "Of course," he confessed, "an absolute cut and dried following of this scheme would mean a dry book, and so I have mixed them up somewhat. . . ."[41] Keyed up by the finished chore, he dashed off a preface for a projected book of cat stories, a volume that was not published until the following year, after the appearance of *The Tiger in the House*, a title that Fania Marinoff substituted before publication in October.

Knopf had made announcement of the book's impending appearance a few months earlier in *The Borzoi 1920*, a collection of pieces by and about the writers whose work he had published during the first five years of his organization. It contained Carl Van Vechten's brief "On the Advantages of Being Born on the Seventeenth of June," dedicated to Knopf's son, who shared that birth date with Carl. There was also a short appreciation by Philip Moeller, who declared that Carl's "mental gesture" was more or less "unique in American literature," with about as much relation to what might be considered the "serious classical output" of writing as "irresistible footnotes had to filling an all too fulsome history."[42] *The Borzoi 1920* concluded with a postscript by its pub-

41 CVV, NYPL.   42 P. 32.

lisher advising readers of projected volumes: "Van Vechten's 'The Tiger in the House' is the only complete account in English of the domestic cat. It is Carlo's *magnum opus* and I have made in it, I think, quite the handsomest of all my books."[43]

A large octavo bound in half canvas with dark blue Japanese Toyogami boards stamped in gold, the book appeared in an initial edition of two thousand numbered copies, printed on India Tint artcraft laid paper, boxed, and illustrated with thirty-two graphics and photographs. *The Tiger in the House* had a lasting sale, and the public's enthusiasm for it was greater than for any of Van Vechten's earlier volumes. The critics were not far behind. A single dissenting opinion, indeed, came from a Philadelphia bookseller who objected to the illustration on the box: a cat performing his daily ablutions in a perfectly natural but not altogether delicate position.

Carl's father objected to "all . . . the French which I suppose was put in to 'fill up,' "[44] but scores of readers—total strangers—wrote either to praise the book or to offer illustrations for the next edition, to suggest anecdotes, to ask for information and cat cures. Some wrote of "grievously ill" cats and "psychotic" cats; California librarians sent obscure quotations for identification. Mabel Dodge was sufficiently excited by the book to write probably the longest letter of her long life, which, two years later, Carl used in *Peter Whiffle*.

Immediately following the publication of *The Tiger in the House*, an English edition of *The Music of Spain* appeared, "chiefly notable for its inspired ugliness,"[45] bound in dark red leather and murky pink cloth, with a preface by Pedro Morales, a Spanish musician; Knopf, about the same time, reissued the "interpreters" from *Interpreters and Interpretations* in a separate volume. In the new edition, there were sixteen photographs of the subjects and an "Epilogue" that served as a final justification for Carl's concern with interpretive art: "Posterity . . . is absolutely dependent upon

[43] P. 133.
[44] CVV, NYPL.
[45] Scott Cunningham, *A Bibliography of the Writings of Carl Van Vechten*, p. 12.

books for its knowledge of the interpreters of a bygone day. For that reason I am perfectly sure in my own mind that of such of my books as are devoted to criticism this is the one most likely to please. . . ."[46]

The appearance of *Interpreters* moved Carl to consider a reissue of *The Merry-Go-Round*, but the plan was never realized, though he did prepare a new manuscript and a tentative excuse for doing the revisions:

> My Merry-Go-Round, on inspection, I perceive, needs new paint. The little horses must be refurbished, garnished, their dingy harnesses must be restored. Some of them I find in such a condition that I have believed it better simply to replace them by new little horses. . . .[47]

The new edition was to be illustrated with scenes of Paris and portraits of Spanish dancers, Isadora Duncan, Margaret Anglin, Mimi Aguglia, Mary Garden, Moeller and Hopwood, and Carl's boyhood idol Della Fox. The piece on Margaret Anglin's Shakespeare productions was to be revised from his 1914 newspaper review: something in the performance that, five years earlier, had delivered a "distinct body blow" was changed, with the passage of time, to "staggering"; the staging, which had originally achieved a "weird effect," became "charming" in 1919. Then, for no particular reason, the whole idea went flat; *The Merry-Go-Round* was never reprinted. Many years later, Carl inscribed a copy of the book: "I just read a few pages, and certainly have forgotten I wrote this one."

In early 1921, two articles went to the *Atlantic Monthly*, both of them refused, and the *Smart Set* rejected a third, though all were ultimately published. It was not until July, however, that another Van Vechten item saw print. Knopf issued *Lords of the Housetops*, a book of cat stories, chosen by Carl, including one by Balzac that he had translated. There were also tales by Booth Tarkington, Mark Twain, W. H. Hudson, Edgar Allan Poe, and several others. By way of introduction, Carl supplied a brief explanation of his choices, and dedicated the collection to Avery Hopwood. The

[46] *Interpreters*, p. 182.   [47] CVV, NYPL.

The Victorian room at 150 West Fifty-fifth Street,
about 1930.

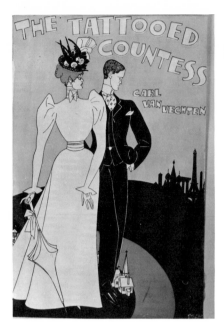

(left) Dust-jacket illustration by Ralph Barton
for *The Tattooed Countess.*

(right) Dust-jacket illustration by Ronald MacRae
for *Spider Boy.*

Alfred A. Knopf, Carl Van Vechten, and Texas Guinan
at the signing of the contract for *Parties*, 1930.

Four Saints in Three Acts, original production, 1934.

Photograph by White Studios
Courtesy Hope White

Carl Van Vechten, Gertrude Stein,
and Alice B. Toklas, 1934.

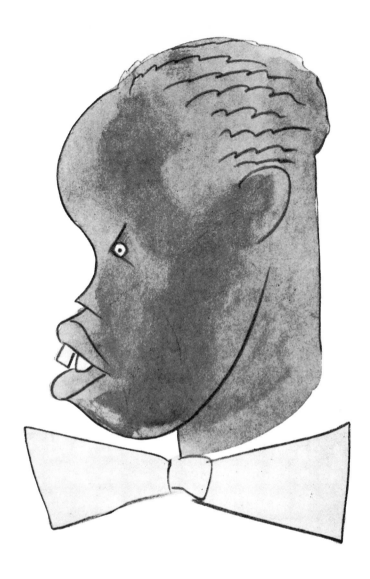

Carl Van Vechten—"A Prediction," caricature
by Miguel Covarrubias.

Carl Van Vechten, about 1936.

Carl Van Vechten, about 1940.

The Stage Door Canteen,
with Langston Hughes as busboy, 1943.

Photograph by Carl Van Vechten

Alice B. Toklas and Carl Van Vechten, Paris, 1949.

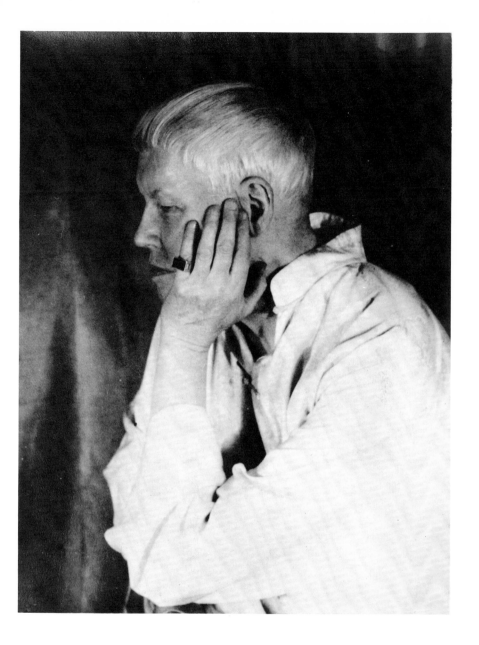

Carl Van Vechten, 1952.

Photograph by Saul Mauriber
Courtesy Saul Mauriber

Carl Van Vechten at the Thalia Theatre, 1956.

Detail of a drawing by Al Hirschfeld. Left to right: Mrs. Gilbert Miller, Mr. & Mrs. Clifton Daniels (Margaret Truman), Mr. & Mrs. Carl Van Vechten (Fania Marinoff); Vinton Freedley, Harold Arlen, Radie Harris, Louise Beck, Allene Talmey, Marlene Dietrich, Herbert Bayard Swope, Cole Porter, Noel Coward, Frank Farrell, and Sol Hurok.

Dr. Carl Van Vechten and Dr. Charles Johnson,
president of Fisk University, on the occasion of
Van Vechten's receiving an honorary doctorate, May, 1955.

Photograph by Fania Marinoff Van Vechten

Fania Marinoff and Carl Van Vechten, 1959.

Photograph by Saul Mauriber
Courtesy of Saul Mauriber

Carl Van Vechten, 1961.

book's binding followed closely that of *Interpreters and Interpretations*: black cloth stamped in yellow and green.

In the fall of that year, while Fania was playing in *The Hero*, two Van Vechten articles appeared that gave some indication of the reasons Carl was soon to forsake musical criticism. "Cordite for Concerts" in the *Smart Set*, and "On Hearing What You Want When You Want It" in the *Musical Quarterly* both complained about programing. What they did not say, however, was that Carl had grown tired of the concert stage, the opera house, the recital hall. The experience of fifteen years—attending musical entertainments or concerts nightly, and writing about most of them—had worn thin; he found that he had little to say. Firmly convinced that after the age of forty (he was then forty-one) the intellectual arteries hardened, Carl was ready to direct his pen elsewhere. Then, too, he had always been a few years in advance of his contemporaries, championing the operas of Richard Strauss and the compositions of Debussy and Stravinsky before they were widely accepted in New York. Further, he realized that musical criticism was never going to pay him a living wage. Carl had no overwhelming desire for money, but, at the same time, he and Fania had been living in genteel poverty long enough.

THE *Reviewer*, stylish and impertinent, first came to Carl's attention through Joseph Hergesheimer, who was already contributing to its pages. Started as a serious lark by Emily Clarke, a young and totally inexperienced Southern girl, the *Reviewer* gained a popularity and enviable notoriety in its brief existence, when it was unique among little magazines. At the end of 1920, Miss Clarke and a few friends in Richmond, Virginia, bemoaning the demise of the only book review column in the city's newspapers, decided to publish a fortnightly periodical. They had no money but they were enthusiastic; they had no training but they had nerve. Further, they had the paternal benevolence of Richmond's resident writer James Branch Cabell, who from the beginning guided their efforts and even acted as editor for a few issues.

Carl Van Vechten

In *Innocence Abroad* (which Cabell insisted on calling *In No Sense A Broad*), Emily Clarke reflected that, when she began the jaunty excursion of the *Reviewer*, the literary scene was "quivering with undeveloped and unexplored potentialities," most of which she took advantage of. Cabell, Ellen Glasgow, Hergesheimer, and Louis Untermeyer were already unpaid contributors when Emily Clarke's first letter to Carl arrived at his East Nineteenth Street address:

> Mr. Hergesheimer has probably told you about The Reviewer as I understand from him that you might consider writing an article for us. I shall be more grateful than I can say if you will do this, as you are one of the people that we would especially like to have. Please be good to us if you can.[48]

Carl responded immediately with "The Tin Trunk," an expanded version of an article that the *Atlantic Monthly* had refused, which he called "an autobiographical rhapsody on American themes." A nostalgic essay of childhood memories in Cedar Rapids, it was published in the *Reviewer* in two installments in November and December, the first of many pieces to appear in Emily Clarke's magazine.

Carl first met Miss Clarke in February, 1922, shortly after her first letter to him. She was in New York on holiday, but no one of mutual acquaintance was in town to introduce them. Carl suggested the Algonquin for lunch, where the young editor arrived "late and breathless, in the manner which Carl has always, perhaps unjustly, called Southern from that day." He was standing by the desk when she got there, Miss Clarke reported in her *Innocence Abroad*,

> ... looking at me with the cold, blank stare which for some reason has never disconcerted me, although it has occasionally enraged me. That day I was neither enraged nor disconcerted, although the first words I ever heard from Carl were not reassuring. "Of course this has been as awkward as possible for me," he said, blank and unsmiling. "I have spoken to every lady who has come in for the last

48 Yale.

124

half-hour, thinking it might be you. You are very late. Now we will go in and get drunk on tea."[49]

They parted amicably only to meet unexpectedly that evening at the opening performance of *Frank Fay's Fables*, a musical revue in which Fania Marinoff was appearing. Carl took Emily Clarke backstage afterward to meet his wife, who was being heartily embraced at the time by Philip Moeller. Florine Stettheimer, standing nearby, was introduced as a "painter of incomparable zinnias."

Emily Clarke recalled another New York episode when she and Carl and Fania were going to a gathering on lower Fifth Avenue. Fania urged an open-topped bus as the only sensible and sanitary means of conveyance; Carl insisted on a taxi as the only comfortable conveyance. "You get no air whatever, Carl," an outraged Fania cried. "A daily bath is now the only healthy habit you still have." And Carl coldly replied, "I shall probably drop that habit soon."[50]

Carl did not meet Miss Clarke again until the following fall. In the summer of 1922, Fania went on tour in *Call the Doctor* after a highly successful run in New York; Carl accompanied her as far as Chicago, and went on to visit his father and stepmother in Cedar Rapids. In November, they were back in New York again, Carl preparing for a trip to Joseph Hergesheimer's Victorian house in Pennsylvania, where Emily Clarke was to be a fellow guest.

"Tawny-haired and super slender," she once moved Carl to declare her the daughter of Sarah Bernhardt by a leopard. Miss Clarke remembered the proposed father as a yellow panther, though in either instance the image was severely strained. Carl often spent too much of his time trying to make exotic what was home-grown, to glamorize the plain, to have fun with the humorless. (He once suggested to Sinclair Lewis that he name his child George Moore Lewis or at least More Lewis as a compromise.) As for Emily Clarke, she did not even remotely resemble Sarah Bernhardt, and was closer to a domestic short-hair than to a Persian, much less a leopard or a panther.

[49] Pp. 129–130.
[50] *Ibid.*, p. 138.

At the time of their visit to West Chester, Hergesheimer was working daily on a projected volume about the West, and Carl and Emily were left to amuse each other. "Your voice and accent are enchanting," he said of her Southern drawl, "but I can understand scarcely a word you say." Then he got down to business: "Do you really intend to go on collecting manuscripts from all of us for nothing?" "I must," Miss Clarke replied openly. "I must have a few celebrated names in each issue for bait, else the new Southerners that we want cannot afford to write for us. They cannot afford to write without pay, and they consider it pay to have their names seen in a table of contents with yours and others like it." Carl brooded a moment over this, and then replied: "Of course you realize that you are the lowest form of prostitute. Honest prostitutes pay for what they get."[51]

Nevertheless, he continued to contribute regularly to the pages of the *Reviewer* without pay, and in spite of Emily Clarke's peculiar business arrangements. Once, in answer to a letter chiding her for neglecting to send out issues on time, she replied:

> I hadn't realized I was so primitive in my methods—naive, they called it—but anyway it isn't so bad a plan in a sophisticated age, and has relieved me of ever having to read a line of Freud. . . .
> From every other standpoint I am, of course, quite middle aged. If I had known then what I know now I should probably not gaily have undertaken to run a magazine with no money or ability, only a trustful disposition which made me quite certain I could get what I asked for.[52]

What Emily Clarke asked for, Carl supplied in a series of six installments, titled each time "Pastiches et Pistaches," their genesis the contents of the volume turned down by so many publishers five years earlier. In the intervening period he had added to the collection from time to time on widely ranging subjects. Occasionally, one or another of the pieces found its way into print as a solo effort. Gertrude Stein's *Geography and Plays* had inspired a piece, for example, that, first included in *Pastiches et Pistaches*, was later lifted

[51] *Ibid.*, pp. 131–132.　　　　[52] Yale.

126

to serve as a review—called "Medals for Miss Stein"—of the Stein book. But, for the most part, these little vignettes that appeared in the pages of the *Reviewer* had remained unpublished since 1916, when Carl Van Vechten had first compiled them.

The first appeared in the *Reviewer* February, 1922. Two years earlier, Carl had tried once again to get the book in its entirety printed privately, through his brother. Carl wrote to Ralph suggesting that perhaps he would want to publish the volume as a gift edition limited to a few copies for his friends. Ralph was not unfriendly to the idea; in fact, he was pleased with the suggestion, and wrote to praise the contents. But Carl, fired by Ralph's enthusiasm, began to specify ivory paper labels and Chinese decorated papers as possible wrappers, sending samples to Chicago. The conservative Midwestern banker fled from the idea by procrastinating, and Carl recalled the manuscript. Publication of "Pastiches et Pistaches" never went beyond the pages of the *Reviewer*.

Over the two-year period during which they appeared, George Jean Nathan, Marguerite d'Alvarez, Florine Stettheimer, Ernest Boyd, and John Dos Passos were given brief attention. So were Gertrude Stein's cook, Ronald Firbank, Paul Whiteman (leader of the "Best Orchestra in America"), and the Richmond, Virginia, Sabbath Glee Club. Even Eva Tanguay's formula—"styleless and loud"—got a nod. There were remarks on first editions; on the Grand Street Follies; on "music and stomachs"; on "law and custom," which suggested that parents give their children bassoon lessons, since orchestras were always in need of bassoon players, and in case "the insurance business or the green grocery company went to pot." The collection concluded with a note of healthy if not very original humor on "Uses for a Million Dollars." Carl Van Vechten's were, predictably, in 1924, literature and liquor. The curious blend of erudition and ephemera, good fun and bad jokes, pretentious sophistication and conscious naïveté exaggerated his best and worst characteristics. His contributions to the *Reviewer* were, however, minor opera in the early 1920's: a new career was already under way.

Carl Van Vechten

In his first letter to Emily Clarke, some months before their initial encounter at the Algonquin, Carl Van Vechten mentioned that he was just putting the finishing touches on a book called *Peter Whiffle: His Life and Work*. He did not specify what kind of book it was; in all probability, he himself was not wholly aware. But Peter Whiffle proved to be the subject of a novel a few months later when Alfred A. Knopf published what became one of the most popular books of the decade just begun. In a way, *Peter Whiffle* justified a long letter Carl had written to his father two years earlier:

> I have been going over old letters, old things in general, cleaning house.... For twelve or sixteen years I seem to have been a subject of perplexity, anxiety, worry, and wonderment to you ... and always, or nearly always, in need of money. I think on the whole you have bourne up with marvelous patience and fortitude, and occasionally hope.
>
> What I have wanted to do has not always been as apparent to me as it is at present, but there has always been the *urge*: I have known that I must do a certain thing, even though I have not known *why*. But looking back, the *whys* seem moderately clear, and even my mistakes seem to have had definite meaning, that is they created a desire to acquire an armor or a mask which should prevent their recurrence. As for the future a clear white light shines on that, so that from now on I think I can march straight, unless Nature or Fate interfere in some unforeseen manner.
>
> Perhaps I have already accomplished enough so that you, in a sense at least can see the meaning of my life, but I have not accomplished one hundredth part of what I hope or expect to: what I am doing is still preparation, for I am well aware that I have been very late in developing, and am still somewhat in that process, although I have passed forty. I remember once you wrote me that you were forty-eight before you found yourself. Well I found myself six years ago, but it takes some time to put all the pieces together.
>
> As for money, I have never sought it in quantity and have no desire for it; my wants are modest and simple. I hope, however, that in a few years we shall be able to live ... without periods of debts which amount almost to hysteria! And that is one reason why I have drawn

so heavily on what I have: to pay debts. . . . In the meantime I have learned to be patient, and I think I could go through ten more years of struggle, for what I know is ahead.

This letter is no more than a small attempt to explain to you how deeply grateful I am to you for your assistance at all times, for I do not remember that you have ever failed me, even when you have thought that I had embarked on uncharted and unlighted seas. My love for you has been very deep, but it grew even deeper when I read over those letters and saw what torments you must have gone through, in your effort to adjust yourself to what must have seemed to you at times a very mad career indeed. And Addie's love and faith has been no small part of this. We both send much love to both of you, Carlo[53]

[53] CVV, NYPL.

VI

The Splendid Drunken Twenties 1

*The world of the nineteen-twenties was a narrow one
easily encompassed without the aid of a bicycle: . . .
with . . . bathtubs so full of synthetic gin that ablutions had to be performed extra mural.*

The Eighteenth Amendment, designed, it was hoped, to keep
the country sober, became official on January 29, 1919, though
another six months passed before anybody paid much attention to
it. Back in the cabaret days of 1912, when Carl and Fania were
turkey-trotting around the town, liquor had been a conveniently
pleasant addition to an evening's entertainment; with the passage of
time, it became more and more the main attraction. During the
war years, there had been a gradual falling off in cabaret popularity
because of inflationary taxes and the automatic increase in tempo
that seems to accompany periods of crisis. The casual evenings at
Rector's and other old and established places gave way to livelier
pastimes in night clubs, exciting hybrids that mushroomed around
the city. By the end of 1919, the cabaret days were nearly forgotten, and the night club era emerged in full bloom, timed appropriately to conflict with the Volstead Act, which became the
law to enforce the Eighteenth Amendment on January 16, 1920.

Farewell parties and elaborate wakes were held around the city,
in commemoration of the day, though behind more than one closed
door the celebrations continued for more than nine years.

That same winter, Carl Van Vechten wrote a decade later, "I
conceived the idea which led to the composition of Peter Whiffle."[1]
Actually, the idea was a little older than that, though the process of
putting the fellow together did come later. As early as 1917, Peter
had turned up in "La Tigresse" as Carl's drinking companion in a

[1] *Sacred and Profane Memories*, p. 229.

New York café. There were also a few pages of manuscript that rolled through the typewriter in January, 1917, about an odd character named Sasha Idonsky, probably based on Avery Hopwood, who used the nickname during the earlier days of his friendship with Carl. The piece was titled "Undecided Sasha," no more than a brief sketch of a writer who could not make up his mind about anything. He became Sasha Broadwood in an unfinished second draft, and then the pages were put aside. Two years later, as Carl Van Vechten was finishing his collection of cat stories *Lords of the Housetops*, an idea came to him in the New York Public Library: the story of a man who never accomplished anything he began, yet who was able to satisfy cravings for experience and novelty through his own invention. Carl called his protagonist Peter Whiffle and, utilizing a couple of Sasha's adventures, began to write a chronicle of Peter's wanderings. Meanderings is a more appropriate word.

In tone, the book was in many ways only an extension of what had gone before. There were discussions of art and literature and music, catalogues of exotic names and offbeat information, incidents involving a few celebrated names—disguised and undisguised. That the material happened to fall into the framework of a novel was fortuitous, for the book freed Carl Van Vechten from the unremunerative shackles of criticism. During the decade that followed, he was to be heralded as one of the most fashionable and popular writers of the period. He roared along with the twenties, and shut up when they came to an end; in the interim, he produced seven novels with varying degrees of success. His recipe was not original, but it was unique: the style and rhetoric were strongly influenced by James Branch Cabell; most of the characters were born this side of F. Scott Fitzgerald's paradise without being self-consciously beautiful and damned; the satire was mordant, with dashes and flavorings of Mencken and Sinclair Lewis. The result was always brilliant, frequently provoking, often instructive. Carl Van Vechten used several patterns of the period concurrently, writing contemporaneously about his own society with the detachment of a historian and the craft of an artist—and the formula worked. *Peter*

Whiffle: His Life and Work, structurally the weakest, got the best reception, which seems to be fairly indicative of the collective state of mind during the decade.

Peter Whiffle begins with several epigraphs, among them Edmund Gosse's remark that "The man who satisfies a ceaseless intellectual curiosity probably squeezes more out of life in the long run than anyone else." A more detailed explanation of the book went to Carl's father, who had not understood *Peter Whiffle* at all: It could be taken as a period picture, as a satire on "authors who make a fetish of method," as a "moral document" explaining man as a "mystic entity . . . studied better in contemplation."[2] But it was amusing too, Carl added, and could be read for fun.

By the middle of February, 1921, the first draft had been completed, giving Carl the form and most of the content he wanted: in a deadpan preface, the reader was to learn that Peter Whiffle, a beguiling youth, had died, naming Carl Van Vechten his literary executor. Peter had written no books, published no essays; but Carl, having "become to Peter something of a necessity, in that through me he found the proper outlet for his artistic explosions,"[3] is asked, in a letter dated two years earlier, to write Peter's story. Peter's one purpose in life has been to have no purpose, for moments are too difficult to recapture. "I should have been compelled to invent a new style, a style as capricious and vibrant as the moments themselves."[4] At least, he concludes, he has given Carl another subject for another book.

In the subsequent pages, Carl, as a player on his own stage, travels to Paris, where he meets Peter Whiffle. They immediately become friends, only to separate shortly, then to meet again, a few years later, in New York. Together they visit Mabel Dodge (masquerading as Edith Dale); they meet again in Europe and again in New York, just before Peter's death. There is no actual plot to the novel—Carl and Alfred Knopf both said later that neither of them

2 CVV, NYPL.
3 *Peter Whiffle*, p. 1.
4 *Ibid.*, pp. 4–5.

really knew that Peter Whiffle *was* the subject of a novel until he had reached the bookshops—and the central characters numbered only three: Carl and Peter and Edith.

By April, the second draft was finished. Knopf, about to leave for vacation, wrote, "Certainly, if it comes off at all, it ought to be far and away your best to date."[5] Carl too had hopes for some success, but he felt as uncertain as his publisher. "I shall give birth to more cats in the fall," he wrote to Arthur Davison Ficke about the upcoming anthology, "and . . . am about to finish . . . my new book which may or may not be something. It has nothing to do with cats or music, but there is a connection with Leda and her swan."[6]

The reference to the egg-laying nymph pointed to a ring that Peter gives to Carl in the closing chapters of the novel. Actually, Fania Marinoff had given the ring to Carl in 1912, having discovered the faintly ribald intaglio in a Sixth Avenue pawnshop. More than one writer had remarked the ring. Mabel Dodge recalled it as a "merry intaglio," as *outré* as Carl himself when they had first met; and one gossip columnist had been horrified by it. But Carl was never very conventional in his accouterments or his attire. The wrist watch of ten years earlier was just a beginning: two or three bracelets joined it—one of gold links, one of dull green jade—in the years that followed. The ruffles on the shirt that Gertrude Stein immortalized gave way to violent silk stripes or red fireman's blouses worn with outrageous cravats. Certainly, the distinctive dress of the era suited him admirably. Lawrence Langner recalled an ornate Carl at a party, garbed in red and gold Oriental robes, looking like "the dowager Chinese empress gone berserk"; Taylor Gordon remembered him in a "phantom red New Mexican cowboy shirt" with green and orange bandanna; his even more familiar silk lounging robes, like Mencken's striped trousers and Knopf's dark-colored shirts and Hergesheimer's plaid plus fours, soon became well known in the twenties. Carl's wife too joined the parade. "Town Topics" reported: "Fania Marinoff, always pic-

[5] CVV, NYPL.
[6] Yale.

133

turesque, on stage and off, has been attending premieres wearing what may have been a stage costume for there is little front and less back to the brocade confection, and a turban is worn which causes the straight, bobbed tresses to protrude on either cheek like side winders."

By the end of the summer, a third draft of *Peter Whiffle* was completed and delivered to Knopf; in November, Fania witnessed her husband's signature on the contract. A week or so later, Carl wrote again to Arthur Davison Ficke, who had supplied several of the pictures for *The Tiger in the House*, "I hope you will like Peter Whiffle, for therein I saunter a trifle more carelessly than usual . . . ."[7]

The saunterings included the first fictional treatment of such pre-1914 memories as a fledgling's-eye view of Paris, the intellectual movement in Greenwich Village at 23 Fifth Avenue, and subsequent footnotes at the Villa Curonia. If the book had its genesis in J. K. Huysman's *À Rebours*, it was unlike any of its six successors. Compiled of conversation and catalogues, nearly plotless, *Peter Whiffle* closely resembled Carl Van Vechten's own critical vagaries of the preceding years.

On the occasion of their first meeting, Carl and Peter are in Paris, where the latter is collecting material for a book of about three hundred pages, "of colour and style and lists, lists of objects, all jumbled artfully."[8] There will be, Peter cries, no morals, no ideas, no propaganda, no preaching, not even any humor. "Thank God, I can start in at once constructing a masterpiece!" When they meet again, five years later in New York, Peter is getting ready for the Second American Revolution. The book is not yet written but is coming fast, he tells Carl with authority, now with a harelipped heroine, "marching up Fifth Avenue with the comrades, her face stained with blood, humbling the Guggenheimers and the Morgans . . . ."[9] The following month, Peter has redecorated his digs

[7] Yale.
[8] *Peter Whiffle*, p. 52.
[9] *Ibid.*, p. 118.

with Marsden Hartley and Marcel Duchamp and Pablo Picasso—
the year is 1912—and the book is forgotten.

Carl and Peter meet again the following year at Edith Dale's Villa
Allegra (the Villa Curonia, of course), and spend an idyllic holiday,
talking about the arts with Edith, giving Carl an excuse for some
casual ramblings in his familiar brash manner. Of writing:

> I think a great book might be written if everything the hero thought
> and felt and observed could be put into it. . . . Nothing should be
> omitted, nothing! One might write a whole book of two hundred
> thousand words about the events of one hour. And what a book!
> What a book![10]

Of critics:

> The trouble . . . is that they are not contradictory enough. They
> stick to a theory for better or worse, as unwise men stick to an
> unwise marriage.[11]

Of himself:

> Good critics, I should like to believe, are always loose writers; they
> perpetually contradict themselves; their work is invariably palinodal.
> How, otherwise, can they strive for vision, and how can they inspire
> vision in the reader without striving for vision themselves. Good
> critics . . . should constantly contradict their own definitions.[12]

When they meet again, after Peter's sudden departure from the
villa, Carl is once again in New York. But the encounter is final;
Peter is dying, and the novel concludes a little ambivalently, putting to shame a whole generation of poseurs, but with some degree
of love. Peter says that sympathy and enthusiasm are something
after all:

> I must have communicated at least a shadow of these to the ideas and
> objects and people on whom I have bestowed them . . . and they are
> just so much more precious because I have given them my affection.

[10] *Ibid.*, p. 177.
[11] *Ibid.*, p. 181.
[12] *Ibid.*, p. 183.

This is something; indeed, next to ... creation ... perhaps it is everything. ... But ... if I had found a new formula, who knows what I might have done?[13]

In February, 1922, just a year after Carl had started the book, Knopf's catalogue carried the first announcement of *Peter Whiffle*, calling it a "curious, gossipy chronicle" that defied "satisfactory classification." But it was, nevertheless, labeled a first novel. One early reviewer disagreed, calling it "empty and left-over." Nearly every other reviewer, however, praised *Peter Whiffle* highly. "The smartest thing of its kind done by an American," said the *New York Herald Tribune*; "the book all of us dream about," said the *Chicago News*; and Carl's old employer, the *New York Times*, found it "sparkling and delightful." Heywood Broun called it distinguished, and Elinor Wylie praised the style and manner. Carl Van Doren analyzed its achievement in greater detail in the *Nation*:

> It is strange how few authors have written biographies of imaginary persons. It makes possible at once the freedom of the novel and the sober structure of the biography. In "Peter Whiffle," Carl Van Vechten has crossed the two literary forms fascinatingly. . . . He deals with it now racily, now poetically. He is full of allusions, of pungencies, of learning in his times. He knows how to laugh, he scorns solemnity, he has filled his book with wit and erudition.[14]

For a couple of months, *Peter Whiffle* moved slowly. Then, suddenly, it began to catch on. Carl wrote Arthur Davison Ficke:

> Peter is getting astonishing reviews, which are amusing me very much. I am even considering writing a review myself after it is all over, just to make it more mysterious. Peter has been praised as a great religious mystic and he has been damned for a cad. He has been identified with my subconscious mind, and with the satirical heroes of Max Beerbohm! I am very content, of course. And if, in my review, I tell the whole truth, no one will believe it, because I will only be repeating what I have already said in the book—for those who have eyes.[15]

[13] *Ibid.*, pp. 244–246.   [14] May 10, 1922, p. 569.   [15] Yale.

Gertrude Stein wrote from Paris that Carl was "indeed the most modern the least sentimental and the most quietly persistent of the romantics."[16] Joseph Hergesheimer liked particularly "the bits about you—the prologue in Paris, in a . . . fine bath of memory, was splendid."[17] And James Branch Cabell, whom Carl had not yet met, wrote, "For weeks I have intended to voice the, in the ultimate not very important, fact that Peter Whiffle delighted me in every respect—and that statement, duly recorded, seems to say all."[18] Emily Clarke found Peter "enchanting"; Mabel Dodge suggested that Carl become "a kind of chronicleer [*sic*] of yr time & do dozens. . . . Times change—it would be an amusing record. Like Saint Simon—& S. Pepys—etc. Only a *lot* of vols. one a year."[19] Thomas Beer, a new writer friend, remarked good-humoredly, "My aunt has read Peter Whiffle and says that it contains a good moral lesson,"[20] and Ficke wrote: "You and the intriguing Peter should be shut up together, and have administered to you the cup of hemlock 'for corrupting the youth of Athens.' How is this book going to help Young America to become better automobile salesmen? I ask you."[21]

But Carl's father was not so enthusiastic:

Someday I will get the courage to say to you my criticism of that book. It will come by way of a caution for the next book you write. . . .

To tell the truth I am not particularly interested though there are many (for me) good things in the book—(have been trying to answer a question—what message did you wish to give your readers? I could answer that quite satisfactorily regarding everything else you have written but this is to me a stumper. . . .) I can't afford on nearly every page to be using the dictionary to look up words that my vocabulary doesn't contain.[22]

[16] CVV, NYPL; *The Yale University Library Gazette* (hereafter cited as *Yale Gazette*), October, 1952, p. 79.
[17] CVV, NYPL.
[18] CVV, NYPL.
[19] CVV, NYPL.
[20] CVV, NYPL.
[21] CVV, NYPL.
[22] CVV, NYPL.

The reaction was understandable: in 1922, Charles Duane Van Vechten was eighty-two years old; moreover, Ralph had recently written Carl that their father had "failed considerably since I last saw him. While he was perfectly well, he seems to be showing his age more than ever before. His hearing is poor and his mind is not so alert. . . ."[23]

By August, the novel had sold more than 5,700 copies. The first edition, limited to fifty copies for Knopf's bookseller friends, had been bound in orange boards and paper left from the covers of *The Music of Spain*. The trade edition, which Carl had had a hand in designing, had a linen spine with paper label and boards covered with batik papers—of which there were ninety-seven variations in color and design—that Blanche and Alfred Knopf had brought back with them after a holiday in Germany. There was of course no way of knowing that the book was going to be so popular. None of Carl's other Knopf volumes had required more than a small edition. But the success of *Peter Whiffle* necessitated using a plain cloth binding after the first few printings had been sold.

Dedicated to the memory of his mother, Carl Van Vechten's literary alter-ego went through eight printings in his first year. By that time it had reached the hinterlands. Someone wrote to say that he had met Peter in Bucharest in 1909; someone else could not help "wondering politely how much of Peter was simply what Carl Van Vechten would wish to be."

Hugh Walpole, wrote the definitive, if not the final, word on the book in a review for the *International Book Digest*:

> When I come to . . . "Peter Whiffle" I am tempted to throw aside all criticism. It is altogether so personal and individual you must either love or detest it. . . . The things that Carl Van Vechten doesn't know about anything out of the way or odd are simply not knowable. His humour is so whimsical that it can frequently be missed unless the observer watches very closely indeed. Its beauty is constant. . . . There are unexpected passages of tenderness and poetry . . . but there is no knowing what he will do in the future. He would

[23] CVV, NYPL.

laugh at anybody who took him seriously. He eludes definition—like his own Peter Whiffle, he is always just around the corner.[24]

In terms of readers, Carl Van Vechten had become a popular success; in terms of critics, he had become significant as an artist, all of which was very good news. But Carl was equally aware that, for the first time in seven years, he was financially solvent. At the beginning of an era that would run rampant to such an extent that elders today grow misty-eyed when speaking of it and youngsters attempt to emulate it in constant revivals of its fashions, Carl Van Vechten had arrived to chronicle the frailties of a singularly extraordinary period. Moreover, he himself fell heir to them with a delight and abandon that were almost always slightly out of hand.

F. Scott Fitzgerald, whose *This Side of Paradise* had invented the twenties a year or so before, decided his generation had "grown up to find all gods dead, all wars fought, all faiths shaken." The heat generated by their flaming youth ignited some older embers without much difficulty; Carl, whose fires had been temporarily banked by the war years, joined the blaze. There was of course a difference: Carl was forty-two years old when *Peter Whiffle* appeared, his own youth having flamed sufficiently around the turn of the century. No one was less lost during the heyday of the lost generation. The conventional period of soul searching had passed long before, and, when the country's inhibition gave way to Prohibition, Carl was much better equipped to tend bar than anybody whose name has ever been associated with the period commonly referred to as the roaring twenties.

If Fitzgerald's flappers and philosophers gathered in prohibition pubs, his peers frequently met for similar purposes in publishers' offices. Bennett Cerf—then a junior clerk at Boni and Liveright—recalls Carl chatting confidentially with Dorothy Parker and Eugene O'Neill. O'Neill became a warm friend a few years later, but Mrs. Parker never overcame her initial aversion. Several years later, meeting Carl by accident in a Philadelphia hotel, she fled through the nearest door. It was the entrance to the men's room.

[24] January, 1923, p. 70.

The publishers' gatherings may have been ostensibly designed for literary conversation, but they frequently turned in the direction of Prohibition parties. As Dwight Taylor said in his memoir of the twenties:

> Our national heritage of freedom seemed in jeopardy, drinking became a patriotic duty, and the average American writer's reaction to the passing of the Eighteenth Amendment was to embark upon a prolonged Boston Tea Party, in which he very often found himself acting like an Indian. Some of the outstanding editors and publishers of the period were enthusiastic leaders in this revolt. . . .[25]

On one occasion Horace Liveright, a rather prim fellow in ordinary circumstances, held his literary tea (as such a gathering was called) at the Brevoort, during which the festivities grew slightly nonliterary: Carl was playing the piano, and Liveright—presumably in good humor—pulled him back, tossed him off the stool, and broke his collarbone.

If parties could grow from literary soirees, so could the reverse easily occur. On another occasion, Carl, with H. L. Mencken and Ernest Boyd, stopped for dinner at the Brevoort before proceeding to Theodore Dreiser's St. Luke's Place apartment. They were joined in the dining room by F. Scott Fitzgerald, then in his early prime and flushed with success. Rather enviously, he expressed an enormous admiration for Dreiser and said he would rather meet him than anybody else he could think of. Despite his pleas, Fitzgerald was not invited to accompany them.

Dreiser's party was variously reported, never quite accurately, according to Carl. Llewelyn Powys, in *The Verdict of Bridlegoose*, and Burton Rascoe, in *We Were Interrupted*, tried their hands at it; so did Carl himself, in a memoir printed several years ago in the *Yale University Library Gazette*. The gathering was arranged on the eve of the publication of one of Dreiser's novels, the guest list being composed of critics and novelists and essayists of the period. The host received in the center of a large room, apparently ignorant

[25] *Joy Ride*, pp. 56–57.

that not all the guests knew one another. In a circle around the room, chairs were arranged on which the assemblage sat, "stiffly and soberly" (for there was nothing to drink but beer), like applicants for a job nobody really wanted. Mencken tried without much success to liven things up with schoolboy jokes; Carl sat silently on a hard chair, according to Powys, "like an aging madonna lily that had lost its pollen and had been left standing in a vase which the parlor-maid had forgotten to refill with fresh water."[26]

In the middle of the wake, Scott Fitzgerald tottered in, a bottle of champagne under his arm. He presented the gift with an eloquent if somewhat fuzzy speech. Dreiser thanked him, invited him in, took his bottle, and put it in the refrigerator. Nobody ever saw it again. After another dismal hour the guests began to realize that the host had no intention of sharing the tribute, and one by one they bade him good night.

Most of the parties during the 1920's were not so dry, however. Everybody gave them and everybody went to them, a somewhat older Van Vechten nostalgically reflected many years later. Food and drink were in abundance, and "lots of talk and certainly a good deal of lewd behavior" as well. In the circumstances, it was not difficult for him to capture some of their flavor, "with the greatest ease," in a second novel, *The Blind Bow-Boy*.

"I AM WRITING A NEW NOVEL," Carl Van Vechten wrote Emily Clarke, "that is amusing me so much that I absolve it from the need of amusing future readers,"[27] and, a few months later: "It is a nice book. If Ben Hecht had written it, it could be called *devastating*, but I shall make it charming."[28]

The charm that resulted—and too often ran away with itself—brought the wrath of the critics ("perverse"; "nasty") and their praise ("deft"; "sophisticated"). He began the book in May, 1922, just a few months before *Peter Whiffle* embarked on the unsteady

26 *Ibid.*, p. 224.
27 *Innocence Abroad*, p. 134.
28 *Ibid.*

seas of public opinion and popularity. *Peter Whiffle* sailed through fifteen different printings during the decade, but Carl Van Vechten certainly could not have anticipated such a success at the time he began "Daniel Matthews' Tutor." The title was changed in the second draft, three months later, to *The Blind Bow-Boy*, a reference to a masked statue in his heroine's garden about to loose its arrow on the unsuspecting but usually willing characters in the novel. The dust jacket advised readers, "The influence of this blinded Eros plays havoc in 'this modern Satyricon' which 'carries sophistication beyond any point it has hitherto reached in American Fiction.'" (An uncredited critic, Ernest Boyd, had sneaked between the inverted commas.) But by the time this explanation reached the public, *The Blind Bow-Boy* was widely known. The original trade edition of 3,500 copies had sold out even before the book was released. When it appeared publicly in August, 1923, the critical reviews helped to deplete three more large printings before the end of the year.

"Done with . . . the bizarre strokes of a Beardsley," Ernest Boyd wrote for the *Nation*,[29] though Mencken qualified Boyd's remarks in a letter to Carl:

> Boyd tells me that he had a hell of a hard time thinking of something nice to say about your book, but that he finally managed it. It will be easier for me. I actually like it, despite the occasional descents to what no right thinking man can fail to regard as lamentable lasciviousness.[30]

Mencken's letter had been written primarily to announce one of his regular visits to New York. Proposing an inscription party, he then wrote: "I shall bring with me a sheaf of your own works so you may occupy yourself decently and reciprocally. Think up some good Scriptural texts. Our widows will reap a harvest when our books are sold."[31]

Other reviewers did not suffer Boyd's affliction. Heywood

[29] September 5, 1923, p. 244.
[30] CVV, NYPL.
[31] Yale.

Broun pronounced *The Blind Bow-Boy* an uplift story in which
the author "propagandizes for all those brave beings who seek, in
spite of tyranny, to follow their own inclinations."[32] Burton Rascoe, in the *Tribune*, labeled it "a clever and roguish book, all icing
and innuendo, deviltry and wit."[33] If John Farrar, on the other side
of the ring, wrote it off as a "scandal sheet," almost everybody else
responded favorably, though most of them missed the point.

In another letter to Emily Clarke, Carl wrote that his formula
consisted of treating extremely serious themes as frivolously as possible; to Henry Blake Fuller, a neglected American novelist, he
wrote, "Milieu, mood and style are all quite different from anything you know of mine."[34] He could declare to intimates that it
was a "tremendously serious book with a sardonic approach," but
to the unsuspecting reader *The Blind Bow-Boy* was more than
faintly salacious. Mencken's criticism was justifiable in 1923; to a
lesser extent, it still is, more than forty years later.

Harold Prewett (Daniel Matthews of the first draft), fresh from
college, is deposited by his father in the care of Paul Moody, a
tutor in the Seven Lively Arts and Deadly Sins who has been hired
because he has served a term in Ludlow Street prison for back alimony. Paul introduces his ward to the sophisticated court of
Campaspe Lorillard, an impervious princess whose credo comes
slyly between a couple of amoral situations, "We are the few; the
rest are fools, and all we have to do to persuade the fools to permit
us to live our own lives is to make them believe that we, too,
are fools."[35]

One of the few is Titus Hugg (called Bunny for obvious reasons—this was 1922), a futurist composer who needs a piano with
quarter and sixteenth notes between the customary blacks and
whites. Mencken was moved to raise a few questions, as a "practical
musician of delicate talents." Early in August, he wondered, after
reading the novel: "How in hell a mechanical piano can wail a

32 *New York World*, May 19, 1923.
33 August 26, 1923.
34 Yale.
35 *The Blind Bow-Boy*, p. 72.

quarter note off key as reported in your instructive work, 'The Blind Bow-Boy'; page 75. Such howlers will fool Boyd and other such boobs, but I defy you to put them over on the undersigned. I am two-thirds through the book, and find my hay fever much improved."[36] Carl upheld the possibility, with some historic pianos to prove it. "Off goes my hat," Mencken replied, "you have discovered something new in music. Let us inspect all . . . those pianolas. I'll bring along a tuning fork; I lost my absolute pitch when I was down with sciatica."[37] Pianos get out of tune, Carl suggested. "Of course pianolas get out of tune," Mencken countered in another letter. "Who denies it? But is getting out of tune the same thing as playing off key? If so Richard Strauss wasted his time teaching me music. I offer such witnesses as Busoni, . . . Gustav Strube and Sousa, and you come up with Louis Sherwin, a brothel pianist. Go to hell."[38]

In addition to the perpetrator of Mencken's musical notes, there were other players in the Van Vechten orchestra: Zimbule O'Grady, a snake charmer from Coney Island who manages to get most of the men in the novel, including Harold, into bed with her at one point or another; Campaspe's frustrated husband Cupid, who shops around for substitutes; Ronald, Duke of Middlebottom, who dresses like a sailor, carries an umbrella, and engraves his stationery with the pronouncement that "A thing of beauty is a boy forever." In the center of this slapdash menagerie, Harold is placed by his father, a cloak and suit man anxious to turn his son against the perverse and the decadent by exposing him to their evils. Eventually, however, Harold learns of the deception and, finding the nimble wits more attractive than he should, embraces the life he is expected to reject, leaves his wife of two weeks and his mistress of a shorter period, and sails for Europe with the infamous duke.

The plot had a more polished structure than that of *Peter Whiffle*; yet it was, again, of secondary importance to the often

36 CVV, NYPL.
37 Yale; *Fragments I*, p. 56.
38 Yale.

brilliant scenes and dialogue. Further, it was subsidiary to what amounted to predictable Van Vechten pronouncements. Originally, in the first draft, the point of view was that of his personal essays, a monologue directed to the reader, as in the opening of the fourth chapter. Following a traffic incident involving Harold and a policeman, Van Vechten spoke:

> The appearance so early in this story of burly Irishmen and sundry taxicab drivers may frighten the sensitive reader. . . . Let me reassure him at once. Let me state distinctly that this is a story of high life, so far as high life exists in New York. This is no drab history of middle class existence, no realistic history of uneventful lives. This is romance, warm-blooded romance and my figures shall be romantic and as far as it is possible to make them, rich.[39]

In the second draft, he deleted the whole passage, cut directly to Campaspe, and decided to let the reader figure things out for himself, by way of Campaspe, who functioned as his spokesman and, indeed, as spokesman for the entire period that frowned on work and lived on play:

> A book . . . should have the swiftness of melodrama, the lightness of farce, to be a real contribution to thought. . . . How could anything serious be hidden more successfully than in a book which pretended to be light and gay? Plot was certainly unimportant in the novel; character drawing a silly device. . . . Growth of character in a novel was nonsense. People never change. Psychology: the supreme imbecility. The long and complicated analyses that serious writers give us merely define the mental limitations of these writers.[40]

If the purpose of *The Blind Bow-Boy* was reflected in a society that coveted the outlandish, knowing that life itself was outlandish, it was almost too successfully hidden. In spite of the Campaspe-Carl avowal, what might be capricious could become simple lunacy: menus of potted blackbirds and pickled walnuts; bathrooms paneled in alternating squares of malachite and lapis lazuli, with a jade tub

[39] CVV, NYPL.
[40] *The Blind Bow-Boy*, p. 163.

and gold faucets. What might be amusing could become what Mencken called "lamentable lasciviousness": "Paul began, unreasonably, to grin. I don't know what reminds me, he said, but have you heard about Bunny? He's had Zimbule's name tattooed on his person so cunningly that it can only be deciphered under certain conditions."[41]

Carl Van Vechten's anonymous statement on the original dust jacket of *The Blind Bow-Boy* was at least superficially justified: "This book is not 'romantic' or 'realistic' or 'art' or 'life' . . . and no ideas are concealed beneath its surface." He managed, nevertheless, in defiance of his own intentions, to prepare a fairly succinct statement on the twenties: that the life of his time might as well be the time of his life. Although it could not be altered, it might, ironically, be accepted for the mélange that it was. Moreover, the engaging surface of the novel never managed—despite Van Vechten's attempt—to overcome his own nudging awareness.

The Blind Bow-Boy sold out four printings within ten days. In England, plans were under way for publication. Grant Richards had published *Peter Whiffle* earlier in 1923, and by March a few "decidedly encomiastic reviews" encouraged Richards to try another Van Vechten novel. In point of fact, the plans were more or less settled before the book was released in America, though the English publisher had some reservations.

For fear of shocking his readers, Richards wanted to alter a few passages: one, about a little good-natured flagellation; another, about the Duke's stationery motto; the third, a comparison of white chrysanthemums to geese's bottoms; and the fourth and longest, a "curious request" made by a boarding school roommate of Campaspe's older son. ("Do you want to?" asks Campaspe. "No, mamma," the boy replies. "Then you don't have to."[42]) Carl Van Vechten replied to Grant Richards' letter:

If you will read it over you will find that there is nothing in it that the reader does not put there. Its importance is to suggest that Campaspe

41 *Ibid.*, p. 135.
42 *Ibid.*, p. 258.

wished her boy to do exactly as he desired in every respect. I have made the nature of the . . . boy's request vague because it is unimportant. Possibly the . . . boy was a Roman Catholic who wished young Lorillard to say his prayers. . . .[43]

The novel appeared in England two months after the American edition was released, with a drawing of a perplexed young man on the cover. Its publication signaled Hugh Walpole—who had witnessed Carl's signature on the contract—to write, "None [of the reviews] seem to realize that this is quite another thing from Whiffle: a brilliantly ordered and shaped thing, creative all through and of a delicious humor by no means depending on your far-fetched erudition!"[44]

In America, other friends wrote about *The Blind Bow-Boy.* Mabel Dodge (by this time Mabel Dodge Luhan), convinced she was Campaspe, wrote to compliment her old friend on "having produced one of the most completely and essentially psychoanalytical works of anyone alive not excepting Freud."[45]

Sinclair Lewis, who had lived down the hall from Carl twenty years before, wrote that the book was

impertinent, subversive, resolutely and completely wicked. I didn't believe any American could do that—I know my own wickedness is so feeble and apologetic. . . . You prove that New York is as sophisticated as any European capital and . . . I think you slap the tradition that highbrow American novels must be either lugubriously and literally "realistic" . . . or else acrobatically "original" like . . . all the writers who are deriving from the solemn theology of Gertrude Stein.[46]

She herself spoke from Paris:

I spent the afternoon at the site of the Assumption of the Virgin reading the Bow Boy and it went very well. You have invented your own brightness. . . . Its all the background and the background, as

[43] Yale.
[44] CVV, NYPL.
[45] CVV, NYPL.
[46] CVV, NYPL.

yet American life is the background. Others have tried to make background foreground, but you have made foreground background and our foreground is our background.[47]

There is no problem in translating Miss Stein's remarks. Van Vechten had successfully managed to mingle his own milieu into his material.

Henry Blake Fuller, a little sadly, seemed to agree: "Each of your books is like a nail in my coffin. After so much youth, spirit, invention, I find myself intoning a Whitmanian Miserere: Goodby My Fancy."[48]

Joseph Hergesheimer congratulated Carl on the book's "wholly formal correctness and the amazing, the sterile, the satirical conclusion. This is a better book for these reasons, dear Carl, than Peter."[49]

Young men wrote asking for explanations, wanting to know just what subversive machinations were taking place between decorated paper-covered boards of *The Blind Bow-Boy*. For example: "I am a young man ready for business like Harold."

Others were not so enthusiastic. Carl's father contented himself with a single line, "A *very well written* picture of depravity." And from Oklahoma came word that the author should be hanged in Times Square, "an Iowa bumpkin with a thin coating of Firbank"; but Firbank thought it was wonderful "to have attracted another butterfly like myself."[50]

To conclude the praises, Alfred A. Knopf said happily, "If all our authors were as amicable as you, sold as well and knew exactly what they wanted, what a nice time we'd have."[51]

After the success of *The Blind Bow-Boy*, Carl began to consider revising *Music after the Great War*; actually, it had never gone out of print, but he started a new introduction. It dwindled after a paragraph. In its place, he got off a hasty note to G. Schirmer, Inc., beg-

47 CVV, NYPL; *Yale Gazette*, October, 1952, p. 79.
48 CVV, NYPL.
49 CVV, NYPL.
50 CVV, NYPL.
51 CVV, NYPL.

ging them not to reprint the "awful book," because it was corrupting the morals of its readers. But they replied that only about twenty-five copies were sold annually. "Hence you are corrupting the morals of only 25 persons a year. Why worry?"[52]

Carl then turned his attention to some final polishing on a novel he had started the preceding March, a second draft of which was completed before *The Blind Bow-Boy* had been published. Concurrently, he contributed his share of noise to the roaring twenties.

CARL VAN VECHTEN later remarked that no one born after World War I could have any faint concept of the epoch during which so much writing blossomed, here and in England, and quickly withered away. It was, in retrospect, a storybook period for storytellers, all of whom seemed to know one another: F. Scott Fitzgerald, Theodore Dreiser, Sinclair Lewis, James Branch Cabell, Floyd Dell, Elinor Wylie, Ellen Glasgow, Hugh Walpole, and W. Somerset Maugham. Van Vechten and Hergesheimer and Mencken had been friendly for a number of years, of course, through the offices of Alfred A. Knopf, but it was not until the "splendid drunken twenties," as Carl called them, were just beginning to get high on bathtub gin and belles-lettres that the circle widened, primarily through a real appreciation of one another's work, but also in part through the Algonquin Hotel, which most of the celebrated names of the period frequented. Alexander Woollcott, Heywood Broun, Franklin P. Adams, Robert Benchley, Deems Taylor, Harold Ross of *The New Yorker*, George S. Kaufman, Marc Connelly, and Robert Sherwood formed the nucleus at the legendary Round Table; but Fitzgerald, Fannie Hurst, Gertrude Atherton, Louis Bromfield, George Jean Nathan, Irvin S. Cobb, Hendrik Van Loon, Burton Rascoe, and Knopf's own literary trio were frequently in attendance. "If the Algonquin exploded," Carl remembered Frank O'Malley's saying, "American literature would stop dead for twenty-four hours."

Nor was the West Forty-fourth Street salon limited to writers:

[52] Yale.

Marilyn Miller and Laurette Taylor turned up now and then before matinees; Mary Pickford and Douglas Fairbanks and the Gish sisters put in appearances between filmings on Long Island; Fania Marinoff and Ethel Barrymore and Noel Coward and Gertrude Lawrence lunched there; and visiting contributors to the arts often moved in while on holiday in New York.

The talk was largely literary because of the clientele, but it must have halted momentarily on those days when a glamorous girl named Tallulah Bankhead swept in—a very young Tallulah on the verge of changing her name to something more suitable for theater marquees. Miss Bankhead went from table to table, sampling this guest's salad, the next guest's entree. At the time she was absolutely broke, and running up astronomical bills at the hotel. Once, passing a table where Carl Van Vechten and Joseph Hergesheimer were lunching together, she was asked to sit down. "If you change your name, we'll neither of us ever write another word," they threatened; and Carl added: "Keep it. It is very odd; also it is very easy to remember."

Carl's connections with Tallulah Bankhead and the Algonquin extended, on at least one occasion, beyond the limits of the dining room. Ralph Van Vechten, in town on a visit, found himself host to a very large and very wet party in his rooms at the hotel. Hergesheimer was there with Carl, and, a little later, Mencken dropped in. As the evening wore on, the crowd grew in size and abandon. With a young actress perched on his knee, Mencken fell fast asleep, let the girl slide to the floor, and snored loudly enough to rouse the guests in the neighboring suite. When he awoke later, he discovered an entirely new set of people at the party, including Miss Bankhead. He took one astonished look and exclaimed to Carl: "Your brother is a wonderful fellow! When he gives a party apparently he has his first set of girls beheaded or baked, only so he can enjoy a second set later."[53] Total strangers began to drift in. Dancing began. Conversations rose and fell: about sex, about the theater, about Prohibition, about Sigmund Freud, about kissing parrots, about the

[53] *Fragments I*, p. 62.

liquor. Then a popular novelist began to cry because the lights of Broadway were only will-o'-the-wisps; and another, of slight build, was invited by the president of the Chicago Athletic Club to jump up and down on his stomach to test its resilience. The invitation was accepted. "I can see it now," Carl recalled wistfully, "the very corner where he jumped." At that point in the progress of his party, Ralph Van Vechten delightedly slapped his knee and cried, "My God, isn't it wonderful to see all these interesting people here together!"[54]

The intellegentsia may have set the pace for the younger generation in books like *Linda Condon* and *The Blind Bow-Boy* and *The Green Hat*, with some lessons in perversity from Cabell, idol toppling from Mencken, and scorning the bourgeois from Sinclair Lewis; but that same intelligentsia turned right around to imitate their imitators. As Mark Sullivan suggested, "On the dance-floor, in the beauty parlor, on the golf course; in clothes, manners, and many points of view, elders strove earnestly to look and act like their children, in many cases their grandchildren."[55] And, as Frederick Lewis Allen echoed, "From the early days of the decade, when they thrilled at the lackadaisical petting of F. Scott Fitzgerald's young thinkers . . . to the latter days when they were all agog over the literature of homosexuality . . . they read about sex, talked about sex, thought about sex, and defied anybody to say No."[56]

Certainly, there was enough in Carl's novels to point the direction. It was a time when the writers almost equaled personalities of the theater in popularity, a position that film actors had not yet usurped and that opera stars had long since relinquished. A new novel by Joseph Hergesheimer or Carl Van Vechten was heralded with trumpet blasts; with Hergesheimer, indeed (then pronounced America's foremost novelist), it was an event of national importance that led to Knopf's extraordinary limited editions, a kind of bookmaking that has assuredly never been equaled since.

---

[54] Emily Clarke, *Innocence Abroad*, pp. 139–140.
[55] *Our Times*, Volume VI, p. 386.
[56] *Only Yesterday*, p. 234.

Knopf had always had a penchant for collectors; in Carl Van Vechten's novels, he gave his readers something really beautiful to collect. Published simultaneously with the trade edition, which was bound in decorated boards and a linen spine, there was a "large paper" edition of *The Blind Bow-Boy*. The sheets were water-marked and all rag, and the binding was of pale green paper-covered boards set off with an orange linen spine. The copies were left un-trimmed and unopened, and inserted in blue boxes—115 of them—each numbered and autographed. The next novel—*The Tattooed Countess*—was even handsomer. Encased in a black box, the book was bound in black boards decorated in circus pink and white and green flowers (a binding shared with Fannie Hurst's *Appassionata*), and the spine was pink linen. There were 160 copies thus issued, signed of course, and numbered. The trade edition was bound in maroon cloth, stamped in gold, and had a dust jacket designed by Ralph Barton, the caricaturist-artist and husband of actress Carlotta Monterey. The first printing was 7,500 copies, more than twice the number of *The Blind Bow-Boy*, and they sold almost as quickly.

The Tattooed Countess differed entirely from its predecessors, but turned to another subject familiar and fashionable during the 1920's: small-town America. Sinclair Lewis, Floyd Dell, and Waldo Frank had written novels on the subject; but, as Arthur Davison Ficke wrote, "It is delightful to see Main Street described in terms of amusement instead of the usual terms of fury."[57]

Turning to his own past and background—called Maple Valley in the novel—Carl Van Vechten began writing his Cedar Rapids saga less than six months after he had completed the final draft of *The Blind Bow-Boy*. *The Tattooed Countess* concerns Ella Nat-tatorini (née Poore), an Iowa girl who has married money, has been widowed early, and returns to her home town after a long series of abortive affairs with beautiful young men in Europe. The home town to which she returns is a provincial community where so many people are old because the younger generation flees as soon as possible. There, just as she begins to verge on social claustrophobia,

[57] CVV, NYPL.

she finds one native who seems to understand her language, a hand-some boy of seventeen, and promptly takes him back with her to Europe.

Such summaries are almost always weightless. Carl Van Vechten's novels, built as they are of a complex but disarmingly simple pattern and texture, rely heavily on atmosphere—the "charm" of which he so often spoke. The appalling realism is made the more bitter because of that charm. Ella, in 1897—the novel begins on June 17 of that year, when Carl would have celebrated his seventeenth birthday—returns to her home, "at that dangerous age just before decay sets in,"[58] to shock the folks back home with a tattoo on her wrist: *Qui sais-je?* Lou, her sallow sister, cries: "But on the wrist, where it *shows*! It wouldn't have been so bad if it had been on the back of the . . . thigh, where it could be covered."[59]

Ella has returned, expecting to find the past, not as she remembers it but as she would like to remember it. The difficulty, predictably, is that she finds too much of the past, too much of the life she had originally deserted. Faced with the stultifying prospects—"How could you stay away so long? . . . Have you seen the new waterworks?"[60]—she turns her attention to those who show some interest in her, beginning with Lennie Colman, a spinster schoolteacher. Lennie introduces Gareth Johns, one of her students, and from then she is stuck with the schoolhouse. Concurrently, Gareth has been suffering in a different way, restless and unhappy, in a stifling town, where he wants "to know everything, *everything*"[61] and finds no opportunity. (After the book was published, Carl's sister Emma wrote that she had taken the boy to be Carl. "Of course not wholly so as there are some things about him that are different, tho generally speaking it is as you were."[62])

By the time the Countess and Gareth confront each other, the reader concludes that the waterworks, the depot, and the new brick

[58] *The Tattooed Countess*, p. 1.
[59] *Ibid.*, p. 43.
[60] *Ibid.*, pp. 54–55.
[61] *Ibid.*, p. 77.
[62] CVV, NYPL.

pavements will run a sad second place for topics of conversation among the natives. They don't even come in third. On the evening after their first meeting, Gareth and Ella are "friends and allies" over a glass of lemonade; the next afternoon, they picnic in the fields outside the town; six weeks later, they are in each other's arms, almost immediately following the death of Gareth's mother:

> The boy began to weep softly. Laying her hand on his head, the Countess caressed his hair. Silently, with great delicacy she stroked; then, very slowly, very carefully, she leaned nearer to him, rubbing her cheek tenderly against his, the tendrils of her hair brushing his face. This slight contact inflamed her. Now, with one palm still back of his head, with the other she grasped his hand, no longer limp, and slowly, softly, she gradually shifted her position until her lips met his. He did not move, nor did he respond. For a second or two she remained poised; then, swiftly, bending forward still further, she kissed him passionately, an embrace which he returned. . . .
> Gareth, she whispered, I love you.
> I love you, too, he replied.
> Do you understand? she went on, almost as if she were explaining something to a child. I love you . . . that way.
> I want you too, was his response. . . .
> Mon petit chou! she cried. Ma soisoif! Ma faifaim! Adorable! . . . I will be everything to you: mother, mistress, wife, Tu es mon bébé!
> Countess, he began . . .
> Call me Ella, call me your fafemme!
> Ella![63]

The scene is both ludicrous and repulsive: the aging Countess, about to embark on her final affair, and Gareth, whose "hour had come; he was at last a man. As he considered the possibilities of his future, he began to walk more slowly, and a smile spread over his face. . . ."[64] Together he and the Countess flee to Paris, leaving behind them the appalling but "pure, one hundred per cent American state, an' it's lookin' up!"[65]

[63] *The Tattooed Countess*, pp. 259–260.
[64] *Ibid.*, p. 264.
[65] *Ibid.*, pp. 285–286.

To any fair intelligence, the Countess was merely a worldly, "sex-beset moron," as Carl once called her in a letter to Arthur Davison Ficke, seduced for purposes of his own by a ruthless youth whose imaginative sophistication transcends all poor Ella's vast experience. The novel's cynical, amoral conclusion—it was subtitled "*a romantic novel with a happy ending*"—moved at least one reader to respond with the same indignation that the Maple Valley residents experienced in the wake of Gareth and Ella:

> Have just read your successful?? book viz:—"The Tattooed Countess." While it is cleverly written, it is vile.
>
> What is the use of writing such filth? Your crime is the greatest crime of all crimes viz:—Poisoning the mind of *youth*. There is certainly enough rottenness in this world—without writing romances about it. You are not very young judging by your knowledge of . . . that little Iowa town.
>
> You dedicate it to Hugh Walpole. Poor Walpole! he must feel honored using *his name* betwixt the covers of such gutter slime.[66]

But Walpole was enormously pleased to be the dedicatee: "On her own bottom, so to speak, she's not I think so good as my beloved Bow Boy—But I think she's infinitely more interesting and more promising. . . . It shows how true an artist you are that you should step out and develop new talents."[67] Other friends admired it too.

Mabel Dodge Luhan called it the most serious book he had written, for whatever that was worth, and Gertrude Stein wrote, more perceptively, "After having been tender to everyone else you are now tender to yourself."[68] M. P. Shiel, a neglected English novelist whom Carl Van Vechten was in the process of resurrecting, said, "Bravo, you are among the Liberators of the Brethren: that's right, slash into them, don't be afraid, kick 'em, the more you bully them, the more they'll buckle under, for the dull are all cowards, au fond."[69] Scott Fitzgerald wrote from Europe that the view of Iowa,

[66] CVV, NYPL (unsigned).
[67] CVV, NYPL.
[68] CVV, NYPL.
[69] CVV, NYPL.

which he had never seen, was "unbeatable." Elinor Wylie called it a "cruel little masterpiece of analysis [that] is the two iron fists of realism in a pair of the most exquisite doeskin gloves."[70]

The gloves, doubtless, covered the real seriousness of the situation: the clever and charming patina that coated the dreadful loneliness of Lennie Colman and the frustration of Gareth Johns and the subversive motives of the Countess, which made the novel all the more upsetting for many readers. Joseph Wood Krutch, reviewing it for the *Nation*, even suggested that the characters had no "gift of life," objecting to the unbelievability of the conflict; and the *Literary Review* and *New York Times* were equally lacking in perspicacity, content to call it "easy reading" and entertaining and light. But Somerset Maugham hit on the novel's real value, in a letter quoted on the dust jacket of subsequent printings:

> It . . . distresses me to think that not one in a hundred of your readers will ever see how witty and brilliant and entrancing it is. I am always looking for light books and in England, at all events, seldom find them, for most writers think that a light book is the same as a frivolous one, and do not realize that it requires really much more thought, knowledge, culture, and experience than a book dealing with the elemental emotions.
>
> I think *The Tattooed Countess* is a triumph in this difficult genre. I admire exceedingly the way in which you have avoided every temptation to force the note, and the discretion with which you have let your exquisite humour get its own laughter with never so much as a nudge in the reader's ribs to bring to his notice that here is something to laugh at.[71]

Sinclair Lewis, whose own *Main Street* had criticized similar territory, commented sapiently:

> In former days we could dispose of Van Vechten by explaining that *Peter Whiffle* and *The Blind Bow-Boy* were merely clever fantasies concerning superficial people in New York. But now, like the worthy but sometimes depressing authors of *Winesburg, Ohio* and

[70] CVV, NYPL.
[71] CVV, NYPL.

Main Street, and *O Pioneers!* he has entered upon the middle west—and he has made it at once real and amusing. . . .

Mr. Van Vechten has hitherto, often and with justice, been compared to Mr. Aldous Huxley, by reason of the insouciant flippance of his fiction. But now he has gone beyond Huxley through the production of a story which, without ever losing wit, dexterity, and instinct for civilized charm, yet presents full length and solidly the portraits not only of the gay countess but of the lugubrious persons whom she is fated to meet, to court, to hurt so pitifully, so inevitably.[72]

The qualities these writers praised in *The Tattooed Countess* were not arrived at without some serious preparation in advance. It was not, like its predecessor, written with the greatest of ease. Carl Van Vechten began by preparing pages of notes, fragments of conversation, remembered incidents and descriptions, bits of information from his youth, all that could lend authority and authenticity to the framework of the novel. There were snatches of popular songs and a compilation of books published during the period (among them *Bel-Ami*, *McTeague*, *The Red Badge of Courage*, which had run serially in the Cedar Rapids newspaper, and Henry Blake Fuller's *Chevalier of Pensieri-Vani*), lists of Iowa jargon, memorable dresses, flower gardens, houses, notes about the Bohemian section of Cedar Rapids, epigrams, and memories. Some of the material was repetitious, but most of it was incorporated into the novel. The result was sufficiently realistic to Carl's family: his Aunt Mary wanted to burn it, and Ralph (who called it a "scream") wrote, "If you don't get murdered when you go to Cedar Rapids I miss my guess."[73]

He missed. Aside from a justifiable chastisement from a Dubuque, Iowa, reader who called Carl's pen "dull and piffling" because he had spoken inadvertently of the corn's being in full bloom during June—a mistake he categorically refused to correct in later printings—there was very little noise from the old folks at home. On a

[72] *Saturday Review of Literature*, August 30, 1924, p. 75.
[73] CVV, NYPL.

visit to Cedar Rapids he discovered several claimants for every character in *The Tattooed Countess*, most of whom he did not even remember. If he had left Cedar Rapids as Gareth, he certainly returned as the Countess—so Carl wrote to several acquaintances when he got back to New York.

On that trip to Iowa, he stopped in Chicago long enough to see Fanny Butcher, who had been, from the beginning, one of his most ardent reviewers and admirers. After he departed, Miss Butcher reported that he was "the last word in cosmopolitanism, reminiscent of what the great world does for the real middle westerner." The sentiment was, curiously, not unlike those expressed by turn-of-the-century townsmen when Ella returned to Maple Valley. The Midwest had not changed very much after all.

The actual process of writing *The Tattooed Countess* took about the same length of time as the earlier novels had. But there were more changes, and the various revisions, though not always so extensive, were always more painstaking; there was more searching for the exact expression, the precise turn of phrase most clearly to establish Carl Van Vechten's growing objectivity. A remark about the Countess' coiffure is an example. In the first draft, he was satisfied with a simple "Her golden-red hair had obviously been dyed"; in the second draft, there was a more precise air of detachment in "Her golden-red hair, parted and waved, quite evidently owed its hue to the art of the dyer"; and in the third draft—not a bad example of what Maugham called avoiding every temptation to force the note—a single change from "dyer" to "hairdresser" effected the subtly sardonic touch maintained so gracefully throughout the novel.

In the beginning, Carl Van Vechten had called his story "Scenes from American Provincial Life in 1897," and the Countess was romantically named Appassionata. Gradually, as the book grew, her past became more sordid, and Gareth, only a shadow at first, more cynical. Progressing through its successive drafts, the novel became more and more a bittersweet tragedy in the guise of humor, rather than the opposite, as it had begun. When the manuscript was

completed in mid-October, Alfred A. Knopf was already prepared
to commit himself on the dust jacket:

> With *The Tattooed Countess* I think Van Vechten takes on a new
> importance as a novelist. . . . Here is a serious, thoroughly original
> and perfectly true picture of American provincial life a generation
> ago. I heartily commend the book to all who have come to admire
> Van Vechten's work in the sure belief that it will not disappoint
> them, for he has lost none of his charm and cunning. *The Tattooed
> Countess* deserves the attention of all who care for the serious Ameri-
> can novel of today. Here I honestly believe you have it at its best.

Two other friends had comments to make on the book, from
even more personal points of view. Mahala Douglas wrote from
California that she had arrived at fame:

> I am known in Hollywood as the Tatooed [*sic*] Countess. Not
> having a tatoo on my person I have been put to great expense and
> pain in having that condition changed. People are so damned curious
> and want to know when and where and how I was tatooed.[74]

And another friend, a writer, confided, *sotto voce*, "God help the
Countess when she gets Gareth to Paris. I've been there with him
and I know."[75]

Almost immediately, Paramount Pictures wrote to Carl that *The
Tattooed Countess* was "sure fire from the box office angle," and
that to bring it up to date for the movies would be "tragic."[76] He
sold the rights without hope of a literal translation. Fania's intrepid
explorations into the early films had given him a fair idea of the
havoc that might result. Further, he had included a ribald sequence about the movies in *The Blind Bow-Boy*, in which Zimbule
and Harold got involved in front of the cameras. Carl could not,
however, have been entirely prepared for what happened to *The
Tattooed Countess*. The title was changed to *A Woman of the
World*, the woman being Pola Negri, a *femme fatale* then fashion-

[74] CVV, NYPL.
[75] Henry A. and Albert W. Berg Collection, New York Public Library (hereafter cited as Berg, NYPL).
[76] Yale.

able in Hollywood. Playing a titled European who comes to America to visit a distant relative by marriage, Miss Negri encounters Chester Conklin, a popular comedian of the period, in a role invented for the movie. Ella is no worldly dowager stalking a cornfed youth—Gareth has about a dozen lines—but instead a black-eyed vamp whose grand passion is the local district attorney. In this Adolph Zukor–Jesse L. Lasky transformation, the Countess sports a skull rather than a motto as tattoo, and, predictably, the scene is updated to the present. At the fadeout, she marries the D.A., and they live happily ever after, but not before (according to the advertisements) "she has lashed him with a blacksnake and taught him to fetch cigarettes."

Carl Van Vechten saw the picture once, gratefully noting that his name in the credits was in relatively small type. When, in 1934, Carmel Myers wrote to him, "Wouldn't The Tattooed Countess make a swell remake?" he did not bother to answer.

THE FINANCIAL SUCCESS of three novels in a row moved Carl and Fania uptown from their East Nineteenth Street flat to larger quarters. But the leave-taking was full of nostalgia. During the several years they had lived in the old "New Yorkish looking brownstone," as Fannie Hurst remembered it, many friends and many books had come and gone. In that sixth-floor garret, Carl had put together his *Music after the Great War* and all the other volumes that followed it, Fania had learned countless roles, and together they had seen the arrival of their own celebrity. But the neighborhood itself was full of friendly memories too: Theda Bara and George Bellows and Elinor Wylie shared the street with the Van Vechtens, and some of the most notorious parties of the whole decade took place next door, where Bob Chanler held his extraordinary entertainments almost nightly.

Chanler, an occasional artist (to be painted by him, Carl later reflected, was a career and a social experience and an education), possessed of apparently unlimited bank accounts, was probably better known for his parties than for his paintings. After one of the frequent gatherings, Ethel Barrymore emerged to declare, "I went there in the evening a young girl and came away in the early morning an old woman."[77] Although Chanler occupied the entire house, he held his ribald soirees on the top floor, adjacent to the Van Vechten's sixth-floor apartment; not unreasonably, they became accustomed to accepting his invitations.

White-haired, white-smocked Bob Chanler was in the habit of inviting thirty or forty people to drop in after the theater for food and drink, served in rooms where silver and magenta fish swam on gold screens, Yorkshire terriers yapped at all intruders and one another, poets wrote verses while perched on top of ladders, ice tinkled continuously in cocktail shakers, and most of the assembled guests joined in violent snake dances that proceeded through various chambers, over beds, up and down flights of stairs, tripping across an occasional prostrate body out cold from Chanler's bootleg liquor. Friends and enemies alike attended, sometimes with disastrous results. E. E. Cummings once unwittingly found himself in the latter category.

He had turned up at a dinner given by Louise Hellström, Chanler's companion of the period. The hostess had set the table with her choicest glasses—Venetian, Bohemian, and Waterford—perhaps six dozen in all. The budding poet arrived, very drunk indeed, took one look at the impressive display, and pulled the tablecloth out from under, sending the glasses crashing to the floor. Chanler knocked him down, sat on him, and proceeded to beat him up. Cummings looked up dazedly and inquired in amazement; "Bob! Are you doing this to *me*?" Later, at Chanler's house, a young Cuban dancer was performing in the salon. Cummings, still drunk, began declaring to anyone who cared to listen that the fellow was a pansy. Some time afterward, Cummings stood chatting fuzzily with Ruth Chatterton when the little Cuban whirled in. Cummings landed one punch before Chanler stormed in, crying, "So this is the way you treat my guests!" and knocked him down again. Carl and Fania, who had witnessed the earlier encounter, stood on the other side of

[77] *Fragments I*, p. 7.

the room with Armina Marshall and Lawrence Langner. Carl said in mock horror: "Let's get out of here. Any minute now, Bob might decide *I'm* impolite!"

IN 1924, CARL AND FANIA moved from East Nineteenth Street to a spacious double apartment on West Fifty-fifth, where, in a black and orange cubist study, and a sea green and purple and raspberry drawing room, they began to emulate the kind of life Carl had invented in *The Blind Bow-Boy*. The twenties may not have roared there, but they sang lustily enough, usually in a minor key. The parties really came into their own a few months later, when Carl began to publicize the sudden interest in Negro arts and letters, and 150 West Fifty-fifth Street became, as Walter White later put it, the midtown branch of the N.A.A.C.P.

If parties were not constant in the new Van Vechten digs, there were always others about, in wide variety: Carl's personal bootlegger ran a speakeasy in the West Forties that served a fair gin; organized literary teas were regularly held under publishers' auspices; there were jaunts up to Harlem—then just being discovered—to investigate the exotic atmosphere and salacious entertainments in Negro clubs; and there were of course plenty of illicit bars around town—momentary oases that quickly appeared and even more quickly disappeared.

New York's Underground Tea Rooms, as they were called in *Vanity Fair*, had become the city's bastard children, spawned by a generation that took its liquor seriously. In damp cellars and brownstone apartments, in abandoned lofts and whole floors of old houses, the dank little clubs rose and fell as regularly as the breathing of their customers. Nobody mourned the demise: the momentary wake quickly turned into a party of its own. In most of these establishments, the washroom, the coatroom, and the cigarette concessions were sold to outside organizations; the costs of the questionable fare in the kitchen—prepared elsewhere and brought in by a catering service—were covered by the menu charges; the cover and minimum paid for the entertainment. So far the whole thing was totally nonprofit; but a markup from sixteen cents to two dollars for a bottle of third-rate booze made the whole endeavor a remarkably worthwhile investment for the owners. When the inevitable raid came, they lost nothing but the rotgut behind the bar.

Gone were the days of the fashionable restaurant and the elegant cabaret; people ate at speakeasies to keep from getting too drunk too soon—and paid for it: $2.50 for a bowl of indifferent chop suey, or a dollar for a club sandwich that might have cost a dime to put together. The cover charges for the floor shows were equally exorbitant, to pay for the rising salaries of performers. Chorus girls, content to prance through a midnight revue for thirty-five dollars a week before the advent of the night club, demanded triple that amount for the same service; the stars of the period drew as much as three thousand dollars; blues singers could command twice as much money for a forty-five-minute stint as they could draw at a theater for a show twice the length. But equally often the speakeasies were simply impersonal rooms with tables and chairs, the real "tearooms" of the times, where one clinked mugs with the celebrated, the not-so-celebrated, and the merely thirsty. It was not unusual to find four or five such bistros in a single short city block; if the owners were privately prepared to supplement the incomes of the mounted policemen who patrolled their area, a club might survive a season. The frequent raids could collapse at the peephole windows in the doors of places that had been warned in advance.

When the parties in New York palled from time to time, as they must have done with repetition, Carl Van Vechten hied himself south to Pennsylvania for a day or a weekend with the Hergesheimers. Occasionally, he traveled even farther south to Richmond, Virginia, to see Emily Clarke and Hunter Stagg of the *Reviewer*, Ellen Glasgow, and James Branch Cabell, whose prose most writers—Carl included—seemed to be imitating.

Carl had first gone to Richmond in November, 1923. He and Cabell were familiar with each other's work through the *Reviewer* and the persuasion of Joseph Hergesheimer. When they finally met, Carl found Cabell "*very* difficult . . . but on the whole we got on better than I expected."[78] A friendship developed rapidly, however, and was insured two years later when they dedicated books to each other. In the interval, there were infrequent formal dinners in Richmond, given by its queen bee, Ellen Glasgow; there was also at least one rambunctious party at Cabell's Dumbarton Grange, attended by Carl, Joseph Hergesheimer, Elinor Wylie, Emily Clarke, and the Knopfs.

On another occasion, Carl and James and Joe met for more sober purposes, as guests of honor at a luncheon given by the Architectural League of Philadelphia. The three were introduced, and each spoke briefly but apparently without much individuality. At the conclusion, one of the members approached Carl with a copy of *Jurgen* under his arm, addressed him as Mr. Cabell, and invited him to sign. Carl was agreeable, and so was James, who signed Carl's name to the architect's copy of *Peter Whiffle*. Then the trio repaired to Richmond to recuperate from the rigors of their performance.

Back in New York, while her husband was investigating Cabell country, Fania Marinoff was gathering some of the best reviews of her career for a stunning performance in *Tarnish*. Interviewed for the *Brooklyn Eagle* by a youthful Nunnally Johnson, she confided how she and Carl kept their home fires burning:

> "It's an ideal combination, in my opinion," Miss Marinoff said in her dressing room at the Belmont Theatre, where she is playing in "Tarnish." She was still in the fancy dress which, as Nettie Dark, she wore in the last act.
>
> "Mr. Van Vechten never has any desire to play a soiled dove for the drama, as I am playing here, and I haven't the faintest ambition to write a story of a tattooed countess as he was just written. Our interests never conflict. We have our separate roads to success and they never cross."[79]

It was, she concluded, an admirable arrangement: Carl never came to the theater during rehearsals; Fania never read his books until they were completed and in page proofs.

[78] Yale.   [79] March 9, 1924.

Judging from the tenor of the times, and Carl's firm entrench-
ment, it is surprising that anything ever got as far as the proof stage.
Like almost everybody else, he drank around the clock, though
more than one friend has recalled that he never seemed to have
suffered from a hangover. Gossip columnists reported that he was
going to write a musical show of backstage life in which Broadway
would be the heroine; he announced a new novel called "The
Divine Monkey," according to another columnist, that would be
about show girls; he attended the theater almost as regularly as he
had during his reviewing days; and, again, like almost everybody
else, he stayed up all night. But his pen was rarely idle, and the call
for copy was fairly constant. By the end of 1924, with *The
Tattooed Countess* in the bookshops and on best-seller lists in a
number of cities across the country, the *American Mercury* could
run Van Vechten essays, like "A Note on Tights" and "A Note on
Breakfasts," that became the subjects of full-length articles in the
New York World and the *National*. (Of "Breakfasts," Mencken
wrote in response to Carl's offer: "Needless to say, I'll be delighted
to see the treatise on breakfasts. A sad subject. I am always sour in
the mornings, and never eat much."[80]

Carl's output at the typewriter was, however, not given over
entirely to such ephemera. He revised *The Tiger in the House* for
a second edition, greatly expanding the already extensive footnotes
in the process; he revised *The Tattooed Countess* for a fourth printing, though the changes were minor and the Iowa corn remained
tasseled in June, in spite of protests from the home town; and he
prepared an introduction for his first bibliography.

The Centaur Book Shop in Philadelphia, which catered to collectors of contemporary writers, had already issued bibliographies
of Hergesheimer, Cabell, Mencken, and Stephen Crane. Three
hundred copies were printed of the one of Carl Van Vechten (including the invariable limited edition); the book listed with painstaking accuracy nearly everything he had written since his days

[80] Yale.

with the *New York Times*. Carl's introduction to the volume was entitled "Overture in the form of a funeral march":

> A casual examination of the record set down . . . in the following pages gives me, quite terrifyingly, the impression that I have been strolling in a graveyard. . . . These, my early books, born too soon, written with too inadequate a skill, collected too indiscriminately from . . . periodicals . . . breathed feebly from the time of their premature birth, exhibiting only occasionally furtive signs of life, and expired, I am convinced, without a murmur, after one small edition was exhausted. Certainly, I did not follow the hearses with a band of crêpe on my arm.[81]

Though some of the prophetic material from the earliest volumes —musical scores for films, space staging décor, the importance of Stravinsky and Strauss, his "interpreters"—did not deserve such harsh treatment, Carl Van Vechten's evaluation was just. Also, at work on a fourth novel (which, assuredly, had nothing at all to do with show girls), he had no time to mourn.

Though written out of chronological order, Carl's first four novels constituted a tetralogy. Clara Barnes, Gareth's adolescent companion and occasional bed partner in the studio-lair behind his house, appears in *Peter Whiffle* as a would-be singer in Paris who becomes Peter's mistress for the better or worse part of a week. In the fourth book—*Firecrackers*—Paul and Campaspe from *The Blind Bow-Boy* and Gareth and Ella from *The Tattooed Countess* are all revived. Chronologically, the quartet of novels had a conceptual order as well, as Carl confided to a friend: *The Tattooed Countess* represented aspiration; the next two, achievement (charm through *Peter Whiffle*, and sophistication through *The Blind Bow-Boy*); and *Firecrackers*, the *Götterdämmerung* of the series, represented disintegration. He wrote about this to Mabel Dodge Luhan as *Firecrackers* reached completion:

> My intention is to create moods, to awaken unconscious echoes of the past, to render to shadows their real importance. I don't think I

[81] P. 5.

ever think of sex at all. It plays around here and there, but that's not what my books are about. They seem to me to be books about a man who is alone in the world and is very sad.[82]

These thoughts were expanded even further in *Firecrackers*. At a cocktail party, Gareth Johns, now a successful writer and not a very happy one, is talking to Campaspe Lorillard about his trade:

> It doesn't seem to occur to the crowd that it is possible for an author to believe that life is largely without excuse, that if there is a God he conducts the show aimlessly, if not, indeed, maliciously, that men and women run around automatically seeking escapes from their troubles and outlets for their lusts. The crowd is still more incensed when an author who believes these things refuses to write about them seriously.[83]

Van Vechten reinforced the contention in his anonymous dust-jacket blurb:

> Another of Carl Van Vechten's unimportant, light novels, disfigured by all of this author's customary annoying mannerisms: choice of a meaningless title, rejection of quotation marks, adoption of obsolete or unfamiliar words, an obstinate penchant for cataloguing, and an apparent refusal to assume a reverent attitude towards the ideals of life which are generally held most precious.

Readers were already well aware of the cataloguing, since it had been going on for twenty years. By 1925, they were used to the deletion of quotation marks around dialogue as well—a practice of George Moore's that Carl had eagerly adopted, probably with an eye toward Gertrude Stein. The title, however, was clearly explained, and readers would have had to be fairly obtuse to miss Gareth Johns's definition, more than adequately borne out by the novel:

> ... you must think of a group of people in terms of a packet of firecrackers. You ignite the first cracker and the flash fires the fuse to the second, and so on, until, after a series of crackling detonations, the

[82] Yale.
[83] *Firecrackers*, pp. 164–165.

167

whole bunch has exploded, and nothing survives but a few torn and scattered bits of paper, blackened with powder. On the other hand, if you fail to apply the match, the bunch remains a collection of separate entities, having no connection one with the other. Explosions which create relationships are sporadic and terminating, but if you avoid the explosions you perdurably avoid intercourse.[84]

Firecrackers was the first of the novels to manipulate several concurrent plots: Roman candles and pinwheels sputter; fountains burst; sparklers flash, most of them lighted by Gunnar O'Grady, a strangely detached fellow who turns up variously as a furnaceman, a florist, a waiter, and an acrobat. Everybody loves him; nobody understands him; everybody pursues him; nobody catches him. When he meets Campaspe Lorillard, however, his composure gives way to hers. In avoiding the sins of her flesh, he turns instead to Wintergreen Waterbury, a kind of second cousin to Lorelei Lee, thus proving himself as human as the rest of the clowns in Van Vechten's circus. There are a lot of them: Paul Moody, Wintergreen's would-be sugar daddy; his elephantine wife Vera; George and Laura Everest and their problem child Consuelo, a real terror who wears sables and orchids and who seems to be as well read as Carl Van Vechten; too many others. There are further involvements with Campaspe's husband Cupid and Paul in big business on Wall Street, with the Pinchon Prophylactic Plan for physical fitness, with echoes of Carl's own trumped-up adultery charge, with the death of the Countess Nattatorini.

In spite of its diffuse structure, *Firecrackers* reflects the twenties with more accuracy than exaggeration. As Louis Bromfield noted in his review, "Mr. Van Vechten is not ponderous in his books, but he comes much nearer to depicting the American scene than many a laborious corn-fed realist."[85]

Perhaps the academies are unwilling to acknowledge the Van Vechten confections as more than sweet-tooth pacifiers because the books are outwardly so frivolous; but the frivolity, so frequently

[84] *Ibid.*, pp. 167–168.
[85] *Bookman*, August, 1925.

chastised, is their ultimate strength. The laughter is hollow. If the point of view of the writers of the twenties was often uncomfortably close to their work—one need only look at the early Fitzgerald —Carl Van Vechten denied it consistently, after a single brush with first-person narrative in *Peter Whiffle*. The observer was detached and omniscient, reporting ironically, but with a constant awareness of the implications. It is, of course, true that the line separating the narrator from his material was occasionally very fine indeed, since so much of the life he chronicled he had created himself. But in the middle of the swim, he had learned how to tread water. No one denies that the twenties worshiped sophistication and modernity— the first demanding style, and the second requiring a constant switch in fads—but if this is true, no one can easily deny that Carl Van Vechten realized it, particularly in view of *Firecrackers*. Similarly, the amorality never overstepped its own boundary lines. He may have written of people devoted to the uninhibited moment, but his interest and affection did not prevent his exposure of their follies. The characters in *Firecrackers* desperately try to outdo one another in perversity and novelty; Carl Van Vechten, reigning over them, derived his own pleasure from an observation made by Campaspe: "It is only . . . those who expected to find amusement in themselves who wandered about disconsolate and bored. Amusement was derived from watching others, when one permitted them to be entirely themselves."[86]

In this, Carl Van Vechten was able to view his subjects with the heavy irony that permeated the memorable cocktail party given by Mrs. Humphry Pollanger, a wealthy follower of the arts. Her husband has just offered a group of his guests a carafe of liquor that he says is 1804 Napoleon brandy, in the middle of the Prohibition era a rare treat for throats corroded by bootleg gin:

> Silent now, each with a glass to his nose, they savoured the rich aroma.
>
> Great stuff, old fellow! Jack's was the first appreciation. Napoleonic, you said?

[86] *Firecrackers*, p. 210.

Yes, I think so. Mr. Humphry Pollanger's face was the façade of his delight. . . .

They all took a sip.

Um.

Um.

Um.

Um . . . .

Marvelous.

Delicious.

Exquise.

An expression of doubt shadowed the face of Mr. Humphrey Pollanger. He held the carafe at arm's length between his eyes and a lamp. Then he sniffed at the unstopped neck. I'm not sure . . . he explained hesitantly. There were two carafes on the shelf. One of them certainly contains 1804 brandy. The other holds some whisky left over from our bootlegger's latest call.

Don't worry, old chap. Jack gave his . . . host a slap on the shoulder. Can't you tell brandy when you drink it? Cognac, fine champagne, that's what this is!

I'm not so sure . . . I think this is the whisky!

Of *course*, this is brandy, George asserted.

Paul executed a few steps of the Charleston while Mr. Pollanger made another hurried journey to his store of supplies. Presently he returned with a second carafe. He held the two to the light together, comparing them one with the other. Precisely the same colour, he muttered in despair.

Well, just to convince you, I'll try a little of the other, was Jack's handsome offer. He extended his empty goblet. This time he did not wait to enjoy the bouquet. He swallowed the contents in one gulp. Whisky! he sputtered. The first was brandy.

I think, Mr. Pollanger put forward timidly, after sampling a drink from the new bottle, that *this* is the brandy.

Whisky!

Brandy!

Let me try the first carafe again, Jack urged.

Madame Madrilena was working on the second. I think this *is* the brandy, she averred.

Let *me* try the new kind, George suggested. . . .

Campaspe was experimenting with the second bottle. Why, they're both the same! she announced.

I think I can tell cognac when I drink it, Jack insisted hotly. The first was cognac, the second Scotch. . . .

Brandy! Nonsense, Jack! You're so squiffy you'd call absinthe brandy. . . .

The second carafe contains the cognac, Mr. Pollanger persisted, almost as if someone had hurt him. . . .

The *first* is cognac. I ought to be able to know cognac, Jack cried. Napoleonic cognac, at that.

Don't be an ass, Jack. They're both Scotch.

I think they're both fine champagne, Madame Madrilena insisted. . . .

One of 'em is brandy. . . . Poor Mr. Pollanger was ready to weep. . . . I'm certain one of 'em is brandy.

I've got it! cried George. We'll ask the barkeeps. They're sure to know. . . .

The servants readily agreed to decide the matter, but when George handed them the carafes it was discovered that both were empty.[87]

Carl Van Vechten completed *Firecrackers* in four months, which fact probably accounts for its fragmentation as the various plot lines develop. The cohesiveness of the earlier books is absent; in its place is a chapter-to-chapter shift that severely weakens its purpose rather than, as he must have intended, strengthening it.

Conversely, individual sections are superb, and a particularly shrewd and unnerving chapter about the death of the Countess is shattering. Amid the poppings of several kinds of fireworks, she reappears, an old woman, her lovers and her beauty behind her, in a scene of bittersweet irony. But, if ironic, the scene refuted a note written to Hugh Walpole about the same time, in which Carl lamented that the one thing he regretted was that he could not write a sentimental novel. The Countess's lust denies her death any dignity, leaving only a repellent fascination. No better off than Lennie Colman, she rouses herself for a last coquettish attempt, convinced

87 *Ibid.*, pp. 157–161.

that the priest—on his way to perform final rites—will be another beautiful youth. Once again, she prepares for the assault, painting her wasted face with cosmetics, strewing the bed with flowers. But the Countess is doomed to disappointment: the holy father who arrives is an old man. "Goya," said Carl Van Doren "never drew a more ghastly picture."[88]

The contract for *Firecrackers* was witnessed by James Branch Cabell, who was "wholly proud to be the dedicatee."[89] The novel appeared in August, 1925, in a trade edition of ten thousand copies—larger than that of any of the earlier books. There was also a limited edition in red and yellow decorated boards and a black spine. The noncollector settled for a *Firecrackers* bound in bright yellow cloth stamped in red.

Henry Blake Fuller, like Cabell, was delighted by the novel: "It's fine, of course, to have a broad, symmetrical plan to please the author himself; but it's a little more important . . . to beguile the reader along, paragraph by paragraph and page by page, and that gift you have."[90]

Uncle Charlie, always interested over the years in his nephew's work, was disconcerted:

> . . . Firecrackers [comes] to assure me that you are still alive and kicking. Why do you do it? i.e. kick. Your last three novels seem to show that you look upon human life as a sort of egregarious blunder on the part of the infinite powers of the universe. . . . Look up, dear boy—not persistently down. Altruism is better than anarchism.[91]

Carl's father did not at first even trust himself to write. "I expect to get a copy of . . . [the] new book soon," he wrote to Fania instead. "He thinks I won't like it—It is decidedly funny how he hates to have me criticize anything he writes—& I have promised hereafter to say nothing except I can say something good. For the boy is very dear to me."[92]

88 *New York Herald Tribune Books*, August 23, 1925.
89 CVV, NYPL.
90 CVV, NYPL.
91 CVV, NYPL.
92 CVV, NYPL.

F. Scott Fitzgerald confided in a friend that he thought the book was *"lousy,"* but he skirted this opinion by writing that he thought it was equal to *The Blind Bow-Boy* and better than the other two novels.

The reviews were contradictory, but that pattern had, by 1925, become standard for Van Vechten novels. The *Tribune* review objected to the book's subtitle—A Realistic Novel—because the same claim could have been made by Lewis Carroll for *Alice in Wonderland*; Donald Douglas, in the *Nation*, before he could have read the *Tribune*, spoke of "the deliberate method and procedure of *Alice in Wonderland*," using verbal fantasies for verbal escapades, and thought Van Vechten "quite right in calling *Firecrackers* a realistic novel. The thing is realistic for its own purposes."[93] H. L. Mencken's dissenting comments were remarkably flat: perhaps he was "out of the mood," he wrote, for the usual pleasures he derived from the "intricate and sanitary adulteries" of the "Van Vechten marionettes . . . frolicking happily in a Christian and infamous world."[94]

The reception given *Parties* a few years later seems already anticipated in the varying reactions to *Firecrackers*: those who liked the book admired it for the wrong reasons; those who disliked it found it too close to their own lives. Once again, Carl Van Doren supplied the most perceptive analysis, this time in the *New York Herald Tribune Books*:

> Is it because Mr. Van Vechten's fancy is really less wayward than austere that his austerest novel is, so far, his best? For the most part, his technique is not well in hand. He has hit upon a world in which his imagination moves easily. He has invented a language which is his and no one else's. . . . Within the limits of his interest, which means also his capacities, almost anything may be henceforth expected of him.[95]

An echo of Van Doren's words came in a letter from Elinor Wylie soon after the review had been printed: "Long before Carl

[93] October 28, 1925.
[94] *American Mercury*, November, 1925.
[95] August 23, 1925.

Van Doren called it austere, I called it tragic. It really is almost un-
bearably tragic; I expected the wit & glitter, but not the dark other
side of the coin."[96]

Miss Wylie's pronouncement contained more truth than could
have been perceived in 1925. The brittle ironies of *Firecrackers*
clearly anticipated the end of the run in 1929, when the impending
depression put almost all the writers of Carl Van Vechten's splendid
drunken twenties between seasons, and those who attempted a
comeback during the thirties died at the box office. Whether they
realized it or not in 1925, everybody was already growing a little
tired of the Fourth of July.

[96] CVV, NYPL.

VII

Some Archaeology, Past and Present

Fame is a quaint, old-fashioned lady who loves to be pursued by the living. She seldom, if ever, runs after anybody save in her favourite role of necrophile.

A FEW MONTHS BEFORE *Firecrackers* was released, Knopf issued a book of Van Vechten reprints, entitled *Red*, "the colour of youth. Oxen and turkeys are always enraged when they see it."[1] The dust-jacket blurb explained the contents to readers familiar only with the author's fiction:

> Before Carl Van Vechten began to write novels he was widely known as an eminent and radical critic of music. This volume contains a collection of his best papers on that subject, three of which, together with the introduction, have never before appeared in a book.

Knopf bound a few extra copies uncut, with a binding a quarter of an inch taller than the red-clothed covers of the trade edition. There was, however, no demand for a second printing. In spite of the three years of popularity for its author, the contention in the introduction to *Red*—that musical criticism was poorly paid because it was poorly read—was once again borne out. Even the favorable reviews did not help much, though so solid a critic as Ernest Boyd, in the *Independent*, called its sophisticated culture "broad and genuine."

Nothing from *Music after the Great War* was reprinted, understandably; Schirmer insisted on keeping the whole volume in print, much to Carl's chagrin. From *Music and Bad Manners*, however, he culled "Music for the Movies." Two other papers on music and the motion picture appeared as well: "The Importance of Electrical

1 Robert Schumann, quoted in *Red*, p. vii.

175

Picture Concerts," which had caused a hullabaloo getting printed seven years earlier in *Seven Arts*; and a relatively new piece, "Movies for Program Notes," which had been printed in 1922 in *Wave*, a short-lived little magazine in Chicago. From the other early books on music, he lifted seven articles, and concluded the new volume with two others, "On Hearing What You Want When You Want It" and "Cordite for Concerts," each of which gave some indication of his abandonment of musical criticism as a career. *Red* contained, as the introduction said, "such papers as I care to preserve, save for a few dealing with specific composers, later to find their niches in a book to be entitled *Excavations*, which will also include papers on certain figures in the literary world."[2]

Excavations appeared under Knopf's imprint in 1926, and included, as Carl had promised readers, a quartet of articles on composers he had chosen to resurrect from obscurity: Léo Delibes, Sir Arthur Sullivan, Isaac Albéniz, and Erik Satie. The first had been printed in *Musical Quarterly* in 1922, the second and third in *In the Garret*, and the fourth in *Interpreters and Interpretations*. These were not essays in criticism, but papers "to provoke the reader to share my own enthusiasm for certain, at the time of writing, more or less obscure figures,"[3] as Carl confessed in his brief "proem." As usual, he charmed without converting and enchanted without really inciting to revolution; perhaps that was only part of the method— to light upon the oddity, the rarity, to publicize the *outré*, to cultivate the forgotten, the unusual, the undiscovered.

Out of books as well as in them, however, the concentrated effort to propagandize was less than circumspect: Carl and Fania and Alla Nazimova standing up to cry, "bravo!" at seventeen-year-old Leonard Sillman's tap dancing at the Palace; Carl organizing— and publicizing—some Charleston classes for Fania and Anita Loos and the Gish sisters; Carl's inclusion of Sigmund Freud, James Joyce, and D. H. Lawrence in his list of "Ten Dullest Authors" for a *Vanity Fair* symposium.

The blue-cloth-bound *Excavations* and its inevitable limited edi-

2 *Red*, p. xvi.   3 *Excavations*, p. ix.

tion included two other musical papers: a reprint of his piece on Sophie Arnould, which, in 1919, had served as a preface to Philip Moeller's play; and "Oscar Hammerstein: An Epitaph," a nostalgic portrait of the head of the Manhattan Opera House during Carl's salad days with the *New York Times*, which the *Nation* called "valuable as biography and moving as characterization."[4]

On the whole, *Excavations* impressed the critics. The pieces were "still interesting and entertaining" to the *Herald Tribune*; in London, the *Saturday Review* complimented backhandedly, "The worst that can be said of the author is that, while he never fails to interest, he does not convince."[5] It is unlikely that Carl had hoped to convince as late as 1926: the epigraph, a quotation from Walter Pater, said clearly what he had hoped to achieve; certainly, he did not proselytize:

> But, besides those great men, there is a certain number of artists who have a distinct quality of their own by which they convey to us a peculiar quality of pleasure which we cannot get elsewhere; and these, too, have their place in general culture, and must be interpreted to it by those who have felt their charm strongly, and are often the objects of a special diligence and a consideration wholly affectionate, just because there is not about them the stress of a great name and authority.[6]

As a footnote, it should be remembered that, as a result of Carl's own "special diligence," some of his excavated writers experienced a rebirth in popularity if not an initial one in some instances. The twenties saw a real interest in the work of Ronald Firbank and Edgar Saltus and Arthur Machen. Later generations are indebted to Carl Van Vechten for having been present at the exhuming of Herman Melville, almost forgotten until 1921, when the digging began.

AMONG THE OTHER AMERICAN WRITERS Carl Van Vechten excavated was Henry Blake Fuller, a Chicago novelist-essayist-poet,

---

[4] August 11, 1926.   [5] Edward Shanks, July 10, 1926.   [6] *Excavations*, p. vii.

"perhaps not the greatest of living American novelists," Carl wrote in an article for the *Double Dealer* in 1922, "but certainly one of the most original and distinguished."[7]

During the preparation of the article, Fuller had written to Carl, "No further novels likely: too much effort and too little return."[8] When the piece appeared in print: "I feel excavated indeed. Notes and additions have brought me—like a favored tut or a Carthage *reconnaissante*—still further into the light of day. . . . You . . . have done for me what scarcely anyone else has ever thought to do."[9]

The article did not boost Fuller's sales appreciably, either in its periodical or *Excavations* appearance, but it did make readers aware of a novelist who wrote as superbly of Italy as he did of the Chicago society matrons at whom Carl had poked fun during his "Chaperone" days on the *Chicago American*. "Quietly amusing and gently melancholy," Henry Blake Fuller was a writer whose sweep was never grand, whose genre was the miniature. Carl Van Vechten said, "In spite of the depressing consistency of my experience in this regard, I still wax melancholy when I recall how many literary reputations lie buried in America, a country which seems to derive a perverse pleasure from indulgence in necrophilic auctorial amours —the longer the bones have bleached the better."[10] Readers familiar with the literary tastes of Peter Whiffle and Gareth Johns could recall that Fuller's *The Chevalier of Pensieri-Vani* was never very far away. But in addition to "the fortunate moment and the felicitous hand"[11] felt in that book and several others, Carl Van Vechten called attention to *Bertram Cope's Year*, a novel of great skill and subtlety about latent homosexuality, and to the ironies of *Under the Skylights* and *With the Procession*.

A critic on one of the Chicago newspapers said, in response to a query of Carl's, that Fuller was a "charming person, not very talka-

---

[7] June, 1922, p. 289.
[8] Yale.
[9] CVV, NYPL.
[10] *Excavations*, p. 129.
[11] *Ibid.*, p. 147.

tive." Later, when Carl asked if a meeting might be arranged, he was advised, rather apologetically, that Fuller rarely went out, that he was a recluse, that he dreaded encounters with strangers. They did meet, nevertheless, through the courtesy of Robert Morss Lovett, whom Carl had known at the University of Chicago, and the "encounter" proved the beginning of a pleasant relationship, carried on primarily by mail. Until his death in 1929, Fuller corresponded regularly with Carl, admiring his books, grateful for his own resurrection.

Continuing his plea for attention to forgotten writers, Carl wrote, in his essay on Fuller, "With my own hands I have exhumed the skeleton of Edgar Saltus, arranging its fantastic contours in a corner of my museum, with the satisfactory result that the author . . . has become a favourite with 'collectors,' and is even read belatedly by a few adventurous spirits."[12]

The Van Vechten paper on Saltus, originally printed in *The Merry-Go-Round* in 1918, occasioned two letters from music critic James Huneker, who had promised himself, twenty years earlier, "the pleasure of writing a definitive article on Edgar. . . . Now you have done it and beautifully. . . . Edgar is a genius. George Moore once told me that Walt Whitman and Saltus were the only two Americans he read."[13]

Edgar Saltus, born in 1855, had made several appearances in *Town Topics*, a magazine that followed the gradual fading of the yellow nineties. (The periodical should not be confused with the later gossip column that often reported on the activities of Carl and Fania and the various sets with which they were identified from their meeting in 1912 into the twenties.) A writer of fiction, history, poetry, criticism, and philosophy, Edgar Saltus drifted toward oblivion long before Carl Van Vechten first wrote about him. In 1907, Elbert Hubbard—somewhere between limp leather covers—had called Saltus "the best writer in America—with a few insignificant exceptions"; although Carl Van Vechten neglected to mention

[12] *Ibid.*, p. 129.
[13] *Ibid.*, p. 91 n.

179

Hubbard's exceptions, he could find no mention of Saltus else-where. When Van Vechten's paper on Saltus appeared in 1918, "the best writer in America" had staled in a forgotten larder. Van Vechten praised the style, of which Oscar Wilde had complained because passion struggled with grammar on every page. But Carl admired the same things that might later be easily said of his own characters in his novels about the decade just ready to begin:

> There is no poverty in his fictions. His creatures do not toil. Usually, they cut coupons off bonds. Sometimes they write or paint, but for the most part they are free to devote themselves exclusively to the pursuit of the emotional experience, eating, drinking, reading, and travelling the while.[14]

Although they corresponded for a time—Saltus addressing his letters to "Dear Mr. Van Vechten," "Dear Interpreter," "Dear Friend," "Dear Genius"—they met only once, after a series of attempts aborted by Saltus' being "gripped and shelved" with ill health. The encounter took place at the Manhattan Club over whiskey and soda. Saltus was an oddly distinguished figure, something of a dandy, Carl remembered, and probably handsome in his youth. "He really *looked* like a man of letters. He is the only author I have ever seen who did."[15] Saltus was by turns sensitive and cynical, inspiring and malicious. That afternoon, he presented Carl with the manuscript of one of his floridly purple romances, a work of his vintage years called "The Paliser Case," hoping for publication by Alfred A. Knopf. Carl wisely demurred after reading the work, and he and the "paradoxical combination of Beau Brummel, Don Juan, and Saint Francis of Assisi"[16] went their separate ways.

In the *Excavations* paper on Herman Melville, Carl Van Vechten turned his attention to a writer who was already undergoing an excavation. In 1921, when he reviewed Raymond Weaver's biography of Melville, *Mystic and Mariner*, for the *Literary Review*, his own article had recently been written and sold to *Double Dealer*, though it was published a month after the Weaver book.

14 *Ibid.*, p. 102.   15 *Ibid.*, p. 93n.   16 *Ibid.*, p. 94 n.

Some Archaeology, Past and Present

Moby Dick had already been rediscovered and accorded a higher station than it had enjoyed during its author's life, but Carl noted that, as late as 1920, first editions of the novel could be picked up for fifty cents or a dollar at the secondhand bookstalls in New York. *Billy Budd* had not yet been unearthed, and the critics—Weaver and Carl Van Doren among them—had dismissed Melville's last novels as second rate. But it was toward these books that Carl directed his attention.

> After Moby Dick . . . [Melville] devoted himself to subjective rather than objective creation, and from this time on he lost credit with public and critics alike. His very next work, indeed, Pierre, or the Ambiguities infuriated the reviewers and drove them to devastating tongue-lashings. The clergy and the one hundred per-cent Americans assisted at the lynching. . . .[17]

> Let us bear in mind Melville's struggle for faith and the apparent collapse of his career as we approach The Confidence Man, his last extended work in prose. . . .[18]

> Readers who are satisfied to stop with Moby Dick will not understand his later life, but those who go on through Israel Potter and The Confidence Man will get a clearer picture of his bitterness and unhappy striving.[19]

He was convinced, moreover, that the day would come when the final novels of Herman Melville would be preferred, just as the later Henry James was proving to be.

> It is possible that the delay in appreciation of the later works has been occasioned by the fact that . . . the public was not ripe for the richer undercurrents inherent therein. These books cannot be investigated by the aid of the critical jargon ordinarily applicable to works of art: they are the man himself.[20]

At about the same time, Carl began to encourage friends of his to investigate Melville's later efforts: "I wish you could read . . . Pierre!! Such a book for 1851. It has never been republished. Moby

[17] *Ibid.*, p. 79–80.   [18] *Ibid.*, p. 87.
[19] *Ibid.*, p. 88.   [20] *Ibid.*, p. 72.

Dick will give you thrills, but not quite such good ones. . . . I am writing about Ouida. I shall gradually work up to 1921! The past is always so amusing in terms of the present."[21]

WITH OUIDA (Louise de la Ramée), Carl Van Vechten's *Excavations* turned toward England to discover a "belated literary liaison." He had a good time ranking her not far below Dickens and Thackeray and "considerably above the turgid George Eliot,"[22] all of which is a clue to his method: in his essays, in his novels, in his journalism, and in his appreciations, Carl *always* had a good time. That both contemporary and subsequent critics were not always able to take his pronouncements seriously may indeed be more their fault than his.

As for Ouida, that "vain, capricious, obstinate, and foolishly proud" lady he had first introduced to his readers in a preface to her *In a Winter City*, he was deadly honest in his adoration and amusement. In dozens of ornate novels of pencil-slender heroes and haunted sirens, she was verbose ("but . . . only for the purpose, Ouida almost convinced herself, of showing the reader how empty is the life of the very rich"[23]); she was redundant ("but how delightful to read an author that one may skip occasionally"[24]); she was compelling ("Ouida wrote of a life she hungered to enjoy. . . . which, even when she most moralized over its fatal rottenness, has almost persuaded me that the life of the idle English is the life for me"[25]). Moreover, he praised her essays in criticism and her influence on a world that had unwittingly adopted the requirements of her fiction:

> Ouida's society is a little wickeder, a little gayer, a little richer than the real thing, but heaven knows that society since her day has done its best to live up to her specifications. Lanky guardsmen with their wasp-waists, the vampire of the silver screen, these we owe to Ouida's imagination.[26]

[21] Yale.

[22] *Excavations*, p. 64.

[23] *Ibid.*, p. 52.

[24] *Ibid.*, p. 55.

[25] *Ibid.*, pp. 52–53.

[26] *Ibid.*, p. 61.

The piece prompted a letter from Arthur Davison Ficke: "You have led at least one unwilling mortal to the edge of Ouida's infinite seas. What a hell of an old girl she is! One starts to laugh, and remains to bray, and God knows just how one finishes!"[27] But Carl's Uncle Charlie decided that the lady was simply tiresome: "It is not enough to say that a room is . . . sumptuously furnished; she has to tell you every damned thing in it. . . . One . . . must wade through endless pages . . . to come to where the King says to the Countess, 'Good morning,' or something equally thrilling."[28] The letters, nevertheless, seemed to bear out a remark of G. K. Chesterton's that Carl included in his paper, "Though it is impossible not to smile at Ouida, it is equally impossible not to read her."[29]

Another English writer came into Carl Van Vechten's orbit, shortly after he discovered Ouida, by way of Hugh Walpole. One February afternoon in 1923, they sat in Carl's yellow library discussing books. Walpole, a temperate Englishman, restricted his refreshment to apples; Carl poured bootleg gin and ginger beer together for himself, reflecting that the ginger beer at least was genuine. His guest's eyes roved over the various collections on the shelves: a row of Melville's works—all, except *Typee*, there in first editions; two shelves of Arthur Machen, including his multi-volumed translation of Casanova (another of Carl's discoveries); a set of Ouida's three-volume novels, bound in battered rust and green bindings; the Saltus shelf; the Fuller books; a few pamphlets and volumes by Gertrude Stein; half a dozen black-bound novels by Ronald Firbank.

Hugh Walpole turned to his host and commented, "just a little triumphantly," Carl recalled, that there was not a single volume by Matthew Phipps Shiel in the room. "I should think," Walpole continued, "that you, who pride yourself on a knowledge of all the byways and crannies of exotic literature, would know at least a little about a strange fellow like M. P. Shiel. . . . His range covers

[27] CVV, NYPL.
[28] CVV, NYPL.
[29] *Excavations*, p. 49.

183

the globe, civilized and uncivilized; his imagination runs a race with facts and beats them." Shortly thereafter, having finished his apple, he departed.[30]

Between then and Walpole's next visit, Carl had ferreted out ten of nearly two dozen books by Shiel. At first his enthusiasm was qualified, and after three novels he was ready to give up. Then he discovered *The Purple Cloud* and *The Lord of the Sea*, and the obscure English exotic had a new champion.

The *Excavations* article on Shiel served first as a preface—"to be read, if ever, only after you have read The Lord of the Sea"[31]— when Knopf issued that novel in America in 1924. A writer whose "imagination and fancy are boundless," Shiel would require readers to "acquaint themselves with several . . . [novels] before they can appreciate with any exactitude the magic of this writer or can capitulate to his special charm."[32] Readers responded sufficiently for Knopf to reissue *The Lord of the Sea* a few years later in his small-format Blue Jade Series (which title Carl had suggested); in 1924, Knopf also issued Shiel's *Children of the Wind*. Carl once spent an afternoon in London with Shiel, the only time they ever met; but for many years thereafter they corresponded, usually about each other's books or their mutual admiration for Arthur Machen, another of Carl's "little known exotics."

Of his own appearance in *Excavations*, Machen, "Dreamer and Mystic," as Carl called him, wrote:

> I was saying to my wife, after reading some of it: "The fact is, Van Vechten likes reading things that other people won't read; that's why he likes reading me."[33]

Carl's essay first appeared in the *International Book Review*. Conceding that a mystic writer had precious little to say to the man in the street or the idle bystander, he nevertheless bemoaned the indifference of the public toward *The Hill of Dreams*, Machen's

---

30 *Ibid.*, p. 149.
31 M. P. Shiel, *The Lord of the Sea*, p. v.
32 *Excavations*, p. 152.
33 CVV, NYPL.

best book. But this particular excavation was almost a two-man chore. Although Van Vechten encouraged and Knopf published, the response was scarcely robust. In an earlier era, it is possible that the literary tastes of that idle bystander of whom Carl wrote might have turned in Machen's direction. During the fickle twenties, however, readers were more attuned to another of Carl Van Vechten's discoveries, Ronald Firbank.

He had first come across this curious writer's work through *Valmouth*, a 1918 novella handed him by Stuart Rose at a party given by the Knopfs. An author *sui generis*, but with some few roots in Jane Austen and Thomas Love Peacock and Oscar Wilde, Ronald Firbank had been issuing annual volumes through Grant Richards's publishing house in London for several years, at his own expense. They did not sell out their first editions, appealing only to a small coterie of readers who were willing to pore through the perverse innuendo, the maddening ellipses, the pages of preciously wicked dialogue. In recent years, Firbank has been given serious evaluation by Edmund Wilson, Osbert Sitwell, Anthony Powell, E. M. Forster, W. H. Auden, and Ernest Jones; but in the early twenties he was read only by the fashionable intelligentsia, primarily through Van Vechten's press-agentry.

When *Excavations* appeared, Firbank wrote to Carl: "A thousand salaams for 'Excavations' just come, I shall read it with delight —not least the chapter on Ronald."[34] But the note was from a pen pal by that time, if that innocent moniker can be applied to somebody as strange as Firbank. Carl had written him in 1922 for information in anticipation of an article for *Double Dealer*. Firbank replied on the large heliotrope cards he used invariably for letters and occasionally for stories. The correspondence blossomed, though most of the plants were characteristically hothouse variety: "I usually write with purple ink. . . . I am older than this, but only admit to 19. . . . My books in England are a cult."[35] When Carl sent him a copy of *Peter Whiffle*, Firbank hoped it would be "revealing, with subterranean touches. . . ."[36]

[34] Berg, NYPL. [35] Berg, NYPL. [36] Berg, NYPL.

Before he first wrote Carl had, however, gone ahead with his plans for the *Double Dealer* article. It appeared in April, 1922, and Carl received twenty-five copies in lieu of payment. A second article appeared the following year in the *Herald Tribune*:

> Sophisticated virgins and demi-puceaux will adore these romances. Married or unmarried persons over thirty will find them either shocking or tiresome, according to the individual temperament of the readers. I have a suspicion that a few delightful old ladies will enjoy a quiet closet-laugh on the sly. These novels are not suitable for public libraries and Brander Matthews and William Lyons Phelps will never review them.[37]

Then Carl arranged a publication in the *Reviewer*, Emily Clarke's Virginia periodical that had so often called upon him for material. Though the staff was not convinced, Ronald was willing: "I lately began you a conte called The Story of Percy Eton and Eunice Cutbush, but Eunice grew *too* terrible, and Percy took to his heels."[38] Finally the *Reviewer* agreed to print a chapter of a new novel, but Firbank procrastinated: "It is stupid being so helpless but I cannot type, which must be so nice, especially when one's hand writing gets depraved."[39] Eventually, the chapter did arrive at the office of the *Reviewer*, typed professionally and tied up in a lavender ribbon by the author.

In 1924, Firbank's *Sorrow in Sunlight* was published in New York by Brentano's, somewhat tastelessly retitled *Prancing Nigger*, at Carl's suggestion, and prefaced with "An Icing for a Chocolate Eclair," in which he likened the novel to a Freudian dream illustrated by Alastair and set to music by George Gershwin. It was probably Carl's preface that inspired the flurry of plans to dramatize the book, with Gershwin songs and an elaborate production by the Theatre Guild. The financial risk involved ultimately cancelled the idea, but *Prancing Nigger* did insure other American editions of Firbank's books, and, additionally, it brought the author his first

37 *Excavations*, pp. 171–172.
38 Berg, NYPL.
39 Berg, NYPL.

Anna May Wong, 1932.

Judith Anderson, 1932.

Helen Morgan in *Showboat*, 1932.

H. L. Mencken, 1932.

George Gershwin, 1933.

Eugene O'Neill, 1933.

Carl Van Vechten, self-portrait, 1934.

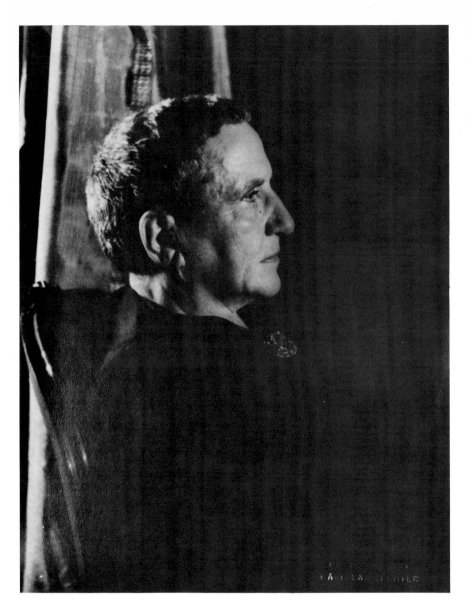

Gertrude Stein, 1934.

Talullah Bankhead, 1934.

Bessie Smith, 1936.

Fania Marinoff as Mrs. Frail in *Love for Love*, 1936.

Thomas Wolfe, 1937.

F. Scott Fitzgerald, 1937.

Thomas Mann, 1937.

Joseph B. Louis, 1941.

Marc Chagall, 1941.

remunerations. Some time earlier he had mentioned to Carl "the sordid and unattractive side of authorship that's best never mentioned. . . ." But he could just as quickly chastise himself for complaining: "What is nine years, anyway, to a publisher, & you will think me impatient & mercenary—But you see I have never made yet a sou in my life, & hate being deprived of a new sensation."[40]

The reviews of *Prancing Nigger* were mixed. Joseph Wood Krutch and Ben Ray Redman wrote serious evaluations, but the *Brooklyn Eagle* complained: "Silly. Bevo-naughtiness. Highly praised by Carl Van Vechten." The novel had a fashionable popularity, nevertheless. When *The Flower beneath the Foot* appeared in America, Firbank remembered the dissenting opinions, and wrote:

> Dear Carl I owe you endless things & my distress would be acute if arrows meant for me went astray. You know my books are quite unconventional, & shock a lot of people . . . & you were brave to champion them. . . . I mean to send you my photograph as San Sebastian, all darts, and reading the Brooklyn Eagle.[41]

In the fall of 1925, there were plans for an American novel, according to another lavender letter, about Negro Aunt Andromeda and her friend Mrs. Storykoff, married to a Pole who ran a dope den off Gramercy Park. There were even plans for Firbank to come to New York to round up material, but these never materialized; the novel was left unfinished when he died in 1926, of tuberculosis. His last letter to Carl came from the Libyan desert, where he was "pitching a parasol," and frivolously lamenting his self-styled life:

> It seems queer for a single soul like me to be writing on a clear moonlit night to one away in the far Americas. . . . I am a spinster, sir, & by God's grace, intend to stay so; I have just been exploring the hotel lobby & [got] left behind . . . by Napoleon's army after the

40 Berg, NYPL.
41 Berg, NYPL.

battle of the Pyramids. Adios, Don Carlos, et bonne nuit. Ronald. The Sphinx has caught a cold.[42]

CARL VAN VECHTEN uncovered several others, even though they did not appear in his 1926 volume. When *Jennifer Lorn,* by his friend Elinor Wylie, threatened to expire for lack of readers in 1923, he said in a review for *Dial* that it was the "only successfully sustained satire in English with which I am acquainted. . . . A permanent masterpiece."[43] Miss Wylie was more or less compelled to inscribe his copy of her novel, "For Carl Van Vechten, without whom this book would never have been read."

He wrote a paper in recognition of Ernest Newman, the English music critic who had continued when Carl had stopped trying to cure the world's musical ills. When Knopf issued a handsome volume of drawings by Alastair, the German artist, which included illustrations for *The Blind Bow-Boy,* Carl supplied the introduction. And for another artist—this time a composer—he performed a different kind of service, one indeed that harkened back to his stint as Luisa Tetrazzini's ghost writer: "I am working on a nasty piece of work," he complained to a friend, "which I am sorry I ever promised to undertake, rewriting a bad translation from the Russian and editing it generally."[44] This referred to *My Musical Life,* the long-winded autobiography of Rimsky-Korsakoff. It was published in America and England in 1924 and, in spite of its shortcomings, was revised and reissued during the late thirties.

Carl's attention was of a more personal nature for Miguel Covarrubias, whose work he first popularized in 1923. The young Mexican painter had recently arrived in New York and was brought around one afternoon by a friend to meet Carl. "He has nothing to show editors but caricatures of Mexicans, unknown here," the friend confessed. "If you like his designs, I thought perhaps you might introduce him to some New York subjects."[45]

42 Berg, NYPL.
43 March, 1924, p. 283.
44 Yale.
45 "Preface," *The Prince of Wales and Other Famous Americans,* p. [7].

Some Archaeology, Past and Present

Carl discovered, through a "volley of quite unrecognizable English," that Covarrubias had recently been staying in Mexico with Witter Bynner and D. H. Lawrence; he had not bothered to draw them, he said, because he was unaware of their celebrity. But he drew Carl that afternoon, and the result prompted the subject to telephone Mencken, Waldo Frank, Avery Hopwood, and Eva Le Gallienne for appointments. As soon as Covarrubias had drawn a few local faces, Carl took him to lunch at the Algonquin, and another career was launched. In the next few years, he produced two volumes of drawings and illustrated a third, designed the scenery and costumes for the Theatre Guild's production of *Androcles and the Lion*, created the décor for three ballets, and caricatured almost everybody. His list of subjects in a volume Carl introduced—*The Prince of Wales and Other Famous Americans*—reads like a biographical dictionary of the 1920's.

As book reviewer, Carl covered two significant contributions to the period: *Gentlemen Prefer Blondes* and *The Great Gatsby*. Anita Loos wrote briefly, "I have read your criticism of my book and am so happy about it that I've nearly gotten over the flu,"[46] and F. Scott Fitzgerald was genuinely flattered.

But Carl's really diligent and most consistent digging was for Gertrude Stein, who, since 1913, when they first met, had found her most ardent champion and sincere sponsor in him. During the war years, he had continued to arrange, from time to time, for periodical appearances; he tried also to get his publisher (and others as well) to issue her work in America. When *Geography and Plays* appeared in 1922, published with Miss Stein's own funds, including her portrait of him, he wrote:

> The book is lovely and I thank you. . . . How nice . . . to be in a big book by Gertrude Stein . . . . What has become of *The Family*? I want to show the ms. to my publisher. It has occurred to me that the time is getting ripe for its publication now that you are a classic & have Imitators and Disciples! Please do something about this![47]

[46] Yale.
[47] Yale; Donald Gallup, ed., *The Flowers of Friendship*, p. 151.

The Family referred to *The Making of Americans*, a prodigiously long and prodigiously difficult novel Miss Stein had written over a five-year period near the beginning of the century. But it was a novel only in the loosest sense of the word. There was little dialogue, little dramatized incident, little description of setting in this "history of everyone whoever was or is or will be living"; and there was no publisher who had ever wanted to touch it.

A dozen years earlier, it had crossed the Atlantic in a large wooden case, all "2428 pages of typewriting 19 lines to the page," as Miss Stein described it, for the consideration of the enterprising B. W. Huebsch, who was to publish James Joyce in 1916. The bewildering book was of course rejected.

At Carl's suggestion, Miss Stein decided to try again, and posted three large volumes to him. "Please don't send any more until you hear from me," he wrote:

> ... my feeling is that you have done a very big thing, probably as big as, perhaps bigger than James Joyce, Marcel Proust, or Dorothy Richardson. Knopf won't be back until the middle of May. I don't know what he'll make of it. You see the thing is so long that it will be hellishly expensive to publish, and can one expect much of a sale? I mean, to the average reader, the book will probably mean *work*. I think even the average reader will enjoy it, however, once he begins to get the rhythm, that is so important. To me, now, it is a little like the Book of Genesis. There is something Biblical about you, Gertrude. Certainly there is something Biblical about you.[48]

Carl's diplomacy did not completely mask his obvious reservations; certainly, he must have anticipated the rejection by Horace Liveright, a second rejection by Huebsch, and Knopf's immediate hesitancy. But there were other Stein matters to occupy Carl's attention. *Vanity Fair* had accepted a prose-poem-portrait entitled "A List inspired by Avery Hopwood" and sought Carl's permission to cut it.

Without any official authority, he had become Gertrude Stein's unsalaried American agent. It was a more felicitous arrangement

[48] *Ibid.*, p. 154.

than any other could have been for her. He knew what she was getting at, and could sometimes readily understand the cryptic convolutions in rhetoric; and he was willing to accept her refusal to use commonplace or working language:

> One thing you must understand is that very often she writes expecting you to read single words instead of a sentence. Each word must give you some image. That's very often the case. Then, she's very difficult for another reason, that she puts in a great many things that are very familiar to her, and unless you know the people and objects that she's writing about, it's very difficult to figure out what they were.[49]

If, when *Vanity Fair* ran that "Ten Dullest Authors" symposium, H. L. Mencken included Miss Stein high on his list, Carl Van Vechten certainly did not. His work in her behalf continued untiringly in spite of the general apathy toward her writing. By October, 1923, there were plans at the Knopf offices to issue *The Making of Americans* in a set of volumes for twenty-five dollars. Brochures were issued to investigate what the audience might be; but the response was slight, and it remained for Robert McAlmon's Contact Editions in Paris ultimately to publish the book.

Carl Van Vechten did not despair. "Medals for Miss Stein," a review of *Geography and Plays*, appeared in the *Tribune*; and, to the chagrin of several of the subscribers, he arranged for an appearance or two in the pages of the *Reviewer*, one of which was a second portrait of himself, "Van or Twenty Years After." He had become her agent, her distributor, her champion in America; moreover, he was her friend, one of the few with whom she never quarreled, though that may easily be accounted for by the several hundred miles of Atlantic Ocean that separated them most of the time. He continued to function in these various capacities until her death, and even beyond it for another dozen years as her literary executor.

ONE OTHER KIND OF EXCAVATION proceeded simultaneously: popular music. Though it was never buried very deeply, Carl Van

[49] Van Vechten, Oral History.

Vechten was one of the first serious diggers. In 1924, he declared that jazz was the only music of value produced in America and although "not the last hope of American music, nor yet the best hope, at present . . . its only hope."[50] In one of his series of "Pastiches et Pistaches" for the *Reviewer*, he had called Paul Whiteman's organization the greatest orchestra in the country. It was not surprising to find him trying to further interest in the medium, or to discover that he was probably the first to recognize the scope of George Gershwin's music.

Carl first met Gershwin at T. R. Smith's apartment in 1919. They soon encountered each other again at a party, where the composer played a number of his songs at the piano, including *Swanee*, shortly to be performed professionally for the first time in a new revue at the opening of the Capitol Theatre. Carl Van Vechten and George Gershwin became warm friends almost immediately. During the next few years, George and Ira Gershwin offered Broadway a series of musical comedies with some of the most infectious music and lyrics of the period. If Carl grumbled now and then at the dismal librettos they used, he was, nevertheless, convinced of the Gershwin talent. When, in 1923, Eva Gauthier announced a "Recital of Ancient and Modern Music for Voice," Carl suggested a group of popular American songs, to be performed with Gershwin at the piano. Mme Gauthier was delighted with the idea, and at Aeolian Hall, between a group of Hindemith and Bartók and the *"Lied der Waltaube"* of Schoenberg, she launched into *Alexander's Ragtime Band*. The set concluded three numbers later with Gershwin's own *I'll Build a Stairway to Paradise*. The response was overwhelming.

Carl had been out of the city on the West Chester–Richmond–Baltimore circuit at the time of the recital, but Mme Gauthier invited him to attend a rehearsal for a repeat performance to be given in Boston. It was at that rehearsal that Gershwin told Carl of Paul Whiteman's invitation to write a special composition for a concert coming up four weeks later. He added, offhandedly, that he hoped

[50] *Red*, p. xv.

to create a concerto for piano and jazz band. It was probably his first allusion to the *Rhapsody in Blue*.

The initial performance took place in February, 1924, at Aeolian Hall at the conclusion of a very long concert with the Palais Royal Orchestra, Zez Confrey (who played his *Kitten on the Keys*), and several groups of numbers by Irving Berlin and Victor Herbert, dance versions of some old chestnuts, and so forth. The capacity audience included, at Paul Whiteman's invitation, Rachmaninoff, Heifetz, Stokowski, Kreisler, Victor Herbert, Walter Damrosch, Ernest Bloch, Gilbert Seldes, Heywood Broun, Fannie Hurst, and of course Carl Van Vechten. Like everyone else in the auditorium, they were bored and restless and hot by the time Gershwin appeared, twenty-second on a program of twenty-three numbers. He darted to the piano, nodded to Whiteman, and his *Rhapsody in Blue* began with its now familiar clarinet glissando.

Two days later, Carl dropped a note to Gershwin: "The concert, quite as a matter of course, was a riot; you crowned it with what I am forced to regard as the foremost serious effort by any American composer. Go straight on and you will knock all Europe silly."[51] Later in the year, he made his initial reaction public, in an article for *Vanity Fair*, convinced that *Rhapsody in Blue* was "the finest piece of serious music that had ever come out of America; moreover, that . . . [Gershwin] had composed the most effective concerto for piano that anybody had written since Tchaikovsky's B flat minor."[52]

Gershwin provided the music for most of the Van Vechten parties during the years that followed. He played until the sun came up, sometimes accompanying Marguerite d'Alvarez when she sang his songs, on another occasion providing the rhythm for Adele Astaire's dancing. He entertained when the Knopfs gave a party for Noel Coward, recently arrived from England; and when Noel Coward threw a party of his own for Anita Loos, Muriel

[51] Edward Jablonski and Lawrence D. Stewart, *The Gershwin Years*, p. 88.
[52] "George Gershwin: An American Composer Who Is Writing Notable Music in the Jazz Idiom," p. 24.

Draper, the Lunts, the Van Vechtens, Eva Le Gallienne, and Lenore Ulric, Gershwin played again.

The enthusiasm for American popular music reached a feverish peak in the mid-twenties, but its success was due only in part to George Gershwin's music. The impact of the Negro revues, beginning in 1921 with *Shuffle Along*, was considerable. It was but a step from Gershwin's rhythms to their roots in the music of the Negro, and scarcely a step beyond that to his poetry, his humor, himself. There was talk, late in 1924, that Gershwin and Van Vechten would collaborate on a "jazz" opera with a Negro subject. DuBose Heyward's *Porgy* was an early suggestion, which Carl declined. Another was a rather elaborate epic based on a Svengali theme, which Gershwin declined.

The idea of working with Negro material, coupled with Carl Van Vechten's growing interest in Harlem, suddenly the most fashionable after-hours area in Manhattan, moved him directly toward another book. Its sky-blue dust jacket announced, anonymously, the intention: "In this, his fifth novel, Carl Van Vechten continues to act as historian of contemporary New York life, drawing a curious picture of a fascinating group hitherto neglected by writers of fiction."

The book was called *Nigger Heaven.*

VIII

The Darktown Strutter's Ball

Race prejudice is an acquired taste, like olives. Children do not have it and whole nations are bereft of it. It is something you have to learn to have.

Sullen-mouthed, silky-haired Author Van Vechten has been playing with Negroes lately," *Time* complained in 1925, "writing prefaces for their poems, having them around the house, going to Harlem."[1]

The attitude was to be expected in the mid-twenties, and even *Time*'s report—having them around the house, like stray cats—would have gone through the press without upsetting the type. It was an era when Negroes had trouble purchasing orchestra seats in theaters and meals in public restaurants; when old minstrel-show terms like "coon" and "nigger" were used conventionally rather than disparagingly; when white and Negro children were not allowed to appear together on the stage in Eugene O'Neill's *All God's Chillun Got Wings*; when indeed a Manhattan shadow of the Mason-Dixon Line fell directly across the island at 110th Street.

The Negro had continued to fascinate Carl Van Vechten during most of his forty-five years, beginning in Cedar Rapids with the Van Vechtens' gentle yardman, who was always politely called Mr. Oliphant. Additionally, Carl's father's co-founding of the Piney Woods School for Negro children in Mississippi (at a time when Negro children did not go to school in Mississippi) helped inoculate Carl against prejudice at an early age. Under his own steam, an enterprising sixteen-year-old Carl practiced his photography by consciously posing two Negro children sitting on the steps of Harriet Beecher Stowe's house in Cincinnati during the winter

[1] CVV, NYPL.

195

holiday he spent with his sister Emma in 1896. From his days in Chicago, where he first encountered Bert Williams and Carita Day and George Walker, through his panegyric review of *Granny Maumee* in 1914, and into the twenties, he had continued to be impressed with Negro talent, Negro beauty, Negro humor. With the passage of time, his interest began to focus not on Negroes who happened to be creative artists but on creative artists who happened to be Negroes. The distinction is significant enough.

It was to be expected that his publicity for popular music would lead him inevitably to the Negro singers of the period. *Shuffle Along*, the 1921 Negro revue—indeed, the first Negro revue—had a great deal to do with this: a happy show with tuneful numbers, Florence Mills and Caterina Jarboro on stage and Hall Johnson and William Grant Still playing in the orchestra. The movement it started at the beginning of the era, continuing through the Harlem Renaissance, reached its peak, as Langston Hughes later wrote, "just before the crash of 1929, the crash that sent Negroes, white folks, and all rolling down the hill toward the Works Progress Administration."[2]

During the noisy decade that preceded the depression, however, Roland Hayes and Paul Robeson joined in the chorus from several recital halls, and the Smith girls, Bessie and Clara and Mamie (united only by name), and Ethel Waters and Rose McClendon and Florence Mills added their notes as well, to make the twenties roar. It was largely through the efforts of Carl Van Vechten that the speakeasy intelligentsia paid any attention to Negro singers and entertainers. As James Weldon Johnson pointed out, Carl's interest developed in advance of almost anybody else's: "In the early days of the Negro literary and artistic movement, no one in the country did more to forward it than he accomplished in frequent magazine articles, and by his personal efforts in behalf of individual Negro writers and artists."[3]

Carl did not, however, invent the Harlem Renaissance, as it was

[2] *The Big Sea*, p. 223.
[3] *Along This Way*, p. 230.

generally called. The popularity of the Negro revue on Broadway, coupled with the bogus nostalgia in Irving Caesar's lyrics for Gershwin's *Swanee*—which almost everybody seemed to be singing—started the whole thing in 1919. White theatergoers found themselves viewing Negro entertainers as Carl had seen them twenty years before in Chicago. Concurrently, James Weldon Johnson and Walter White, working through the National Association for the Advancement of Colored People, could see new reasons for social acceptance begin to form. Johnson's *The Autobiography of an Ex-Colored Man*, the poetry of Paul Lawrence Dunbar, and the writings of Booker T. Washington and W. E. B. Du Bois—all before the twenties—began to echo in the work of a new generation of Negro writers. When Carl Van Vechten first went to Harlem to find out what was going on, he very simply discovered a new world waiting to be claimed. As Mrs. James Weldon Johnson put it: "Carl was a force, a spur in a labyrinth of individual effort, but for that which was already in process. . . . He recognized it first, and he dramatized it."

In 1924, Carl read a Knopf publication called *The Fire in the Flint*, a bitter indictment in novel form by Walter White, a young Negro of pale complexion but dark anger. The book was "not very good, but it told a nervous story of the Atlanta riots." Carl immediately asked Alfred Knopf to introduce him to White. The meeting was, for both men, propitious: White, anxious to strengthen contact with a society that shunned his race; Van Vechten, already impressed with Negro music and theater, anxious to move beyond the confines of periphery. "Walter and I got on like a house afire," Carl later recalled, "and we began calling each other by our first names. (This was Walter's invariable custom and he did the same with Mrs. Roosevelt when he met her. She said in an interview later that he was practically the only person alive who called her Eleanor.)"

Within a matter of weeks, White had introduced Carl to almost every continent in the Negro world; when White arranged a meeting with James Weldon Johnson, Carl's enthusiasm became incandescent. Almost immediately, he and Johnson were warm friends as well as sympathetic guides into each other's societies. Johnson was of course unique: he had been a teacher, a lawyer, a writer of popular music; he had served as a United States consul in Venezuela and Nicaragua; he had written books, edited magazines, and was then secretary of the N.A.A.C.P. At first, Carl's encounters with him were careful, discerning, in the nature of interviews. Then, Johnson's widow pleasantly recalls, "He wrote a letter to Carl, after two or three visits, inviting him back, not as sociologist but as friend."

Johnson and White took Carl to his first N.A.A.C.P. cabaret party, held at Happy Rhone's Club, where he met the fledgling poets Langston Hughes and Countee Cullen and other members of the growing Harlem literati (which Wallace Thurman and Zora Neale Hurston, Negro novelists, later telescoped into "niggerati").

If Harlem was like a great magnet for the Negro intellectual, pulling him in from all parts of the country, as Langston Hughes suggested, its pull was equally strong for Carl Van Vechten. By the end of 1924, he knew almost every important Negro in Harlem and many who were not so important. It was an easy step from the N.A.A.C.P. balls to Harlem's night clubs. At Bamville, the Nest, the Club Alabam', and dozens of other clubs now nameless and forgotten—"They didn't last more than two or three weeks,"Nora Holt recalled—Carl seems to have begun to reside more or less permanently. *Vanity Fair* declared he was getting a heavy tan, and, because he appeared on the street only after dark, he must have acquired it in a taxi, bound for Harlem; Covarrubias caricatured him in blackface, titling the drawing *A Prediction*; in Andy Razaf's popular song of the day, *Go Harlem*, singers advised, "Go inspectin' like Van Vechten!"[4]

Small's, where the waiters did the Charleston while balancing full trays of bad whiskey, became Carl's headquarters, a Fifth Avenue basement that lived up to its name. Guests at the tables cried, "Get off that dime!" continuously to the slow-motion dancers, laminated

4 Yale.

to each other on the floor. In time, Small's became one of the show spots to which Carl escorted out-of-towners. He and Bennett Cerf took William Faulkner there one evening. "The people up here are soft," Faulkner murmured slowly; "they couldn't get along down south." On a more felicitous occasion, Mabel Dodge Luhan, in town at the Plaza with part of her Taos entourage, deposited her Pueblo husband Tony in Carl's care. (Carl once confided to a friend that he suspected it was the U.S. government that drove Mabel to this marriage since, with Mabel, it "was but a spring-board to the higher life.") Witter Bynner also was in town. Tony, Witter, and Carl were high by the time they got to Small's after midnight. Tony had never seen anything like it in New Mexico, but he made himself immediately at home, wandering around the tables, draping the girl's scarves, Indian fashion, on the heads of their escorts. Bynner had no fears, though Carl was a little uneasy: downtown visitors came to observe, not to participate. But the crowd was enchanted, particularly when Tony joined the band to play the drums. Van Vechten and Bynner deposited him at the Plaza at five in the morning. "I never went to bed in those days," Carl always took pleasure in recalling. Nor, apparently, did anyone else. His friends were quick to follow his lead: at almost every Harlem soiree of any public nature, the races mingled, danced, drank, made small talk.

The cultural exchange that so suddenly got under way in New York did not, however, necessarily split its dividends equally. Langston Hughes remembered that many Negroes—laborers, wait-resses, clerks, all unaware that a renaissance was supposed to be going on—despaired at finding bars and clubs where visiting whites did not sit and stare at them. House-rent parties evolved as a retalia-tion, where bootleg whiskey, fried fish, and chitterlings were sold at nominal prices, and a guitar augmented a piano for dancing. Ad-vertised on brightly colored cards in elevators and hallways, these "whist parties," "tea-cup parties," "rent-raising parties," as they were called, were attended solely by Negroes. At the same time, ironically, the Cotton Club and several other palaces of entertainment stooped to some Jim Crowing of their own, catering to the white clientele as it arrived in droves from downtown, not infrequently excluding Negroes in the process. "Have you noticed," Negro writer Nella Imes once asked Carl, "that when Nordics talk against the admission of Negroes to their homes . . . it is rank prejudice, but when we take the same attitude about white folks it is race loyalty?"[5] Carl worked hard to alleviate the paradox, though the effort never really verged on conscious propaganda.

In their chambers on West Fifty-fifth Street, Carl and Fania entertained most of the Negroes whose work had even then commanded some attention, in addition to white celebrities of the period: Somerset Maugham, Hugh Walpole, Fannie Hurst, Witter Bynner, Arthur Davison Ficke, Louis Untermeyer, Lawrence Langner and Armina Marshall, Salvador Dali, Helena Rubinstein, Regina Wallace, Marie Doro, Nickolas Muray, Horace Liveright, Lilyan Tashman, Eugene Goossens, and many others, as well as the amusing nonentities and aspirants of the period. If the guests found Carl's Prohibition bar impressive, they could easily find themselves equally intoxicated on the entertainment, usually supplied by one another. One evening Bessie Smith came in with Porter Grainger, tossed down a healthy tumbler—about half a pint—of bootleg gin, and sang the blues for the assembled guests. The Peruvian contralto Marguerite d'Alvarez followed her with an operatic aria. Afterward, an impressed Bessie embraced her, saying, "Don't let *nobody* tell you *you* can't sing!" On another occasion, Chief Long Lance performed Indian war dances; and on still another, there was a weird gossip party, where everyone went around whispering the worst things he could think of about the others. Langston Hughes remembered another when a woman—not a guest—unwittingly supplied the entertainment by standing outside the next-door apartment, a loaded gun in her hand, waiting for her husband to emerge, while Carl fortified her with cups of coffee during her vigil. She left at dawn as Carl's guests departed, the neighboring apartment door still firmly closed. Emily Clarke recalled a June evening in 1925,

[5] Yale.

200

when George Gershwin sat at the piano playing his current show tunes, while "Theodore Dreiser sat, heavy and brooding, the direct antithesis, almost a contradiction of all that Gershwin means. And Elinor Wylie sat, aloof and lovely, a contradiction and denial of all that both Dreiser and Gershwin mean."[6] Later in the evening, Paul Robeson sang spirituals with Lawrence Brown at the piano; still later, James Weldon Johnson recited "Go Down, Death" from his *God's Trombones*.

Carl and Fania were not, of course, the only people who integrated their guest lists, but only their parties were reported as a matter of regular record in the Negro newspapers in New York. The notoriety gave rise to strongly varying reactions. From a scornful Southerner: "The only man I ever heard of who made a career out of being a nigger-lover." From the folklore of the twenties: At Grand Central Station, a Negro porter picked up a woman's luggage. "Good morning, Mrs. Astor," he said. "How do you know my name, young man?" she asked. "Why, ma'am, I met you last weekend at Carl Van Vechten's."

In turn, Carl was frequently included in literary evenings at the Johnsons', where Clarence Darrow read from *Farmington* and Paul Robeson recited "The Creation," from *God's Trombones*; not long thereafter, Carl signed his name to an endorsement—a sincere but breathless panegyric—on a Robeson-Brown recital program.

At the integrated transvestite costume balls at the Rockland Palace Casino, Carl and Avery Hopwood occasionally served as judges while "the Astors and the Vanderbilts sat regally in boxes" to observe the parades of pretty boys in gilt and feathers and elegant gowns. Once, for a Harlem drag at the Savoy, he joined Bob Chanler and an old enemy, Muriel Draper, in awarding first prize to a lad almost "stark naked, save for a decorative *cache-sex* and silver sandals and he was painted a kind of apple green." But the balls became too smart, "in a sort of Vassar fashion," and Carl's participation at the Savoy occurred at Chanler's insistence to mend the breach with Mrs. Draper. In 1925, Edith Grove and the Villa

----

[6] *Innocence Abroad*, pp. 144–145.

Curonia existed only in legend; more and more regularly, Mrs. Draper and Carl turned up at the same parties. Finally, an unspoken truce was made and, as the twenties progressed, so did a friendship; but it ripened slowly.

Although the costume balls served as occasional encounters with Harlem society, Carl was more regularly an attendant at the parties of A'lelia Walker, the immensely wealthy daughter of Mrs. C. J. Walker of Indianapolis who many years before had invented the hair-straightening process.

Carl had met A'lelia Walker at the height of the Harlem vogue, and often visited her Villa Le Waro, built for half a million dollars at Irvington on the Hudson. She had an apartment in Manhattan as well, but she gave her startling parties in a town house on 136th Street, later destined to be transformed into the Harlem branch of the New York Public Library. Negro poets and Negro bolito kings mingled there with downtown writers and stock exchange racketeers; marini queens like Nora Holt and the African black A'lelia provided the glamour; and visiting celebrities like Osbert Sitwell (who remembered being received by the hostess in a Parisian tent room of the Second Empire) supplied an international atmosphere. Harold Jackman, a handsome Harlem schoolteacher whose homework entailed showing visiting dignitaries around town, recalled the Walker gatherings many years later:

> One couldn't help being impressed with the brilliance of the evenings. . . . Literature, politics, painting and music were always discussed. Something interesting was constantly happening. Madame Walker made certain that there was always more than enough elegant dishes and drinks to go around.

Jackman also remembered being one of a regular group who did not need an invitation to attend, "along with Countee Cullen, Mac Stinnette, Jules Bledsoe, Carl Van Vechten and Langston Hughes. . . ."[7]

It was not long before Carl's name was as well known in Harlem

[7] "Those Were the Fabulous Days, *Pittsburgh Courier*, October 11, 1952.

as those of Negro celebrities. "I don't want to be unduly suspicious," Walter White wrote to him, "but I am beginning to be convinced that these colored newspapers are in your employ."[8] There was, however, more than entertainment involved. The Van Vechten trumpet sounded with increasing frequency, calling downtown attention to the efforts of aspiring Negro writers. He helped foster the career of Countee Cullen, supplying a *Vanity Fair* introduction for some of the young poet's work, and another for the poetry of Langston Hughes. They had met briefly—Hughes, Cullen, and Van Vechten—at Carl's first N.A.A.C.P. cabaret party; several months later, the acquaintance was renewed in Washington, when *Opportunity*, a Negro periodical, sponsored a literary contest.

James Weldon Johnson, Witter Bynner, and John Farrar awarded the first prize of forty dollars to a twenty-two-year-old Langston Hughes—an amount he had spent going after it. When the ceremonies concluded, Carl went to congratulate the winner. He suggested that Hughes give him a sheaf of poems to offer Knopf for publication. These appeared as *The Weary Blues* (with a Van Vechten introduction) in January, 1926; but Carl had already persuaded Frank Crowninshield to print some of Hughes's work in *Vanity Fair*, stanzas that "recapture[d] the spirit of Negro folklore. The Blues are not yet as famous as the Spirituals," Carl Van Vechten advised readers, "but all the world is now learning about their beauty."[9]

Two months later, Carl reviewed James Weldon Johnson's *Book of American Negro Spirituals*, a labor of love for a man who was to become one of his closest friends. Like Carl's own father, Johnson was "kind, gentle, helpful, generous, tolerant of unorthodox behaviour in others, patriarchal in offering good advice, understanding in not expecting it to be followed, moderate in his ways of living, and courageous in accepting the difficulties of life itself. As a matter of fact," Carl wrote after Johnson's death, "Jim possessed at

[8] Yale.
[9] "Langston Hughes: A Biographical Note," *Vanity Fair*, September, 1925, p. 62.

least two other desirable qualities which were lacking in my father: tact and discretion."[10]

With reviews and prefaces behind him, Carl Van Vechten contributed a number of his own articles to periodicals. *Theatre Magazine* published his "All God's Chillun Got Songs," a paper about Paul Robeson and Lawrence Brown, for whose debuts he had been responsible. *Vanity Fair* ran half a dozen of his pieces. The first, "The Folksongs of the American Negro," declared that these were "the most important contribution America has yet made to the literature of music. . . . They contain, indeed, every element of modern jazz, save the instrumentation."[11]

In "The Black Blues," he pleaded, again in terms of hyperbolic propaganda, for wider recognition, predicting that the blues would "enjoy a similar resurrection which will make them as respectable, at least in the artistic sense, as the religious songs."[12]

Carl's "Prescription for the Nigger Theatre" in 1925 bemoaned the absence of so much Negro material on Broadway because of the constant repetition of what had preceded. *Shuffle Along*, and its formula-following imitations *Runnin' Wild*, *Dixie to Broadway*, *The Chocolate Dandies*, held to a single doctrine, "which varies so little that only once in five years or so after the customers have forgotten the last one is it possible to awaken interest in a new example."[13] Blacking up the comedians and whiting up the chorus girls did not help. Carl Van Vechten's own suggestions for improvement were several: advertise for a Negro chorus and forget about autonomy in color; forget the false make-up, the mammy songs, and the ghost-in-the-graveyard skits; insert some spirituals; do a Harlem cabaret sequence; do a Striver's Row sequence; and hire Bessie Smith for a number. He could have suggested, with equal facility, Taylor Gordon or Nora Holt, two disparate singers in whose careers Carl had become passionately involved.

[10] "My Friend, James Weldon Johnson," *James Weldon Johnson (1871–1938)*, p. 22.
[11] July, 1925, p. 52.
[12] August, 1925, p. 92.
[13] October, 1925, p. 92.

The Darktown Strutter's Ball

Taylor Gordon "somehow got himself on paper, lanky six-feet, falsetto voice, molasses laugh,"[14] in his autobiography, *Born to Be*, for which Carl wrote a foreword in 1929. They had met four years earlier, when James Weldon Johnson's brother was preparing a book of spirituals, engaged Gordon to join him in performing them, and took the young tenor around to meet "the Abraham Lincoln of negro art." Carl's "pure blue eyes" had a piercing effect that "mighty near stopped my breath for fear," Gordon wrote. ". . . at last I am before Old Pilate himself. If I can pass this examination I will be O.K. and if I can't, never no more singing." While they were performing, Fania came in, "clad in a Japanese robe . . . a bewitching creature five feet six, exquisite figure, dark eyes, fascinating face with a head full of jet black hair and keen feet!" That afternoon, he concluded, "led to all our success."[15]

Taylor Gordon missed on the color of Carl's eyes and added a few inches to Fania, but his closing remark was accurate. The Van Vechtens introduced him to Lawrence Langner, who arranged the first Gordon-Johnson recital for the Theatre Guild. After that, Gordon's career was assured, and his social life too: at Van Vechten parties, at those of the Knopfs, Muriel Draper, and Robert Chanler. He was at the latter's house when Carl's portrait was being painted. Gordon sang *The St. Louis Blues* while Chanler slashed paint at the canvas. Chanler surrounded his models with guests and refreshments, an appropriate atmosphere for his subject that day, though Carl balked when, as a final double stroke, Chanler's brush shot forth to add the famous fangs. Even at forty-five, Carl had not totally reconciled himself to his unspeakable teeth. Over the years he had learned to smile with his lips closed; indeed, he had trained the muscles of his mouth to do his bidding.

Nora Holt met Carl under entirely different circumstances, in a Harlem speakeasy that had just opened; certainly, no singer could have been farther removed from Taylor Gordon. A girl of surpassing beauty, she had come to New York a few days earlier from

14 P. v.
15 *Ibid.*, pp. 185–86.

Chicago, where she had been singing a rowdy repertoire in a voice that ranged from "deepest bass to shrillest piping." Carl, as enchanted with her steamy tunes as he was with Gordon's spirituals, began to see Nora regularly, and within weeks she was an intimate friend and a frequent guest.

Between parties and recitals and Harlem jaunts, Carl continued the articles for *Vanity Fair*. In "Moanin' wid a Sword in Ma Han' " he conceded that Negroes need not refrain from offering conventional recital programs, though he felt a real need for authoritative renditions of spirituals. Similarly, although there was nothing to prevent the Negro from investigating foreign fields, it was unfortunate that he chose not to investigate his own:

> Until novels about Negroes, by either white or coloured writers, are regarded as dispassionately from an aesthetic standpoint as books about Chinese mandarins, I see little hope ahead for the new school of Negro authors. . . . [He] readily delivers his great gifts to the exploitation of the white man without—save in rare instances—making any attempt, an attempt if doomed to meet with success, to capitalize on them himself. It is significant, however, that the great Negroes almost invariably climb to fame with material which is the heritage of their race.[16]

Such an attitude may be responsible for the hostile reception Carl's Negro investigations received from some Negroes. They accused him of glamorizing the culture, of giving them the kind of chichi publicity they wished to avoid. But a number of sympathetic Negro intellectuals, far removed from the speakeasy life, came into Carl's orbit—or he into their orbits—as his *Vanity Fair* articles reached a wider audience that winter of 1925–26: Dorothy Peterson, the beautiful West Indian girl who, a few years later, got a leave of absence from her teaching chores in the New York public school system to play Cain's girl in *The Green Pastures*; Harold Jackman, also a teacher, who subsequently established the Countee Cullen Memorial Collection at the Trevor Arnett Library in Atlanta; Arna Bontemps, the writer turned scholar who became the

16 February, 1926, p. 102.

librarian at Fisk University. Of Carl's new acquaintances, however, Zora Neale Hurston was probably the most colorful, the most memorable.

The daughter of a self-ordained Southern Baptist minister, she had come up from Florida to attend Barnard College on a scholarship and through the financial assistance of friends, casual acquaintances, and strangers, who all instinctively adored her. Fannie Hurst once wrote, "Regardless of race, Zora had the gift of walking into hearts." She walked into Miss Hurst's heart almost immediately after her arrival from Barnard, but without much enthusiasm for the secretarial position for which she was applying. "Her shorthand was short on legibility, her typing hit-or-miss, mostly the latter, her filing, a game of find-the-thimble"; but Miss Hurst hired her on the spot.[17] When Carl met her, he too fell under the spell of the Hurston charm, and she under his: "If Carl was a people instead of a person," she confided in Miss Hurst, "I could then say, these are my people."[18] Raffish and irresponsible, careless and unpredictable, she roared through the Negro Renaissance to become a writer herself, leaving in the wake of a sudden disappearance some years before her death half a dozen books and an invariable topic of conversation for Fannie Hurst and Carl Van Vechten.

In March, 1926, *Vanity Fair* published a fifth paper of Carl's, this time on blues singers Bessie Smith, Clara Smith, and Ethel Waters. If he never knew the first two intimately, the third became a warm friend. Carl first met Ethel Waters backstage following a performance during the days when she was known as Sweet Mama Stringbean. Almost immediately, she was invited to attend one of the parties on West Fifty-fifth Street; but the expensive furnishings and exotic foods made her uncomfortable: caviar, "little grey balls," and borscht, "beet soup and clabber . . . enough to curdle your gizzard."[19] Shortly thereafter, she reversed the situa-

[17] *Yale Gazette*, July, 1960, p. 17.
[18] *Ibid.*, p. 19.
[19] Ethel Waters, *His Eye Is on the Sparrow*, p. 195.

tion by preparing a home-cooked meal for Carl; ham and mustard greens, lemon meringue pie, and iced tea. They were friends forever after. Bessie Smith offered an equally happy story. Several months before she had first sung at his apartment, Carl had met her through Leigh Whipper, then the manager of a theater in Newark where she was singing on Thanksgiving Day in 1925. Bessie was at that time the size of Fay Templeton in her Weber and Fields days, "which seemed very large, and she wore a crimson satin robe sweeping up from her trim ankles, and embroidered in multicolored sequins in designs."[20] Carl recalled a beautiful face, "with the rich, ripe beauty of southern darkness, a deep bronze brown, matching the bronze of her bare arms," and a voice "full of shouting and moaning and praying and suffering, a wild, rough Ethiopian voice, harsh and volcanic, but seductive and sensuous too, released between rouged lips and the whitest of teeth." Backstage, he said: "I believe I kissed her hand. I hope I did."[21]

A final article, in the *Crisis*, "The Negro in Art: How Shall He Be Portrayed?" echoed the sentiments of an earlier piece on subject matter, "Are Negro writers going to write about this exotic material while it is still fresh or will they continue to make a free gift of it to white authors who will exploit it until not a drop of vitality remains."[22]

Carl had followed his own lead by writing a novel that was to have a profound effect on the Negro and the white man in New York and across the country as well. Although there was no intention to exploit, there was, assuredly, intention to instruct. He wrote Gertrude Stein about it in June, 1925: "This will not be a novel about Negroes in the South or white contacts or lynchings. It will be about Harlem. . . . about 400,000 of them live there now, rich and poor, fast and slow, intellectual and ignorant. I hope it will be a good book."[23] It was—though the critics and the public were not so certain in the beginning.

[20] "Negro 'Blues' Singers," *Vanity Fair*, March, 1926, p. 67.
[21] "Memories of Bessie Smith," p. 7.
[22] March, 1926, p. 219.
[23] Yale.

The Darktown Strutter's Ball

With *Nigger Heaven*, Carl Van Vechten had hoped to strengthen ties between the races, but instead he became the scapegoat of the whole movement, blamed for the work of all Negro writers thereafter. Langston Hughes said: "The critics of the left, like the Negroes of the right, proceeded to light on Mr. Van Vechten and he was accused of ruining, distorting, polluting, and corrupting every Negro writer from then on, who was even known to have shaken hands with him."[24]

Although a few perceptive Negro critics praised the book, most of them sided with the opposition, sending Carl Van Vechten out to sea from the Harlem shores, with the influential W. E. B. Du Bois doing most of the splashing:

> A blow in the face, an affront to the hospitality of the blackfold and to the intelligence of the white. . . . A caricature of half-truths . . . an astonishing and wearisome hodgepodge of laboriously stated facts, quotations and expressions illuminated here and there with something that comes near to being nothing but cheap melodrama.[25]

On the other hand, James Weldon Johnson found it an absorbing story that comprehended "nearly every phase of life from dregs to the froth, the most revealing, significant and powerful novel based exclusively on Negro life yet written."[26] Johnson also called attention to the chagrin of Negro objectors who were resentful of such disclosures to a white public.

Now, more than forty years later, *Nigger Heaven* probably belongs halfway between the hysterical cheering and the irrational condemnation. Certainly, there were stylistic faults in the novel. An unconscious attempt to make Van Vechten Negroes talk like Van Vechten whites occasionally ended in their talking in a grotesque parody of the author's own manner. For the serious intentions of the book, this was out of place and probably open to justifiable criticism. The curious mixture of sophistication and

[24] *The Big Sea*, p. 271.
[25] *Crisis*, December, 1926.
[26] *Opportunity*, October, 1926.

sociology was dichotomous; but, more than the content, it was the title that confused and irritated.

Negroes whom Carl had known intimately turned on the use of "nigger" with loathing, not bothering to read as far as the middle of the first chapter, where the word was explained in a footnote: "While this informal epithet is freely used by Negroes among themselves, not only as a term of opprobrium, but also actually as a term of endearment, its employment by a white person is always fiercely resented."[27] Two passages in the novel itself clearly stated the purpose in his having ironically used the expression. The first comes from Ruby, a Lenox Avenue prostitute:

> Does you know what Ah calls dis . . . . place, where Ah met you—Harlem. Ah calls et, specherly tonight, Ah calls et Nigger Heaven! I jes' nacherly think dis heah is Nigger Heaven![28]

Later in the book, Byron Kasson, Carl Van Vechten's bitter protagonist, cries out:

> Nigger Heaven! That's what Harlem is. We sit in our places in the gallery of this New York theatre and watch the white world sitting down below in the good seats in the orchestra. Occasionally they turn their faces up towards us, their hard, cruel faces, to laugh or sneer, but they never beckon.[29]

Unfortunately, the average reader, if he had not been repelled by the title alone, read only as far as the prostitute's definition, thereby failing to realize the ostensible intentions. Carl was accused of white supremacy, of trying to lower the Negro in the eyes of the white public. A letter from his own father was probably a good indication of the first impression many readers formed:

> Your "Nigger Heaven" is a title I don't like. I remember what . . . was said of some Democratic candidate for the presidency because he spelled negro with two g's, & I have myself never spoken of a colored man as a "nigger." If you are trying to help the race, as I am

27 *Nigger Heaven*, p. 26n.
28 *Ibid.*, p. 28.
29 *Ibid.*, p. 149.

assured you are, I think every word you write should be a respectful one towards the black.[30]

Charles Duane Van Vechten did not live to see the time, many years in the making, when the Negro—beyond the confines of his son's circle—began to recognize the author of *Nigger Heaven* as the Negro's persistent white patron, his most beneficent white champion. Carl's father died of pneumonia at the age of eighty-six, seven months before the novel was published. The loss was a painful one for Carl. A very long time had passed since he had first decided to travel a different road from the one expected of him, such a long time since he had begun to write books that he hoped—in spite of his hedonistic vows—would please the man who had for so many years endured the puzzle of a creative offspring.

Certainly, the elder Van Vechten's letter about *Nigger Heaven* caused some concern on Carl's part. Even earlier, he had anticipated trouble, writing to Alfred A. Knopf:

> Ordinarily . . . books should not be advertised so long in advance, but this book is different. It is necessary to prepare the mind not only of my own public, but of the new public which this book may possibly reach . . . . so that the kind of life I am writing about will not come as an actual shock.[31]

Knopf was "delighted that Nigger Heaven is making such fine progress. We shall definitely schedule it for August 15 and I am taking care of the advertising as you suggest."[32] A few days later, he wrote again, "I feel more and more that it is going to be a big success."[33]

Carl's precautions did not stop with the advance publicity: James Weldon Johnson and Walter White read galley proofs; and, in the final stages of polishing the Negro novelist, Rudolph Fisher, gave it a last check for authenticity and factual accuracy. Another set of proofs went to a lawyer, who, for a two-hundred-dollar fee,

[30] CVV, NYPL.
[31] *Yale Gazette*, April, 1950, p. 154.
[32] CVV, NYPL.
[33] CVV, NYPL.

checked for words and expressions and situations that might incur difficulties. The tenor of the cuts suggested by the lawyer seems quaintly tame today. It is surprising to find, as recently as 1926, that "he could feel her leg pressed against his" had to be altered to "he was conscious of her nearness." Nor was Byron allowed to rest his head between the "nude, golden breasts" of Lasca Sartoris, his sexy seductress; he pillowed it, instead, "on her shoulder." The graphic "eel-eater" as a slang expression for homosexual was replaced by "queer," and, rather than "pressing his lips against her thigh," Byron had to be content with raising his eyes in supplication. Other questionable passages were left intact—the book was banned in Boston—though actual descriptive passages never appeared in terms of erotic realism; implication could suggest more: "There were rages, succeeded by tumultuous passions; there were peaceful interludes; there were hours devoted to satisfying capricious desires, rhythmical amours to music, cruel and painful pastimes; there were artificial paradises."[34] But "whore" and "bastard" and "God damn" were largely excised from the text.

Another two hundred dollars came out of Carl's pocket for last-minute changes in the approved page proofs. Everything was carefully checked—with one expensive exception. Inadvertently, Carl had included the lyrics of a popular song of the period, *Shake That Thing*, the words to which he had taken down from a record, without thinking to get permission from the song publisher. At the height of the early sales of *Nigger Heaven*, the copyright holders demanded an accounting, and with the powerful ASCAP on the side of the composer, Knopf's lawyers could make no progress toward a settlement: the book would be removed from bookstores, and sales would be suspended.

A woebegone Carl began to appear daily in Knopf's offices, with a hip flask of whiskey to soothe the pain as the wrangling wore on. Then, he frantically telephoned Langston Hughes, the young poet, temporarily a student at Howard University. Would he write original lyrics, to be used instead of the published song, for the

34 *Nigger Heaven*, p. 261.

subsequent editions—if ever, alas, there were any? He would. Hughes came to New York immediately and, in one grueling night at Carl's apartment, he composed nearly a dozen verses. At least once during the splendid drunken twenties, Carl closed the bar, and, bolstered by Fania's strong coffee, he and Hughes set about fitting the new verses into the pages of *Nigger Heaven*, line for line, so that the demand from booksellers for copies of the novel might be filled with a new printing.

Meanwhile, Knopf happened to mention the legal troubles involving *Shake That Thing* to a lawyer friend from Pittsburgh. By coincidence, he had something to do with ASCAP; in a few days he had arranged for a settlement claim of a staggering $2,500. Carl earned the money back with subsequent sales, to be sure, but Knopf later reflected that most publishers and writers "know better today than to risk copyright difficulties with this particular breed of Broadway cat."[35]

Langston Hughes's new lyrics went into the seventh printing of the book; there were nine printings in the first four months of publication, after an immediate sellout of the original sixteen thousand copies. The controversy in the press of course had a lot to do with the book's popularity: "Cheap French romance, colored light brown," according to the *Independent*. "A frontier work of enduring order," according to the *Saturday Review of Literature*. "Far and away the best of its author's novels," declared another reviewer; still another called the book "A slumming party for the entertainment of jig-chasers anxious for an excuse to be base." D. H. Lawrence, busy in New Mexico discovering the Indians, called it "Just another nigger book."[36] But Louis Kronenberger disagreed: "To get beneath the skin of another people , . . . even though imperfectly, is a conspicuous achievement. *Nigger Heaven* is possibly not Mr. Van Vechten's most delightful book . . . but all in all it is the truest book he has written and it is the most powerful."[37] If this

---

[35] "Reminiscences of Hergesheimer, Van Vechten, and Mencken," *Yale Gazette*, April, 1950, p. 154.
[36] CVV, NYPL.
[37] *International Book Review*, October, 1926.

evaluation seems less true today, one may blame the experience from which most white critics could not speak.

Most other white publications made favorable—if platitudinous—comment. The Negro press, however, lacked such tact. Its condemnation was fearful and destructive, not only to prospective Negro readers but to the emotional equilibrium of the author, who had hoped to improve the Negro's position in a white-centered society. In September, Carl wrote to James Weldon Johnson about some of the terrible publicity the book had received:

> I thought Grace might like to read Charles Johnson's letter which the Pittsburgh Courier printed. I'm sorry I haven't a copy at hand of the editorial in the Age. A lot of rotten characters who come to a bad end, is Fred Moore's report: hence a fine book. The New York News (colored) says that anyone who would call a book Nigger Heaven would call a Negro nigger. Harlem, it appears, is seething in controversy. Langston, the other night, . . . suggested to a few of the knockers that they might read the book before expressing their opinion, but this advice seems to be superrogatory.[38]

To populate his *Nigger Heaven*, Carl Van Vechten chose Mary Love and Byron Kasson, two young Negroes caught up in the exotic Harlem nightmare of the 1920's: Mary, an underpaid librarian at the 125th Street branch, who longs to break free from the casual vulgarity of the uneducated and still avoid the affectations of the bogus sophisticates among the Negro intellectuals; Byron, a bitter boy who wants to be a writer but manages only to secure a job as an elevator operator. As a background to the tragic pattern of their lives, the author applauded without apologizing for, and criticized without condemning, the sensuousness and brilliance of the Negro world in New York.

The novel began with a dozen pages of Carl Van Vechten's silky prose, describing the passing scene on Lenox Avenue—the whores and numbers racketeers, the pimps and bootleggers—in a heightened essence of his own ironic nihilism, in shet-mah-mouf dialogue full of all the usual clichés, wholly in keeping with the average white man's

[38] Yale.

idea of Negro indulgences. Then, turning abruptly to a straight-forward narrative, he moved to other planets in his Nigger Heaven: society balls and formal dinners; serious (and familiar) discussions of literature and the other arts; fashionable conversation.

The recognizable Van Vechten mannerisms were, for the most part, avoided though not completely obliterated. Occasionally, the writing lacked its customary grace and, instead, became pedantic and patronizing in its attempt to justify the Negro intellectual. Mary Love, who cherishes "an almost fanatic faith in her race, a love for her people in themselves, and a fervent belief in their pos-sibilities,"[39] admires all Negro characteristics and desires earnestly to possess them. But somehow, many of them elude her:

> Savages! Savages at heart! And she had lost or forfeited her birth-right, this primitive birthright which is so valuable and important an asset, a birthright that all the civilized races were struggling to get back to—this fact explained the art of a Picasso or a Stravinsky. To be sure, she, too, felt this African beat—it completely aroused her emotionally—but she was conscious of feeling it. This love of drums, of exciting rhythms, this naïve delight in glowing colour—the colour that exists only in cloudless, tropical climes—this warm, sexual emo-tion, all these were hers only through a mental understanding.[40]

Particularly in the early passages of *Nigger Heaven*, there is some self-consciousness apparent in the usually felicitous style, probably because Carl purposely tried to avoid his usual, light-fingered, sleight-of-hand manipulations of syntax. In an early sequence, the reader meets the wrong kind of Negro intellectuals—those who deny the gifts of their own race—in the persons of Hester Albright and her dreadful mother, who pretend offense at the "hopelessly vulgar" primitive art, and Hester's sterile friend Orville, who mincingly translates everything into phony French. Here, the Van Vechten manner worked with first-rate satiric effect; at a later party, it did not. Mary Love meets Gareth Johns, who is dining in the home of a Negro for the first time, and attempting, not very

[39] *Nigger Heaven*, p. 89.
[40] *Ibid.*, pp. 89–90.

successfully, to be easy in his manner. "What a charming place you have . . . he began in a rather high key, from which the note of astonishment was not entirely lacking." Later in the evening, Mary quotes some poetry of Wallace Stevens at the dinner table, in a well-meant attempt by Van Vechten to mirror the intelligence of her character; but the scene is faintly Firbankian in tone:

> So you know Wallace Stevens! Gareth cried with enthusiasm.
> Not all by heart, but . . . Peter Quince at the Clavier, and The Emperor of Ice-Cream, and . . .
> Tea! Gareth interrupted. Oh, do, for my sake, recall Tea!

> When the elephant's-ear in the park
> Shrivelled in frost,
> And the leaves on the paths
> Ran like rats,
> Your lamp-light fell
> On shining pillows,
> Of sea-shades and sky-shades,
> Like umbrellas in Java.

> Will you have any more of the fish? Mrs. Sumner inquired.[41]

But, additionally, the scene at the dinner table supplies a look at Harlem from the Negro's point of view:

> To us on the outside it seems magnificent, a dream come true, the doctor continued, sipping his Sauterne. A Negro city almost as large as Rome! We couldn't have counted on that a few years ago. You have everything here: shops and theatres and churches and libraries. . . .
> And cabarets, added Mary. You should have mentioned them first.[42]

As the novel progresses, however, the reader begins to suspect that perhaps some of the stilted phraseology is present only in his own eyes; he forgets, as Carl must have intended him to do, that he is reading about Negroes, even when they are talking about themselves:

[41] *Ibid.*, pp. 100–101. [42] *Ibid.*, p. 102.

Try Harlem, will you? Dick's lip curled cynically. I guess you won't find that much easier. Howard here is a lawyer, but the race doesn't want coloured lawyers. If they're in trouble they go to white lawyers, and they go to white banks and white insurance companies. They shop on white One hundred and twenty-fifth Street. Most of 'em, he added fiercely, pray to a white God. You won't get much help from the race.

Don't they want a member of the race to get on?

Say, Dick inquired, where have you been living? They *do* not. You'll have to fight your own race harder than you do the other . . . every step of the way. They're full of envy for every Negro that makes a success. They hate it. It makes 'em wild. Why, more of us get on through the ofays than through the shines.[43]

This kind of conversation moved Charles Johnson of *Opportunity* to write to Carl, "Your observations and honesty are to be thanked for this, although you managed to get what many Negroes will regard as 'family secrets.' "[44] Another example comes through Mary and Byron:

What can we do? Byron demanded, clasping and unclasping his hands. Here we are in an alien world. We think, we feel. We do our best to fit in. We don't want *them*. All we want is to be let alone, a chance to earn money, to be respectable.

I believe, Mary said, that they actually prefer us when we're not respectable.[45]

The two speakers in this passage meet in the first chapter, at a weekend house party given by Adora Boniface (who is clearly A'lelia Walker, Carl's Harlem hostess). Almost immediately, Byron and Mary fall in love, though the romance is doomed: Mary, at war with herself, is an idealist, impatient but content to look forward to improved conditions for her people; Byron, jostled and enraged at every turn by a rising feeling of racial inequality, is unwilling to wait in his determination to succeed. Mary is not strong

[43] *Ibid.*, pp. 119–120.
[44] CVV, NYPL.
[45] *Nigger Heaven*, p. 148.

217

enough to give him the stability he needs to survive in an unfriendly white world, and he succumbs to the steamy charms of Lasca Sartoris, "a legend in Harlem . . . who had married a rich African in Paris and had eventually deserted him to fulfill her amorous destiny with a trap drummer. . . ."[46]

With several considerable alterations, Lasca is a full-blown portrait of Nora Holt, the glamour girl Carl had met during his Harlem forays. When *Nigger Heaven* was published, she wrote from France: "The cries of protest from the Harlemites reach me even in Paris. . . . Strange that in such a short time you caught the attitude of the Negro toward the Negro and not one in a thousand of them will admit it."[47]

The affair between Lasca and Byron eats through the pages of two or three chapters with an erotic sensuality, in spite of the lawyer's pre-publication deletions, and ends in a hopeless shambles when Lasca's attentions turn to a gross but wealthy numbers racketeer. When the racketeer is slain by the Scarlet Creeper, a first-class Harlem stud, Byron is ironically arrested for the murder, bringing the novel to a melodramatic but nevertheless affecting conclusion. Like Harold and Peter and Gareth, Byron Kasson was, in spite of his color (or perhaps, in the Van Vechten canon in 1926, because of it), another lonely youth, echoing Carl's letter to Mabel Dodge Luhan, "a man who is alone in the world and is very sad."[48]

Nigger Heaven appeared in August, 1926, dedicated to Fania Marinoff. The contract for the book was witnessed by James Weldon Johnson, who wrote, off the cuff, an epitaph for Carl:

> *Here lies the tallow-headed late*
> *Idol of the sophisticate:*
> *He kneads his dough with a dingy leaven;*
> *He rolls his own and shouts "Come seven!";*
> *He's got wings in Nigger Heaven.*[49]

[46] *Ibid.*, p. 81.
[47] CVV, NYPL.
[48] Yale.
[49] Yale.

Much earlier—nearly a year before Carl started on the novel—Johnson had written: "I am quite . . . anxious for you to write on the subject now out of your larger knowledge & more intimate experiences. Besides, as I once said to you, no acknowledged American novelist has yet made use of this material."[50]

Nigger Heaven proceeded with fantastic speed. Nora Holt remembered more than one time when, following an all-night bender at the Van Vechten apartment, Carl would move from the bar to the typewriter, consume several cups of strong coffee, and, at seven in the morning, begin to write. On other occasions, after watching the winter sun rise over some Harlem cabaret, he would weave his way to a taxi, return to West Fifty-fifth Street, and start to work on the book. This behavior was not particularly unusual; it was expected, it was accepted. Donald Angus, a close friend of Carl's through the whole period, reflected in all seriousness that nobody ever completely sobered up. They moved from party to party, from club to club, drinking anything offered them. People drank all night, every night; when they slept has never been ascertained. Carl apparently went without sleep for months at a time; he worked as long as twelve hours a day on *Nigger Heaven*.

One wonders how. During that 1925–26 winter, he later admitted, he was wholly or partly drunk around the clock. Such a path would have doubtless led to alcoholism, had it not been for a sharp turn it took in October, 1929, when almost everybody sobered up in a hurry. But that was a long way away. Usually with Donald Angus—a young man he had met a few years earlier, first a fan, then an intimate friend—Carl took off for Harlem in the evenings. In the beginning, they went to places like Small's, popular, well known, fashionable; but later investigations led to Philadelphia Jimmy's and Leroy's, tough places he had been warned against, where whites never went, where regular fights occurred, where indeed he could have been slugged or robbed or both. Six A.M. breakfasts of scrambled eggs and tomatoes and Scotch highballs could as easily begin a new bender as end another. Trips

[50] Yale.

to the theater could intervene: Noel Coward sniffed cocaine in his own *The Vortex* that season; Lunt and Fontanne had revived Shaw's *Arms and the Man*, and Helen Hayes his *Caesar and Cleopatra*. Local celebrations could intervene: Jimmy Walker became New York's mayor with a 400,000-vote majority. Minor excursions could intervene: John Colton, the playwright, escorted Carl and Angus and the visiting Somerset Maugham and his secretary Gerald Haxton on a field trip to a whorehouse in Harlem. And, occasionally, the composition of *Nigger Heaven* could intervene.

The three drafts were completed between November and March, but the successive versions were altered considerably. Passages were cut that might adversely reflect on the Negro in the eyes of white readers; for example, "We're most of us lazy, and indirect, and careless, and if we get anywhere it's usually luck." The working over of dialect was almost mathematical, as in the change from the conventional and inaccurate "Dis am Nigger Heaven" to "Dis heah is Nigger Heaven" in Ruby's apostrophe to Harlem. Negro phrases and catchwords were substituted for customary expressions, and a glossary was appended to explain them. *Nigger Heaven* is the most thorough piece of writing Carl Van Vechten ever accomplished; if not his best novel, it is certainly his most polished one and in many ways his most significant. Published simultaneously in England and America, it appeared also in translation, during the next half-dozen years, in almost every country where American literature circulated: Czechoslovakia, Denmark, France, Germany, Hungary, Italy, Norway, Sweden, Poland, and even in Estonia.

The first American edition was—appropriately—bound in tan cloth, stamped in blue; the large-paper, limited edition appeared in yellow flowered cloth, boxed in a black and tan slipcase. As usual, Carl sent out dozens of copies to his family and friends. Brother Ralph sent his congratulations: "You have done more for the Negro than anyone since Abraham Lincoln, and I say this advisedly."[51] From Michigan, Uncle Charlie appended a few ideas of his own:

[51] CVV, NYPL.

The Darktown Strutter's Ball

You have one perceives the modern way of stopping without an ending, leaving it to the reader's imagination to carry on. The mid-Victorian writer and some too of the moderns, would have added some twenty to forty chapters after you quit work. Following your last sentence would have been something like this:

> Then there flamed within Byron all the long pent-up hatred of the savage for the conquering dominant white race. For the moment he was endowed with superhuman strength. Seizing the policeman with marvelous celerity he for an instant held him high above his head, then dashed the officer to the floor with a force that carried with it death. Then, before the astonished spectators could do a thing to stop him, even if they wished so to do, he gained the door and was gone. After that, of course far and away and under an assumed name, he could achieve his wished-for literary success and acquire a respectable standing, always with nemesis on his trail. After his inevitable capture, the trial, the appeal, the final sentence, the execution. O you miss a lot by being born so late.[52]

Several writers to whom copies had gone, though not so loquacious as Uncle Charlie, sent their appreciation. "Broad, barbaric, and so alive that it bleeds," wrote Ellen Glasgow.[53] Avery Hopwood dashed off one of his rare but characteristic notes:

> I am explaining to ... [readers] that you really see little of Harlem, these days, but that you saw a great deal of it before you *passed*. They are all so surprised to hear about your Negro strain, but I tell them that your best friends *always knew*.[54]

From Gertrude Stein:

> You have never done anything better it is rather perfectly done and that is one of the things I like about it most ... neither too delicate nor too anything and yourself in it ... really Carl the way you have kept it delicate and real it is the most perfect workmanship, and the first party ... is one of your best parties and you know what I think of your parties, the rest of it is all good and the interest as the critics

[52] CVV, NYPL.
[53] CVV, NYPL.
[54] CVV, NYPL.

say never stops, I am awfully pleased that it is so good more pleased than I can say.[55]

The customarily reserved James Branch Cabell wrote from Richmond, Virginia:

> After a purposeful leisured reading of Nigger Heaven I abound in the most honest sort of admiration. Here is, I am sure, upon a number of counts, your most excellent book. . . . I have no way of conjecturing in how much the book is "true" to the . . . life of the Negro colony. Yet if the volume is relatively "true" I incline to think you have prepared an astounding and invaluable contribution to sociology, a thing of permanent scientific value, whereas if it is not all, or even not at all, "true," it ranks as a work of the most remarkable creative genius. Either way, you thus seem to me to have done a splendid thing. . . .
>
> I can but repeat . . . I very heartily admire this book. But I repeat that utterance with the most profound sincerity. And I hopefully await the row this book must almost inevitably arouse in all camps.[56]

The row was, of course, inevitable. Carl Van Vechten must have realized this from the beginning. Perhaps it was the speed with which he had discovered and documented the Negro world which offended so many people; perhaps it was the extent—which also implies the limitations—of his knowledge which rendered it invalid for numbers of readers. On the other hand, perhaps it was the excitement of finding Harlem (in an age that thrived on fads) which popularized Carl's writings about the Negro. In either instance, the response was myopic and even occasionally silly. College sophomores wrote for explanations of Negro cant, and would-be writers constantly requested permission to send him manuscripts on Negro subjects. Other letters from strangers were vicious, contending that his work had done permanent damage to Negroes connected with the arts. But, as Langston Hughes said: "To say that Carl Van Vechten has harmed Negro creative activities is sheer poppycock.

[55] CVV, NYPL; *Yale Gazette*, October, 1952, p. 80.
[56] CVV, NYPL.

The Darktown Strutter's Ball

The bad Negro writers were bad long before *Nigger Heaven* appeared on the scene, and would have been bad anyway, had Mr. Van Vechten never been born."[57] Nevertheless, more than occasionally Carl was attracted to Negro writing, Negro performing, or Negro painting simply because it was Negro, not because it was necessarily good. Bad, it may have been before *Nigger Heaven*, as Langston Hughes contended; publicized, it was not.

Carl Van Vechten's point of view tempered in time, but although the Harlem renaissance died along with the decade, his interest and affection persisted with growing conviction. Several years after *Nigger Heaven's* first appearance, James Weldon Johnson noted: "Has anyone ever written it down—in black and white—that you have been one of the most vital factors in bringing about the artistic emergence of the Negro in America. Well—I am glad to bear witness to the fact. . . ."[58] A quarter of a century later, another old friend, Nora Holt, remarked how much he had done to "engender social equality . . . through the good old American tradition of the family—in the parlour and the dining room!"

Still—almost as an aside, nearly forty years later—in terms of years and intimacy his oldest Negro friend could not understand how Carl could have been so thoughtless, so unkind, as to call the novel *Nigger Heaven*.

[57] *The Big Sea*, p. 272.
[58] Yale; *80 Writers*.

223

IX

The Splendid Drunken Twenties 2

I possess only sufficient skill to write about what happens to interest and please myself; and in the manner that pleases myself; with the further limitation that I never entirely succeed even in doing that. If, then, I succeed in pleasing others, that must largely be in the nature of an accident.

THE MONTH AFTER THE PUBLICATION OF *Nigger Heaven*, Carl and Fania went to Europe to escape the monotony of New York's vacuous search for pleasure. They stopped in Paris long enough to renew acquaintance with Gertrude Stein and Alice Toklas, who were just then seeing the monumental *The Making of Americans* through something less than the success they had anticipated. The publication of Ernest Hemingway's *The Sun Also Rises* had already begun to convince his generation that it was lost, and life on the Left Bank, Carl discovered, was not very different from life in Manhattan. The twenties may have been roaring in French instead of English, but the noise was very nearly identical.

He spent part of the trip in London, enjoying some of the publicity that accompanied the English editions of *Nigger Heaven* and *The Tattooed Countess*, both issued just before his arrival, renewing British memories and seeing British friends, and staging apocryphal orgies at the Savoy. Twenty years later, Burton Rascoe remembered that it had been said that "Van Vechten took several floors of the hotel, stocked them with liquors and vintage wines, and held open house for days and nights,"[1] though Carl never gave a party at the Savoy.

Back in America, *The New Yorker* was again requesting a piece on A'lelia Walker, and *Vanity Fair* wanted a new article about George Gershwin or perhaps Lotta Crabtree, the New York girl who had toured the mining camps of the West. Carl returned to

[1] CVV, NYPL.

224

New York in January, 1927, but not to write for magazines or to approve any of the Theatre Guild's suggestions—Sidney Howard or Maxwell Anderson or Laurence Stallings—as a possible dramatizer of *Nigger Heaven*. Memories of that curious film version of *The Tattooed Countess* nudged him into a Hollywood visit, and he paused in New York only long enough to change his English tweeds for garments more suitable for California.

He stopped along the way in Taos, New Mexico, where Mabel Dodge Luhan had opened a Western version of her 23 Fifth Avenue salon. She had first visited New Mexico in 1916 with Maurice Sterne, her third husband. After that divorce, she stayed on to marry Antonio Luhan. Gradually, an art colony developed: Witter Bynner was a permanent resident in the neighborhood; so was Spud Johnson and, later, Lady Dorothy Brett. D. H. Lawrence was the first of many artists and writers who paused for a time at Mabel Dodge Luhan's oasis; but Carl's visit was only momentary. He headed for Hollywood.

His introduction to the "fourth largest industry" (as it was called then) was effected through a new acquaintance, Aileen Pringle, whose wit and beauty had made her the darling of the literary lions of the 1920's. For Carl Van Vechten, however, she became something considerably more than another fancy fad of the period—indeed, one of the warmest friends of his entire life. The devotion, it should be added, worked both ways, for they eventually became a mutual admiration society.

Aileen Pringle had first come to New York to study at the American Academy of Dramatic Arts. Shortly thereafter, she played the ingénue role in a play starring Marguerite Namara, in which an unknown actor named Rudolph Valentino played the villain. Later, after a run in *The Green Goddess* with George Arliss, Aileen returned to her home in California for a rest, and suddenly found herself in the movies.

In 1924, she starred in Elinor Glyn's *Three Weeks*, based on a novel that Carl certainly remembered from his Paris correspondent days when he had interviewed the glamorous author. Mrs. Glyn, delighted that the ebullient Aileen had been cast in the leading role, fancied a marked resemblance between the two of them. Mrs. Glyn had an extraordinary imagination. In *Three Weeks*, Aileen Pringle alternately reclined on beds of roses, tiger skins, and chiffon-draped chaise longues, in spectacularly beautiful settings designed by Cedric Gibbons. After that, she seems to have made most of her movies from a supine position, perpetually typecast as an Elinor Glyn heroine. But she differed from her sister sirens to a considerable degree: Aileen Pringle could laugh at the absurdities of her roles on the silent screen and the single-mindedness of the casting directors. "They invariably cast me as queens and duchesses," she recalls. "I don't think they even reduced me to a countess."

An outlandish but nevertheless true story about her is, however, not very regal—the kind of story that endeared her to the literati of the twenties. In another Glyn opus, a romantic epic of old Scotland, Edmund Lowe was required by the script to bound up a great flight of stairs, wrap the lady in a slippery sealskin cape, sweep her into his arms, and descend again. During the several takes, Aileen could feel herself imperceptibly slipping, each time a little farther, from Lowe's rather short arms. The director, a rangy fellow more than six feet tall, in a rage over the delay, tossed Aileen on his hip to demonstrate with ease. Finally, the scene was printed, but the wrath of several lip readers in the audiences descended when they "read" Aileen's words on the silent screen during the staircase journey: "If you drop me, you bastard, I shall murder you!"

In 1925, she returned to New York on holiday, an established movie queen. Aileen Pringle had already known Joseph Hergesheimer in California and, through him, the Knopfs and Mencken and several other writers. Carl Van Vechten shortly joined the fan club. During the eight-day visit to New York—which extended to one of eight months—T. R. Smith brought Carl around to Aileen's apartment while she was down with a cold. Wearing an Inverness cape and carrying a bunch of violets for the beautiful mascot of the literati, Carl began a long and pleasant friendship. When he went to

Hollywood two years later, Aileen showed him the town. The Pringle tour outdid anything he could have dreamed up in his fiction.

He visited the studios to watch Cecil B. DeMille film the earthquake sequence for *The King of Kings*, and Aileen swoon in the arms of Norman Kerry, and Emil Jannings waste his talents on a foolish script. He attended parties where he met the "Cream of American loveliness [that] had hopefully migrated to Hollywood": the "effulgent, orchidaceous" Joan Crawford; the "barbaric and sullenly splendid" Pola Negri, who dined alone in state in her Ambassador Hotel bungalow, complete with candelabra and butler; Lois Moran, who wanted to have Scott Fitzgerald play in a movie with her; Clara Bow, who wanted to play Zimbule O'Grady, the snake charmer in *The Blind Bow-Boy*. At Marion Davies's house, where the hostess did imitations of Lillian Gish and Mae Murray and Pola Negri, Carl renewed acquaintance with Elinor Glyn and for the first time met William Randolph Hearst. Sometime during the evening Carl found an opportunity to recall that the *Chicago American* had fired him in 1906 "for lowering the tone of the Hearst papers." Hearst's laughter verged on hysteria. Since his interests were financial rather than literary, he could appreciate Carl Van Vechten's celebrity in 1927: "Now," he said, "I have an excuse for having founded that paper!"[2]

A few days later, Carl attended a première with Mary Pickford and Douglas Fairbanks, mobbed along the way because he was a member in a party that included the god and goddess of the movies. "They adore, they worship these modern divinities," Carl reflected a few months later in an article for *Vanity Fair*, "and did more to convince me that democracy is an unpopular form of government than all the editorials H. L. Mencken has ever written."[3]

Vanity Fair published three other articles as well in the summer of 1927. In "Fabulous Hollywood," Carl had already written that it was "incredible, fantastic, colossal," if only because there was *more*

[2] *Fragments II*, p. 54.
[3] "Hollywood Royalty," July, 1927, p. 38.

of everything: money, sunlight, distances, jewels, oil wells, fur coats ("in a climate where they are not required"), work, poverty, bad luck, flowers ("a young man unable to come to a tea party I attended apologized for his absence by sending the hostess five dozen orchids"), police dogs, heartbreak, courage, Italian villas, Spanish houses, beautiful girls, and dissatisfaction.[4] In "Hollywood Parties," the second of the series, *Vanity Fair* readers learned that Louella Parsons had carted off to a party at Bebe Daniels's house, where the hostess's latest movie was being shown but that nobody bothered to watch ("certainly Miss Daniels didn't"); that at a party given in Beverly Hills he was stranded forty-five minutes across town from his quarters at the Ambassador Hotel; that at another party, introduced as one of the great authors of the world, the introducer asked immediately thereafter, "What have you written, Mr. Van Vechten?"[5] Aileen Pringle gave a party for him too, and, not unreasonably, Carl tossed a party of his own, attended of course by Miss Pringle. By that time he was her biggest fan, and he remembered to say so in one of the articles.

In the final member of the *Vanity Fair* quartet, called "Understanding Hollywood," he made an attempt to explain the West Coast phenomenon:

> The walls of the Hollywood houses are constructed of plaster with wire netting between so that it would be quite possible to kick a hole through the average domicile. A good deal of the Hollywood attitude is equally hollow, but I never found the occasion to kick a hole through it.
>
> There is, one senses immediately, a group spirit which unites to confound the inimical stranger or to welcome the trusted stranger, but no visitor is entirely trusted. It is obvious that the native sons wish us to regard the bright side of their existence. No attempt is made to tell the guest the number of people killed in the super-specials, or to relate stories of down-and-out extras and superseded stars. No one offered to present me a list of films, already shot at considerable expense, which later were banned by Mr. Will Hays. . . .

[4] May, 1927, p. 54.
[5] June, 1927, p. 86.

I do not mention the gnawing envy of the extra gal who sadly takes her bus from studio to studio seeking anxiously for work while she watches the Rolls Royces roll by.[6]

In addition to writing his Hollywood investigations when he returned to New York, Carl revised *Peter Whiffle* slightly—primarily spellings and accent marks—for an illustrated edition. Printed from newly set plates in a larger typeface, it was bound in a cartoon-map of Paris by Ralph Barton and boxed. To satisfy collectors, Knopf went through the real absurdity—at Carl's suggestion for sublime snobbery—of beautifully, superbly printing the Barton map for twenty copies on pure silk; and he inserted a limitation notice to prove it. Years later, Carl said that Joseph Hergesheimer was "the conscious artist, perhaps the first on such a grand scale I had met."[7] But, by the fall of 1927, Carl had tried hard to replace him, and not only with silk bindings. The extravagance and the elegance of the period, compounded by the considerable income from his books, led in other directions. If Hergesheimer liked to claim "there are only a few of us left," Carl wanted to be included: always a hoarder and a saver, he had bundles of pamphlets and clippings, magazines and advertising broadsides that included his own work all packaged into beautifully upholstered file boxes, across the spine of each were his name, *Opera*, and a "volume" number; he had entire collections of various periodicals—*Trend*, the *Reviewer*, *Vanity Fair*—sewn into gay cloth bindings; he had his own name watermarked into the paper he used for stationery; he slipcased rare pamphlets and first editions of his various excavated writers. All of which, admittedly, was preservative; all of which, equally admittedly, was outrageously extravagant, expensive, unnecessary, and symptomatic.

A couple of curious letters awaited Carl when he returned to New York from California, the first from an autograph hunter who did not promise to cherish but to sell Carl's signature: "Frankly I think that an author who is in a position to pay someone's rent for three days simply by signing his name to a letter is practically an

[6] August, 1927, p. 78.
[7] *Fragments I*, p. 13.

Economic Menace anyway, and ought to pacify the proletariat, on all possible occasions, just in case of revolution."[8] Carl accused Mencken of perpetrating a hoax. The Baltimore oracle pleaded innocent, but suggested that the fellow handle autographs in bulk and pay a commission. He and Carl could use the money, he said, in the gin traffic.

The other letter was from Theodore Dreiser, singing a hymn to the bucolic life in Pennsylvania: "There is something quite marvelous about a cross country junket at this time of year. I have done something like 150 miles so far, have lost weight, and regained a jaded appetite. . . . Come out and do a day with me."[9] Carl demurred; walking was scarcely one of his major pastimes, and Dreiser was an uneasy companion at best. From time to time in the period, they did meet—Carl included Dreiser at an occasional party in the West Fifty-fifth Street apartment—but not always happily. He was neither a natural partygoer nor a party giver: Anita Loos once reported to Carl that, in the middle of one of Dreiser's own crowded gatherings, she "discovered him in the butler's pantry, dissolved in tears, shed no doubt for the sorrows of the world."[10] And the disastrous evening involving Scott Fitzgerald and the bottle of champagne—after which Mencken reported to Carl that he and Ernest Boyd were "sinking for the third time when the St. Bernard dogs of the monastery in Irving place" found them ready to expire as a result of poor Dreiser's ineptitude—is reasonable evidence.[11]

On the occasion of the sale to the movies of *An American Tragedy*, Dreiser decided to celebrate with a first-class blast. He asked Dwight Taylor, the son of actress Laurette Taylor, then very much a flaming youth of the twenties, how to go about it. He wanted the "most fashionable" night club in town; he wanted dinner and entertainment and "plenty of champagne." The guests—Ernest Boyd and his wife, Covarrubias, Carl and Fania among them—arrived as bidden. Taylor remembered that they found

8 Yale.
9 Yale; *The Collected Letters of Theodore Dreiser*, Vol. II, p. 455.
10 *Fragments II*, p. 12.
11 Yale; *Fragments I*, p. 57.

Dreiser and his mistress . . . established as a sort of receiving line of two inside the foyer. Helen wore an evening gown, bought especially for the occasion, shimmering with red spangles like a circus rider's. Dreiser, big as he was, had managed somehow to find evening clothes that were even bigger, and . . . [he] clutched an enormous pair of white cotton gloves in his left hand, in some dim, elephantine memory of dancing school.[12]

There were, indeed, champagne buckets and bottles at every other place, and the table was strewn with large American Beauty roses that became entangled in the food as the dinner progressed. In desperation, nearly everyone drank as much as he could hold, arguing violently all the time about art and life, while Dreiser sat with his back to his guests to watch the floor show. The evening was of course another disaster.

But in spite of his behavior, Carl later reflected, Dreiser was "actually perverse enough to enjoy the company of people," and he loved asking questions. Once, to liven up the generally dismal proceedings, Carl brought along a boy named Max Ewing. As usual, Dreiser was "concerned with an idea." What became of handsome men, he wanted to know; what would become of Max in ten years?[13] An attractive figure during the twenties, Max Ewing had come into Carl's orbit in 1922, when, still a student at the University of Michigan, he had written a front-page piece about *Peter Whiffle* and his author that so astonished readers of the campus newspaper that it was reprinted in the *Detroit Free Press* shortly thereafter and then suppressed. Carl was delighted enough (and flattered enough) to write to Ewing, telling him he was too bright to fritter away his life in college. Very shortly, Max Ewing had camped permanently in Manhattan and, in the ensuing years, became another symptom of the social disease that blighted the era. Among other things, Max's "art gallery"—actually his own apartment, papered, pasted, and otherwise covered with a risqué and ribald collection of photographs—became one of the seven wonders of a world that began on Armistice Day and ended with the stock

12 *Joy Ride*, p. 230.   13 *Fragments II*, pp. 10–11.

231

market crash. Theodore Dreiser's question about the future of beautiful youth remained unanswered: Max Ewing drowned himself a few years later, despondent over his mother's death.

Carl was, however, harder hit by Avery Hopwood's death, which "nearly knocked me flat. I don't think anything before ever affected me so much,"[14] he wrote Gertrude Stein. The immediate reaction of the press and even of some acquaintances was that, Hopwood being a notorious drinker, he had drowned in a drunken stupor at Juan-les-Pins. But Fania, holidaying in the south of France at the time, wrote to Carl to squelch the rumors: Avery Hopwood had suffered a sudden heart attack—in scarcely two feet of water. Hopwood's death was the third in quick succession for Carl to endure: in 1926, his father, simply of old age, at eighty-six; the following autumn, his brother, of a heart attack, at sixty-five.

At that time, Ralph Van Vechten was the director of several banks and three railroad companies, with sound investments and considerable stock holdings. The estate amounted to six million dollars. The bulk went to his wife, Fannie, with a stipulation that at her own death two-thirds would then pass in trust to their adopted daughter Duane; the other third was to be divided equally in trust between Carl and his sister Emma's son Van Vechten Shaffer. When Fannie Van Vechten died eight months after her husband, Carl found himself with a considerable fortune: one million dollars in trust. Additionally, Avery Hopwood's will left him about forty thousand dollars. All this, coupled with the royalties from the fantastically successful *Nigger Heaven* and the less popular but nevertheless remunerative earlier novels, put far behind him the difficult years before *Peter Whiffle*.

The shift from man of letters to man of means, however, had little immediate effect upon his working habits—at least in the beginning. For more than a dozen years, he had always written almost compulsively, the successive versions of his several books rolling through his typewriter in a matter of months, usually in three complete drafts. He once announced—about *Firecrackers*—that he would write a chapter a day until the book was completed, and he

[14] Yale.

232

did, or very nearly so. He once advised Langston Hughes to write a specified amount every day—three hundred words, for example—and stick to that amount, even if on the preceding day he had turned out two thousand; this method, he admitted, was "hard at first and very easy after a week or two."[15] Whether or not he adhered to the suggestion himself, Carl Van Vechten did continue work on a new novel in the fall of 1927. Predictably, it dealt with Hollywood.

CARL BEGAN THE FIRST DRAFT of *Spider Boy* in August and completed it in nine weeks. The second took about the same length of time; a month later, in January, 1928, the third was finished. There were, however, few corrections along the way. The complete typing of the three full drafts of the novel seems to have been largely a matter of routine, accomplished between regular house calls from the bootlegger. The Van Vechten touch had become assured through the decade, swift, acid, and clever. As the note on the dust jacket averred, *Spider Boy* was his "gayest novel." It was also his slightest: a neatly constructed, slapdash, and merry myth of the papier-mâché life in Hollywood, with some lamentable lapses into Mack Sennett slapstick that cannot be excused as purposeful, because much of the book was a tirade against the "fourth largest industry" in the country. It is insufficient, for example, that Carl Van Vechten's hero balance precariously on the mudguard of a milk truck, in which he tries to escape the clutches of a Theda Bara vamp; he is required to fall "flat on his belly in the street" afterward. Similarly, he is slammed by a reflector in one of the studios and knocked to the floor. He upsets fingerbowls, stumbles over his own feet, and most of the time behaves like a silent-screen comedian. If these and other kindred incidents were designed as part of the "scenario for a motion picture," as the book was subtitled, they were not important enough to be justified. The satire in one direction was too extravagant and in the other not sharp enough to be incisive.

To many readers, the book was certainly "riotously funny," as the *Boston Transcript* called it; assuredly, it was an early treatment

[15] Yale.

233

of that mythological kingdom on the West Coast, and perhaps this current view stands only because Hollywood itself has poked much fun at the silent era.

Ambrose Deacon, a shy and unknown writer with a sudden Broadway hit, flees New York to visit a friend in New Mexico (just as a not-so-shy writer had done on his way west the preceding year), only to be accosted en route by a Pola Negri type named Imperia Starling. She has some ideas about Ambrose's future:

> I want you to write me a love scene such as no one has ever played before . . . a scene flaming with passion . . . but kind, sympathetic, sweet passion. . . . I see a Russian empress with her jewels, her fans, her laces, lying on a couch with an American boy. . . .[16]

The satire in *Spider Boy* has already thickened by the time Ambrose meets the Great Greisheimer, a producer who tells him:

> The very ushers in our moving picture cathedrals . . . ain't permitted to smoke. Morals, even outside business hours, is one of our great concerns.[17]

Later he hires Ambrose:

> When you write a story for the pictures always keep in mind . . . the wages of sin is death, but if the motives is moral you can get in quite a bit o' necking.[18]

The story Ambrose finally writes, not for Imperia Starling but for Auburn Six, a thinly disguised Aileen Pringle, grows from his pursuit by the several women he has encountered. Actually, the script is thought up by an idea man on the lot, including its title, "Spider Boy":

> Don't you know about the male spiders?
>   The females eat 'em and the males try to escape.
>   . . . Our theme—*your* theme— is the pursuit of the male by the female. They'll pursue him in aeroplanes, in motor-cars, on bicycles,

[16] *Spider Boy*, p. 50.
[17] *Ibid.*, p. 130.
[18] *Ibid.*, p. 193.

in catamarans, canoes, coracles, gondolas, and luggers, in brigs, clippers, yawls, and junks, in trucks, jinrickshas, landaus, and droshkies, in Marmons, Rolls-Royces, Jordans, Chevrolets, Buicks, and Citroëns, on Arabian steeds, zebras, elephants, and camels. They'll even pursue him on foot.[19]

Carl's old delight in cataloguing came into play in *Spider Boy*, but the humor of abundance overshadowed the fascination of erudition. The happy combination of amusement and instruction in the old days, when criticism was his preoccupation, had upset its own balance under the influence of satire.

Before Ambrose has even finished the script, the studio turns his spider boy into a circus ceiling walker, then a Russian spy in the employ of the tsar: "Really, Auburn in boy's clothes. I had to put her in trousers occasionally," the ghost writer explains to Ambrose, "to justify the title."[20] But that too is changed, to his "other lovely old title . . . Love and Danger . . ."[21] though not before he has married, with predictable Hollywood pomp, a new starlet. The movie is a hit, and Ambrose can write his own contract. Instead, he flees, like Harold and Byron and Peter and Carl Van Vechten, back to New York.

Aileen Pringle "hated it . . . enjoyed it . . . disliked it & ended by loving it,"[22] observing that *Spider Boy* caused no stir in Hollywood "because nobody out there read any books." Gertrude Atherton and Henry Blake Fuller wrote to praise its folly. Fania read it at sea during a cruise and adored it, doubtless from her own experience in movies. George Jean Nathan called it "a thoroughly amusing job. Its drollery has just the right degree of cruelty."[23] Florine Stettheimer "would be disappointed if you don't get Ufa to do it when you go to Germany."[24] James Branch Cabell, not so voluble as he was over *Nigger Heaven*, called it "a very wildly delightful

19 *Ibid.*, pp. 200–201.
20 *Ibid.*, p. 256.
21 *Ibid.*, p. 282.
22 CVV, NYPL.
23 CVV, NYPL.
24 CVV, NYPL.

volume."[25] Even the editor of a currently popular movie magazine had words of praise: "A much better job than any of the hard-hitting literary blacksmiths have done."[26]

But at least two reviewers scorned *Spider Boy*, and for perfectly valid reasons. Clifton Fadiman declared the satire

> without sparkle or good nature and . . . so obvious that the attentive reader . . . scents it twenty pages ahead. On the whole, Mr. Van Vechten is a mediocre reporter of the smart cracks of five years ago and a fairly good purveyor of the appetites of the upper-class fourteen year olds.[27]

Nor was Dorothy Parker, the "Constant Reader," very happy:

> It appears that your correspondent is in a minority amounting practically to an isolation in her attitude. . . . People think that this fantastic satire on Hollywood is keen, amusing, brilliant, and important. Well, I don't. People say it sparkles, entertains, and instructs. I just keep quiet. People cry that Mr. Van Vechten is light-headed, erudite, gifted, and inspired. And I go right out and take a good rousing walk around the reservoir.[28]

Bound in pink cloth and stamped in gold, *Spider Boy* had a first edition of twenty thousand copies—an increase of four thousand over that of *Nigger Heaven* and nearly seven times that of *Peter Whiffle*—and appeared in late 1928, dedicated to Blanche Knopf ("with pansies and kinkajous and love"). But there was no immediate need for further printings. By the end of September, the sales had begun to dwindle. Two thousand copies were left, and Ronald McRae's clever dust jacket began to function, as its name implies, on another five hundred in the Knopf offices.

To match the novel's extravagance, Knopf had given *Spider Boy* the snootiest of all the limited editions by issuing not only 220 signed and numbered copies on rag paper, bound up in blue boards

[25] CVV, NYPL.
[26] CVV, NYPL.
[27] *Bookman*, circa August, 1928.
[28] *The New Yorker*, August, 1928.

with pink spines, but also an extra 75 in red vellum, their heavy Inomachi Japan pages shot with strands of silk, uncut and untrimmed of course, signed and numbered too, a red satin ribbon bookmark depending from the top of the spine. It was an old Knopf trick—two limited editions—that had served for Joseph Hergesheimer's novels for years. The sales of *Spider Boy* were not improved, however, by Carl's having been asked into the club. Several months earlier, he had made a second trip to Hollywood, ostensibly to get Charlie Chaplin's signature as witness on the contract with Knopf for *Spider Boy*, but he stayed long enough to renew acquaintance with Aileen Pringle and to make a few new ones. Miss Pringle remembers introducing Carl to Greta Garbo during his reinvasion of the film colony. The first encounter went well: they got on amicably, and Carl promised to send the "painfully shy" actress a Swedish translation of *Nigger Heaven*, then just released; Miss Garbo, ordinarily terrified of strangers, seemed to be enchanted by him. A few days later, she rang up Aileen Pringle for a game of tennis on Matt Moore's court. After the match, Aileen said that Carl was coming over to call for her, thinking that Garbo would be pleased to see her new acquaintance again. "No," she said gloomily, "I would not like to do it again," and she disappeared into the house until he had come and gone.

After his return to New York, Carl sailed almost immediately for Europe. Between this trip and the preceding one, there had been no apparent letup in the local high jinks. He occupied—quite by accident—part of the royal suite on the *Mauretania*, and gave a going-away party that everybody he knew in New York seems to have attended. There was nothing to drink but champagne; as the celebration progressed, the guests got increasingly drunk on the wine and one another's company: Witter Bynner composed twelve verses on the spot in commemoration of the occasion, and in the final moments Nora Holt belted out *My Daddy Rocks Me With One Steady Roll*. When she finished, an unidentified Southern lady tottered up to her to confide, "How well you sing spirituals, my dear." Two days out to sea, Carl wrote to Emily Clarke, "I am sure the personnel of the ship must have decided that Booker T. Washington was sailing . . . ."[29]

CARL AND FANIA JOURNEYED SOUTH to Italy that fall. In October, they were in Florence, and one bright day, fourteen years after the harried events of Carl's escape from Europe in 1914, he and Fania drove out to Mabel Dodge Luhan's Villa Curonia.

When she deserted it, Mrs. Luhan—then Mrs. Dodge—had said to Carl: "I'm glad I don't want *this* any more. I've done it all, sixteenth, and seventeenth, and eighteenth century art. I've made a perfect place of this and now I'm ready for whatever will come after the war. I am through with all property, as every one will have to be."[30] Her leave-taking was a little dramatic, Carl reflected, but apparently she meant it. No one had occupied the Villa Curonia since 1914. Both Mrs. Dodge and her husband Edwin had sent for quantities of furniture and pictures, and the place was largely dismantled, "yet when the caretaker opened the windows and the sun poured into the gracious rooms," Carl later wrote, "it was easy to reconstruct the past."[31]

The following February, back in New York, Carl and Fania invited their absent hostess at the villa over to meet a relatively unknown composer named Virgil Thomson. The Van Vechtens had asked him to play his score for an opera libretto Gertrude Stein had written, entitled *Four Saints in Three Acts*, "to a select crowd . . . & everybody liked it so much that yesterday I cabled you," the host wrote to Miss Stein in Paris. "I liked it so much that I wanted to hear it all over again right away. Mabel liked it so much that she said it should be done & it would finish opera just as Picasso had finished old painting."[32]

The curious mixture of liquor and literature—Carl and Thomson took off for an all-night celebration in Harlem following the recital—may not have been unique with the Van Vechten clan in

[29] Emily Clarke, *Innocence Abroad*, p. 140.
[30] *Sacred and Profane Memories*, pp. 119–120.
[31] *Ibid.*, p. 120.
[32] Yale; Donald Gallup, ed., *The Flowers of Friendship*, p. 228.

1929, but it was hardly *de rigueur* on the sidewalks of New York. Opera and old painting, and nearly everything else, verged on extinction as the speakeasy became a fashionable preoccupation for almost everybody. Liquor alone was apparently sufficient diversion. There were more than a hundred thousand speakeasies that winter, all trying to keep up with a whole city hellbent on drinking itself under a Prohibition-laden table. As the demand increased, so did the prices. Inferior champagne went for about twenty-five dollars a quart; bourbon and gin, tasting approximately the same, sold for not much less. At Texas Guinan's celebrated cabaret, brandy brought fifteen dollars a pint, cocktails $2.25 apiece, and cigarettes ten cents each. Texas Guinan yelled to the suckers from her piano perch, and the suckers—including Carl on occasion—yelled happily back. Unlike most of the customers, however, Carl was an old friend, dating back to the prewar days when he and Fania had known Texas through the theater. She and he had at least one inexhaustible topic of conversation: two celebrated sisters, who ran a famous brothel in Chicago, where Carl had first met them. Later, when the sisters had become respectable and moved to a New York suburb, Carl and Texas often threatened to go calling, but the visit never materialized. Texas Guinan was much too busy adding fuel to the fire that kept the twenties flaming.

Her establishments, on and off Manhattan Island, were legendary during their own time. Her cover charges went as high as twenty dollars a customer, and plenty of customers gladly paid it to watch Ruby Keeler dance. When Texas got raided and locked out during the great reform of 1928, she merely opened again on Long Island, where Ruby Keeler was replaced by a girl who danced with an eight-foot boa constrictor while the proprietress sat on the piano wearing a necklace of padlocks. Night-club entertainment at the close of the decade was of a kind not seen again for a whole generation. Bea Lillie broke up the patrons at the Sutton Club; Helen Morgan sang laments from Fifty-fourth Street; Libby Holman crooned at the Lido; Clifton Webb danced at Ciro's; Fred and Adele Astaire polished the floors at the Trocadero with ballroom routines; at the Casanova, Helen Kane sang "I Want to Be Bad" from a Broadway show called *Follow Thru*, and the customers went right out afterward to illustrate the lyrics. When the hours grew late, the superintelligentsia taxied up to Harlem, to the Cotton Club—by that time having Jim Crowed the Negroes out completely—or to the Savoy to watch the Negro boys and girls gyrate to the rhythms of the Lindy Hop. When the after-hours places finally closed, the customers stopped at Child's for hot cakes and coffee, lacing the latter with what may have remained in their hip flasks, or they tottered home to their own home-brew, or—like Scott Fitzgerald, who once carried his party on to the city morgue at five o'clock in the morning—they invented their own speakeasies wherever they happened to be at the moment.

It was not difficult to join the parade. Carl Van Vechten may not have led it, but he twirled a few batons of his own. With the exception of an introduction for a reissue of James Weldon Johnson's *The Autobiography of an Ex-Colored Man* and a brief paper on Ellen Glasgow, Carl wrote nothing for more than a year after the proofs of *Spider Boy* were completed. His days began when the sun set, and his nights continued until it rose again. The forays into Harlem increased in regularity, and the evenings he was not there he spent at private clubs with "perverse entertainments," as he recalled them, or sampling drugs, or inventing new amusements, or investigating the latest slumming grounds, or simply boozing at his bootlegger's speakeasy. It was a "modest place of business" in the West Forties, "furnished with sufficient number of chairs and tables of Grand Rapids manufacture, a piano, a radio, a phonograph, a few cheap rugs, and some framed lithographs of nude women."[33] The clientele could be described as various:

> There gathered not only many of the very best people—whose names appeared on the passenger lists of the Majestic or the Ile de France and who headed the reports of balls at Palm Beach or those of Reno divorces—but also others far richer, but not so well known to a

[33] *Parties*, p. 29.

tabloid public, and yet others: painters, writers, chauffeurs, actors, sailors, soldiers, and firemen.[34]

Infrequently, there were out-of-town parties at the Langners' house in Westport, Connecticut, where Carl and Fania joined Clifton Webb and Nora Holt and Marilyn Miller for holiday celebrations. But Carl, having escaped the bucolic pleasures at an early age, was never very happy in the country. Bennett Cerf remembers him there, "sitting on a throne apart, with the lordly air of a potentate." But Cerf also remembers the Van Vechten Christmas parties in New York, when it was Carl's and Fania's habit to invite all the Manhattan strays they knew—those without families, those away from home—over to celebrate the holiday.

In May, 1929, Carl was off for Europe again, in an alcoholic haze he shared with almost everyone at the time, giving dinner parties on the *Majestic* for Eva Gauthier and Gilda Gray, the shimmy queen. Once in England, he sobered up long enough for a brief visit to Hugh Walpole's country house, close on the heels of Sinclair Lewis and Gene Tunney, where he was "very happy at Brackenburn"— he gladly admitted in Walpole's English edition of *Nigger Heaven* —for a few days. Walpole's hospitality returned that which Carl had shown him on several visits to New York, and faltered only once. Carl proposed calling Fania in London, which horrified his host; the telephone had apparently never been used for long distance before, and Walpole disapproved of such extravagance. Fania took a tour of the cathedral cities with Armina Marshall and Lawrence Langner while Carl was at Brackenburn; then she joined him for a summer on the Continent.

They stopped in France at Tours, to visit Eugene O'Neill and his new wife, Carlotta Monterey, at their rented chateau. The O'Neills had just returned from the Asiatic trip that followed their marriage. Although Carl and Fania had met O'Neill fifteen years earlier at the Provincetown Playhouse in Greenwich Village, they knew Carlotta Monterey intimately at the same time as the wife of Ralph

[34] *Ibid.*

Barton, the dust-jacket artist for Carl's *The Tattooed Countess* and Paris map maker for *Peter Whiffle*. After a divorce, Carlotta's subsequent marriage to O'Neill, and Barton's early death, the Van Vechtens saw neither the playwright nor his bride until that 1929 holiday.

From there, Carl and Fania moved on to Berlin, "which was like Rome under Caligula" when they arrived: in Germany too, life had begun to imitate art, as the atmosphere of the Brecht-Weill *Threepenny Opera*, the drawings of Caspar Neher and George Grosz, and Dietrich's *Blue Angel* permeated the city. They traveled on to Salzburg for some of the concerts, and then returned to New York in the fall, back to the frenetic limbo about to be liberated by the stock market collapse a few weeks later.

Since January, 1928, when he had put the final revisions to the manuscript of *Spider Boy*, a period of eighteen months, Carl had written nothing at all. Certainly, the inheritance from his brother's estate and the financial success of a couple of his novels had something to do with the abrupt change in his working habits; but the rowdy milieu in which he moved was equally influential. In 1923, Carl's Campaspe had declared: "Is there such a thing as a tired businessman in America? I suppose so . . . . But we try not to be aware of it. It is the smart thing to do nothing. It is even a trifle démodé to write or paint."[35] Two novels later, in *Firecrackers*, Carl devoted a whole chapter to the absurdities of the business world, in which a day on Wall Street very much resembled a day "at the country club . . . or an opening night at the Follies."[36] By 1929, he had begun to believe it himself.

The vogue for a new decadence following the World War I had manifested itself in what Frederick Lewis Allen rightly called a "series of tremendous trifles." In an age gone mad for extravagant first editions, song-writing mayors, speakeasies, Harlem slumming, mah-jongg, rouged knees and bee-stung lips, opium pipes and cocaine sniffing, the Charleston, and all the other fads and crazes,

[35] *The Blind Bow-Boy*, p. 133.
[36] *Firecrackers*, p. 107.

there is something both alarming and depressing in Carl Van Vechten's involvement. He becomes, all too easily, a middle-aged playboy, the chorus line's oldest living juvenile.

When Anita Loos's *Gentlemen Prefer Blondes* appeared, he ranked it as a "work of art."[37] When Mae West undulated on Broadway in *Diamond Lil*, he ran backstage afterward, "blond, buck-toothed, bored and chi-chi," according to Miss West,[38] with John Colton to pronounce her the greatest actress since Sarah Bernhardt. Once, after commandeering Texas Guinan into witnessing his signing the contract for a novel, they roared away together from the Knopf offices in a gangster's armored car.

Carl was drunk most of the time that season, on a fairly steady diet of sidecars, but regularly interspersed with anything else his bootlegger could deliver; for, because someone or other was always giving a cocktail party, "a man with an extensive acquaintance . . . could drink steadily . . . from the beginning of cocktail time until eleven in the evening without any more expense than that entailed by car- or cab-fare."[39] After that hour, all-night benders usually ensued, with Donald Angus, with Max Ewing, with Scott and Zelda Fitzgerald when they were in town, usually in Harlem.

The parties and literary teas given by the intelligentsia seemed to one observer largely second-rate in retrospect, booze and snobbery being such curious companions. Thomas Wolfe attacked them in his novels *The Web and the Rock* and *You Can't Go Home Again*, and Carl too, as Van Vleeck, the author of "books about tattooed duchesses, post-impressionist moving picture actresses, and negro prize fighters who read Greek."[40] Carl also appeared as Wolfe's Stephen Hook, "a proud, noble, strangely twisted and tormented man" with a "white flabby face."

Carl had met Thomas Wolfe at a party given by Philip Moeller. Aline Bernstein, Wolfe's companion, was there of course, as was Elinor Wylie, who, Wolfe reported, was a horrible woman. He

[37] "Fast and Loos," *Book Review*, January 1926, p. 20.
[38] *Goodness Had Nothing to Do with It*, p. 99.
[39] *Parties*, p. 172.
[40] The Web and the Rock, p. 481.

remembered Carl through Stephen Hook's "elaborately mannered indirection," which had "provided a key to his literary style."[41] As the twenties ran out, Carl's behavior had become more "elaborately mannered," to be sure; but Wolfe's remarks applied to the past rather than to the present. By the time they met, there was no lock for the key to fit.

Like an actor who gets stuck in a very long run, Carl's performance had become a gross imitation of the role he had begun playing nearly a decade before. "It is not the novelties that make happiness, but it is their repetition," he presently quoted Raymond Radiguet in an epigraph.[42] By that time, however, the repetition had become a shallow search for anything to replace a gradually insufficient good-natured hedonism. The show had had a long run too, but the curtain finally dropped, and with a sobering thud, on October 29.

Two weeks later, Carl sat down at his typewriter, a little shakily, to write its obituary in *Parties*, his seventh and necessarily final novel.

HELD UP TO THE ARTIFICIAL LIGHT of the 1920's, *Parties* is just another Van Vechten cocktail: equal parts of irony, frivolity, topical erudition, and sex; sampled several years after those lights have been extinguished, there is a strong flavor of bitters. It is the only novel of the seven to stand as a terrible indictment of the period: the others had laughed at the foibles of the whole drunken generation; this one wept. Curiously, the reviewers were remarkably imperceptive in seeing what the novel had attempted to do; "Unsavory," "sniggering," "dull," "tasteless," "specious," they said. Clinton Simpson, in the *Saturday Review of Literature*, completely missed the point of view. Van Vechten had talents, Simpson admitted; was it not surprising then that he used them "for books such as this one, which is flippant at best and occasionally a little— even more than a little—cheap?"[43]

[41] *You Can't Go Home Again*, pp. 126–127.
[42] *Parties*, p. [ix].   [43] September 6, 1930.

Carl's Uncle Charlie did not even believe it:

> I think that you have greatly exaggerated conditions, for not even
> in New York City—the modern Babylon—can it be that people exist
> who do nothing but drink and engage in illicit amours, and who
> converse about nothing except their, or their neighbor's sexual
> peccadilloes. It is well to remember that Parties is a work of fiction.[44]

Subtitled *Scenes from Contemporary New York Life*, *Parties*
was only partly fiction, however; though most of the letters that
would have verified this were simply blank and depressing. "It is . . .
grandly amusing and . . . it makes me feel so proud to think that I've
been on so many—many such parties with you,"[45] wrote one acquaintance. Another was equally myopic: "Parties arrived yesterday, all green, yellow, bunches of grapes, sidecars and drunk; and
caught me just in the mood! DRUNK—I've been drunk for a fortnight, absolutely blind. . . ."[46]

Complete strangers reacted violently in newspapers that had
never before even bothered to review Carl's novels. In Peoria,
where he was called Van Hechten, *Parties* was a "stupid book, in-
excusably vulgar." In Ohio, it was labelled "vulgar, inane, and
rotten" in Dayton, and a "drunken debauch" in Columbus. In
Oklahoma, the book proved that "Harlem and Park Avenue are
brothers under the skin, and the skin is fairly thin." In Maine,
"theme and manner are outworn." In the Midwest again, someone
wanted to "take Mr. Van Vechten to one side and explain to him
that nobody is interested. . . ."

A single perceptive analysis appeared in the pages of *Bookman*, by
George Dangerfield.

> Like a whole classification of literature from *The Feast of Trimal-*
> *chio* onward, *Parties* promises entertainment, but offers something
> quite different and far more important. . . . And it establishes what
> one believes to be the truth—namely that the body of Van Vechten's
> work, whether good or bad or indifferent, represents in its own way

[44] CVV, NYPL.
[45] CVV, NYPL.
[46] CVV, NYPL.

a modern tragedy of manners, and that the same fate has befallen it which overtook an earlier comedy of manners; that it has been forced from the unmoral to the moral, not by outside influences but by inner compulsion.[47]

The fragmented manipulation of several plots with which Carl had experimented unsuccessfully in *Firecrackers* worked to advantage in *Parties*. Structurally, the book seems to be made up of a series of vignettes, but the total effect is staggeringly cohesive, at times surrealistic, though the surface is familiar: recognizable characters from the current set, or literati, or supper clubs, with brilliant backgrounds for them, an extravagant wit and exaggeration and satire. But the impact on the reader must have canceled all memory or recognition of any familiar manner. To anyone sobered by the stock market crash, a perusal of *Parties* must have been rather like reading excerpts from a diary that he would rather forget had ever been kept. With the oblique effect of a morality play about an aimless society, living from drink to drink, avoiding pause for fear of what sobriety might bring, *Parties* was not very entertaining.

To populate his final charade, Carl chose familiar types, as outrageous as those in earlier novels, but with the marked difference that readers who, six or eight years before, had begun to imitate the Campaspes, the Pauls, the Zimbule O'Gradys suddenly discovered they were reading about themselves and finding the identification none too pleasant. There is Simone Fly, for instance, who resembles a "gay death" with her chalk-white face, depraved mouth, and bobbed red hair. There is Donald Bliss, who is known as "the handsomest bootlegger in New York but the ladies who were clever enough to remember the old proverb, Handsome is as handsome does, had no cause to complain in the end."[48] There are Roy Fern, a homosexual drug addict; and Beauty Butcher, a pianist thus called "because his name was Marmaduke and he was very ugly"; and King Swan, Donald's chauffeur, whose habit of stowing cigarette ashes in his trouser cuffs moves a certain wag to remark that "this

[47] September 1930, p. 72.
[48] *Parties*, p. 26.

was Swan's way." There is Noma Ridge, "a young English girl with dimpled, rosy cheeks who did not drink or smoke, but who atoned for the lack of these semi-precious vices by describing in an endless monotone the various forms of her amorous transports and the characteristics of the persons with whom she enjoyed them."[49] There is Midnight Blue, a film star who, according to a friend, "takes off her drawers mentally when she talks." ("She takes them off literally when she doesn't talk," replies another.)[50] There is the aged Gräfin von Pulmernl und Stilzernl, drawn from a tiny, aristocratic lady Carl and Fania had seen in Salzburg on their European trip in 1929, who finds all the Old World pleasures she missed in the false and glittering New World of the speakeasy.

To head the cast of characters there is Hamish Wilding, the descendant of earlier Van Vechten protagonists. Finally, there are his friends David and Rilda Westlake, based to a degree on Scott and Zelda Fitzgerald, who pause momentarily to deliver the whole theme of the novel:

> We're swine, filthy swine, and we are Japanese mice and we are polar bears walking from one end of our cage to the other, to and fro, to and fro, all day, all week, all month, forever to eternity. We'll be drunk pretty soon and then I'll be off to Donald's to get drunker and you'll be off with Siegfried and get drunker and we'll go to a lot of cocktail parties and then we'll all turn up for dinner at Rosalie's where you are never invited. She won't want you, and I shall hate you, but . . . we'll get drunker and drunker and drift about night clubs so drunk that we won't know where we are, and then we'll go to Harlem and stay up all night and go to bed late tomorrow morning and wake up and begin it all over again.[51]

Not only in action, as this passage suggests, but in structure as well, *Parties* moves in a circle, going nowhere but back to its vacuous beginning. From the brilliantly constructed opening chapters, related in terms of an alcoholic nightmare involving David and

[49] *Ibid.*, p. 67.
[50] *Ibid.*, p. 69.
[51] *Ibid.*, p. 87.

Hamish, to the concluding, bitter denouement, *Parties* revolves monotonously on its own axis, unable to break its prescribed orbit. After a series of cocktail parties in New York and casual acquaintances behind unfamiliar bedroom doors, the novel travels to London and Paris through David, who leaves America in search of himself, prompted because "nobody we know does anything but drink in this crazy town." But liquor alone is not the cause of his discontent; the amorality of the milieu in which he and his wife exist contributes its share to David's ennui. He believes, he says, that they should separate because of their "damned faithfulness." He wants to get away, not so much from Rilda but

> from *us*, from what it is that makes us hate and love and drink, from this intensity of "clean" fidelity, as you call it. I want to be actually unfaithful to you in feeling and imagination as well as physically, so that I can return to you free. . . . I never make a move or commit an action without considering whether it will annoy you or not. I swear that the strongest sensation I experience when I look at another woman is to wonder what effect it will have on you. That's why I get drunk so often. That's why you get drunk so often. We get drunk to forget we belong to each other and when we are drunk we remember harder than ever.[52]

The repetition of the novelties has, apparently, begun to wear thin, but the escape to Europe offers David no solution. There is only further repetition, which certainly does not lead to happiness: with Midnight Blue on board ship ("Now, my dear . . . I never allow anything but silk and flesh to touch my body. Do we or don't we?"[53]); with Hamish Wilding's wife and a passing fancy named Mrs. Alonzo W. Syreno in London; with Malvina Crane, a dancer, in Paris—and each of the encounters liberally fortified with liquor. David returns to New York neither a sadder nor a wiser man than he was when he started. Whether he wants to admit it or not, love is for him as it is for Noma Ridge, "like picnicking. . . . It's all right when one is very young to eat one's lunch lying about on the damp

52 *Ibid.*, p. 82.
53 *Ibid.*, p. 103.

248

grass, but later in life we are likely to be more comfortable at the Ritz. It's more convenient in the long run to substitute affection or passion for the grand emotion."[54] David ends where he began, back in the vacuum, along with the others. Nobody escapes.

This jagged sophistication, apparent in the earlier books though not as bitter coating on a much more bitter pill, was even more pointedly directed when, later in the novel, one of David's casual dalliances gives a party to which a Negro seeress comes, pronouncing some unpleasant truths for several of the characters: their shallowness, their vanity, their "misdirected thought through self." Of Hamish Wilding, however, she is more explicit:

> You do not know yourself. . . . You don't know where you are, or who you are, or what you are, or what you want. You are not unhappy, you are miserable. You do not understand. . . . You want so much so badly, and you do not know what it is you want. . . . Poor, dear creature, poor boy, I would like to help you, so many people would like to help you, but we do not know what it is you want.[55]

Suddenly, late in the novel, Hamish Wilding becomes the focus of attention. Apparent from the first chapter, Hamish hovers on nearly every page; sardonic and sentimental, he touches the reader only subtly because of the more flamboyant David. In the scene with the seeress, however, one realizes with a kind of shock that the real tragedy of *Parties* lies not with David and Rilda Westlake but with Hamish Wilding. Like his older brothers—Byron and Harold and Peter and Gareth—he is, once again, Carl Van Vechten's "man who is alone," caught up in a senseless drive toward self-destruction, in a desperate need to identify, even when that identification leads to moral suicide. In *Parties*, he "must occasionally do something, out of the way, to behave in a manner that would be considered almost bad form by some of his friends."[56] But even this is rendered futile by his own unwillingness to break away. He does not, as the seeress says, know what it is that he wants. David

[54] *Ibid.*, p. 156.
[55] *Ibid.*, pp. 232–233.
[56] *Ibid.*, p. 237.

is the mover and shaker of the duet, suffering a common malady, but Hamish is infinitely more tragic, unable to function independently: immediately, on David's return from Europe, they are once again "as drunk as anyone had ever seen them."[57]

In spite of the perversions, the immorality, the sophistication that, paradoxically, both dull and sharpen every situation and character in *Parties*, the novel's conclusion leaves no doubt about its ultimate purpose. With the stock market crashing down about their heads, the whole zoo of them converges in the Westlake apartment for a final cocktail party. "It's just like the opening chorus of an opéra-bouffe," Simone Fly gaily remarks, "all of us here clinking glasses like villagers on the village green." The wise old Gräfin corrects her: "Somehow, it's more like the closing chorus. . . . I think we're all a little tired."[58] But the singing does not stop until David supplies a hopeless, flippant coda:

> . . . Hamish and I will get drunk as usual this afternoon, and . . . we shall somehow manage to arrive at Rosalie's in time for dinner where, of course, we shall meet Rilda and . . . we shall spend most of the evening at Donald's and probably end up in Harlem. That is the life of our times in words of two syllables. I am not bitter about it. I accept it as the best we can do. . . .
>
> We're here because we're here, and we should be extremely silly not to make the worst of it.[59]

Readers who had been making the worst of it for ten years were in no mood to read about their chic sins and petty vices. Perhaps it is not so curious after all that *Parties* was misinterpreted, not only by those who hated it but by those who liked it. In neither instance did the novel sell. Its beautiful format—a lemon yellow binding stamped in green and silver for both the trade and vellum editions— did not help, nor did Carl Van Vechten's faintly cerebral dust-jacket note:

> Exhausted by wars and peace conferences, worn out by prohibition

57 *Ibid.*, p. 225.
58 *Ibid.*, p. 259.
59 *Ibid.*, p. 260.

and other dishonest devices of unscrupulous politicans, the younger generation, born and bred to respect nothing, make a valiant and heart-breaking attempt to enjoy themselves.

In 1930, probably nothing could have saved *Parties*, and it was therefore, inevitably, the end of the series. Carl had said all he could say about his era, concluding with an almost wistful condemnation of all the pleasure seekers of all his novels and, additionally, of himself. Concurrently, writing had grown more difficult: in part because of the material; in part because the books had come to birth without any serious gestation; more pertinently because he lacked the temperament and the philosophical equilibrium to develop much further—and he knew it. Although his talent was scarcely slender, it was not enormously robust, initially because of the restrictions he placed upon himself, finally because of his own involvement with the period. With the publication of *Parties*—and, it must be admitted, because of the reception *Parties* received—he closed his garret window to turn his attention elsewhere.

Outside, the fallout from the stock market explosion settled on a suddenly sobered nation.

X

The Friendly Advocate

I am never foolish enough to believe that I can do anything for anyone else, BUT I do hope to improve myself.

THE WAKE OF THE CRASH and the collapse of the twenties sent most of the creative artists of the period into one kind of oblivion or other. James Branch Cabell retired even further into the shell of his mythical kingdom of Poictesme; Joseph Hergesheimer stopped masquerading as the Great American Novelist to grind out indifferent tales for the pages of the *Saturday Evening Post* and the *Woman's Home Companion*; H. L. Mencken stopped trying to change the country's mores and returned to the country's language through the scholarly series he had begun in 1919, called in its published form *The American Language*; F. Scott Fitzgerald's *Tender Is the Night* suffered the fate of *Parties*—with which it shared an undue amount of coincidence—but sent its author toward Hollywood and alcoholism; Sinclair Lewis's bad-tempered books became worse-tempered, and without their occasional salvation through humor; Elinor Wylie was wise enough—literarily at least—simply to die the year before the crash; and Carl Van Vechten stopped writing of his own accord. From his point of view, there was nothing else to say. Later he could reflect nostalgically: "We were a rough lot in those far-off days, ready with the quip and the shocker. . . . It was a great life, a dazzling life." But Carl Van Vechten's own hangover lasted a year.

He had finished *Parties* in April, 1930. After revising its page proofs, he left again for Europe to begin the recuperation, though it may be assumed he did not travel by wagon. In July, he was a dinner guest of the Princess Violet Murat, an old acquaintance from

The Friendly Advocate

A'lelia Walker's parties. Afterward, he strolled around to the Place du Calvaire and the Place du Tertre, which he had vividly described fifteen years before in "Au Bal Musette," a piece in *The Merry-Go-Round*. But the old Montmartre had completely disappeared. The whole district was filled with professional postcard sellers and cheap souvenir shops. When he returned to New York, he could have seen a similar change along Broadway and Forty-second Street, where burlesque houses and dozens of dance halls had begun to turn the Street of Dreams into a Nightmare Avenue. Those "far-off" days were, assuredly, dead.

Conditions continued to be "rotten, and advance sales for all books . . . [were] pitifully small," Knopf advised him.[1] Carl was not directly affected by the financial crisis, however, because he had owned no stocks on margin. It had been a common practice in the late twenties for investors—and investors included stenographers, cabbies, bellhops, writers, actors, singers, and janitors—to buy stock, using other stocks as collateral, even before the first purchases had begun to pay off. "When people are young they can stand a good deal," Carl wrote to Anna Marble Pollock. "It's the middle-aged, richer people who lost their money who are more to be sympathized with. Altho as I say it was largely their own fault, playing for high stakes on big margins."[2]

Carl Van Vechten may have been middle-aged and rich, but he had been wise enough in this direction to emerge relatively unscathed, even if the excesses of the times had led him astray in others. He was of course not completely untouched by it: some stocks did collapse, and a considerable amount of cash was lost through the closing of the banks. Brother Ralph, however, had been a careful and conservative businessman, and his own fortune had been safely invested: Carl's inheritance in trust remained unblemished. But neither Carl nor Fania was prepared to settle for a quiet life of leisure.

In August, 1931, Fania was off to Westport, after a few years'

[1] CVV, NYPL.
[2] Yale.

253

holiday from the boards. Armina Marshall and Lawrence Langner were in the process of founding a repertory company, and asked her to join. It began with a substantial old chestnut, *The Streets of New York*, and found itself with a surprising hit during a rather dry season in Manhattan. Meanwhile, Carl advised Addie Lawton Van Vechten in Cedar Rapids that, in Fania's absence, he was doing "a little writing in town." He referred to a final volume of essays, the last book of his own he would ever prepare for publication.

In the pages of *Peter Whiffle*, Carl Van Vechten had remarked that his autobiography would be published by Knopf in 1936, in two volumes. With the depression upon him and his own era behind him, he had no desire to commit his memoirs to paper, nor, indeed, would there have been much audience for them. Carl did, however, at Alfred A. Knopf's request, gather together a selection of essays of a more or less autobiographical nature for a new book; but it could not be classified as an autobiography unless its entire contents fell in the same category. Several of the papers were concerned with isolated incidents, frequently dealing with people other than their author and in every instance originally written for purposes far removed from personal reminiscence.

The book appeared in April, 1932, bound in blue cloth, imprinted with a stylized sheaf of corn not unlike a fleur-de-lis on the front cover. Limited to two thousand numbered copies and dedicated to the Stettheimer sisters, *Sacred and Profane Memories* was neither "sufficiently sacred nor yet sufficiently profane," according to the *New York Herald Tribune*.[3] But M. P. Shiel saw in it "a fresh fellow who has the merit of being himself, and shrewd in the corner of one eye."[4] James Branch Cabell found it extraordinary that "you should get more of yourself into these casual essays than into a novel, and I like vastly the intimate and companionable result."[5] Friends of course read as friends rather than critics.

The book began with "The Tin Trunk," the extended paper

3 Virgilia Ross Peterson, April 17, 1932.
4 Berg, NYPL.
5 CVV, NYPL.

that had run in two consecutive issues of Emily Clarke's *Reviewer* in 1922. This was followed by "The Folksongs of Iowa," lifted from *In the Garret*, a hypothetical search for native music among the farm folks back home, in which the intrepid investigator hears only *Hitchy Koo, From the Land of the Sky Blue Water*, and *Onward, Christian Soldiers*.

Two papers from *The Merry-Go-Round* appeared, but slyly revised. In "An Interrupted Conversation," Carl's companion changed his name from Dickinson Sitgreaves to Mark Colfax, probably after a new friend, Mark Lutz, and several remarks were altered to suit the passage of fifteen years, though not always without some self-conscious writing in the result: "I became entangled, God knows how," was changed to "I was upset, top hat and all." On other occasions, the revisions served to tighten the writing: learning "things about oneself" was altered to "simple facts," and some of the wide-eyed enthusiasm in "Au Bal Musette," destroyed by Carl's view of Montmartre the previous summer, was lost in the subtle transitions to a more detached point of view.

In "The Nightingale and the Peahen," the changes were even less noticeable but probably more telling in a close look at the original version as it appeared in *Rogue* in 1915. If exclamation points had been necessary when Carl was thirty-five in 1915, at fifty-two he no longer required them; the content of the paper seemed—at least in its author's eyes—sufficiently significant.

An unpublished autobiographical fragment, "July–August 1914," dealt with the few days before Carl Van Vechten and Neith Boyce Hapgood boarded the *San Guglielmo* in their escape from Italy. Some of the material had been incorporated into the *Trend* article about the actual voyage, but much of it was new. Originally "July–August 1914" included all of "Once Aboard the Lugger, San Guglielmo" except for a final paragraph about rich and poor living together amicably. (Once again, an older Van Vechten hand erased the obvious.) Then, in the first set of galley proofs, four complete columns—about a dozen pages—were killed. Even in manuscript, the paper had been so extensively rewritten that it hardly qualified as a paper in which the author had "striven to preserve the original mood, removing only what time had taught me to believe are excrescences, adding only what may serve to accentuate my primal intention or at any rate to clarify it,"[6] as he claimed in the foreword to *Sacred and Profane Memories*.

Revisions of "The Holy Jumpers," his paper about the religious sect in the Bahamas, and "La Tigresse" were included, though neither of these pieces was altered extensively. Vocabulary was changed here and there; italics and quotation marks were deleted; and, faced with what must have been feelings of guilt over the enthusiasm of his salad days, Carl simply left out some of the greenery. In "The Holy Jumpers," the practice worked to advantage, tightening the paper, focusing on the subject; in "La Tigresse," the cuts rendered the piece something less than successful. When it first appeared in 1919, "La Tigresse" opened with as evocative and exciting a look at New York City as Carl Van Vechten—or perhaps anybody—could have mustered. In its revised state, he slashed away unmercifully at the enchantment the metropolis had held a dozen years before; and, though he admitted in a footnote that New York was still his favorite city, the hyperbolic sentimentality in this passage from the original version was missing:

> And so I feel that I shall never be able to do New York justice: I love her too much and I am too inconstant to any one part of her. From her feet in the Battery to the hair of her head in the Bronx I lavish my caresses unsparingly and gregariously. And if I do not linger with her heart and head it is only because I am too sure they are always there.[7]

"La Tigresse" may have emerged a more mature composition, ridded of its oompah bass and grace-noted treble, but the tune lost most of its harmony in the process of revision.

The next piece in *Sacred and Profane Memories* was called "Feathers," a touching portrait of one of the Van Vechten cats. It had originally appeared in 1930, issued by Random House as a

[6] *Sacred and Profane Memories*, p. vii.
[7] *In the Garret*, pp. 270–271.

"prose quarto," one of six handsomely bound pamphlets, boxed in black cloth, and limited to 875 unnumbered sets. The other five pamphlets in this endeavor were by Stephen Vincent Benét, Theodore Dreiser (the wordiest of the group), Sherwood Anderson, Louis Bromfield, and Conrad Aiken. Carl's contribution grew from an affection begun long before *The Tiger in the House* was written.

Beginning with his grandmother's patient tabby and, later, the tailless Parisienne who loathed sandboxes, Carl had frequently shared his digs with cats. When he and Fania lived on East Nineteenth Street, there were friendly neighborhood felines around: the ugly tom who lived in the cellar and came to call by means of the elevator; clown cats in the grocery store where the Van Vechtens shopped; a short-haired blue who rolled eggs from the counter in a nearby delicatessen. For a time an orange tabby-Persian named Ariel lived with them, an invalid from birth. Later there was Scheherazade, a strange and independent puss whose affections were severely limited and given only after time had passed and trust had grown. But Feathers meant more than any of the others, and her "biography"—reprinted more often than anything else Carl ever wrote—created for him as for the reader "an emotion which . . . is very difficult even for time to destroy,"[8] again refuting Carl's cry from the mid-twenties that he could not write with any sentimentality.

Sacred and Profane Memories concluded with a couple of memoirs: "A Note on Breakfasts," reprinted from the *American Mercury*; and "Notes for an Autobiography," from the *Colophon*, in which he confessed to some early ambitions: "At one period I craved a career as a concert pianist; at another, as a jockey—but I do not think at first it occurred to me that I wanted to write a book."[9]

Most of the reviewers would have been happier if it had not occurred to him to publish *Sacred and Profane Memories*. "A collection of old stories, many of them long out of print. So what," wrote

---

[8] *Sacred and Profane Memories*, p. 208.
[9] *Ibid.*, p. 225.

an unhappy critic. "An unfortunate introduction to this author's writings," wrote another. The Stettheimer girls were somewhat happier, both with the book and with its dedication to them. Carrie, the dollhouse maker, with "elated superiority complexity," thanked Carl "for giving me a new emotion. Is it sacred or profane?"[10] Florine, the painter, "bound up with you/for life/chained/cob-webbed,"[11] asked to be undedicated. And Ettie, the writer, "suf-ficiently inflated," proposed reviving her own pseudonym, her "material shell/Henri Waste/into the realms of productiveness."[12] But few readers shared in the enthusiasm. Carl's book did not sell well, and, almost as if he had known his writing career was finally at an end, he appended a fairly complete bibliography to *Sacred and Profane Memories*. Then he turned his attention to a new interest.

"I am working hard at my photography," he wrote to Fania's brother Jacob early in 1932. "She probably told you I had taken it up. Well, it has hit me very hard and I don't do anything else now. I spend most of my days in the darkroom."[13]

PHOTOGRAPHY WAS NOT REALLY A NEW HOBBY, but it soon became an important one—in fact, the major preoccupation of Carl Van Vechten's life. That it became a major occupation as well is an understatement. Back in the dreary days of Cedar Rapids, a youth-ful Carl with an eye toward the dramatic even then had experi-mented with several box cameras, indulging his theatrical predilec-tions with contrived and elaborate pictures of friends. On photo-graphic plates, printed in blue, he captured Louise Henderson, the daughter of the local impresario, pretending to sing opera on his back porch, and Clara Deacon, swathed in veils and strewn with flowers, as Juliet in the tomb. Grandmother Van Vechten posed in a rocking chair against a long window in Uncle Giles's house, and a quartet of girls, among them an awkward and self-conscious Anna Snyder, song-and-danced in a chorus line in Carl's backyard.

10 CVV, NYPL.
11 CVV, NYPL.
12 CVV, NYPL.
13 CVV, NYPL.

The Friendly Advocate

More as a matter of pastime than as passion, he photographed as most people do, from time to time dragging out the camera for a picnic or a party or an hour's diversion; but the interest never left him, even during his writing days. He photographed several of the opera singers whom he knew through his work on the *New York Times*, snapping their pictures in New York and on the banks of the Thames in London. Once, escorting Luisa Tetrazzini to the Times Building tower, he paused to take her ample likeness a time or two; in Paris, he had Olive Fremstad pose for him along the boulevard and Charles Dalmorés in Tuileries. If the shutterbugging was not constant, it was certainly present until the end of the twenties, when he became sufficiently encouraged to renounce his amateur snappings. Miguel Covarrubias, the Mexican artist whose work Carl had called attention to earlier in the decade, returned from a European jaunt with a Leica. After an initial lesson in the camera's various possibilities, Carl purchased one of his own.

In the beginning, and for several years thereafter, Mark Lutz served as a willing and patient subject through the various experiments, as Carl continued to refine a hobby into a fine art. In Richmond, Virginia, where his family lived, Lutz, during his childhood, had been Emily Clarke's next door neighbor, and he knew many of the contributors to the *Reviewer*: Cabell, Mencken, Lewis, Walpole, Frances Newman, all of whom were friends or acquaintances of Carl Van Vechten. (Perhaps Miss Newman should be called, rather, an enemy: she publicly announced her delight at Carl's inheritance, circa 1927, since it would obviate his ever writing another word.) When Mark Lutz met Carl, in the summer of 1931, a lifelong friendship and correspondence began.

Mark Lutz was with Carl when he tried out the new Leica for the first time. Carl's "outraged cries of indignation" reached him in a letter when the photographer saw his first roll of developed film. Within a few weeks a darkroom had been installed in one of the kitchens in the double apartment on West Fifty-fifth Street, tapestries and props began to accumulate, and Carl suddenly found himself passionately involved in a new profession.

Carl Van Vechten

Carl frequently served as his own subject in the beginning, though very quickly the wide circle of friends made during the passage of twenty-five years in New York—most of them closely connected with the various worlds of theater, films, painting, writing, and music—gave him a broad range of subjects. Anna May Wong, the Chinese-American actress, was the first to come for a sitting, to be caught on film, atmospheric and exotic, her dark Oriental features framed in a cloche of white feathers. Eugene O'Neill was the second caller. When he and Carlotta Monterey returned to New York, Carl arranged for an immediate session with the Leica. He photographed the O'Neills, together and separately, in conjunction with his mother's rosewood square grand piano in the Victorian room of the apartment. The Van Vechten photographs of the playwright and his wife made at a second session, unencumbered by any props and taken against a dark background, are typical of his best work: striking in their use of lighting to emphasize the particular temperament of the subject and accurate as document, since Carl never did any retouching. Additionally, he managed one or two of O'Neill laughing, a rare trick echoed a few years later with Theodore Dreiser.

Between these two dour gentlemen, he repeated the magic with Helen Morgan, the wistful Julie from *Show Boat*. Donald Angus, who gave Carl a hand with the lights from time to time in those days, remembers her late arrival one evening after a performance on Broadway in 1932. When the session began, she was "only slightly tipsy and after a few shots asked Carl for a drink. He had *everything* but brandy (Prohibition was rampant, remember) which was the only thing Helen drank." Undeterred, she simply telephoned down to her chauffeur, asleep in the car parked outside Carl's apartment house, to bring up a bottle. Then, heavily fortified but "with great reluctance, she was made to tear herself away . . . and we finished the . . . session after which she and I also finished the bottle." Helen did not depart until four-thirty in the morning, but during the interim Carl had captured both the bitterness and the ebullience of the story of her wretched life, which she told at length as the time passed and the brandy dwindled. The photographs that resulted are startling and frequently beautiful.

"Photography is a very personal thing," Carl once declared, "even a magical act."[14] Readers of *Town and Country* could agree in 1933, when the magazine ran a quartet of Van Vechten portraits. The subjects were Judith Anderson, whom he would photograph during the ensuing years in nearly all her major roles; Fannie Hurst, an old acquaintance from the twenties; Ona Munson, wife of the painter Eugène Berman; and Ina Claire. Shortly thereafter, Bergdorf Goodman had a show of the work of Cecil Beaton, Edward Steichen, Man Ray, George Platt Lynes, and Carl Van Vechten. Carl was in excellent company, and, moreover, his experiments were widely heralded. "What is literature's loss is photography's gain," wrote Henry McBride in the *New York Sun*. "Quite distinctly, Mr. Van Vechten is the Bronzino of this camera period. He works in the large and with a boldness of design . . . that makes his work carry emphatically."[15]

During those first years, Carl's range was extraordinary: the volatile Tallulah Bankhead subdued momentarily with great clusters of flowers; Henri Matisse recumbent on some Matisse-like tapestries; Scott Fitzgerald outside the Algonquin, his face painfully mirroring the fragments of his flaming youth; James Branch Cabell, not very successfully posed; Alfred Knopf, sartorially dashing, lordly; Grace Moore; Gertrude Atherton; Mary Garden in a paper-sculpture wig; Iturbi; Heifetz; Robert Nathan; an almost adolescent architect named Philip Johnson; a matronly Mabel Dodge Luhan; Laurette Taylor; Muriel Draper; Diego Rivera; Hugh Walpole; Somerset Maugham; Sandor Szabo; Gene Tunney; Cesar Romero; Bernard Faÿ; Max Eastman; two of the three Stettheimer sisters, Florine demurring in spite of pleas; Max Ewing; Reginald Turner; George Antheil; Emily Clarke, no longer editor of the *Reviewer* but a celebrated Philadelphia matron; Clemence Dane; Constance Collier; and of course, Gertrude Stein.

[14] Van Vechten, Oral History.
[15] "The Leica Exhibition," November 30, 1935.

"YOU'D BETTER COME OVER and be photographed," he had written Miss Stein near the end of 1933. Plans for *Four Saints in Three Acts* were under way, thanks to Virgil Thomson's persistence; so, in point of fact, was a whole Stein movement. *The Autobiography of Alice B. Toklas* was having a great success, first in installments in *Atlantic Monthly* and then as a surprise best seller and Literary Guild selection. Additionally, the Modern Library at Random House had been moved to issue a new edition of *Three Lives*, Miss Stein's first published volume, for which Carl supplied the sympathetic introduction. More a portrait of Miss Stein herself, the introduction concluded with a brief analysis in the form of an appreciation of the book, which he called "an authentic milestone on the long road of American letters, were it entirely ignored, for the time being, by the public."[16]

In September, Carl wrote Miss Stein to suggest that Bernard Faÿ's condensed French translation of *The Making of Americans* be published in English in this country; it was, in 1934, by Harcourt, Brace. A few months later, his letters to Gertrude Stein were filled not with publication information but with opera news. *Four Saints in Three Acts* was about to open, with scenery by Florine Stettheimer and choreography by Frederick Ashton, with an all-Negro cast. When it was premiered in February, 1934, sponsored by the Friends and Enemies of Modern Music, in Hartford, Connecticut, Carl called it "in our vivid theatrical parlance, a knockout and a wow."[17]

When Random House issued the text a few months later, Carl supplied another Stein introduction, including a good example of his turning fact into embroidered fiction and back again into fact. Following Carl's initial audition of the work in 1929, he and Virgil Thomson, on their way from one Harlem party to another—so readers were led to believe by his introduction to the opera— traversed the distance in a Rolls-Royce temporarily shared by an obliging fellow neither of them had ever seen before. Unavoidably

16 "Introduction," p. xi.
17 Yale; Donald Gallup, ed., *The Flowers of Friendship*, p. 275.

eavesdropping on the conversation about Miss Stein's curious work which would, as Mabel Dodge Luhan had claimed, do to opera what Picasso had done to painting, the fellow was moved to demand anxiously, "Whatever . . . will I do with my Thursday nights?"[18] Readers familiar with *Parties* might be similarly moved to remember a remark of Claire Madrilena's at one of the interminable drinking bouts in the novel:

> I went to Isabel Pollanger's the other night . . . to hear Virgil Thomson's new opera with words by Gertrude Stein. It is called Four Saints in Three Acts and I was so thrilled by it that on the way home I said to the banker who had taken me that a performance of this work would end all opera, just as Picasso with his imagination had put a stop to repetition in painting. My rich escort looked at me in consternation and exclaimed, End all opera! What would I do Thursday nights?[19]

Thomson's decision to use only Negro singers in *Four Saints in Three Acts* delighted Carl of course, and he reported the composer's reasons in his introduction: "They alone possess the dignity and the poise, the lack of self-consciousness that proper interpretation of the opera demands." Then he concluded on a note of his own:

> There are those, of course, who seek a key to some more perfect understanding of Miss Stein's text, just as there are those who wish to find representation in an abstract Picasso painting. It is unfortunate, perhaps, that I can have very little to say to these people. It becomes more and more evident to me that if appreciation of the text of Miss Stein is not instinctive with a person he never acquires it.[20]

The success of *Four Saints in Three Acts* and the Toklas *Autobiography* prompted Carl Van Vechten to encourage a Stein lecture tour of America in the fall. On a summer holiday abroad in 1934— after a momentary stop in London to photograph Somerset

[18] "A Few Notes about *Four Saints in Three Acts*," p. 6.
[19] *Parties*, pp. 68–69.
[20] "A Few Notes about *Four Saints in Three Acts*," p. 9.

Maugham—he and Mark Lutz visited Miss Stein and Miss Toklas at their summer house in Bilignin in the south of France. Several years before, he and Fania Marinoff had stopped with the ladies when they were living in Belley, just a few miles from the quarters they now inhabited during the warmer months.

For many years Miss Stein and Miss Toklas had gone south on holidays to various resorts. Then, one summer in the late 1920's, they had spotted an eighteenth-century manor house across the Rhône Valley. Without even seeing the inside of it, Miss Stein set about trying to have the resident—a captain in the army—promoted to major and transferred far from the house in which she and Miss Toklas longed to live. The plan did not work out immediately—apparently the captain had advanced as far as the army dared promote him, for dark reasons—but he was ultimately transferred and they were able to move into the place. There, on a brief visit, Carl photographed them from many angles: Gertrude Stein by the trellis roses; Gertrude Stein with her dogs; Gertrude Stein hoeing in one of the several garden beds; Gertrude Stein from the side, from the front, even from the rear; and Alice Toklas nearly as often. Additionally, they talked at length of the American tour; Miss Stein was slightly uneasy about the possible reception she might receive. Although she approached the projected chores with a degree of trepidation, Carl Van Vechten had no fear.

He returned to America and set to work. "Her chief apologist to American readers," as one newspaper called him, had no apologies to make; the whole thing was a labor of love that had commenced in 1913. One of his first moves was to encourage Bennett Cerf at Random House to become Gertrude Stein's permanent and exclusive American publisher. Then he began lining up people to act as legmen during the lecture tour. From Virginia, James Branch Cabell and Ellen Glasgow wrote delightedly of their willingness to entertain the ladies when they arrived. But Gertrude Atherton in San Francisco was less than enthusiastic, complaining, with characteristic jealousy of anyone else who dared put pen to paper, that Gertrude Stein, having been denied a creative brain, had been

obliged to become a freak in order to make herself known.[21] The
Van Vechten charm persisted, however, and Mrs. Atherton gave
in, if to little avail: when Gertrude Stein got to California, she
loathed it. Mrs. Charles Goodspeed and Thornton Wilder, then an
instructor at the university, would fill the requirements of hosts in
Chicago; and W. G. Rogers, whom Miss Stein and Miss Toklas had
known as a doughboy in World War I when they were driving a
Red Cross ambulance in France, and who, indeed, had been instrumental in getting Gertrude Stein to agree to a tour, would arrange
things in Connecticut. Scott Fitzgerald would host the ladies in
Maryland; and, of course, New York presented no problem: Carl
Van Vechten would be very much there.

By the time Gertrude Stein and Alice Toklas arrived in America,
in October, everything had been taken care of. Carl, Bennett Cerf,
and a cousin of Miss Stein's from Baltimore, met them at the boat.
W. G. Rogers had taken the pilot boat out to meet them before the
ship docked. Miss Toklas handed over the keys for their luggage to
the customs official. When he was finished, she proposed tipping
him and later wrote: "Carl threw up his hands in horror and said,
Of course not. Well, I said, can I shake hands with him and thank
him? Not shake hands, said Carl, you will not be doing that here."[22]
Then he swept the ladies down the gangplank, leaving Bennett Cerf
behind to gather up the bags. Later Cerf reflected, not without
amusement, "Carl only became the Great Author when there was
dirty work to be done." The following week *The New Yorker* ran
its version of the arrival at customs by way of a cartoon by Alan
Dunn, depicting a harried checker looking at the ladies' papers and
saying: "It begins like this: 'gertrude says four hats is a hat is a hat.'
What the hell can you make out of a declaration like that, chief?"[23]

Carl arranged a more or less preview lecture before a small but
sympathetic private audience. After the initial fear passed, Miss
Stein blossomed into one of her own roses. A week later, the ladies

21 Yale.
22 *What Is Remembered*, p. 143.
23 *Ibid.*, p. 124a.

were photographed again, this time at the West Fifty-fifth Street apartment. It was during one of these sessions that the frequently reproduced picture of Gertrude Stein in profile was taken, like some magnificent, benevolent Caesar, handsomely mirroring the head that was, as Peggy Bacon had it, "striking as stonehenge."

In November, Miss Stein took time out from the lecture tour for the Chicago premiere of *Four Saints in Three Acts*. The sponsors agreed to pay the travel expenses for her and Miss Toklas to fly out to the Midwest, but the ladies had never flown before and were ready to decline. Miss Toklas was neutral, but Miss Stein was "superstitious." Finally, she agreed to try the then novel means of transportation, but only when Carl agreed to accompany them: he was a seasoned air traveler by that time, presumably insuring their safety. Once aloft, Miss Stein immediately wrote on her tablet, "The air is solid," capitulated completely to planes, and insisted on them, whenever available, for the rest of the tour. But Carl called that Chicago jaunt "the bumpiest ride I've ever had."

The opera was a gala affair. The celebrated trio occupied the box of honor, but at intermission Miss Stein, still deaf from the plane ride, moved down to the sixth row to catch her "pigeons on the grass alas" as they flew out over the footlights. After the performance, the ladies flew back east to attend the Yale-Dartmouth football game with Alfred Harcourt, who had just published the condensation of *The Making of Americans*. Carl traveled west from Chicago to Cedar Rapids for a visit with his stepmother, but he returned in time to photograph Miss Stein and Miss Toklas again during the Christmas holidays. Between sessions, Gertrude Stein managed to inscribe all Carl's volumes and pamphlets and periodicals in what was certainly the most complete collection of her work. A single example is indicative of the debt she felt for "her chief apologist." In the book he had tried so hard to get published in America, she wrote: "To Carl, The Making of Americans which is not more connected with him than all the others because it and all the others are all connected with him. Always and always Gtrde."

About the same time, Fania received great critical acclaim for her

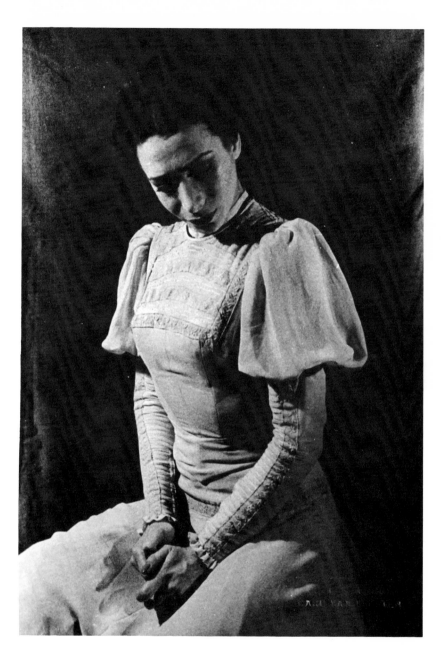

Nora Kaye as Hagar in *Pillar of Fire*, 1942.

Alicia Markova and Hugh Laing in *Aleko*, 1942.

Virgil Thompson, 1947.

Truman Capote, 1948.

Billie Holiday, 1949.

Roald Dahl and Patricia Neal, 1953.

Leontyne Price, 1953.

William Faulkner, 1954.

William Warfield, 1955.
("I consider this the finest photograph I have ever taken!")

Alvin Ailey, 1955.

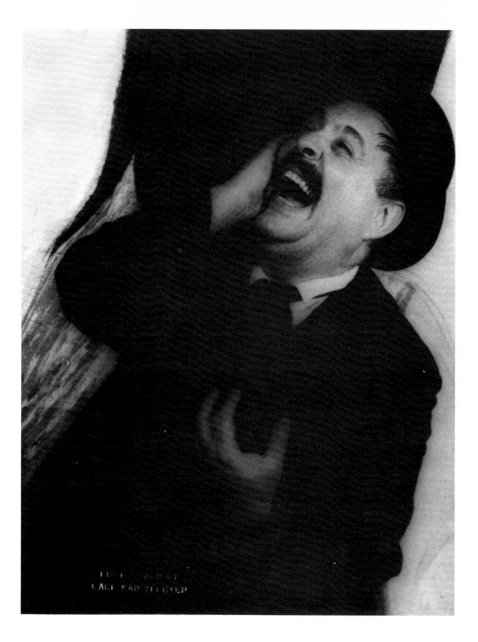

Zero Mostel as Bloom in *Ulysses in Nighttown*, 1958.

Kim Stanley as Elizabeth in *A Far Country*, 1961.

Edward Albee, 1961.

Martha Graham and Bertram Ross in *Clytemnestra*, 1961.

Lotte Lenya, 1962.

Mahalia Jackson, 1962.

role in Elmer Rice's *Judgment Day*. Between performances and photographic sessions, there were parties of course. Carl and Fania gave several for Gertrude Stein and Alice B. Toklas, one including "all the Negro intellectuals he could get together." Bennett Cerf gave the ladies a luncheon, and Katharine Cornell had them over for lemon pie. When they went south to Richmond, Carl accompanied them, for a lecture at the university and, later, for a large dinner party at Ellen Glasgow's house. That evening, James Branch Cabell, "slightly roguish but not too perplexed," asked Carl what Gertrude Stein meant by the phrase "outer and inner reality." Cabell got a literal answer. Then he turned to Miss Toklas. "Is Gertrude Stein serious?" he asked. "Desperately," Miss Toklas answered. "That puts a different light on it," he said. "For you," Miss Toklas concluded, "not for me."[24]

The next lap of the tour took them farther south and then west, gaining the momentum of a track meet as it proceeded. Carl's letters greeted them at nearly every stop:

> No one except Sarah Bernhardt and William Jennings Bryan has ever seen so much of our country. You will have fabulous stories to tell for years and when some one mentions Blue Bell City, Maine, or Sight Unseen, Idaho, you will pipe up and say I spent several weeks there during the Great Freeze of 1934.[25]

In the spring, they returned to Paris. Before Carl saw them off at the pier, he had already dubbed them with the names he would use forever after: Miss Toklas was Mamma Woojums, and Miss Stein was Baby Woojums (and he was Papa Woojums). The almost old-fashioned conceit of inventing pet names for friends had always been one of Carl's peculiar passions. Early in the century he had called Avery Hopwood Sasha, and the name persisted until Hopwood's death. During the twenties, Alfred Knopf was Freddo, and his wife Blanche was either Blanchette or the Grand Duchess Cunegunde Wilhelmine Schwartz (the latter an invention of Menc-

[24] *Ibid.*, p. 150.
[25] Yale; Gallup, ed., *The Flowers of Friendship*, p. 292.

ken). Equally often, Carl liked to number people: Donald Angus, for example, was Donald I, and some years later Donald Gallup was Donald III (the latter often addressed in letters as "Dear III"); Edward Lueders, responsible for two Van Vechten biographical studies, was Edward XV. Then, just to be captious, Carl abjured most customary familiarity: although no one ever considered calling James Branch Cabell Jim or Jimmy, Sinclair Lewis was either Red or Hal to everybody but Carl; Hergesheimer was Joe to his friends, though often Joseph to Carl; Mencken was invariably addressed by Carl as Henry rather than as Menck, which George Jean Nathan used. After a few years of Fan, he began addressing his wife as Marinoff or Miss Marinoff. Carl himself was of course, for more than fifty years, called Carlo. During an earlier period he had been called Van, which he loathed: "Van? Van? That just means *of!*" he once despaired. But Gertrude Stein called him Van for years, and he never complained. She switched to Papa Woojums before she and Alice Toklas had left America, and persisted in it until her own death in 1946.

Gertrude Stein never returned to this country, but the success of her trip remained behind. Though Carl's hopes for a Stein anthology in 1936 did not materialize, Bennett Cerf kept his promise and for the next half a dozen years—until the war cut off communications with Europe—brought out annual volumes of her work, for which Carl supplied several photographs.

A few months later, Carl returned to Europe again for a holiday in Spain, where his camera documented some sights from earlier visits and discovered some new ones. Some of these photographs give further indication of his facility. Far removed from the portrait lights and preplanned wall hangings and attractive celebrities for subject matter, the Spanish pictures are often compositionally fascinating and beautiful: monumental stone trees, rough pillars crowned with miniature jungles, behind which stretches the skyline of Barcelona; Antoni Gandé's artificial caves, their slanted columns photographed obliquely against one another; *santos*, reclining Christs in the agony of Crucifixion, borne aloft by dark-robed monks; the gatehouse of the Parque Güell in Barcelona, like a myth-ical candy palace against a flat and cloudless sky; a detail of the spires of the Templo de la Sagrada Familia, resembling modern windowed office buildings, or New Year's Eve hats, or honey-combs; perspective views of the baroque balconies on the Casa Batló in the Paseo de Gracia; Domingo Ortega, the first matador during the thirties, in action in the practice ring at El Soto, his farm near Madrid.

When Carl returned to New York, he found a manuscript by Mabel Dodge Luhan awaiting him. His old friend had composed another volume of her staggeringly long autobiography, though Carl found little excitement in what he read. His silence demanded an explanation, Mrs. Luhan complained, so he replied:

> Of course I'm not mad. It didn't seem very important to me to write to you about the book because I don't like it and I didn't see any sense of telling you that! You seem to belittle every character in it including yourself . . . and the characters I know I would hardly recognize from your dealings with them, but maybe that's the way you see it and feel it and maybe you are right. I suppose "truth" can always be no more than one's own point of view. . . . In the circum-stances I wonder if telling the "truth" is what Miss Loos' blonde would call education?[26]

But Mabel Dodge Luhan was not easily placated: she neither saw nor corresponded with Carl for the next sixteen years. No official break occurred, no further argument or conversation—only silence. Mrs. Luhan had simply mustered her customary stoicism, letting "life express itself in whatever form it will," letting "it" decide, as she had long before synthesized her whole point of view, letting "it" happen. As for Carl, it was never very difficult to lose interest in someone who had lost interest in him—but without malice. "Do not dislike people," he advised another friend many years later; "it is a waste of time, energy, and personality. Cultivate indifference. You cannot possibly dislike any one you haven't loved. It is the reverse of the shield."[27]

[26] Yale.   [27] Yale.

Carl Van Vechten

THE FOLLOWING SPRING—in May, 1936—Carl and Fania went to Sea Island, Georgia, to visit Carlotta Monterey and Eugene O'Neill at their Casa Genotta, where another chapter was added to the Van Vechten photographic iconography of their hosts. When they returned to New York, the camera continued to click. Indeed, since the day of the first sitting, with Anna May Wong, it had almost never ceased.

Earlier that year, Willa Cather had come to be photographed, strong and somber, like one of her Nebraska characters, but she was unhappy with the results. She had agreed to a sitting only after several months' urging, and, because she had lost much of the demeanor in Edward Steichen's famous portrait, very probably her vanity intervened. The photographs were superb but scarcely flattering. The Van Vechten portraits were often too accurate to satisfy the subjects.

A month later Carl's friend Al Moor brought Bessie Smith to the West Fifty-fifth Street apartment so that she might join the Van Vechten roster. Bessie was making one of her final appearances at a night club in New York at the time, and she arrived for the sitting between shows, "cold sober and in a quiet reflective mood." If Carl could recall a happier Bessie from happier days, he was able, nevertheless, to get "nearer to her real personality than I ever had before and the photographs, perhaps, are the only adequate record of her true appearance and manner that exist."[28]

Through that year and the following one, 1937, an astonishing gallery emerged: Eugène Berman, Lillian Gish, Dame Myra Hess at Carl's mother's rosewood piano, Zora Neale Hurston, Thomas Wolfe looming toward the ceiling in Carl's studio, Thomas Mann with cigar and homburg outside Knopf's offices, John Gielgud and Judith Anderson in their 1936 *Hamlet*, William Saroyan, Brooks Atkinson, Julie Haydon, Philip Moeller, Paul Cadmus. He photographed W. C. Handy against the American flag because his *St. Louis Blues*, Carl never tired of telling people, should have been the national anthem.

28 "Memories of Bessie Smith," p. 7.

The Friendly Advocate

The photographic sessions were transferred to a new location that gave Carl a real studio when he and Fania moved to the quieter Central Park West. A garage had opened on West Fifty-fourth Street, just under Fania's bedroom windows, and commenced a daily racket at eight in the morning which continued until evening. The entrance hall in the new apartment was lined with part of Carl's staggering collection of books; the overflow spilled into his bedroom, which functioned also as a library. The Victorian room was nearly duplicated, but the drawing room's appointments were somewhat more conventional than the pink and purple and emerald green Chinese combination at West Fifty-fifth Street. The new photographic studio, for all its improvements, did not necessarily relax the subjects who came—still by invitation only—to sit before Carl's camera eye.

A session in the Van Vechten studio was never the easiest thing to survive with savoir-faire. Sometimes, the background was already chosen; sometimes, one had to be dragged out of the catalogued rolls of materials and papers stacked on shelves against one wall of the studio. Another wall bore a fantastic collection of posters, paintings, and sketches; gimcracks and gewgaws perched on every available ledge or edge. A third wall, heavily hung with two or three sets of draperies, contained a casement window through which the subject might see, while waiting for the lenses to be focused, a lovely view of Central Park, just across the street.

Carl always puttered a little; an assistant set up the lights. Carl adjusted his camera on a wooden easel; the assistant supplied stools, chairs—indeed, chaise longues or beds—against the draped or otherwise decorated fourth wall. Then the subject sat. The lights were excruciatingly hot, and the room was stuffy. Carl stood behind his camera, staring like a mad scientist in the movies, waiting for the "exact moment," in which he always believed. Then the shutter began to snap, sometimes quickly, sometimes with syncopated hesitations, always with Carl's embalmed stare above. Occasionally, there were stops while the composition was improved or compli-

271

cated with props: robes, costumes, banshee hats, Easter eggs, masks, feathers, cats, marionettes.

The results always followed with amazing speed, a doubly astonishing circumstance because Carl always did all his own developing, all his own printing, all his own enlarging. The whole process remained, for the most part, a hobby. Occasionally, photographs were solicited for reproduction in books, and more recently on phonograph albums, but they were primarily gifts to their subjects and for the pleasure of their maker. By the end of the decade, photography had become a full-time occupation. If Carl appeared outwardly to be in semiretirement, he remained constantly active. Always an early riser since forcible youthful routings out at dawn in Cedar Rapids and 3:00 A.M. beats in Chicago, he was in the darkroom daily as early as he had been at his typewriter during the twenties. Always possessed of an uncompromising will—though he never really began anything he did not want to do and therefore always finished anything he began—he could work with photography for hours at a time, constantly experimenting, constantly learning.

He liked to brag about spending "whole months, whole years" in his pajamas and elegant dressing gowns, too preoccupied to get dressed, as others came to join the growing catalogue of photographic subjects: Laurence Olivier, in New York for *Romeo and Juliet*; Franz Werfel; Sidney Lumet, then a child actor in *My Heart's in the Highlands*; W. H. Auden and Christopher Isherwood, young expatriates from England; Julian Green, expatriate American novelist living in France; Marc Chagall; Ferenc Molnár; and, soon, dozens of ballet dancers.

For all professional purposes, except an occasional book review, usually concerning cats or Negroes or music, Carl's pen extended its silent sojourn in the inkwell; but over the years he had privately withdrawn it for the voluminous correspondences he conducted: with Gertrude Atherton and Neith Boyce since the beginning of the first world war; with Mabel Dodge Luhan, until their break, for an even longer period; with Emily Clarke, Gertrude Stein, Edna Kenton, Mark Lutz, with regularity; and only less so by comparison with Witter Bynner, James Branch Cabell, Arthur Davison Ficke, Ellen Glasgow, and—right in New York City a great deal of the time—with Langston Hughes, Fannie Hurst, Alfred Knopf, and Muriel Draper, and, an almost oldest acquaintance, Anna Marble Pollock. The advent of the telephone and the telegram seems largely to have destroyed the *art* of letter writing; it never did for Carl. Intensely personal, full of information but also inquiry, unbuttoned humor, and graceful phrase, he may have been the last writer of any significance to practice that art so extensively. A remark in a letter from Carl to Lin Yutang about his own novels explains probably better than he realized why his letters stand as a literary contribution of considerable significance: "I imagine that I am at my best when I am writing nonsense out of the overflowing of a temporary mood & without the desire to achieve immortality."[29]

CONCURRENTLY, Carl's friendship with, and interest in, Negroes continued. The passing of the Harlem Renaissance only intensified his involvement. The warmest of these associations came to a sudden, shocking halt in 1938 when James Weldon Johnson was killed in an automobile accident. Carl served as a pallbearer for his great friend and then, within the year, became engrossed in the plans for a Johnson memorial at Seventh Avenue and Lenox in the heart of Harlem. When this proved financially and architecturally impractical, an infinitely wiser kind of memorial occurred to him, when Johnson's widow was approached to start a Poetry Room in her husband's name at the Library of Congress, using the Johnson papers as foundation. Grace Nail Johnson remembers Carl saying at the time, "I wish to God they had asked for *my* things." The "things" referred of course to the gigantic collection of Negro material Carl had amassed over a quarter of a century. Carl was not convinced, however, that the Library of Congress was the best place for such a collection. A university library, on the other hand, would be a superb location for the kind of collection into which the idea might grow. He asked the board of directors of Yale Uni-

[29] Yale.

273

versity Library if it would be interested in housing the genesis of a collection of Negro contributions to the various arts. With the library's enthusiastic endorsement, Carl began clearing out his vast accumulation of material.

Fortunately for Yale, he was as meticulous about his collecting as he was about his writing and photography. Manuscripts and books were slipcased or boxed; clippings, programs, catalogues, advertisements, pamphlets, brochures—anything that dealt with the Negro as a creative artist—had been carefully preserved in as pristine a condition as possible. There was probably as much truth as joke involved when, during an interview, Fania Marinoff once ventured to suggest that her husband would prefer she read worn rather than new copies of books.

Carl called his gift to Yale the James Weldon Johnson Memorial Collection of Negro Arts and Letters. During the succeeding decade, it grew to mammoth proportions, one of the most important cultural collections of any kind.

WHEN THE THEATRE GUILD AGREED to lend its support to a Stage Door Canteen, Fania Marinoff was one of its first members to volunteer. Carl followed her shortly thereafter, to the then un-friendly-looking basement under the Forty-fourth Street Theatre, where, on March 2, 1942, the first group of hundreds of thousands of servicemen began the invasion. Within a few weeks, the publicity seekers had disappeared, and this extraordinary phenomenon, born of America's rampant patriotism during the early forties, began to operate effectively. The various shifts of busboys, hostesses, dish-washers, and captains fell into place, "hour after hour, week after week, with a lack of friction, a sense of responsibility and timing, that were well nigh magical."[30]

For three years, Carl never missed his regular Monday and Tues-day shifts, while soldiers and sailors of many nationalities and many races surged into the canteen. They came for food and affection and

[30] "An Ode to the Stage Door Canteen," p. 230.

entertainment and companionship: to dance to the music of name bands; to watch Frank Piro, better known as Killer Joe; to jitter-bug with Shirley Booth; to amuse themselves with a whole floor show put on for one another; to hear Gertrude Lawrence or Celeste Holm sing numbers from their current Broadway musicals; to listen to Irving Berlin warble *I Left My Heart at the Stage Door Canteen*.

As a captain on the American Theatre Wing, Carl was respon-sible for his own crews of busboys. The almost frantic devotion he was able to inspire may be illustrated, in part, through his crews, whose members were just as loyal to their jobs as he was to his. Nor did his work stop at the canteen. Carl became further involved in helping to organize tea dances on Sunday afternoons at the Hotel Roosevelt for the women members of the armed forces and their enlisted dates. His specific job was to get the entertainment to-gether, a chore that would have been a headache to most people; but the difficulties encountered seemed to spur him on to try to secure the "best people, just to see if I could do it." He usually could.

The entertainer's guest book for the Roosevelt Tea Dances, now on permanent file in the theatre collection at the New York Public Library, reads like selections from a theatrical *Who's Who*: every-one from pianist Josef Hofmann to Gypsy Rose Lee; dozens of singers and dancers and actresses; and the entire ballet sequence from Rodgers and Hammerstein's *Carousel*.

At the height of these activities, Carl took time to print and mount more than a hundred photographs for an exhibition of his work at the Museum of the City of New York, called "The Theatre through the Camera of Carl Van Vechten." The show included, among many others, photographs of Luise Rainer, James Stewart, Deems Taylor, Agnes De Mille, Orson Welles, Ethel Waters, George M. Cohan, Walter Slezak, Clifton Webb, Alexander Woollcott, Sinclair Lewis, Alicia Markova; and he added to his own files, during the run of the exhibition, a brilliant selection of dancers from Ballet Theatre, notably Nora Kaye and Hugh Laing, young musicians like Menotti and Barber and Bernstein, Joe Louis at his training camp, and a full documentation of the Stage Door Canteen.

At some time in the early forties, the vast collection of photographs—until then suffering under a complicated and confusing organization—found a patient curator. One evening Carl took a number of the workers from his Tuesday crew at the canteen to the apartment on Central Park West to be photographed. Somehow, a young man named Saul Mauriber found himself holding the portable lights while Carl took pictures. During the ensuing twenty years Saul Mauriber rarely put the lights down. His devotion, moreover, resulted in the entire collection's being collated and cross-indexed with a mathematical accuracy that still makes possible the finding of any picture with ease. Saul was a student when he began working with Carl; today he is an independent designer, but until Carl's death he faithfully gave every Tuesday of every week to helping his old boss from the Stage Door Canteen.

Saul and Carl were still working at the canteen when it finally closed in 1945. After the last evening, several of the old canteeners stayed for the wake. "The end was inspiring and beautiful," Carl wrote to Anna Marble Pollock, "and everybody cried, including Jane Cowl, who doubtless has had more practice than we others."[31] At midnight they all sang *Auld Lang Syne*, led by Lucy Monroe, whose many renditions of the national anthem at baseball games and rallies were more familiar, the band played Irving Berlin's *I Left My Heart at the Stage Door Canteen*, "and everything was over."

But the canteen's demise did not bring Carl's associations with the services to a close. Prints of photographs, books and letters, magazines and clippings, kept the fleet and army post offices busy. In turn, service personnel helped him out. Overseas mail was restricted, even after peace was declared, but several friendly military messengers came to Carl's rescue when he wanted to send parcels to Gertrude Stein and Alice Toklas in Paris, on whom the privations of the occupation had been rigorous. Also, he sent them most of

[31] Yale.

the American army. At his instigation, soldiers he had known at the canteen, now stationed in Europe, frequently went to Paris on brief passes "to see the Eiffel Tower and Gertrude Stein."

While Miss Stein was writing *Brewsie and Willie*, about American servicemen waiting to be released after the war, Carl was writing to her about their fears and frustrations in this country: "A GI friend came in last night and like all the others nowadays he seemed very depressed. They want to get out of the army but they wonder what in hell they are going to do when they DO get out. They just don't know. Nor does anybody else."[32] Of the Van Vechten ménage, he wrote: "Everything is the same except we have no servants. Nobody has. Fania and I scrub floors and make beds and wash dishes, and there isn't much meat or butter but we are well and happy."[33]

And, once again, he was writing about Miss Stein as well as to her. Early in 1946, he edited and wrote an extended introduction for a volume of selected writings. Gertrude Stein's book about the occupation years in France, *Wars I Have Seen*, had made the best-seller lists in America, her first to make money since *The Autobiography of Alice B. Toklas* more than a dozen years before. The new success moved Bennett Cerf to issue the omnibus volume, a fat one of more than six hundred pages. For its contents Carl chose to include almost every style from Miss Stein's long career with letters. His persuasive introduction began with a paragraph he had written for a catalogue of modern writers, published by the Gotham Book Mart in 1940:

> Gertrude Stein rings bells, loves baskets, and wears handsome waist-coats. She has a tenderness for green glass and buttons have a tenderness for her. In the matter of fans you can only compare her with a motion-picture star in Hollywood and three generations of young writers have sat at her feet. She has influenced without coddling them. In her own time she is with honor. Keys to sacred doors have been presented to her and she understands how to open them. She

[32] Yale.
[33] Yale.

writes books for children, plays for actors, and librettoes for operas. Each one of them is one. For her a rose is a rose and how![34]

His introduction went to the printer in April, 1946. Gertrude Stein never saw it or the book it introduced; three months later, she died in France, at the age of seventy-two. The news came first over the radio and later through a telegram from Alice Toklas. Not long afterward, Carl learned that Gertrude Stein, dying, had named him her literary executor, leaving funds and instructions to publish what material of hers still remained unpublished.

Carl's initial feeling, as he later wrote, was that "Gertrude had bitten off more than I could easily chew...."[35] There was a natural hesitancy on the part of publishers to accept a chore that could promise little or no financial return. In time, however, the presses began to turn. At Yale, where Miss Stein had deposited all her manuscripts and correspondences, *Four in America* was published in 1947; the following year, Houghton Mifflin issued *The Gertrude Stein First Reader*, dedicated "To Carl Van Vechten Who Did Ask for a First Reader." The Banyan Press, one of the last of the private printing houses of really beautiful books, handset the type for Miss Stein's strange detective story *Blood on the Dining-Room Floor*. (In an advertising brochure, Carl called it "hair-raising," though it scarcely tickled the temples, nor did it sell.) In 1949, Rinehart published *Last Operas and Plays* with a Van Vechten introduction entitled, after a line from Miss Stein's *Four Saints in Three Acts*, "How Many Acts Are There in It?" The essay was edifying but not very exciting in its attempt to prepare prospective readers for the various situations and characters employed in the curious dramatic pieces. Two years later, one of these plays, *Doctor Faustus Lights the Lights*, was produced in New York by the Living Theatre. An opera libretto originally written for Lord Berners (who never composed a score for it), Miss Stein's version of the Faust legend was ultimately performed as a play, with a program

---

[34] "A Stein Song," p. ix.
[35] "A Few Notes apropos of a '*Little*' *Novel of Thank You*," p. vii.

essay supplied by Carl called "Some Notes Written on Stone" and some persuasive incidental music by Richard Banks, a commission—although an unpaid one—that Carl had arranged.

In the meantime, the Van Vechten photographic catalogue had continued to swell: Pearl Bailey, Pierre Balmain, Truman Capote, Paul Robeson, Marianne Moore, Marlon Brando. Occasionally, a name is worth dropping because of a memorable sitting, none more so than the night Billie Holiday came to be photographed. It took the whole of one night and seemed like "a complete career," Carl later wrote.

He had asked her to wear an evening gown, but she arrived at the appointed hour in a plain gray suit and a "facial expression equally depressing." The session was verging on failure: the singer was unco-operative and indifferent. Then Carl remembered the photograph he had taken a dozen years before of another great singer, Bessie Smith. Looking at the picture, Billie burst into tears, recalling that Bessie Smith had been her inspiration at the beginning of her own career. After that, "she was putty in my hands," and Carl's remarkable photographs resulted. About midnight, Billie told him she had to go home briefly. Carl assumed the journey was to procure narcotics; so, to insure her reappearance, he sent Saul, who was assisting him that night, along to Harlem as an escort. They returned an hour later with Mister, her dog. "She was now on a different plane, all energy, sympathy, cooperation and interest," Carl wrote, and the photography went on for two more hours. Afterward, in the drawing room, Billie told her steamy history, "a heartbreaking story, one no one could invent . . . told simply, but with a good deal of feeling and, on occasion, of dramatic intensity."[36] Fania, awakened by the sound of voices, came in while Billie was telling her story, and in a short time, like both Saul and Carl, was in tears. At four in the morning, Billie's current husband appeared; her story continued until five; then they left. Neither Saul nor the Van Vechtens ever saw her again.

[36] "Portraits of the Artists," *Esquire*, December, 1962, p. 256.

Carl Van Vechten

NEAR THE CLOSE OF THE FORTIES, Carl wrote to a friend that he had a "vague intention" of giving away another section of his enormous library to a university. The success of his James Weldon Johnson Memorial Collection of Negro Arts and Letters at Yale had begun to give direction to a gradual dispersal of his possessions. By 1947, the Yale collection had grown sufficiently for the James Weldon Johnson Memorial Committee to donate its funds—originally collected for the proposed monument in Harlem—to establish an endowment for future purchases.

"It is enchanting and exciting and touching how people are behaving about this Yale Collection," Carl wrote to Harold Jackman, an old friend from the Harlem days. "Everybody is doing a great deal more than they are asked to do and you are doing more than anybody."[37] Jackman had been instrumental in securing manuscripts from several Negro writers, and many others gave freely to the project of their own volition. The year 1925 had begun all over again: The James Weldon Johnson Literary Guild initiated Carl, along with Johnson's widow, as an honorary member; George Schuyler contributed "The Van Vechten Revolution" to *Phylon*; Hugh Gloster included "The Van Vechten Vogue," from his *Negro Voices in American Fiction*, which assessed *Nigger Heaven*, both its value as publicity and its limitations as fiction; and, in 1944, when a dinner was given for Walter White, Carl was called upon to speak. Never much of a public orator—his voice had the flat resonance of a cardboard bell—he managed a touching tribute in spite of himself. Carl spoke warmly and, not without humor, reminded the audience that he and White had been associated in so many projects that at one time White had said that the Van Vechten apartment was "situated half way between 695 7th Avenue and his Harlem home, the midtown office of the NAACP."[38]

The title was not inappropriate. There had been no flagging of affection during the years between Carl's introduction to Negro society and his establishment of his collection at Yale, which opened

[37] Yale.
[38] Yale.

officially on January 7, 1950, nearly a decade after its beginnings. By that time, it included work by nearly every Negro writer in the world. After the opening ceremonies, guests were invited to browse around in a collection that ranged from Booker T. Washington to Billie Holiday. There was no question that day that the resolution expressing gratitude from Yale, adopted by the president and fellows of the university, was justified.

The collection must certainly have suggested the "vague intention" regarding another gift to another university. If a Negro collection would draw Negro scholars to a white university, why would a white collection not draw white scholars to a Negro university? Carl Van Vechten invited the Fisk University Library in Nashville, Tennessee, to accept as a permanent acquisition his George Gershwin Memorial Collection of Music and Musical Literature, as he called the extensive musical material he had gathered over the years. Named after Gershwin—in part because he was a member of a minority group but, more important, because he had worked successfully in both the popular and serious avenues of music with Negro rhythms—the collection was established with a double motive. First, it was Carl Van Vechten's hope that serious musical scholarship in the South might flourish more bravely with this added resource; second, he wanted to use his personal library as a nucleus, which could expand and develop through contributions.

When the George Gershwin Memorial Collection of Music and Musical Literature officially opened in 1947, students and faculty at Fisk discovered, in their modest library, first editions of John Gay's *The Beggar's Opera*, Strauss's *Elektra* and *Salome* and *Der Rosenkavalier* in their original bindings, and several works by Rimsky-Korsakov; there were manuscripts by Auber and Victor Herbert from the past, and by Samuel Barber, Gian Carlo Menotti, Deems Taylor, Paul Bowles, Virgil Thomson, Aaron Copland, and of course George Gershwin from the present. A collection of scores was included, and another of phonograph records, many of them inscribed by Gershwin, Humperdinck, Puccini, and Thomson. There were concert programs dating back to 1909 and inscribed photographs of the greatest singers of that more noble day in the opera house. There was a selection of musical novels and, finally, there were a few rare letters, from composers Gounod, Meyerbeer, Weber, and Wagner and from singers Adelina Patti, Nellie Melba, and Mary Garden.

At the same university, Carl established a second collection, named after Florine Stettheimer, of his books about the fine arts. In turn, Fisk houses its part of the Stieglitz Collection—donated by Georgia O'Keeffe at Carl's instigation— in its Carl Van Vechten Gallery. It must be admitted that his fervor for these various endeavors occasionally ran away with his judgment. At one period, when he discovered Karl Priebe and began flooding Fisk's collection with that artist's elegant but perverse, beautiful but precious paintings, Carl was severely chided by a friend—indeed, an art collector of some repute—for sending so much "bad camp" to the Negro university in Tennessee.

Other interests were at work when Carl presented an extensive group of his photographs of celebrated Negroes to Wadleigh High School in New York City; even Cedar Rapids benefited when he presented its high school with a similar selection of photographs.

The Anna Marble Pollock Memorial Library of Books about Cats, which was no more frivolous in content than was the neo-Victorian lady after whom it was named, had its genesis when Carl wrote *The Tiger in the House* in 1920. For the ensuing thirty years, he continued to add to it until, on its presentation to Yale, it had grown into an extensive, rare, and assuredly unique library.

Yale was once again recipient when Carl deposited his personal correspondence with several American writers or copies of their books, or both, beginning chronologically with Herman Melville and working its way forward to Donald Windham and James Purdy. These collections inspired others at Yale: through Carl Van Vechten's encouragement, the Stieglitz Archive has been established by Georgia O'Keeffe, and the Theatre Guild Collection by Lawrence Langner and Armina Marshall; also, Carl was instrumental in having the papers of Max Ewing, Arthur Davison Ficke,

Mabel Dodge Luhan, Gertrude Stein, and the Stettheimer sisters deposited in the Yale University Library.

To the Berg Collection in the New York Public Library, Carl presented his correspondence with English writers and their books; and to its dance collection he gave a considerable library of material dealing with the ballet as well as a thousand photographs he had taken of dancers. A collection of theater photographs and, more recently, a selection of Negro subjects went to the Museum of the City of New York.

The most fascinating section of the Van Vechten personal holdings went to the New York Public Library manuscript division: the Carl Van Vechten Collection, comprised of everything he had ever written, in all various manuscript drafts, proofs, published versions, and revised editions. In a bibliographical listing of more than one hundred single-spaced, typed pages, he catalogued everything relating to his own career: a dozen fat scrapbooks housing his newspaper criticisms; a complete file of family photographs and snapshots; bound volumes of *Vanity Fair* and *Reviewer* and *Trend*; carefully preserved copies of the short-lived *Wave, Rong-wrong, Double Dealer*, and even the *University of Chicago Weekly*, which contained his first attempts at fiction; and correspondence dealing with his published work, from both friends and enemies, and other letters from various members of his family.

From so prolific a writer, the amount of material entailed might easily prove anathema to most libraries. Yale, for example, must have paled ever so slightly when Gertrude Stein began to send over her papers, with no more organization than a Girl Scout paper drive; but there was no such problem for the New York Public Library. Although Carl was an insatiable collector, he was a meticulous one: his work received the care he had devoted to that of other writers. His own record is probably as complete as any ever kept by a writer. Even objectively, to students and scholars who have never even heard of Carl Van Vechten, his collection is a tempting invitation to anyone interested in following the path traveled as an author develops from practicing writer to professional artist.

The giving away of these various collections was not simply an easy way of disposing of accumulated material. Nor with his own personal manuscripts could it be dismissed as the preposterous behavior of an egomaniac. Although most men nearing seventy settle into a retirement of near inactivity, Carl spent a large part of an already busy photographic schedule keeping the collections up to date. Regular shipments went out to Yale and Fisk and the New York Public Library. Carl's scouts were legion, constantly on the lookout for books, programs, and newspaper and magazine clippings that might be pertinent, though Carl himself usually discovered things before anybody else had; and, as new photographs were taken, they too were sent out to join one collection or another, sometimes more than one collection. Finally, the hobby that had commenced in 1932 began to progress with definite purposes.

If the forties had begun with Ballet Theatre and the Stage Door Canteen as subject matter, they concluded with Betty Field, Alexander Calder, Thornton Wilder, and, on a 1949 holiday in Paris, Jean Cocteau, André Maurois, and Jean Marais and Valentine Tessier while the latter two were filming Colette's *Chérie*. More for business than for pleasure, Carl had flown over to consult Alice Toklas about the posthumous Stein publications, and he photographed her too of course, stooped and lonely, with Basket II on the steps of 5 rue Christine.

The Parisian jaunt was the first of three holidays after a long spell—since 1937—in New York. The following year Carl and Fania went to Port-au-Prince. In 1951, he took a trip, with Saul Mauriber, to New Mexico to visit Witter Bynner, Georgia O'Keeffe, and Christopher Isherwood; to meet Frieda Lawrence, D. H. Lawrence's widow; inadvertently but happily to conclude a feud. On the sidewalk outside La Fonda in Santa Fe, an ample woman plunged toward Carl and then embraced him heartily. "You old fool, you," she cried several times, "you old fool!"[39] She was Mabel Dodge Luhan. The sixteen-year silence had broken, and for the remaining eleven years of her life this woman, who had "done

[39] *Fragments II*, p. 37.

more to encourage a point of view, if it was only by way of argument, than any one else I have known,"[40] remained in constant touch with Carl. When, a few months later, Edward Lueders, a young instructor at the University of New Mexico, drove up to see her with a draft of a dissertation, eventually published as *Carl Van Vechten & the Twenties*, Mrs. Luhan sent him on to Carl with pleasure; when Carl urged her to deposit her papers at Yale, she happily complied by sending off an initial shipment weighing fifteen hundred pounds; and when, in January, 1952, Carl's memoir about "Literary Ladies" he had known appeared in the *Yale University Library Gazette*, he paid her public homage: "I think I owe more to her, on the whole, than I do to any other one person."[41]

"Some 'Literary Ladies' I Have Known" was not the only piece of writing to disprove Carl's ancient avowal that he had stopped. The *Yale University Library Gazette* had carried almost annual Van Vechten essays in connection with the various gifts Carl had made the library: on H. L. Mencken, Joseph Hergesheimer, James Branch Cabell, Theodore Dreiser, and Anna Marble Pollock. The *Saturday Review of Literature* contracted for half a dozen articles and reviews about sopranos and ballerinas. The Gertrude Stein prefaces and introductions from the late forties attest to his activity at the typewriter, though in these instances the labor had become gratuitous.

Finally, however, in 1951, some of the burden was eased when a permanent plan for the remaining Stein material took shape. With the assistance of Donald Gallup, the curator of the American Literature Collection at Yale and, more pertinently, of the Gertrude Stein Collection, Carl arranged for the Yale University Press to undertake the publication of the rest of the posthumous manuscripts. With an advisory committee composed of Van Vechten, Gallup, Donald Sutherland (who had just completed his "biography of her work"), and Thornton Wilder, the Yale University Press issued the first in a series of eight annual volumes.

About the same time, Carl asked Gallup to serve as his literary

[40] *Ibid.,* p. 38.   [41] *Ibid.,* p. 36.

trustee. There was reason to believe that his work might require one: though he kept reminding himself that he had ceased to write in 1930, requests for reprint rights continued to come in, usually in connection with his writings on ballet and cats. *Nigger Heaven* was reissued as an Avon paperback with a new introduction, but the cries of protest—once again over the title—caused it to be withdrawn when a well-meaning but apparently illiterate group threatened to picket the publishing house. Also, there were some new articles published in the forties: "An Ode to the Stage Door Canteen," in *Theatre Arts*; a moving obituary for Gertrude Stein, composed with Carl's customary care in three drafts, but tastelessly titled by the editors of the paper in which it appeared "Pigeons and Roses Pass, Alas"; and a memoir of Bessie Smith for a phonograph record guide, and of Florine Stettheimer for *Harper's Bazaar*.

On the verge of seventy, Carl had dismissed what is commonly referred to as old age because he had no time for it. Though his hearing had begun to weaken about 1945—an affliction he did not really admit to for another ten years—and his gait had slowed somewhat, though thick-rimmed glasses depended from a black cord around his neck—he was too vain to wear them constantly—and his voice had grown softer, he never missed very much. Certainly, he was aware of his years. "So far I have avoided the usual gifts of old age, such as cataracts and prostate trouble," he wrote to Mabel Dodge Luhan at seventy-two, "but doubtless, like Job, I'll be afflicted by these later."[42] Some time before, a similar reflection, written at Easter to H. L. Mencken elicited a commiserating reply: "I am always glad when the happy day of resurrection dawns, for as I grow older the rigors of Lent fatigue me severely. . . . It is not, however, the fasting that knocks me out, but the long hours on my knees in church."[43] A few years later, when Carl did undergo a minor prostate skirmish, Mencken was suitably sympathetic, having undergone a similar operation himself. But this was confidential, he warned, since the women might overrun him.[44] And, again in a letter to Mabel Dodge Luhan, Carl spoke of having grown tired—of

[42] Yale.   [43] Yale; *Fragments I*, p. 62.   [44] Yale.

the opera, of ballet, of parsnips, of things: "God, how tired I am of THINGS."[45] But he contradicted himself almost constantly.

The apartments on Central Park West—first at 101, and then at 146, where he and Fania moved in the fall of 1953—always overflowed with "things": dozens of glass and ceramic and china and porcelain cats, the inevitably useless and extravagant Christmas or birthday gifts of friends desperate for something to give; French glass paperweights; paintings and photographs on every wall, in every room; articulated, metal-linked, and glass-eyed silver fish in Chinese bowls on lacquered tables; Venetian chandeliers; miniature orange trees; Polynesian shadow puppets; Oriental headdresses; hundreds of books, even after Carl's various collections had been established. Old "things" simply made room for new ones.

As for the theater—in all its forms—he attended almost with the regularity of a critic; and if he and Fania no longer bothered to attend first nights, they rarely missed an actor's benefit performance, their tickets always procured through their old friends at the Theatre Guild, Lawrence Langner and Armina Marshall. He never stopped attending the opera, even when he was dissatisfied with it. "I am hearing Salome . . . next week," he wrote me in 1952, "but the opera and I are not very good friends at the moment. Performances are so inferior to what I am used to." Nor did he miss recitals and concerts: "It is amazing that the technique and style of contemporary violinists and pianists is a great advance over their predecessors. So is that of the ballet which is far ahead of earlier ballets . . . but singers have deteriorated steadily and vastly." But he was patient: though Ljuba Welitsch's *Salome* was "a ghastly embarrassing experience, like seeing a favorite maiden aunt washing her pants at a public dinner," the advent of Leontyne Price renewed his faith, and "after a respite of twenty years I am mad for opera again. I dare say it is the approach of senility." Nor did he limit himself to the concert hall: when Carl discovered Dave Brubeck and Paul Desmond, he "swooned" over "those long Rossini-like monotonous crescendos that stretch out endlessly like the moon of my delight in the orient."

45 Yale.

Moreover, he continued to read omnivorously, his reactions less critical than they might have been in earlier years but never less fervent. "The Rainbow Bridge," he advised me of a book about Olive Fremstad, "is as exciting as atom-bombing on skis or self-baking in a fast oven." About the "goddam bloody fine volume called From Here to Eternity," he was more loquacious: "I never knew soldiers who used quite such expressive lingo . . . but somehow I wish they did and I did. Somehow I am sure it is true, even the parts of it that are not true. . . . In fact I LOVE this book, as much as if it were Henry James, or Gentlemen Prefer Blondes, or Carl Van Vechten." Colette was "one hell of a writer and without writing anything but variations of sex, food, flowers, and cats, she is the most INTELLECTUAL writer I know because she does her job so stunningly." About Mickey Spillane, he was more circumspect: "Of course it is not nearly as tough as From Here to Eternity and not nearly as REAL. But it's good fun, not too dirty, and I wouldn't say sexy at all, except perhaps to novices. In fact I am sure Mickey has a success in nunneries." Almost simultaneously: "Have you read Isak Dinesen? Somehow I hadn't until day before yesterday when I devoured both Out of Africa and Seven Gothic Tales. I am MAD about them and have written a love letter to the Baroness Blixen."

Concurrently, Carl continued to photograph: Harry Belafonte; Julie Harris, in *I Am a Camera*; William Faulkner, in makeshift lighting, one evening when he was brought by a mutual friend, unannounced, to Carl's apartment; Dave Brubeck and Paul Desmond; George Szell; Marjorie Kinnan Rawlings, Cousin Marjorie as Cousin Carl called her after they discovered a mutual ancestor in Anneke Jans in the eighteenth century; Eartha Kitt; Frederick Buechner, before he had published his first novel; and several sets of Alicia Markova, whose niche in the Van Vechten archives includes a documentation of all her roles.

The "friendly advocate," as John D. Gordan once called him, never really stopped working.

XI

Carlo Beau Patriarch et Mage

So many people think that in old age you feel differently from what you were when you were young. That's not true at all. I feel exactly the same way I felt when I was eighteen years old.

O<small>N</small> J<small>UNE</small> 17, 1955, Carl began his diamond jubilee, when he reached the age of seventy-five; but the celebrations had really begun six weeks before with the publication of Edward Lueders's *Carl Van Vechten and the Twenties,* an entertaining expansion of his Ph.D. dissertation at the University of New Mexico.

Carl sent out copies to friends as soon as the shipment arrived at the Central Park West apartment. At least one old acquaintance wrote about it in terms of the past rather than the present. James Branch Cabell, "ill all spring with a complication of disorders mostly due to extreme old age," was depressed by it in spite of his "pleasure and admiration: Our prime seems nowadays so very long ago; and as a friend of mine said lately, 'Everybody we knew is either dead or getting ready to be.' And I agreed with him perforce...."[1]

Mencken, his mind already badly deteriorated, had been too ill even to acknowledge his copy of the book except through a note from his secretary. He died in 1956; Cabell followed him in 1958; Hergesheimer, long out of touch, had died in 1954; Sinclair Lewis was dead; Scott Fitzgerald was dead; so were Theodore Dreiser, Ernest Boyd, and Eugene O'Neill. Several years later, when Margaret Cabell edited a volume of her husband's correspondence among his contemporaries, Carl's introduction "seemed to be a matter of necessity."[2]

[1] CVV, NYPL.
[2] "An Introduction with Some Candour and Some Little Truth," in *Between Friends,* p. ix.

Carl, himself was, however, very much alive in 1955, and his letters to me that spring speak best of the excitement. Most of them carried news of fresh accolades. Early in March:

> As my 75th year draws to a close, events seem to CLUSTER. There's more to see and do than there ever has been before and more and more firecrackers are being heaped on my head and more and more wreaths burned at the stake.

A month later:

> Fisk is giving me a doctorate! . . . I dare say all this extra activity will bring on some fatal disease, if it is only exhaustion. . . .

In mid-May:

> What times I am living in! What times I am going through! More and more honors. More things to do. More things that HAVE to be done. Will I get through all of it? . . . On Sunday . . . I fly to Nashville for my degree. I do hope people will not begin to hail me as Doc, but I expect the worst.

At the end of the month:

> Tomorrow I become by magic an LLD—without writing a thesis.

Two weeks before his birthday:

> I am as busy as two birddogs. . . .

Finally, after his birthday:

> The 17th lasted for two full days and nearly did me in. I never drank more champagne . . . and I attended innumerable lunches and dinners and after theatre suppers formal and informal. The two big shows are grand (on all summer). The one in the Berg Collection . . . is devoted entirely to me. . . . 2,389 persons have visited this one in the last two weeks.

The *New Republic* printed an article late in May, by Edward Lueders; and the July number of the *Bulletin* of the New York Public Library, featured a chronological account of his work, by

Carlo Beau Patriarch et Mage

John D. Gordan, curator of the Berg Collection, "Carl Van Vechten: Notes for an Exhibition in Honor of His Seventy-fifth Birthday." It was the first exhibition ever given a living writer by the library.

The second show to which Carl referred in his letter took place at Yale, organized by Donald Gallup to include a sampling from each of his various collections. Yale's acknowledgment did not stop there: later in the year, the library published the first major addition to the Van Vechten bibliography in two decades. Commencing with a quotation from *Peter Whiffle*, "my autobiography, which Alfred A. Knopf will publish in the fall of 1936," *Fragments from an unwritten autobiography*, bound into two little red volumes and boxed in a black slipcase, was issued just in time for Carl to distribute them as Christmas gifts. They contained the seven essays originally published in the *Yale University Library Gazette*.

During that same spring, there were photographic exhibitions at the Universities of Atlanta and New Mexico; and a new bibliography appeared. Alfred A. Knopf issued an edition of four hundred copies of an excellent but only partly collated compilation by Klaus Jonas of the University of Pittsburgh, with a "preamble" by Grace Zaring Stone, another of Carl's "literary ladies."

The year 1955 had been a busy one, with—Carl complained with amusement—enough recognition to last for a while, though his own vanity refused to neglect any of the attention. "I'm never interested very long in anybody who isn't interested in me," he once admitted, not without some considerable pride; and more than once, his white-fringed forehead raised, his eyes uplifted in mock ecstasy, he cried, "I *love* attention!" Not long after, during one of the intermissions at a Lewisohn Stadium concert, two preteeners came up for his autograph. The audience was particularly celebrated that evening, and the girls had been circulating frenetically for signatures. "Do you know who I am?" Carl asked in that slow, flat, unnerving voice of his. Obviously, they did not, and they nudged each other and giggled a little, staring all the while at the white bangs and great teeth and gold-linked bracelet and violently colored shirt, avoiding all the while the scary penetration of Carl's merry eyes. Finally, one of them mugged awkwardly, "Well, you never can tell." Then they giggled again, as Carl signed his name with suitable flourishes in their books. They squinted momentarily at the indecipherable scrawl. "Thanks a lot, Mister!" they cried, running off. "They probably thought I was Carl Sandburg," he said, giggling a little himself.

One accolade, however, he took seriously enough, circulating widely a letter that had come to me from Alice Toklas in Paris, written in her fine calligraphy, like delicate spider's web:

> What a fitting and beautiful celebration C. Van V. was given for his anniversary celebration—not one inch more than he deserved. . . . Wonderful Carl who has excelled in so many important directions. U.S. has had no one to approach him and other countries not since generations. We were fortunate to have known him, to have seen his glory, to hear his words in our ears.

"FM GOES TO THE COUNTRY on Monday," he wrote, shortly after the excitement surrounding his birthday had died down, "so I shall be leading a dissolute and sinful life, eating all the wrong things, drinking to excess, and entertaining my most disreputable friends. I will have a ball." Instead, he became involved almost immediately in a new project when Knoedler's art gallery telephoned to say they wanted to give a show of Gertrude Stein's pictures, borrowing the ones she had already sold, flying over from Paris the remainder of the collection and Alice Toklas with them. Carl awaited her reply, he wrote me, "with baited breath. If this comes off probably Yale will give a Gertrude Show TOO and perhaps we can persuade Virgil to revive one of the operas." Then a follow-up: "Alice is probably coming to New York . . . but nothing is definite YET, altho she has nodded approval." Then resignation: "Miss T is no longer tentatively on her way. . . . Perhaps she has no further inclination to shake hands with the public. Anyway I have written her to concern herself no longer with the project. Perhaps this will make her determined to come. I HOPE SO." It did not of course, but Carl was too busy in the darkroom and the studio to worry about it.

In the passage of nearly twenty-five years, Carl's photography had undergone some considerable changes. No one easily mistakes a Van Vechten photograph, regardless of its date, but the theatrical poses and arty lighting of the thirties gave way to a more straight-forward, documentary approach during the forties. The latter does not of course necessarily deny dramatic effect, and, as Carl said on more than one occasion, the intentions of documents need not be construed as an argument against their being beautiful. He dis-approved of retouching in any circumstances, though, in spite of his frequent avowals to the contrary, he did crop pictures from time to time, pointing up or intensifying what might have remained otherwise ordinary. There were mistakes, of course, bad photo-graphs, plenty of them. Although Carl liked to say that he always "threw out anything that isn't perfection," he often neglected to do so, particularly in the later years. On more than one occasion, he printed copies of every shot he developed, good or bad. Did the eye grow less discriminate as age encroached?

During this same period—the late fifties—Carl discovered the movies. Or perhaps he only rediscovered them after a long hiatus. Ordered in no uncertain terms to desert the darkroom during the hot summer months, Carl bowed to his doctor's judgment. His boyhood in Cedar Rapids had conditioned him to withstand almost any kind of rigorous temperature—hot or cold—but the Central Park West apartment was never air-conditioned; and one June morning, when the mercury reached 110, he had blacked out. The movies made a comfortable respite. But he avoided most American films ("they bore the pants off me") and English films ("I need sub-titles to understand what they are saying"), and concentrated on foreign imports and silent films, not only during the summers but into the later seasons as well. Part of this was due to his in-creasing deafness, but part was nostalgia too: he loved to go again and again to see a treasured picture.

Carl never forgave anybody who was guilty of having missed his *favorite* film, which he saw by actual count at least twenty-three times: "There is a new French film called Casque d'Or with a wonderful woman named Simone Signoret which I have seen twice and will see again," he wrote to me in 1952, and then said much the same thing whenever it turned up again. He was wild about Hayley Mills in a melodrama called *Tiger Bay* ("a MUST"), and the German *Gervaise* ("the best picture ever, perfect in every way"), and "the fabulous new Briggete [*sic*] Bardot." He really doted on Cocteau pictures, even when "the film broke THREE times and it took so long to mend it that I fear they tore its bowels out." A few years later, he went often to see Ingmar Bergman films, sitting through most of them twice and returning a day or so later for a third view. For a time he took in all the spectaculars: "I am beginning to prefer long pictures. . . If I go to a bad one I can leave early." Having come to the movies seriously in his vintage, Carl brought to it the enchantment of his youth, with a happily noncritical approach most of the time. "It's the best film I've ever seen" must surely have occurred more often than any single phrase whenever he got excited by a *Viridiana*, a *Hiroshima, Mon Amour*, an *Around the World in Eighty Days*, a rereleased *Son of the Sheik*. Carl reached some zenith in hyperbole in 1961: "Over the weekend I saw . . . Tiger Bay at the Thalia and went completely mad and then saw Room at the Top at the Beacon and cried my eyes out. Simone [Signoret] and Hayley [Mills] have even improved their performances!" Or perhaps he had finally heard them. "I have a new hearing aid. What have you got?" he wrote at about the same time.

Since 1945, his deafness had steadily increased; one was always obliged to speak up to Carl. Then, in 1957, he tried out his first hearing aid—but secretly, at the movies. When the lights went down, Carl took out what looked like a cigarette case, though I knew he had given up smoking thirty years before when he had himself locked in an Atlantic City hotel room for one long weekend. He detached a small plug, inserted it in his ear, dialed up the batteries, and settled back. At the conclusion, before the lights went up, he stowed the whole apparatus back in his pocket. I must have smirked disapprovingly at his vanity. "It doesn't really help much, anyway, you know," he sheepishly explained.

The movies were usually preceded by lunch or dinner at a nearby restaurant, with Fania or Saul or Aileen Pringle—his most frequent companions—or by himself. Carl never tired of eating out. When he first arrived in New York, he made a pact with himself to try every restaurant in town before he died. Shortly thereafter he altered this to include only the Chinese restaurants, and even then quickly realized the task was an impossible one. His investigations, nevertheless, led to an amazing knowledge of dining rooms, cafés, and even an occasional hash house worthy of a discriminating palate. He had a longstanding fondness for the Capri, an Italian establishment where osso buco always claimed his attention. Before his discovery of the Capri, Carl had been enamored of Mercurio, but once turned away because he did not have a tie on—I believe he was wearing a thin white Cuban shirt covered with tiny tucks—he never returned. For a time he patronized La Potinière and liked to lunch at Sardi's with champagne splits, but he was equally happy over bratwurst and sauerkraut and steins of German lager at Lüchow's or the Blue Ribbon. From experience, one learned to accept Carl's suggestions: garlic soup in a Greenwich Village Spanish restaurant; snails in a French place on Second Avenue; dozens of popovers—we made a whole meal on them once—in a place devoted to Southern cookery; ratatouille at Le Brasserie when it first opened; pigs' snouts and ears and tails in an Argentinian stew at La Fonda del Sol. I balked only once, at the Canton Village, probably Carl's favorite restaurant in all Manhattan, when he insisted we have "ancient eggs," duck eggs buried underground for six months or so, that were "divine with ginger." When I demurred, he fixed me with his customary glacial stare and said, "There is an old Arabian proverb: it is unsafe to say, out of this fountain I will never drink."

On an earlier occasion, he had already made himself clear on the subject in a letter:

But I used to be more intolerant in that respect than you. I deliberate-
ly decided at last that I would eat EVERYTHING and now, on the
whole, I do. Certainly I enjoy some food more than others, but now
I CAN eat almost anything, although I've never eaten locusts
(Egypt) or live shrimps (Chinese) but doubtless I shall some day.

Almost in the following post, he could reverse the situation:

For the moment I am not drinking at all and am eating less than a
ballerino in a successful attempt to lose 20 pounds (at least I have
already lost half of this).

Or exaggerate it slightly:

I have had nothing to eat for the past six weeks but pâté de foie gras
and champagne jelly.

But Carl's letters never concentrated at great length on any
single subject unless, as was true occasionally, there were business
matters under discussion. More often than with his most recent
meal or restaurant, his letters were filled with what can be considered only—but in the best sense of an exhausted word—gossip.
Usually in the robin's-egg blue, square envelopes he affected, engraved in emerald or red or white inks with his name and address,
and stamped on the back in sealing wax with his Leda ring, they
arrived with devoted regularity. When the letters accompanied
shipments of photographs, they came in great gray envelopes,
covered with twelve or fourteen different commemorative stamps
for the postage, which he himself always judged by means of a
largely inaccurate small scale on his desk. Certainly, they always
gave their recipients the most immediate sense of Carl's presence,
which, even with the passage of time, does not weaken, whether he
was writing about a new celebrity register:

I am in it but to my disgust Signoret is not. . . . However it is FULL
of Negroes and even begins with a Negro baseball player. . . .

Or his own health:

I have a bad cold, but my income tax is settled. . . .

Carlo Beau Patriarch et Mage

Or a recent outing:

> Wednesday of the current week, Fania . . . and I visited the Palladium and watched Killer [Joe Piro] teach the mambo to two or three hundred boys and girls simultaneously. . . . Killer is a card and plans to be the richest man in America. I have no doubt he will be. He is just as he was in the Canteen only more resolute about it.

Or Elvis Presley:

> I heard him with amazement and I am convinced that his appeal is purely (or impurely) sexual. And as he does not appeal to me on that basis, I have discarded him forever, unless he comes around with his hand-organ to sing at my door.

Or the opera, when a substitute singer appeared, unannounced:

> The Tristan . . . acted like a sick stick or a frozen marshmallow and sang like a sardine in a frigidaire, but he is a thin boy and when the curtain rose on Act III to expose the fattest boy in captivity, I believed I had lost my mind.

Or simply a busy schedule:

> I am down to solid bedrock work: furnishing an Yvette Guilbert piece for Angel Records (done today), a piece about Olive Fremstad for the Sat Review (done yesterday) and a piece about Marguerite d'Alvarez (to be done next week), any amount of photographs to develop and print, more printed photographs to be put in order . . . strange social adventures . . . new books to read, new pictures and plays to take in, new hands to kiss, new feet to wash, and new hours to LIVE.

Too busy:

> I barely have time to breathe these days or even sleep, and I scarcely eat at all. . . . My mail is scattered all over my desk and the adjacent floor. I always put the most important letters on the floor.

Some subjects certainly continued from letter to letter, usually various interests in common: books, plays, both of which clearly delineated Carl's tastes and prejudices and, at the same time, his personality. "I may have a blind spot," he conceded about J. D. Salinger, "but I may be unable to appreciate this great genius." On other occasions he could be more loquacious:

> I have just finished reading Sartre's Saint-Genet. It is certainly the most extraordinary book I ever read & perhaps the most fascinating, translated . . . in the most remarkable way, even metaphysically and mystically. It is over six hundred pages and every page is a series of black text. There are so few dialogues, you could say there are none. It is difficult to get into but when I did get into it I couldn't put it down and every chapter progressively gets easier to comprehend and better. No other living writer of any period has ever paid such a tribute. It is catharsis and glory, everything a great book should be, I feel overwhelmed and free. Everything beautiful. What a book!

Sometimes, if equally enthusiastic, more circumspect:

> I have just finished reading the most beautiful book I have read in years: The Ten Thousand Things, by Maria Dermout. . . . It is downright marvellous. We have such different tastes that I will not recommend it to you, but there is no law against your getting curious.

When a book hit too close to home, he could become almost hurt, in a wistful way:

> I have been reading B. L. Reid's Art by Subtraction, re Gertrude Stein. I have two things to say: Anybody who can write a whole book about somebody else to defame her, is pretty fond of that person; Reid is harder to read than Gertrude in her most hermetic moments. Consequently, his quotations from her books stand out like diamonds from his DULL comment. . . .

Occasionally, he just gave up:

> I find myself utterly unable to read Ivy Compton-Burnett. I have tried several times and never get farther than the twentieth page.

But he was always willing to take a chance on a friend's recommendation:

Carlo Beau Patriarch et Mage

I have always been terrified by Kinder, cher Bruce, a condition augmented by reading The Innocent Voyage, What Maisie Knew, and The Bad Seed, and watching performances of The Children's Hour. Now I have had the piss scared out of me by reading The Lord of the Flies, and nothing will induce me to remain in the same room with the murderous little brats. A remarkable performance, as you alleged.

About Robert Graves's *Goodbye to All That*:

I've taken a violent dislike to Graves himself and doubt if I will read any more. It's his inevitability that sets me off. He is ALWAYS right. The fact that this is the truth doesn't influence me.

About Christina Stead's *The Man Who Loved Children*:

I am in sack-cloth and ashes. It is a great book.

Albert Camus' *The Myth of Sisyphus* was "too much for my small brain," but he worshiped James Purdy's *Malcolm* and Anthony Powell's *A Dance to the Music of Time*, and in the last year of his life such strange companions as Jean Genet and Anthony Trollope.

Carl's letters never neglected to report on his various theater activities or his inevitable reactions to them, usually violent in one direction or the other. Of concerts and recitals:

I am in my usual state of gaping enthusiasm. (Will it never end? Probably NOT.) I heard André Watts at the Stadium and sans doute he is the greatest living pianist. He has everything, including good taste and he will end in glory, as he has begun.

Or, more succinctly:

Oistrakh impaled me at the Philharmonic yesterday.

Of the ballet, he could be by turns vindictive and panegyrical. Carl actually loathed the Royal Ballet. "Essentially middle-class British," he said more than once, "appallingly dull, like eating marshmallows in the late afternoon with the curate." But he adored the New York City Ballet, and attended almost religiously. At the age of eighty-four, he was as excited about Mimi Paul, a nineteen-year-old dancer, as he had been about Pavlova and Nijinsky fifty years before. "I can't wait for the next season when I can loll at her feet in Lincoln Centre," he wrote. "Please respect my passion and understand it." Conversely, he could exercise his wrath on individual performers as well, sometimes indirectly and largely for fun: a husband and wife team were "so sublime" they made a more celebrated pair of actors "look like made-up superannuated curlews or snapdragons"; sometimes nastily and on purpose: Maria Callas was "a disagreeable bad-singing slut, and I have no intention of ever taking the trouble to hear her again." When I reminded Carl that the critics usually praised in Callas the very attributes he had most admired in Mary Garden and Olive Fremstad—their "interpretations" even at the expense of vocal grandeur—he neatly sidestepped the issue by writing, "I will not argue with you about what you have told me, because if you have told me things at different times I have not thought of them together."

Most often, Carl's letters were designed without any particular instruction in mind but as casually intimate rambles. He could gently chide:

> It seems ages since we corresponded. . . . However, I propose to continue, unless you have other ideas. Even tho' we don't agree on most subjects, I like to argue with you and watch you grow up (slowly).

Or compliment, while observing the way of the world:

> Your limerick is almost as good as Pope. No fresh dirt comes my way any more. The new youth seems to be pure or at any rate incredibly naïve. Some of them drink Dubonnet and their eternal desire is to stay THIN.

Occasionally, the observations were personal, and more revealing, perhaps, than Carl would have liked to admit:

> One of the amazing things about my life is that so many people, through a strange fatality, I am destined to see only once or twice,

and sometimes these make such a vivid impression that I feel I have known them forever and often like them better than old friends. . . .

Sometimes he seemed to include entries for a diary:

It is now 9:30 and I think I will go to bed, for a change. I have been leading a shamelessly external life.

And again:

The place is a shambles today. Floor and desk covered with old letters. When I get through with all this I promise never to read or write a letter again!

Sometimes he would drop a remark about his own mortality, though not often; Carl was always a rather casual atheist, "never religious about anything but music":

I have no fear of death or the angels. The idea of seeing all those people is appalling to me.

He was too interested in life to worry about death, but he did worry about his health and liked to send along the latest developments:

Today I went to three doctors. I have housemaid's knee and the foot & mouth disease!

Or, after a bad fall on the street:

I . . . have a few bumps as souvenirs, but nothing interior seems to be damaged. The adjacent peasantry were surprisingly wonderful when the accident occurred and picked me up tenderly and carried me to the nearest chemist where I was bathed and annointed. I felt like Christ after the Cross!

Then, as age did finally begin to encroach:

I still fall down occasionally (today for instance, on Fifth Avenue, where three handsome gentlemen picked me up).

But, after a medical checkup, he proudly crowed:

There is nothing the matter with me after all. I have the arteries of a boy of 16!

Carl Van Vechten

Some years earlier, his letters had been filled with dentistry:

> I had a wisdom tooth pulled this week. No one else ever kept a wisdom tooth till the age of 77, but you will admit I am exception to most rules.

Sometime later, there was more tooth trouble. One of the famous fangs had to be removed, and very shortly the other one had to follow:

> I have another ulcerated tooth. These always make their appearance on Saturday night or Sunday when no dentist is available.

Then a day later:

> My tooth is okay and the base can be preserved in which a new version can be set. No more pain and trouble.

A few months later, I was astonished to discover that the new version was no different from the old: Carl still looked like an amiable beaver. "Well," he sighed, looking toward heaven in supplication, setting his head to a quick jiggle in mock irritation, "I've lived with them for so long that nobody would recognize me without them."

He liked to drop remarks in his letters from time to time that could only perplex:

> Aromarama is terrific, all but the smells which are accurate and as bad as they would be in real life.

Or astonish:

> Balanchine has had a stroke, had a finger cut off and is not very well.

Or fascinate:

> I am being regenerated by a new variety of massage which exhausts the operator and excites me.

Sometimes he could be indignant:

> Stop calling me grandpa at once. I can do that, but I want no such impertinence from you. . . .

Carlo Beau Patriarch et Mage

Or really distressed, as occurred when an extended squib about him appeared in the Cedar Rapids newspaper that I had neglected to send along, his rejoinder to which is accurately reproduced:

> Dearest Bruce, You certainly are a stinker. My relatives are stinkers. Not one of you has srnt me hst spprsrf.z do.So busy as you a hasbest get on the telephone and get TEN copies for me subito. All Ny is clamoring. ij cludinh nr of the producerd.

And sometimes he could add at the foot of a letter the kind of remark that made the heart sing:

> I find you the easiest of all my friends to write to. . . .

He loved to sign his letters fancifully, occasionally at the expense of good taste but never at the expense of good humor:

> Skis and Skates to you, and fourteen Baltimore Orioles,

> Bread Fruit and Baking Powder Biscuit to You,

> I enclose some tidbits and ditties and wish you well, comme toujours,

> Hearts and flowers to you,

> Curds and whey to you,

> Thunder and lightning to you,

> Huckleberry Finn and Haddie to you,

> Faster horses to you, parsnips (in gold paper) and 14 fanciful beagles with strange names and gilded toenails,

> Wild cries of Sirens to you, pink hippopatami, and other distinguished gadgets,

> Bright Red Strawberries to you, a robin, and a proud guitar,

> Grace to you, indigence and indolence, and porridge!

Sometimes he closed by identifying the date of the month:

> Tomorrow is LABOR DAY. It sounds like the end of a pregnancy.

Sometimes with cryptic autobiography:

I am now a Begum and wear a green circle on my forehead.

Or, when inspiration flagged:

Love, Carlo.

AT HIS SEVENTY-NINTH BIRTHDAY PARTY, Carl got a new name, and he kept it until the end of his life, signing himself "Carlo Patriarch" or "Carlo le beau Patriarch" or "Carlo Mage" or "Carlo PM" or variations thereon. He had no recollection of who had first delivered up the name, for the party was as wet as its predecessors in the twenties had been. Also, with paella and mangoes and champagne, and William Warfield singing, and Carl "reduced to putting posies into toilet bowls and bath tubs," the gathering was fairly typical. Carl and Fania liked to entertain regularly, always with good food and drink, occasional entertainment, brilliant guests. If rarely different from the exciting standards set during their heyday thirty years before, the parties were somewhat smaller. The apartment to which Carl and Fania had moved in 1953, just up the street from 101 Central Park West, was a little more confining.

There was no Victorian room—Carl gave his mother's Gilbert square grand piano to a niece in Connecticut—and the dining room had been appropriated for a library. A first impression of the apartment was inevitably contradictory: enormous space, enormous clutter. The rectangular foyer, book-lined on two sides, sported a Persian wall hanging, antique mirrors, a Spanish chest, and for several years a gigantic poster of Simone Signoret's *Casque d'Or*. To the left was a huge drawing room, with a Venetian chandelier over a round center table covered with photographs and feather quills, candied ginger in Italian boxes, and Mexican toys. The walls held most of the important paintings, important from Carl's point of view because he liked them best: a self-portrait of Giorgio di Chirico, Florine Stettheimer's "incomparable zinnias," a tempera portrait of Fania circa 1920, a Raoul Dufy seascape, some small paintings by Diego Rivera and Miguel Covarrubias and others, a huge "Frou-Frou" by Clairon, and Carl's own portraits by Martha Baker and Richard Banks. Some sculpture—heads of Paul Robeson and Ethel Waters, a Philip Grausman heifer in bronze and cat in papier-mâché—and a variety of artifacts and gimcracks—articulated silver fish, tin birds, pottery candelabra, ceramic cats, jugs of greenery—ranged around the room. There was a grand piano, its closed top laden with various photographs that changed from time to time, perhaps a dozen chairs, love seats, divans, two low tables with pedestals of Venetian blackamoors, the collections of a lifetime.

To the right of the foyer was a white, antiseptic-looking kitchen and butler's pantry; behind them was Carl's darkroom, fashioned from what would have been servant's quarters. At the end of the foyer were two doors: one leading to the book-jammed library, the other to a long hall lined with prints and photographs and paintings. Four more doors opened here: to the tiny photographic studio; to a bathroom with a scabrous collection of drawings by Jean Cocteau and Gaston Lachaise, a ribald Leda and the swan, some Balinese erotica, and scattered prints and photographs; to Carl's yellow bedroom, with its French folding screen and antique glass paperweights, and bathroom papered with old *Le Rire* magazine covers; to Fania's elegantly cool and beautiful blue suite at the end of the hall.

It was a pleasant place to visit, a fascinating place to tour, presumably a happy place to live—in part, because of its arrangement: small enough to serve Carl and Fania as an intimate and friendly home but still large enough and suitably divided to allow them their separate lives. One would have never referred to the Marinoff–Van Vechten alliance as serene. They had first met in 1912, and had "quarrelled almost incessantly about important and unimportant matters" ever after, Carl easily admitted. "She is more frequently governed by her heart, I by my head."[3] They were, however, never very far apart, even though "she has her friends and I have mine, but actually this gives us the necessary variety to bring

3 Van Vechten, Oral History.

us more closely together. . . . In short, we adore each other."[4] Friends might wonder on occasion, when violent discussions erupted into volcanic arguments; yet five minutes later Carl would have moved on to something else, and Fania would be "all smiles and charm." Once, Carl wrote me that he was never very much in love until he reached the age of thirty-four, when "love hit me hard, but I'm more in love now than I was then." The letter was dated shortly before their fortieth wedding anniversary. Nearly ten years later, one evening after dinner when Fania had just excused herself—she liked to retire early—Carl said, very carefully and in an even more measured voice than usual, "I . . . simply . . . cannot . . . imagine my life . . . without her."

In their later years, Carl and Fania liked to dine at home. Several gastric bouts denied Carl most salt and Fania all fibrous foods, not always easy conditions to fulfill in restaurants. They liked small dinner parties too, with a couple of guests, arranged at a small table set up in the library, a large chamber flanked with books and filed photographs, easy chairs, a daybed, and Carl's desk, usually in a state of organized turmoil, under Florine Stettheimer's portrait of him in lavender socks against a vermillion background. There was always some degree of astonishment and pleasure in reflecting that dinner with the Van Vechtens was not, after all, so very different from dinner with one's own affectionate if slightly eccentric relatives. Mildred Perkins, their excellent cook for more than twenty-five years, would clang a brass camel bell to penetrate Carl's deafness and announce the meal. Carl always seemed to arrive first, usually outfitted in a Greek or Hawaiian or Mexican shirt and baggy pajama bottoms; Fania would appear a second later, lost in a mumu, a bright ribbon in her cropped silver hair, and a variety of pretty jewels and assorted bangles. Sometimes there was a wine, sometimes not; an appetizer, frequently one of Fania's own amazing soups, cucumber or sorrel or watercress, pureed to liquid velvet; an entree of broiled baby turkey or rare roast beef with some vegetables; a light dessert; some coffee.

4 Van Vechten, Oral History.

Carlo Beau Patriarch et Mage

On Mrs. Perkins' day off and during her intermittent absences over the years, dinner was served in the kitchen, with guests or without them. When Carl cooked—occasionally while Fania was off visiting the Langners in the country or on one of her infrequent cruises—the result was often nothing more than an icebox raid: smoked tongue, some succotash inspired by leftovers, a blender dessert made from equal parts of mashed chestnuts, whipping cream, and honey; and all courses liberally punctuated with too many cocktails, usually stingers with a dash of Pernod. When Fania performed in the kitchen, one got what might best be described as a good, home-cooked meal: leg of lamb roasted conventionally but perfectly to a sentimental pink and laced with garlic; or prime rib, barely wounded; or boeuf à la mode with pot-roasted potatoes and carrots; or, once for a small Thanksgiving dinner around the white kitchen table, baked Virginia ham.

For larger groups—Carl considered twenty an absolute maximum, but the number sometimes doubled—the dinners and supper parties were served buffet, and the dishes exotic variations on old favorites: curried crab salad; thick Southern gumbo; jambalaya; and, almost invariably, a Theda Bara invention called garlic ice cream, a tabasco-loaded frozen mayonnaise, flavored with Cowboy's Delight and served in avocado halves. ("Goddammed chichi food!" a guest muttered under her breath one night after the shock of a first bite.)

The guest lists always constituted a cross section of the arts but also of Carl and Fania's joint as well as individual tastes, both the celebrated and the unknown, always a mixture of the races, and with the informality of a family reunion. Fania would change her mumu for an enchanting dress of Siamese silk or for one of her own expert creations; Carlo Patriarch would change his pajamas for a pair of beltless trousers and a cardigan jacket. Then they would greet their guests, who always tried to arrive on time since their host was never late—indeed, they were usually early. First the regulars: Donald Angus, Saul Mauriber, Aileen Pringle, Nora Holt, Mark Lutz when he was in town, Regina Wallace; then a number of old friends and renewed acquaintances; then new ones, as they rose on the Van Vechten horizon. If Carl was too easily blinded by the stardust of an occasional sycophant, Fania was not, and such interlopers quickly faded. Those who remained in that charmed circle gave unstintingly of their attention and their affection, and gladly so; for Carl and Fania gave unstintingly of theirs in return.

THE INFLUENCE OF PERSUASIONS—even during so brief a period as five years—occasioned several celebrations when Carl reached the age of eighty. He had continued to write: a preface for a Chinese cookbook; another for a George Gershwin biography; a revised version of a speech he had delivered at the Fifth Annual Capezio Award Luncheon about some early balletic recollections; and, finally, the introduction to the last volume of the Yale series of posthumous Gertrude Stein work, in which he turned over his literary executorship to Donald Gallup. Also, he had continued to photograph: Isak Dinesen on her 1959 American visit, when Carl had complied with her request for a Negro party; Carson Mc-Cullers; Marvin David Levy, presently to compose *Mourning Becomes Electra*, for which permission Carl arranged with Carlotta O'Neill; Sammy Davis, Jr., in almost total darkness at an Urban League benefit; Tyrone Power; Raymond Massey; and Barbara Bel Geddes, Mildred Dunnock, Ben Gazzara, and Burl Ives in *Cat on a Hot Tin Roof*.

In 1960, eighty of Carl's friends gathered at Jimmie Daniels's Bon Soir in Greenwich Village to celebrate his eightieth birthday. His gift from them (and others, not in attendance): two thousand dollars for the endowment fund of the James Weldon Johnson Memorial Collection of Negro Arts and Letters at Yale. And Yale itself surprised him with a handsomely printed pamphlet called *80*, a bibliographical compilation of the correspondence and published works of eighty writers whose materials Carl had given to the library. The *American Record Guide* devoted most of its June issue to him, with a reprint of his 1917 "Why Music Is Unpopular," and a gallery of twenty of his photographs of musicians.

Carlo Beau Patriarch et Mage

That same spring, the University of Pittsburgh held a Van Vechten exhibition, through the auspices of Klaus Jonas. I arranged a somewhat more comprehensive one at Coe College in Cedar Rapids. There was one brief moment when I thought Carl might actually break his twenty-three-year expatriation and come out for the show; he even entertained the possibility in a letter or two. Then, as I suspected, "I am determined never again to visit that unloved town."

Carl sent nearly three dozen photographs for the exhibit, including, at the last minute, one of Anthony Armstrong-Jones, who was just then very much in the newspapers. Carl had photographed him a couple of years earlier in New York. At the opening tea in Cedar Rapids, two people appeared whose presence no other exhibition had ever boasted, would ever boast: Edward Howell, Carl's boyhood friend, and Clara Deacon Taylor, his Juliet in the tomb.

Concurrently, Carl had accepted an invitation to tape-record his reminiscences for Columbia University's Oral Research Collection, the typescript of which ran 366 pages. A last accolade came on June 15, two days before his eightieth birthday, when the New York Public Library acknowledged its debt of gratitude by inscribing Carl's name in stone, joining it with the names of other generous benefactors, on the columns of the main lobby.

A year later, Yale presented its gold medal award to Carl for outstanding service; and, on May 24, he joined Leonard Bernstein, George Biddle, Norman Dello Joio, Langston Hughes, Ludwig Mies van der Rohe, Jacques Lipchitz, Conrad Richter, and Arthur Schlesinger, Jr., for induction into the National Institute for the creative arts. A day or two before, Langston Hughes had telegraphed him, "I see you and I are to represent the race at the National Institute of Arts and Letters which delights me to have such genial company therein."[5]

Also, that eighty-first year, a musical version of *The Tattooed Countess* made its appearance. As early as 1957, there had been some talk of it, when a young man named Coleman Dowell "sat at

[5] Yale.

309

the piano and played and sang me seven songs with the most enchanting music and lyrics that Cole Porter or W S Gilbert might envy." More than once in the past, Carl had rejected requests to make musicals of some of his novels, but this one was "exactly the right mood, even the scenes he had invented. In fact I was delighted."

During the ensuing three and a half years, Dowell played and sang the score on more than one occasion, at Carl's invitation, at the Central Park West apartment for friends; and the music and lyrics were, as Carl had said, "enchanting." But something happened before it reached the stage: a coy and cloying libretto substituted sentimentality for irony, and even the countess's tattoo was altered from *Qui sais-je?* to *Je m'en fiche*, which indicates some of the difficulty. Almost everybody seemed to be scheduled at one time or another to play the lead and, for a while, Carl's letters were punctuated with new possibilities: Risë Stevens, Patricia Morison, Eileen Herlie, Gloria Swanson, Margaret Leighton, Celeste Holm, Simone Signoret. Finally, Irene Manning was engaged, after an absence of fifteen years from the New York stage. Judith Crist's review of the opening summed up the majority of critical opinion: "Haste, Miss Manning, makes waste."[6]

Carl did not mourn its quick demise, but he did lose some of his enthusiasm for a projected film version, by Jerome Lawrence and Robert Lee, of *Peter Whiffle*: "I do not translate easily," he wrote, "and there you are." Also, there were other things to occupy his time: *Esquire* solicited an article about the subjects of a dozen Van Vechten photographs for its 1961 Christmas issue, though it remained unpublished until 1962. "I got my list of pictures from Esquire this morning," he wrote me, "a rather peculiar list, but not unreasonable. They might have been happy businessmen's choices." Then the following year, *Esquire* invited him for a two-page color photograph called "The Last of the Lost Generation." "It was intended to be a group from the twenties and thirties," he wrote to me, "but all of these are dead; so they decided on a group of any

[6] *New York Herald Tribune*, May 6, 1961.

310

old timers. And there we sat, like the Last Supper. . . ." The photograph appeared just in time to coincide with Carl's eighty-third birthday, and shared that distinction with a paperback edition of *The Tattooed Countess*, dressed up in a pandering cover announcing "an underground reputation among certain readers."

There were new articles—about Wallace Stevens, Muriel Draper, Florine Stettheimer; new photographs—of Martha Graham, Lotte Lenya, Mahalia Jackson. Certainly, Carl never sat around between those final birthdays waiting for the time to pass. The morning after Dick Banks's champagne supper for his eighty-third, he was up at dawn and in the darkroom as usual; the same thing occurred twelve months later after a party "even better than last which as you know was a whopper. It was *here* this year and . . . I had so many letters, telegrams and cards that it will take me weeks to reply." But he always replied, unfailingly so; and, between the acknowledgments, he continued to write, during the following months, a paper about *la belle epoque*, to service his various collections, to photograph or develop or print the famous and infamous, handsome and homely.

Doubtless, Carl was either in the darkroom or at his desk the morning after a small dinner party on October 21, 1964, when he and Fania quietly celebrated their fiftieth wedding anniversary; and, two months later, he was still at work the day before he died in his sleep.

On June 17, 1966, his ashes were scattered in the Shakespeare Gardens in Central Park.

No one was ever a less likely candidate for a home for the aged or more ill equipped for a senior citizens' club than Carl Van Vechten. Would anybody deny that some of the last essays went slack? Would anybody hesitate to admit that the photography slipped severely from time to time? Well: one forgives the flat note, the careless chord, the missed cue, for the glory of a total performance.

A few years ago, when Carl recorded his "rudimentary narration" for Columbia University's Oral History Research Office, he said: "If I had my way, I would do three thousand times more things a day than I do. But I have to realize that my physical self is run down to some extent, and I have to take naps. . . . But it's hard to find time to take naps. I never have time to, there is so much to do. There's a great deal to do, all the time."[7]

Small wonder: it wasn't easy trying to keep the twentieth century up to date.

[7] Van Vechten, Oral History.

A Photographic Catalogue
of Carl Van Vechten

THIS LIST, neither definitive nor complete, has been compiled of subjects not elsewhere referred to in the text, to indicate the scope and range of Carl Van Vechten's photographic record of twentieth-century arts and letters.

1932
Bennett Cerf, publisher
Lynn Fontanne, actress
Robinson Jeffers, poet
Alfred Lunt, actor
H. L. Mencken, writer
Paul Muni, actor

1933
Louis Bromfield, writer
Marcel Duchamp, painter
George Gershwin, composer
Edna St. Vincent Millay, poet
Ravi Shankar, sitarist
Hendrik Van Loon, writer

1934
Salvador Dali, painter
Jacob Epstein, sculptor
Emma Goldman, anarchist
Serge Koussevitzky, conductor
Elmer Rice, playwright
Rebecca West, writer

1935
Aaron Copland, composer

Norman Douglas, writer
Libby Holman, singer
Joan Miró, painter
Isamu Noguchi, sculptor
Luigi Pirandello, playwright

1936
Langston Hughes, writer
Giorgio di Chirico, painter
Lin Yutang, writer
Jules Romains, writer
Alec Waugh, writer
Glenway Wescott, writer

1937
Ethel Barrymore, actress
Cecil Beaton, designer
Frank Crowninshield, publisher
Raoul Dufy, painter
Clifford Odets, playwright
Artur Rubinstein, pianist

1938
Byrher (Winifred Ellerman),
    writer

313

Margaret Bourke-White, photographer
Erskine Caldwell, writer
Paul Vincent Carroll, playwright
Edna Ferber, writer
Guthrie McClintic, director

1939

Sherwood Anderson, writer
Marsden Hartley, painter
Oscar Hammerstein II, lyricist
Fredric March, actor
George Jean Nathan, theater critic
Stefan Zweig, writer

1940

Theda Bara, actress
Katherine Dunham, dancer
Ella Fitzgerald, singer
Janet Flanner, writer
Charles Laughton, actor
Henry Miller, writer

1941

Countee Cullen, poet
Dean Dixon, conductor
Lena Horne, singer
Jerome Robbins, dancer
"Bojangles" Robinson, dancer
Sigrid Undset, writer

1942

Shirley Booth, actress
Paul Horgan, writer
John Kriza, dancer
Killer Joe Piro, dancer
Vincent Price, actor
Walter White, writer

1943

Kermit Bloomgarden, producer

Howard Lindsay, playwright
Pearl Primus, dancer
Hiram Sherman, actor
Dorothy Stickney, actress
Anthony Tudor, choreographer

1944

Paul Bowles, writer
André Eglevsky, dancer
Celeste Holm, actress
John LaTouche, librettist
Janet Reed, dancer
William Seabrook, writer

1945

Eugene Goossens, conductor
Chester Himes, writer
Susan Reed, folk singer
Rufino Tamayo, painter
Vera Zorina, dancer
Richard Wright, writer

1946

W. E. B. Du Bois, writer
Lamont Johnson, actor
Ulysses Kay, composer
Beatrice Pearson, actress
Philippa Duke Schuyler, pianist
Josh White, singer

1947

Marian Anderson, singer
Marc Blitzstein, composer
Donald Gallup, curator
Carlo Levi, writer
Oliver Smith, designer
Virgil Thomson, composer

1948

Alexandra Danilova, dancer
Norman Mailer, writer
Ann Petry, writer

314

A Photographic Catalogue

Gore Vidal, writer
Evelyn Waugh, writer
Tennessee Williams, playwright
1949
Philip Barry, playwright
Juanita Hall, singer
Marcel Jouhandeau, writer
Marie Laurencin, painter
Mary Martin, actress
Jessica Tandy, actress
1950
Hurd Hatfield, actor
Charles Jackson, writer
Frieda Lawrence, writer
Georgia O'Keeffe, painter
Marcel Vertès, painter
Harold Rome, composer
1951
Jane Bowles, writer
Josephine Baker, singer
Ralph Bunche, humanitarian
Ossie Davis, actor
Alfred Drake, singer
Richard Rutledge, educator
1952
Jean-Louis Barrault, actor
Judith Evelyn, actress
Arthur Fizdale, pianist
Robert Gold, pianist
Edgar Mittelhölzer, writer
Frederic Prokosch, writer
1953
Beauford Delaney, painter
Ruth Ford, actress
Klaus Jonas, bibliographer
Earle Hyman, actor
Leontyne Price, singer
Zachary Scott, actor

1954
Roald Dahl, writer
Roland Hayes, singer
William Inge, playwright
Iris Mabry, dancer
Patricia Neal, actress
Marian Seldes, actress
1955
Adele Addison, singer
James Baldwin, writer
Dizzy Gillespie, trumpeter
Al Hirschfeld, caricaturist
Louis Kronenberger, writer
Donald Windham, writer
1956
Carol Channing, actress
Lehman Engel, producer
Melissa Hayden, dancer
Peter David Marchant, writer
John Martin, dance critic
Ned Rorem, composer
1957
Edward Jablonski, writer
Geoffrey Holder, dancer
Bruce Kellner, educator
Carmen de Lavallade, dancer
Claudia McNeil, actress
James Purdy, writer
1958
Althea Gibson, athlete
John Hersey, writer
Peter Feibleman, writer
Robert Morse, actor
José Quintero, director
Billy Strayhorn, musician
1959
Diahann Carroll, singer
Padraic Colum, writer

Carl Van Vechten

Zero Mostel, actor
Russell Oberlin, singer
Christopher Plummer, actor
William Warfield, singer
1960
Harold Arlen, composer
Maureen Forrester, singer
Kim Hunter, actress
Edward Lueders, educator
James Lyons, editor
Paul Taylor, dancer
1961
Edward Albee, playwright
Ruby Dee, actress
Marilyn Horne, singer
Jerome Lawrence, playwright
Robert Lee, playwright
Kim Stanley, actress
1962
Christopher Davis, writer

Pierre Dominique Gaisseau, cine-
matographer
Lotte Lenya, actress
Karinska, designer
Alexander King, writer
Andrew Turnbull, writer
1963
Richard Banks, painter
Malcolm Cowley, critic
Lukas Foss, composer
Chaim Gross, sculptor
Mabel Mercer, singer
Paul Padgette, bookseller
1964
Sanford Allen, violinist
Roscoe Lee Browne, actor
Lincoln Kirstein, writer
Beni Montressor, designer
Frances Steloff, bookseller
Gloria Vanderbilt, artist

Bibliography

CARL VAN VECHTEN: EX LIBRIS

FOR MORE COMPLETE ACCOUNTS of Carl Van Vechten's work, the reader is directed to the bibliographies compiled by Scott Cunningham (1924) and Klaus Jonas (1955, 1961), to Frank Paluka's *Iowa Authors* (1967), and to the continuing bibliographical record kept active by Paul Padgette of Anagram Books in San Anselmo, California.

The following chronology includes the materials called upon for quotation or extended consideration in this volume. Periodical articles, later reprinted in published volumes, are not listed. Unless otherwise noted, all Carl Van Vechten's books were published by Alfred A. Knopf., Inc.

"The Change in Harlowe," *University of Chicago Weekly*, January 9, 1901, pp. 331–333.

"A Relief," *University of Chicago Weekly*, July 31, 1902, pp. 942–943.

(alumni letter) *Pulse*, January, 1904, p. 4.

"Gossip of the Chicago Smart Set," *Chicago American*, inconsistently dated clippings in the Carl Van Vechten Collection of the Manuscript Division of the New York Public Library.

"The Whirl of Society," *Chicago Inter-Ocean*, inconsistently dated clippings in the Carl Van Vechten Collection of the Manuscript Division of the New York Public Library.

"Salome: The Most Sensational Opera of the Age," *Broadway Magazine*, January, 1907, pp. 381–391.

Various articles, reviews, news squibs, gossip notes from the *New York Times*, inconsistently dated clippings in the Carl Van Vechten Collection of the Manuscript Division of the New York Public Library.

"The Coming Opera Season," *Bookman*, November, 1907, pp. 256–265.

"Story of My Operatic Career" (ghostwritten for Luisa Tetrazzini), *Cosmopolitan Magazine*, June, 1908, pp. 49–51.

"Facts, Rumors, and Remarks," *New Music Review*, December, 1909, p. 26.

Various reviews from the *New York Press*, inconsistently dated clippings in the Carl Van Vechten Collection in the Manuscript Division of the New York Public Library.

"Drama: The Dying Audience," *Trend*, April, 1914, pp. 109–113.

"A Cockney Flower Girl and Some Negroes," *Trend*, May, 1914, pp. 231–238.

"How to Read Gertrude Stein," *Trend*, August, 1914, pp. 553–557.

"Once Aboard the Lugger, San Guglielmo: An Account of a Flight from Italy in War Time," *Trend*, October, 1914, pp. 13–24.

"The Editor's Work Bench," *Trend*, October, 1914, pp. 100–101.

Music after the Great War (New York: G. Schirmer, 1915).

Music and Bad Manners, 1916.

Interpreters and Interpretations, 1917.

The Merry-Go-Round, 1918.

The Music of Spain, 1918.

In the Garrett, 1919.

Interpreters, 1920.

"On the Advantages of Being Born on the Seventeenth of June," *The Borzoi 1920*, 1920, pp. 48–51.

The Tiger in the House, 1920.

Peter Whiffle: His Life and Works, 1922.

"Pastiches et Pistaches," *Reviewer*, May, 1922, pp. 455–459.

The Blind Bow-Boy, 1923.

"Pastiches et Pistaches," *Reviewer*, January, 1924, pp. 98–103.

"The Lady Stuffed with Pistachio Nuts," *Dial*, March, 1924, pp. 283–286.

The Tattooed Countess, 1924.

"Overture in the Form of a Funeral March," *in* Scott Cunningham, *A Bibliography of the Writings of Carl Van Vechten* (Philadelphia: Centaur Book Shop, 1924), pp. 5–9.

Red, 1925.

Bibliography

"George Gershwin: An American Composer Who Is Writing Notable Music in the Jazz Idiom," *Vanity Fair*, March, 1925, pp. 40, 78, 84.

"The Folksongs of the American Negro," *Vanity Fair*, July, 1925, pp. 52, 92.

"The Black Blues," *Vanity Fair*, August, 1925, pp. 57, 86, 92.

Firecrackers, 1925.

"Langston Hughes: A Biographical Note," *Vanity Fair*, September, 1925, p. 62.

"Prescription for the Nigger Theatre," *Vanity Fair*, October, 1925, pp. 46, 92, 98.

"Preface," *in* Miguel Covarrubias, *The Prince of Wales and Other Famous Americans* (New York: Alfred A. Knopf, Inc., 1925), pp. [7–10].

"Moanin' Wid a Sword in Ma Han'," *Vanity Fair*, February, 1926, pp. 61, 100, 102.

"The Negro in Art: How Shall He Be Portrayed," *Crisis*, March, 1926, p. 219.

Nigger Heaven, 1926.

Excavations, 1926.

"Fabulous Hollywood," *Vanity Fair*, May, 1927, pp. 28, 54, 108.

"Hollywood Parties," *Vanity Fair*, June, 1927, pp. 47, 86, 90.

"Hollywood Royalty," *Vanity Fair*, July, 1927, pp. 38, 86.

"Understanding Hollywood," *Vanity Fair*, August, 1927, pp. 45, 78.

Spider Boy, 1928.

"Foreword," *in* Taylor Gordon, *Born to Be* (New York: Covici-Friede, 1929), pp. v–vii.

Parties, 1930.

Sacred and Profane Memories, 1932.

"Introduction," *in* Gertrude Stein, *Three Lives* (New York: Modern Library, 1933), pp. v–xi.

"A Few Notes about *Four Saints in Three Acts*," *in* Gertrude Stein, *Four Saints in Three Acts* (New York: Random House, 1934), pp. 5–10.

"My Friend, James Weldon Johnson," in *James Weldon Johnson (1871–1938)* (Nashville: Fisk University, no date).

"An Ode to the Stage Door Canteen," *Theatre Arts*, April, 1943, pp. 229–231.

319

Carl Van Vechten

"A Stein Song," in *Selected Writings of Gertrude Stein* (New York: Random House, 1946), pp. ix–xv.
"Memories of Bessie Smith," *Jazz Record*, (September, 1947), pp. 6–7, 29.
Fragments from an unwritten autobiography. 2 vols. New Haven: Yale University Library, 1955.
"A Few Notes à propos of a '*Little*' *Novel of Thank You*" in Gertrude Stein, *A Novel of Thank You* (New Haven: Yale University Press, 1958), pp. vii–xiv.
"Portraits of the Artists," *Esquire*, December, 1962, pp. 170–174, 256–258.
"The Origins of the Sonnets from the Patagonian," *Hartwick Review* (Spring, 1967), pp. 51–56.

SELECTED REVIEWS

THE FOLLOWING LIST is comprised of only those critical notices of individual books by Carl Van Vechten from which extended quotation has been incorporated.

Music after the Great War
Mencken, H. L., "The Tone Art," *Smart Set*, July, 1916.
"*Music after the Great War*," *Cedar Rapids Gazette*, December 31, 1915.
Music and Bad Manners
Bellows, Henry Adams, "Musical Criticism and Readable English," *Bellman*, December 23, 1916.
Mencken, H. L., "The National Letters," *Smart Set*, May, 1917.
Peyser, H. F., "*Music and Bad Manners*," *Musical America*, February 17, 1917.
Interpreters and Interpretations
"*Interpreters and Interpretations*," *New Republic*, November 17, 1917.
The Merry-Go-Round
Bourne, Randolph, "The Light Essay," *Dial*, November 16, 1918, pp. 419–420.
In the Garret
Terrill, Mary, "About Essays, and Three," *Bookman*, April, 1920, pp. 192–195.

Bibliography

Peter Whiffle: His Life and Works

Van Doren, Carl, "The Roving Critic," *Nation*, May 10, 1922, p. 469.

Walker, Harry. *"Peter Whiffle," New York Herald Tribune*, April 16, 1922.

Walpole, Hugh. "Six Best American Novels of 1922; an English Critic's View," *International Book Digest*, Vol. 1, January, 1923, p. 70.

The Blind Bow-Boy

Boyd, Ernest, "Van Vechten's New York," *Nation*, September 5, 1923, pp. 244–245.

Broun, Heywood, *"The Blind Bow-Boy," New York World*, May 19, 1923.

Rascoe, Burton, *"The Blind Bow-Boy," New York Herald Tribune*, August 26, 1923.

The Tattooed Countess

Krutch, Joseph Wood, "Artifice," *Nation*, September 3, 1924, p. 241.

Lewis, Sinclair, " 'Ioway' and the Countess," *Saturday Review of Literature*, August 30, 1924, p. 75.

Firecrackers

Bromfield, Louis, *Bookman* (August, 1925).

Douglas, Donald, "Damp Powder," *Nation*, October 28, 1925, pp. 491–492.

Mencken, H. L., "Fiction Good and Bad," *American Mercury*, November, 1925, pp. 380–381.

Van Doren, Carl, "Under Stained Glass," *New York Herald Tribune Books*, August 23, 1925.

Nigger Heaven

DuBois, W.E.B. "Books," *Crisis*, December 1926.

Johnson, James Weldon. "Romance and Tragedy in Harlem," *Opportunity*, Vol. 4 (October, 1926), pp. 316–17, 30.

Kronenberger, Louis. *"Nigger Heaven," International Book Review*, October 1926.

"Nigger Heaven," Independent, Vol. 117 (August 28, 1926), p. 248.

Niles, Abbe. "Aunt Hagar's Children," *New Republic*, Vol. 48 (September 29, 1926), pp. 162–63.

Walrond, Eric. "The Epic of a Mood," *Saturday Review of Literature*, Vol. 3 (October 2, 1926), p. 153.

Spider Boy

Fadiman, Clifton. "*Spider Boy,*" *Bookman*, Vol. 68 (October 1928), p. 223.

R. M. L. "*Spider Boy,*" *New Republic*, Vol. 56 (September 12, 1928), p. 107.

Parker, Dorothy, *The New Yorker*, August, 1928.

Parties

Dangerfield, George. "*Parties,*" *Bookman*, September, 1930, pp. 71–72.

Simpson, Clinton. "So This Is New York," *Saturday Review of Literature*, September 6, 1930, p. 23.

Sacred and Profane Memories

Ross, Virgilia Peterson. "On the Thread of Memory," *New York Herald Tribune Books*, April 17, 1932.

SECONDARY SOURCES AND RELATED READINGS

Adler, Elmer, ed., *Breaking into Print* (New York: Simon & Schuster, 1937).

Allen, Frederick Lewis, *Only Yesterday* (New York: Blue Ribbon Books, 1931).

Amory, Cleveland, and Frederick Bradlee (eds.), *Vanity Fair* (New York: The Viking Press, 1960).

Anderson, George, and Eda Lou Watson (eds.), *This Generation* (Chicago: Scott, Foresman & Company, 1949).

Atherton, Gertrude, *Adventures of a Novelist* (New York: Horace Liveright, 1932).

Barrett, John Townsend, "Analysis and Significance of Three American Critics of the Ballet: Carl Van Vechten, Edwin Denby, and Lincoln Kirstein" (Columbia University M.A. thesis, 1955).

Beach, Joseph Warren, *The Outlook for American Prose*, (Chicago: University of Chicago Press, 1947).

Bean, Theodora, "Readable Musical Criticism: A Talk with One Who Writes It—Carl Van Vechten," New York *Morning Telegraph*, February 24, 1918.

Bibliography

Beer, Thomas, *The Mauve Decade* (New York: Alfred A. Knopf, Inc., 1926).

Benkovitz, Marian, "Ronald Firbank in New York," *Bulletin of the New York Public Library*, October, 1960.

Bontemps, Arna, "Foreword," in *Selected Items from the George Gershwin Memorial Collection of Music and Musical Literature* (Nashville: Fisk University, 1947).

———, "The James Weldon Johnson Memorial Collection of Negro Arts and Letters," *Yale University Library Gazette*, October, 1943, pp. 19–26.

Brooks, Van Wyck, *The Confident Years 1885–1915* (New York: E. P. Dutton & Company, Inc., 1952).

Cabell, James Branch, *As I Remember It* (New York: The McBride Company, 1955).

———, *Jurgen* (New York: The Robert M. McBride Company, 1923).

Cargill, Oscar, *Intellectual America* (New York: The Macmillan Company, 1941).

"Carl Van Vechten: Novelist of the Twenties Now a Superb Portrait Photographer," *Cue*, April 9, 1949, pp. 418–419.

Clarke, Emily, *Innocence Abroad* (New York: Alfred A. Knopf, Inc., 1931).

Churchill, Allen, *The Improper Bohemians* (New York: Dutton & Company, Inc., 1959).

Colum, Padraic, and Margaret Freeman Cabell, eds., *Between Friends* (New York: Harcourt, Brace & World, Inc., 1962).

Cone, John F., *Oscar Hammerstein's Manhattan Opera House* (Norman: University of Oklahoma Press, 1966).

Cowley, Malcolm, *Exile's Return* (New York: The Viking Press, 1951).

Cunningham, Scott, *A Bibliography of the Writings of Carl Van Vechten* (Philadelphia: The Centaur Bookshop, 1924).

Dorfman, Joseph, *Thorstein Veblen and His America* (New York, The Viking Press, 1934).

Dreiser, Theodore, *The Collected Letters of Theodore Dreiser* (3 volumes) (Philadelphia: University of Pennsylvania Press, 1959).

Evans, Donald, *Sonnets from the Patagonian* (New York: Claire Marie, 1914).

Ewing, Max, *Going Somewhere* (New York: Alfred A. Knopf, Inc., 1933).

Farrar, Geraldine, *Such Sweet Compulsion* (New York: The Greystone Press, 1938).

Firbank, Ronald, *The Complete Ronald Firbank* (London: Gerald Duckworth and Company, Ltd., 1960).

——, *The New Rhythum and Other Pieces* (London: Gerald Duckworth and Company, Ltd., 1962).

Fitch, Morgan Lewis, *A Letter Written in 1837* (privately printed) Chicago, 1919).

Fitzgerald, F. Scott, *The Collected Letters of F. Scott Fitzgerald* (Andrew Turnbull, ed.) (New York: Charles Scribner's Sons, 1963).

Fitzgerald, F. Scott, *The Portable F. Scott Fitzgerald* (New York: The Viking Press, 1945).

Fuller, Henry Blake, *Bertram Cope's Year* (Chicago: Ralph Fletcher Seymour, The Alderbrink Press, 1919).

——, *Under the Skylights* (New York: D. Appleton, 1901).

Gadan, Francis, and Robert Maillard, *Dictionary of Modern Ballet* (New York: Tudor Publishing Company, 1959).

Gallup, Donald, "Carl Van Vechten's Gertrude Stein," *Yale University Library Gazette*, October, 1952, pp. 77–86.

——, ed., *The Flowers of Friendship* (New York: Alfred A. Knopf, Inc., 1953).

Garden, Mary, and Louis Biancolli, *Mary Garden's Story* (New York: Simon & Schuster, 1951).

Gelb, Arthur, and Barbara Gelb, *O'Neill* (New York: Harper & Brothers, 1960).

Gloster, Hugh M., "The Van Vechten Vogue," *Phylon: The Atlanta University Review of Race & Culture*, pp. 310–314.

Glyn, Elinor, *Three Weeks* (New York: Duffield and Company, 1907).

Gordan, John D., "Carl Van Vechten: Notes for an Exhibition in Honor of his Seventy-Fifth Birthday," *Bulletin of the New York Public Library*, July, 1955, pp. 331–366.

Gordon, Taylor, *Born to Be* (New York: Covici-Friede Publishers, 1929).

Bibliography

Handy, W. C., *Father of the Blues* (New York: The Macmillan Company, 1941).

Hapgood, Hutchins, *A Victorian in the Modern World* (New York, Harcourt, Brace and Company, 1939).

Harriman, Margaret Case, *Blessed Are the Debonair* (New York: Rinehart and Company, 1956).

Hart-Davis, Rupert, *Hugh Walpole* (New York: The Macmillan Company, 1952).

Hayes, Dorsha B., *Chicago: Crossroads of American Enterprise* (New York: Julian Messner, Inc., 1944).

Hergesheimer, Joseph, *Cytherea* (New York: Alfred A. Knopf, Inc., 1922).

———, *Linda Condon* (New York: Alfred A. Knopf, Inc., 1919).

Hicks, Granville, *John Reed: The Making of a Revolutionary* (New York: The Macmillan Company, 1937).

Hoffenstein, Samuel, *The Tow-Headed Blind Boy* (privately printed) (Chicago, 1923).

Hughes, Langston, *The Big Sea* (New York: Alfred A. Knopf, Inc., 1940).

———, *The Weary Blues* (New York: Alfred A. Knopf, Inc., 1926).

Huneker, James Gibbons, *Old Fogey* (Philadelphia: Theodore Presser, 1913).

———, *Steeplejack* (New York: Charles Scribner's Sons, 1920).

Hurst, Fannie, "Zora Hurston: A Personality Sketch," *Yale University Library Gazette*, July, 1960, pp. 17–21.

Jablonski, Edward, and Lawrence D. Stewart. *The Gershwin Years* (Garden City: Doubleday and Company, 1958).

Jack, Peter Monro. "The James Branch Cabell Period," *New Republic*, January 13, 1937, pp. 323–326.

Jackman, Harold, "Those Were the Fabulous Days!" *Pittsburgh Courier*, October 11, 1952.

Jackson, Holbrook, *The Eighteen Nineties* (London: Grant Richards, Ltd., 1918).

Johnson, James Weldon, *Along This Way* (New York: The Viking Press, 1933).

———, *The Autobiography of an Ex-Colored Man* (New York: Alfred A. Knopf, Inc., 1927).

Johnson, Nunnally, "The Actress-Wife and Writer-Husband Who Maintain One Home and Two Professions," *Brooklyn Eagle*, March 9, 1924.

Jonas, Klaus, *Carl Van Vechten: A Bibliography* (New York: Alfred A. Knopf, Inc., 1955).

Kazin, Alfred, *On Native Grounds* (New York: Reynal and Hitchcock, 1942).

Kirstein, Lincoln, "Carl Van Vechten (1880–1964)," *Yale University Library Gazette*, April, 1965, pp. 157–162.

Knopf, Alfred A., "Reminiscences of Hergesheimer, Van Vechten, and Mencken," *Yale University Library Gazette*, April, 1950, pp. 145–165.

Kolodin, Irving, *The Metropolitan Opera 1883–1935* (New York: Oxford University Press, 1936).

Langford, Gerald, ed., *Ingénue among the Lions: The Letters of Emily Clarke to Joseph Hergesheimer* (Austin: University of Texas Press, 1965).

Langner, Lawrence, *The Magic Curtain* (New York: E. P. Dutton, 1951).

Leighton, Isabel, ed., *The Aspirin Age: 1919–1941* (New York: Simon & Schuster, 1949).

Lifar, Serge, *Serge Diaghilev: His Life, His Work, His Legend* (New York: Putnam, 1940).

Loos, Anita, *Gentlemen Prefer Blondes* (New York: Horace Liveright, 1925).

Lovett, Robert Morss, *All Our Years* (New York: The Viking Press, 1948).

Lueders, Edward, *Carl Van Vechten* (New York: Twayne Publishers, 1964).

———, *Carl Van Vechten and the Twenties* (Albuquerque: University of New Mexico Press, 1955).

———. "Mr. Van Vechten of New York City," *New Republic*, May 16, 1955, p. 36.

Luhan, Mabel Dodge, *Movers and Shakers* (New York: Harcourt Brace and Company, 1936).

McBride, Henry, "The Leica Exhibition," *New York Sun*, November 30, 1935.

Bibliography

Machen, Arthur, *The Hill of Dreams* (New York: Alfred A. Knopf, Inc., 1923).

Magriel, Paul, ed., *Chronicles of the American Dance* (New York: Henry Holt and Company, 1948).

———, Isadora Duncan (New York: Henry Holt and Company, 1947).

———, *Nijinsky: An Illustrated Monograph* (New York: Henry Holt and Company, 1946).

———, *Pavlova* (New York: Henry Holt and Company, 1947).

Marchant, Peter David, "Carl Van Vechten: Novelist and Critic" (Columbia University M.A. thesis, 1954).

Mencken, H. L., *A Book of Prefaces* (New York: Garden City Publishing Company, 1927).

———, *Happy Days* (New York: Alfred A. Knopf, Inc., 1943).

———, "The Library," *American Mercury*, March 1924, p. 3.

Mizener, Arthur, *The Far Side of Paradise* (Boston: Houghton Mifflin Company, 1950).

Moeller, Philip, "Van Vechten," in *The Borzoi 1920* (New York, Alfred A. Knopf, Inc., 1920).

Nathan, George Jean, *The Intimate Notebooks of George Jean Nathan* (New York: Alfred A. Knopf, Inc., 1932).

Nelson, John Herbert, *Contemporary Trends since 1914* (New York: The Macmillan Company, 1936).

Newman, Ernest, *A Musical Critic's Holiday* (New York: Alfred A. Knopf, Inc., 1925).

Overton, Grant, *When Winter Comes to Main Street* (New York: George H. Doran, 1922).

Padgette, Paul, *Carl Van Vechten, 1880–1964* (Catalogue for a memorial exhibition at the San Francisco Public Library) (San Francisco: The Bindweed Press, 1965).

Paluka, Frank, *Iowa Authors: A Bio-Bibliography of Sixty Native Writers* (Iowa City: University of Iowa, 1967).

Parry, Albert, *Garrets and Pretenders: A History of Bohemia* (New York: Dover Publications, 1960).

Poole, Ernest, *Giants Gone: Men Who Made Chicago* (New York: McGraw Hill Book Company, 1943).

Putnam, Samuel, *Paris Was Our Mistress* (New York: The Viking Press, 1947).

Rascoe, Burton, *We Were Interrupted* (Garden City: Doubleday and Company, 1947).

Richards, Grant, *Author Hunting* (New York: Coward McCann, 1934).

Rimsky-Korsakoff, Nikolay Andreyevich, *My Musical Life* (New York: Alfred A. Knopf, Inc., 1923).

Rogers, W. G., *When This You See Remember Me: Gertrude Stein in Person* (New York: Rinehart and Company, 1948).

———, *Wise Men Fish Here* (New York: Harcourt Brace and World, 1965).

Saltus, Edgar, *Imperial Purple* (New York: Mitchell Kennerley, 1906).

Schorer, Mark, *Sinclair Lewis: An American Life* (New York: Mc-Graw-Hill Book Company, 1961).

Schuyler, George S., "The Van Vechten Revolution," *Phylon: Atlanta University Review of Race and Culture*, Fourth Quarter, 1950, pp. 362–368.

Shattuck, Roger, *The Banquet Years* (New York: Anchor Books, 1961).

Shiel, M. P., *The Lord of the Sea* (New York: Alfred A. Knopf, Inc., 1924).

Sitwell, Osbert, "New York in the Twenties," *Atlantic Monthly*, February, 1962, pp. 38–43.

Steffans, Lincoln, *The Autobiography of Lincoln Steffans* (New York: Harcourt Brace and Company, 1931).

Stein, Gertrude, *Everybody's Autobiography* (New York: Random House, 1937).

———, *Geography and Plays* (Boston: The Four Seas Company, 1922).

———, *Selected Writings of Gertrude Stein* (New York, Random House, 1946).

———. "Van or Twenty Years After: A Second Portrait," in *Morrow's Almanac for 1928* (New York: Morrow, 1927).

Stettheimer, Florine, *The Crystal Flowers of Florine Stettheimer* (Pawlett, Vermont: The Banyan Press, 1949).

Strong, Lewis C., *Prima Donnas and Soubrettes of Light Opera and Musical Comedy in America* (Boston: L. C. Page and Company, Inc., 1900).

Sullivan, Mark, *Our Times* (New York: Charles Scribner's Sons, 1936).

Bibliography

Swanberg, W. A., *Dreiser* (New York: Charles Scribner's Sons, 1965).

Taylor, Dwight, *Joy Ride* (New York: G. P. Putnam's Sons, 1959).

Thomson, Virgil, *Virgil Thomson* (New York: Alfred A. Knopf, Inc., 1966).

Toklas, Alice B., *What Is Remembered* (New York: Holt, Rinehart and Winston, 1963).

Tyler, Parker, *Florine Stettheimer: A Life in Art* (New York, Farrar, Straus and Company, 1963).

Wagenknecht, Edward, *Cavalcade of the American Novel* (New York: Henry Holt and Company, 1952).

Waters, Ethel, *His Eye Is on the Sparrow: An Autobiography* (Garden City: Doubleday and Company, 1951).

Wedekind, Frank. "Spring's Awakening," *The Modern Theatre*, Volume 6 (New York: Doubleday Anchor Books, 1965).

West, Mae, *Goodness Had Nothing to Do with It* (New York: Prentice Hall, 1959).

Wilson, Edmund, *The Shores of Light* (New York: Farrar Straus and Young, 1952).

Wolfe, Thomas, *You Can't Go Home Again* (New York: Dell Publishing Company, 1965).

——, *The Web and the Rock* (New York, Harper, 1939).

Wylie, Elinor, "Carl Van Vechten," in *The Borzoi 1925* (New York: Alfred A. Knopf, Inc., 1925).

——, *Jennifer Lorn* (New York: George H. Doran Company, 1923).

Index

331

Index

Index

Index

337

Index

339

Index

Index

343

Index

Index

Index

Index

351

Index

308; letter to Harold Jackman quoted, 280; honors, 290, 309; awarded doctorate by Fisk University, 290; death, 311; *see also* titles of novels and essays

Van Vechten, Charles Duane: 6, 8, 12, 91, 92, 138, 204; background, 5–7; letters to Van Vechten, 31, 39–40, 91, 121, 137, 148, 210–11; letters from Van Vechten to, 37, 128–29, 132; letter to Fania Marinoff, 172; death, 211, 232

Van Vechten, Duane: 232

Van Vechten, Emma: 6, 7, 18, 20, 33, 196; letter to Van Vechten, 153

Van Vechten, Fania Marinoff: *see* Fania Marinoff

Van Vechten, Fannie Maynard: 232

Van Vechten, Gilbert: 5

Van Vechten, Giles Fonda: 5ff., 24, 258

Van Vechten, Ilona Bent: 8, 257, 258

Van Vechten, Mary Pickney: 8

Van Vechten, Ralph: 6, 7, 34, 91, 127, 150, 151, 242, 253; letters to Van Vechten, 90, 115, 138, 157, 220; letter to Fania Marinoff, 115; Van Vechten letter to, 115–16; legacy to Van Vechten, 232

"Van Vechten Revolution, The": 280

"Van Vechten Vogue": 280

Veblen, Thorstein: 28, 32

Venice, Italy: 82

Verdict of Bridlegoose, The: 140

Verlaine, Paul: 21

Vertès, Marcel: 315

Victoria Theatre (New York City): 42, 43

Vidal, Gore: 315

Villa Curonia (Florence): 64, 69, 71, 76, 82, 83, 90, 134, 135, 201–202, 238; *see also Peter Whiffle: His Life and Works*

Viridiana: 294

Vogue: 103

Voight, Hans (Alastair): 186, 188

Volstead Act: 130

Vortex, The: 220

Voyage en Suisse: 11

Wagner, Richard: 39, 55, 282

Waiting for the Robert E. Lee: 108

Walker, A'lelia: 202, 217, 224, 253

Walker, George: 22, 196

Walker, Mayor James: 220

Walker, Mrs. C. J.: 202

Wallace, Regina: 200, 307

Walpole, Hugh: 171, 199, 241, 259, 261; quoted, 138, 183; letters to Van Vechten, 147, 155

Walsh, Blanche: 62

Ward, Artemus: 117

Warfield, William: 304, 316

Wars I Have Seen: 277

Washington, Booker T.: 197, 238, 281

Waste, Henri (Ettie Stettheimer): 119, 120, 254, 261, 283; letter to Van Vechten, 258

Waters, Ethel: 196, 275, 305; quoted, 207

Watts, André: 299

Waugh, Alec: 313

Waugh, Evelyn: 315

Wave: 176, 283

Way of Ambition, The: 107

Weary Blues, The: 203

Weaver, Raymond: 180–81

Web and the Rock, The: 243

Webb, Clifton: 239, 241, 275

Weber, Carl Maria von: 282

Weber, Max: 70

Weber and Fields: 208

Wedekind, Frank: 47, 109

Weill, Kurt: 242

Welitsch, Ljuba: 287

Welles, Orson: 275

Wellesley College: 20, 24, 41

Werfel, Franz: 272

Werther: 54

Wescott, Glenway: 313

West, Mae, quoted: 243

West, Rebecca: 313

West Chester, Pa.: 105, 117, 125, 126, 192

Westernland: 40

Westport, Conn.: 241, 253

We Were Interrupted: 140

Wharton, Edith: 107–108

What Maisie Knew: 299

353